D1739866

'For anyone interested in the relationships between warfare, information, communication and public opinion this is a must read. The book's great value is that it helps lift the curtain on how informational/psychological warfare is currently deployed in battles over public opinion. This is a timely contribution towards lifting some of the fog of war.'

Eric Louw, University of Queensland, Australia

'I recommend this book for its impressive contributions to news framing of war-related and terrorist events and for its emphasis on hybrid warfare and informational war (such as Russia's "alternative" or "PsyOp" war).'

Professor Jonathan Matusitz, University of Central Florida, USA

'Simons and Chifu address the complexities of the contemporary conflict environment, capturing the weakened mainstream media environment and the dramatically increased importance of "strategic communication" and propaganda activities. The case studies, covering the post 9/11 era are detailed and important contributions to the existing stock of knowledge on media, security and conflict. Essential reading.'

Professor Piers Robinson, Chair in Politics, Society and Political Journalism, University of Sheffield

The Changing Face of Warfare in the 21st Century

This study discusses salient trends demonstrated by contemporary warfare of these first years of our 21st century. The authors reinforce previous notions of Fourth Generation Warfare, but most importantly explore the workings of new components and how these have modified the theory and practice of warfare beyond the basic divisions of conventional and unconventional warfare as witnessed in the preceding century. Throughout history there has been a close interaction between politics, communication and armed conflict and a main line of investigation of this book is to track changes that are presumed to have occurred in the way and manner in which armed conflicts are waged.

Using cogent examples drawn variously from conflicts of the Arab Spring, the Islamic State and Russian adventurism in South Ossetia, Crimea and Eastern Ukraine, the authors demonstrate the application of Information Warfare, the practice of Hybrid Warfare, and offensive use of diplomacy, communications, economics and international law to obtain political and military advantages against the status quo states of the international community.

The authors combine a theoretical framework with concrete empirical examples in order to create a better understanding and comprehension of the current events and processes that shape the character of contemporary armed conflicts and how they are informed and perceived in a highly mediatised and politicised world.

The Changing Face of Warfare in the 21st Century

Greg Simons and Iulian Chifu

Routledge
Taylor & Francis Group

LONDON AND NEW YORK

First published 2018
by Routledge
2 Park Square, Milton Park, Abingdon, Oxon OX14 4RN

and by Routledge
711 Third Avenue, New York, NY 10017

Routledge is an imprint of the Taylor & Francis Group, an informa business

© 2018 Greg Simons and Iulian Chifu

The right of Greg Simons and Iulian Chifu to be identified as authors of
this work has been asserted by them in accordance with sections 77 and 78
of the Copyright, Designs and Patents Act 1988.

All rights reserved. No part of this book may be reprinted or reproduced or
utilised in any form or by any electronic, mechanical, or other means, now
known or hereafter invented, including photocopying and recording, or in
any information storage or retrieval system, without permission in writing
from the publishers.

Trademark notice: Product or corporate names may be trademarks or
registered trademarks, and are used only for identification and explanation
without intent to infringe.

British Library Cataloguing-in-Publication Data
A catalogue record for this book is available from the British Library

Library of Congress Cataloging-in-Publication Data
Names: Simons, Greg, author. | Chifu, Iulian, author.
Title: The changing face of warfare in the 21st century / Greg Simons and
Iulian Chifu.
Description: 1st edition. | Milton Park, Abingdon, Oxon, New York, NY:
Routledge, [2017] | Includes bibliographical references and index.
Identifiers: LCCN 2017002081 | ISBN 9781472482129 (hardback) |
ISBN 9781315614441 (e-book)
Subjects: LCSH: Military art and science–History–21st century. |
War–History–21st century. | Military history, Modern–21st century–Case
studies.
Classification: LCC U42.5 .S55 2017 | DDC 355.02–dc23
LC record available at https://lccn.loc.gov/2017002081

ISBN: 9781472482129 (hbk)
ISBN: 9781315614441 (ebk)

Typeset in Times New Roman
by Cenveo Publisher Services

 Printed and bound by CPI Group (UK) Ltd, Croydon, CR0 4YY

Contents

Author biographies

Professor Iulian Chifu has been President of the Conflict Prevention and Early Warning Centre Bucharest since 2014. He was Counsellor for Foreign, Security and Defence Policy for the President of the Romanian Chamber of Deputies between 2015 and 2016. He has served as Counsellor of the Romanian Senate since July 2016. Chifu has been Presidential Counsellor for Strategic Affairs and International Security, Romanian Presidency, between 2012 and 2014 and Presidential Counsellor for Strategic Affairs, Security and Foreign Policy between 2011 and 2012. Iulian Chifu is specialised in Conflict Analysis, Crisis Decision-making and Post/Conflict Reconstruction, teaching at the Department of International Relations and European Integration SNSPA, Bucharest (Romania) since 2000. Since 2005, Chifu has been Associate Professor at the National Defence College, Bucharest. Between 2007 and 2008, Mr. Chifu was Associate Professor at the National Academy for Information, Bucharest. Between 2002 and 2007, he was Scientific Secretary at the Department for International Relations, SNSPA, Bucharest. Moreover, between 2002 and 2005 he was Associate Professor at the Centre for NATO Studies, Bucharest.

Associate Professor Greg Simons defended his doctoral dissertation in 2004 at the University of Canterbury (Christchurch, New Zealand) on *Ideology, Image-making and the Media in Putin's Russia*. He currently has a number of institutional affiliations as a researcher at the Uppsala Centre for Russian and Eurasian Studies (UCRS) at Uppsala University, and as a lecturer based at the Department of Communication Science at Turiba University (Riga, Latvia). His primary research interests include: communicational aspects of the Russian Orthodox Church (Moscow Patriarchate); Russian public diplomacy and notions of soft power; crisis communication; the relationships between politics, information and communication within the context of armed conflict. Dr Simons has participated in conferences and given lectures, researched and published extensively on these issues. He currently runs an undergraduate course at the Department of Peace and Conflict Research (Uppsala University) on *Mass Media and Contemporary Armed Conflict*.

Colonel Anghel Gabriel gained his PhD in Military Science and Intelligence title, National Defence University "Carol I", Bucharest in 2012. At present he is a senior analyst in the Romanian Ministry of Defence. His research interests include new aspects of hybrid approach in current conflicts, a topic about which he has published and presented at conferences.

1 Introduction

Waging war in the 21st century

Greg Simons and Iulian Chifu

Motivation for the book

This book has been conceived and written as the result of a number of years of working with the subjects of security, mass media, politics and armed conflict by the authors. The elements of communication and politics inform much of the content and the cases contained within the pages of this book. These aspects and the resulting issues have been carefully considered and engaged in from an academic and a practical perspective. War and the manner in which it is waged have been evolving gradually, something that has been noticed by both authors, which prompted the motivation to work on this book to capture the whys, to what extent, the how and the results of those changes (presumed and real). Some of those changes are related to how the public view, perceive and relate to wars and armed conflicts.

After the triumph of the end of the Cold War, the world breathed a sigh of relief after living on the brink for decades, and the 'end of history' was announced. However, currently this short-lived optimism seems to be on the wane as new sets of risks and security challenges evolve and emerge. When wars break out, there are distinct parts to it – the physical fighting that takes place on the battlefield and the informational part that takes place in living rooms across the globe.

The manner and means with which wars and conflicts are communicated is a highly important and pivotal aspect of armed conflict in contemporary times. As such, there are significant implications for mass media, journalism, public opinion and perception. Mass media and journalism have become much more widespread and easily accessible; they have also made the old geopolitical constraints of time and space more or less obsolete to an increasing proportion of the globe's population. When it comes to mass media and journalism, owing to Western traditions in this area, there can be the assumption (although this is diminishing) that these key social institutions are objective and serve the public interest in their presumed capacity as a fourth estate. However, others and including those that have worked in journalism, differ in their opinion and assumptions. Kenneth Payne has gone as far as to declare that mass media are an instrument of war (Payne 2005). This is owing to the fact that no matter what the intention of the journalist (positive or negative), by the mere fact that they report on an armed conflict they influence public perception and opinion.

This situation creates a certain tension and dilemma in a 'democratic' society, where the assumption is that good and reliable information drives good and reliable decisions on a given issue. However, this becomes an unattainable utopia when the different actors engaged in political and/or armed conflict are communicating to the public using media and informational channels with subjective information that is designed to mobilise and prime them to a predetermined set of ideas and actions. Many of the held beliefs on what constitutes how a war should or should not be fought can be found in the different cultural traditions and approaches to war that have evolved over time and experience (Tse-Tung 2000; Nagl 2005: Thornton 2015: Pierman 2015).

Given the dominance of Western capital in the instruments of global mass communication, it is a Western understanding of warfare that dominates. The problem is, there are other traditions and approaches to war, historically and contemporarily, which differ from this view. It has been noted that with the growth of different forms of mass media communication (including non-Western forms) and the means with which to instantaneously communicate to and with larger audiences, there is increasingly less consensus on history and even current events (Kissinger 2015: 330–360). Does the appearance of different forms of conceiving and waging war constitute a change in the prosecution of warfare or merely signify a greater awareness of those alternative styles?

Tangible and intangibles in war

There are tangible and intangible aspects to armed conflicts and attention is certainly more easily drawn to those that are tangible. This can include geographical concerns, such as terrain and climate, but also includes those highly visible aspects of the quantity and quality of personnel and military equipment available. All of these aspects are clearly observed and can be touched. The intangible elements of war cannot be seen, but they can have a significant impact upon operational aspects of an armed conflict. Intangible elements can include the strength or weakness of belief and faith in the political and military leadership, and in the will of a population and an army to go to war or to continue fighting (Simons 2012). This is an important element to consider: although military means determine the outcome of individual battles, wars are increasingly being determined and decided by political considerations (Payne 2005: 81). Therefore, in order to be able to effectively use the tangible elements to the best effect, the intangible elements need to be carefully cultivated.

Intangibles are an important aspect of any contemporary armed conflict, and they ultimately exert a certain influence on the tangibles and along with that impact upon the operational capacity of an actor. Branding has proven to be an increasingly popular tool of choice with which to prime and mobilise target publics. People were captivated by the notions, symbolism and promise of the set of branded revolutions referred to as the *Arab Spring*. Brands can also be exploited in order to leverage political advantage, such as when the Russian Federation moved from narrating the Second Chechen War as an 'internal issue' to one that was part of the Global War On Terrorism (GWOT) (Simons 2010: 59–93). States have not been the sole actors to engage in intangibles, the use of branding and reputation management.

Terrorist organisations have been making increasing use of branding to enhance their reputation and visibility in an increasingly crowded 'marketplace' of terrorist organisations. This is intended as a means of enhancing their intangible value and to differentiate them from other competing (for attention, funding, recruits … etc.) terrorist organisations (Beifuss & Bellini 2013; Simons 2016a). This is a world where perception, which is guided by emotion, rules and affects the nature of the relative choices made by individuals and groups across societies. A strong element of lobbying is present via a system of opposing sets of values and norms, and projected visions of civilizational ideals (Simons 2016b; Simons & Sillanpaa 2016). In a number of instances, terrorist groups have been able to out communicate governments on the informational battlefield. Unlike governments, where information operations play a supporting role to military operations, these groups subordinate military operations to information operations in order to better shape the intangibles of the environment owing to the disparity in available hard power with their enemy.

Politics, communication and contemporary armed conflict

Throughout the history of man there has been a close proximity and an interaction between politics, communication and armed conflict. One of the lines of investigation of this book is to track changes that are presumed to have occurred in the way and manner in which armed conflicts are waged. Such an assumption could be based upon the massive strides and advances of technology and means of communication (Betz 2015). However, perhaps a more prudent initial question to ask would be, have the fundamental nature of wars changed so significantly in the 21st century compared to their historical form(s)? A lot of what may be termed as being hybrid tactics today has already been witnessed in theory and in practice historically (Greene 2006). This is a matter of trying to steer the rules of the game: the actor that is able to create their own rules of international relations can put their adversary on the back foot and gain at least a temporary advantage on the physical and psychological battlefields.

The nature of the conflicts that have been faced, allies, enemies and alliances are constantly shifting and evolving with time and circumstances. In reality, a stable and predictable Cold War has ended already some decades ago. Changes in the global balances and international political relationships have resulted in a much more unpredictable security environment with various emerging risks and threats (Maoz & Gat 2001). This has caused some commentators to announce a divide between what are termed as being 'old' and 'new' wars (Kaldor 2006). Wars are thought of as constituting a last resort, when all other avenues and means of achieving peace have been exhausted. However, this is not always proving to be the case, and this is often attributed to the manner in which they are fought.

Wars are increasingly involve the use of covert military operations and tactics that have little or no transparency or accountability, including by democracies (Scahill 2013), which has a tendency to push the boundaries of war at the same time as blurring them. Gradually the balance of power is shifting away from the West and away from governments, it has also been noted that military force alone is insufficient to ensure the maintenance of defending the international interests of modern states. A report from the House of Lords in the UK concluded that:

> In the context of shared global threats and high economic and political inter-dependence between states, and because coercion alone is proving insuffi-cient for defending nations' interests, being able to build positive international relationships and coalitions – as well as being able to export goods and services – is vital for modern nations' security and prosperity. The degree to which populations now form networks across borders gives this soft power a newly increased impact because it relies to a significant degree on popular perceptions (House of Lords 2014).

The mix of politics and information within the context of communication within an armed conflict is geared towards persuading and influencing a target audi-ence's perception and opinion of it. This is treated as a zero sum game in an environment of conflict and/or competition, which compels the opposing sides to attack the credibility and reputation of the other in order to better position them-selves in the influence stakes. It is clearly seen in the current situation, for exam-ple, where observers deride RT (formerly Russia Today TV channel) as being an instrument of propaganda (Nelson et al. 2015). However, even if it does contain propaganda in its informational products this is not its main purpose; rather it is an instrument of public diplomacy – to reach out to, attract and influence foreign audiences (Simons 2014). Accusations and insinuations are made by different actors as a means of damaging the brand and reputation of media outlets (rightly or wrongly) as a means of attempting to hobble their ability to effectively communicate, influence and persuade audiences. In addition, accusations of propaganda and harm to the public good can be used by governments to crack down on and impose censorship (Layer & Ryjouk 2015). The aim of censorship is not to stop unwanted materials from being made public (this is the means), but to be placed to better shape and determine the perceived reality of the human environment based upon the notion and practice of information dominance.

At times, it is noticeable that the flow of politicised information into the public information sphere, either by accident or design, acts as a barrier rather than a bridge to understanding. It is a rather mainstream and common view that Russia is an outsider, which is not playing by the 'common' understanding of the rules of international relations that have been established by the West (Shirreff & Olex-Szczytowski 2016; Thornton & Karagiannis 2016). This is often based upon a universal set of given norms and values that include such notions as the rule of law, human rights and democracy. But this has a tendency to obscure the other side of the coin, which is less well known. That is the point of view and the perspective of the other party that is often not given without some form of subjective commentary. Some argue for a need to understand the other side's perspective, such as Russia, in order to adequately and effectively engage with them (Kuhn 2015).[1] Engagement does not mean capitulation or appeasement, but rather to know the perspective of the other side in order to more effectively communicate.

Wars are undergoing an increasing level of mediatisation as a means to manage the flows of information, and the public perception and opinions that stem from this practice. This creates a tension between the journalists' mission and the military mission. 'At whatever level media interact with the military during times of conflict, there is always an inherent tension between the ostensible goals of impartial and balanced media reporting and the military objectives of combatants' (Payne 2005: 84). Media have certainly been used by political and military leaders during times of conflict, where impending military offensives have been announced openly in advance or the highly orchestrated televised operation when Osama bin Laden was supposedly killed. The battle of Mosul in 2016 is seen as a good example of a public relations approach to war, where the US and Iraq hope to gain strategic benefits through explaining and justifying the military operation, and determining the perceived reality of the battle (such as a tangible demonstration of success).[2]

Structure and description of the chapters

There are a total of nine individual chapters that make up the contents of this book, which cover a wide range of topics that engage in the theme of the changing nature of warfare in the 21st century. The authors use their experience and knowledge to tackle the increasingly complicated and intricate issue of how wars are now fought, and from different empirical perspectives and academic disciplines. It is the desire of the authors to combine a theoretical framework with concrete empirical examples in order to create a better understanding and comprehension of the current events and processes that shape the character of contemporary armed conflict and how they are informed and perceived in a highly mediatised and politicised world.

The chapters from this book contain examples from Eastern Europe, the Caucasus, the Middle East and Central Asia. It opens with a chapter by Greg Simons on attempts to control the flow of news within the setting of ongoing military operations. *Attempts at Controlling the News Flow: Good News Wars* examines the role and importance attached to information on and about armed conflicts by Western governments. This particular chapter takes events from around the year 2010 when there had been a withdrawal of Western armed forces from Iraq and there were preparations for the eventual drawing down of armed forces from Afghanistan that was scheduled some years later in 2014. The role of information operations within the context of governmental use is shown to be subordinate to military operations. However, those military operations do need to be explained and have at least some semblance of political legitimacy.

Iulian Chifu is the author of the following chapter, *Hybrid Warfare, Lawfare, Informational War: The Wars of the Future*. This chapter engages with concepts of waging war by other means, and acknowledging the centuries long understood dictum that war is an extension of politics, albeit with the use of coercive force in order to compel one's opponent to submit to a situation that they would not ordinarily willingly accept. Thus the 'old' delineations of warfare into regular and irregular have become much more complex, and in some cases there is a blurring of lines with regards to actors and tactics.

The next chapter is co-authored by Iulian Chifu and Gabriel Anghel that follows from the subject of the previous chapter. *Hybrid Warfare: Comparative View ISIL Versus 'Little Green Men'* develops the application of the term and practice of hybrid warfare with two examples from currents tensions and conflicts that have captured the attention of politics, the public and the news media in international relations and affairs. An effect of these new ways of waging warfare is to blur the distinctions between what can be considered war and that what is considered to be peace.

Chapter 5 is authored by Iulian Chifu on the subject of *Fighting Within the Legal Framework and Reaching Military Objectives by Using the Law*. Military operations and war have been regulated by codes of conduct, laws and treaties for some time now. These legal frameworks have sought to impose constraints on the 'lawful' use of military force by the belligerents in order to curb the excesses of organised armed violence in the past in order to protect vulnerable parties and to bestow a seemingly more 'legitimate' way of waging war. This chapter seeks to explain the terms and use of *lawfare*, and its conceptual development in the contemporary world.

Iulian Chifu examines the issue of *The Pattern of Russia's Informational War* in Chapter 6. This is certainly a very hot topic in the current times, attracting a lot of attention and publicity, but also some misunderstandings concerning the development and practice of informational war as conducted by Russia. It is the contention of the author that Russia's approach to informational war lies within the realm of hybrid war, and the informational aspects that play on the creation of alternative realities that drive people's opinion and reaction to events and processes in a manner that can possibly benefit Russian policy, goals and interests.

On the subject of the use of creating and projecting realities during times of political and armed conflict, in Chapter 7 Greg Simons researches the *Strategic Messages in the August 2008 Georgian-Russian War*. As in the previous chapter, this concerns actors involved in an armed confrontation communicating to wider audiences in order to try and project their version of reality and the 'truth' in order to subjectively explain their actions, to gain a sense of political legitimacy, and to win the war of the hearts and minds of various target audiences. This particular war was marked not only by the asymmetry of the physical armed struggle (the comparative sizes and strengths of Georgia and Russia), but also the asymmetry in terms of the intangible functions of communications (Georgia was deemed to have had the upper hand in the war of the narratives).

Chapter 8 concerns *Communication Management and the Humanitarian War Blueprint: The Libya War* and is by Greg Simons. Libya was one of the cases of the so-called Arab Spring that was selectively applied across revolutionary waves affecting the Middle East and North African region. This chapter engages in the issue of hybrid war, but managed by Western countries, which involves the invocation of humanitarian wars in conjunction with a sustained media-based information war that creates a very diametrically opposed set of projected realities in the public information sphere. This is in line with the practice of governments using information operations to support and be subordinate to military operations. However, as the author demonstrates, there were problems in sustaining the desired image and official message of the conflict by Western political and military leaders.

In the next chapter Greg Simons researches the issue of *Propaganda and the Information War Against Syria: The Latest War for Peace*. This represents a second case study from the Arab Spring revolutions, although the war continues, the chapter looks at the first years of the war when actors were attempting to set the narratives. It was an attempt to limit the allowable leeway in describing this event in order to gain hegemony on the discourse. The chapter makes the case of media being used as an instrument of waging war. There are a number of striking similarities in this case with the informational tactics used in Libya against Gadaffi, especially in terms of the employment of Orwellian Double Speak.

Greg Simons continues the topic of regime change in Chapter 10, *Power Through Subversion: Shaping Perception and Opinion on Ukraine's Euromaidan Through Manufacturing Knowledge*. This chapter covers the use of the elements of subversion and perception within hybrid warfare. The beginning of Euromaidan and up to the period of the Anti-Terrorist Operation (ATO) are covered, providing a glimpse of a period when actors try to establish informational dominance in order to better influence public opinion and perception. There is an observable clash of values and norms employed by opposing sides in the struggle for political legitimacy and public sympathy.

Notes

1 Kissinger, H. A. & Shultz, G. P., Building On Common Ground With Russia, *The Washington Post*, http://www.washingtonpost.com/wp-dyn/content/article/2008/10/07/AR2008100702439.html, 8 October 2008 (accessed 7 December 2016)
2 Lee, C., *Warning Orders: Strategic Reasons for Publicising Military Offensives*, War On The Rocks, http://warontherocks.com/2016/10/warning-orders-strategic-reasons-for-publicizing-military-offensives/, 28 October 2016 (accessed 14 November 2016)

Bibliography

Beifuss, A. & Bellini, F. T., *Branding Terror: The Logotypes and Iconography of Insurgent Groups and Terrorist Organisations*, New York: Merrell Publishers, 2013
Betz, D., *Carnage and Connectivity: Landmarks in the Decline of Conventional Military Power*, New York: Oxford University Press, 2015

Greene, R., *The 33 Strategies of War*, New York: Penguin Books, 2006

House of Lords, *Persuasion and Power in the Modern World*, Select Committee on Soft Power and UK's Influence, Report of Session 2013–14, HL Paper 150, 28 March 2014

Kaldor, M., *New and Old Wars: Organised Violence in a Global Era*, 2nd Edition, Cambridge: Polity Press, 2006

Kissinger, H., *World Order*, New York: Penguin Books, 2015

Kuhn, U., Understanding Russia, *Russian Analytical Digest, Analysis*, No. 162, 10 February 2015

Layer, Y. & Ryjouk, O., The Challenges of Pro-Russian Media Bias in Ukraine, a Case Study of the Vesti Newspaper, *Russian Analytical Digest, Analysis*, No. 177, 8 December 2015

Maoz, Z. & Gat, A., *War in a Changing World*, Ann Arbor: The University of Michigan Press, 2001

Nagl, J. A., *Learning to Eat Soup with a Knife: Counterinsurgency Lessons From Malaya and Vietnam*, Chicago: University of Chicago Press, 2005

Nelson, E., Orttung, R. & Livshen, A., Measuring RT's Impact on YouTube, *Russian Analytical Digest, Analysis*, No. 177, 8 December 2015

Payne, K., The Media as an Instrument of War, *Parameters*, Spring 2005, pp. 81–93

Pierman, G., The Grand Strategy of Non-state Actors: Theory and Implications, *Journal of Strategic Security*, 4(8:4), Winter 2015, pp. 69–78

Scahill, J., *Dirty Wars: The World is a Battlefield*, London: Serpent's Tail, 2013

Shirreff, Gen. Sir R. & Olex-Szczytowski, M., Arming for Deterrence: How Poland and NATO Should Counter a Resurgent Russia, Brent Scowcroft Centre on International Security, Atlantic Council, July 2016

Simons, G. & Sillanpaa, A. (Eds.), *The Kremlin and DAESH Information Activities*, Riga: NATO Strategic Communications Centre of Excellence, 2016

Simons, G. (a), Islamic Extremism and the War for Hearts and Minds, *Global Affairs*, 2(1), 2016, pp. 91–99

Simons, G. (b), Rethinking Communication Within the Global War on Terrorism, *Small Wars Journal*, 6 July 2016

Simons, G., Russian Public Diplomacy in the 21st Century: Structure, Means and Message, *Public Relations Review*, 40, 2014, pp. 440–449

Simons, G., Understanding Political and Intangible Elements in Modern Wars, *State Management: Electronic Herald*, 34, October 2012

Simons, G., *Mass Media and Modern Warfare: Reporting on the Russian War on Terrorism*, Farnham: Ashgate, 2010

Thornton, R. & Karagiannis, M., The Russian Threat to the Baltic States: The Problems of Shaping Local Defence Mechanisms, *The Journal of Slavic Military Studies*, 29(3), 2016, pp. 331–351

Thornton, R., The Changing Nature of Modern Warfare, *The RUSI Journal*, 160(4), 2015, pp. 40–48

Tse-Tung, M. (trans. Griffith II, S. B.), *On Guerrilla Warfare*, Champaign (IL): University of Illinois Press, 2000

2 Attempts at controlling the news flow

Good news wars

Greg Simons

News is a means for ordinary citizens to be connected to events that would otherwise prove to be remote from their personal experience. How these events are told and represented to the public has an effect upon public opinion of the event and those tasked with managing that event. There are three different possible avenues of investigation when it comes to news. 1) News as an object of policy formation; 2) news as an object of commodification; and 3) news as an object of public opinion (Allan 2001: 3–4). The stakes are even higher for an incumbent government that launches or continues a potentially unpopular war.

The so-called CNN-effect has been in existence for some time, however, some argue that it is difficult to understand if media move governments into 'humanitarian' wars or vice versa (Robinson 1999). Others argue explicitly that media are in fact an instrument of war (Payne 2005). It is the intention of this chapter to explore the why and the how of trying to get 'good' and positive stories into the news programmes. This is intended to be oriented from the perspective of a government, which is responsible for launching or continuing an armed conflict. What is the motivation and reason for trying to 'weave' positive information into the news? How is this achieved in a practical sense (operationalised)?

There is an attempt to influence public opinion through the nature and style with which the news is related to the public. On the whole, news concerning conflict is descriptive rather than analytical. This provides those who wish to influence the news agenda and themes with an opportunity to do so. Attempts are made to try and convey a positive and upbeat narrative of the conflict in order to influence the public perception into believing in a 'good' and successful war. In the framework of this work, mass media and journalism are used in an interchangeable sense.

Before covering the issue of the interactions and relationships between mass media, political and military actors and contemporary armed conflict, it is critical to understand recent changes to news management and production. There have been numerous changes to operating procedure, management and personnel in their responses to the 24/7 news cycle and economic hardship that has meant checks and balances have disappeared and lowered the quality of news standards, which in turn affects society and the ability of active members in a democracy to make well-informed decisions.

This chapter shall look at a number of events within the Global War on Terrorism (GWOT) that shall demonstrate the dilemma faced by authorities and governments engaged in combating insurgencies and terrorism campaigns. Afghanistan is the primary focus of this work, and in this way the information and research relates to one particular event and bypasses the possibility of mixing narratives, actors and events. The dilemma being that if no sign of progress can be demonstrated then the public may assume that the conflict is being lost. Even if there are lull periods in such conflicts, which can last for many years. Therefore there is an attempt by governments and authorities to accentuate the positive (or seemingly positive) and to try and mitigate the negative in order to try and shore up the vulnerable political aspect linked to modern conflict.

A significant factor for choosing to focus upon Afghanistan within the context of the GWOT is that in terms of international public perception it was initially seen as being a legitimate military action. This contrasted with the much more controversial case of Iraq in March 2003, which was perceived in the wider international public as lacking legitimacy and bearing the hallmarks of aggressive military opportunism by the Bush administration. Material for this chapter is sourced from media reports from around the year 2010 in order to capture the essence of the type and nature of the discussions taking place at a time when the 'forgotten war' of Afghanistan was moving towards the spotlight owing to the gradual withdrawal from Iraq and the necessity to generate more positive news on Afghanistan in order to try and demonstrate progress and success by the ISAF forces stationed there.

News as a shaper of public consciousness

The mass media is the source from which the public 'experiences' events that occur remotely, in a physical sense from their lives, and which they may not normally witness otherwise. If the ability to gain information on an event is difficult to source, for any number of reasons, an impact is exerted by the nature (or lack) of information that is acquired. The mass media, especially in the late 20th century, have come to be viewed as being an all-powerful influence on society.

> As the late twentieth century history of moral panics and food scares demonstrates, the journalistic media have become steadily more important as 'reality defining' institutions. They have become synonymous with the public sphere – that intermediate zone between governors and the governed where public opinion is formed and reformed. The journalistic media are the main source of our information about politics and public affairs in general as well as setting the agenda. Politicians and public organisations – social actors in general – have gradually come to understand this and adapt their organisations and practices accordingly (McNair 2004: 55).

This potential power has not gone unnoticed by those seeking to influence the news content and agenda. In the United States one of the noted trends that are occurring is the establishment (bankrolling) of start-up news organisations around the country by conservative groups. These news organisations are aggressive in their coverage of government and politics, which comes precisely at the time when newspapers are cutting back their statehouse bureaus. The new news organisations almost exclusively use the internet and appear (visually) like traditional news media outlets. On the political level, this type of journalism is viewed with scepticism and organisations that issue press credentials for statehouse reporters have denied some of the outlets membership. This decision is motivated by citing their links to pressure groups.[1]

Effects by and on journalists

An important point that is brought out in this quote is that mass media can act as a 'bridge' between the authorities and the public. The exact way that the mass media goes about acting as a 'bridge' is determined by a number of different factors. Those who bring the public the news are an important factor in the news production cycle. Journalists are influenced by the environment in which they work, the influences being drawn from the nature of their profession, their workplace and an individual journalist's particular world view. Brian McNair highlighted the importance of journalists in the frame of the nature of the effects upon communication.

> Journalism, therefore, like any other narrative which is the work of human agency, is essentially ideological – a communicative vehicle for the transmission to an audience (intentionally or otherwise) not just of facts but of the assumptions, attitudes, beliefs and values of its maker(s), drawn from and expressive of a particular world-view (McNair 2004: 6).

The effect of the human element upon the news production process is an important one to consider, and it is likely to ensure that the utopian ideal of 'truly' objective news is unlikely to be ever reached. Therefore a question that should be investigated is whether high quality news is needed in order for a citizen to be adequately informed and to make sound judgements based upon that information. If this good quality news is absent from mass media, does this mean that this adversely affects the public from making the appropriate decisions?

A number of studies have shown that there are serious concerns about the quality of newspaper content. The University of Technology in Sydney, Australia conducted a six month survey of content of ten newspapers, seven of which were owned by Rupert Murdoch's *News Corporation*. The aim of the study was to gauge the level that Australia's major newspapers relied on PR to generate stories. Some 2203 articles were analysed over a five day period.

- Nearly 55 per cent of the stories were initiated by public relations;
- More than 24 per cent of stories 'had no significant extra perspective, source or content added by reporters';

- 70 per cent of the *Daily Telegraph* (Murdoch owned) stories were PR driven, the worst performer;
- 42 per cent of the *Sydney Morning Herald* (Fairfax) content was PR driven, the best performer.[2]

These findings, albeit for a period of one week only, reveal a dismal performance of Australian newspaper journalism, some relying heavily on sources that have a vested interest in the story being reported. This raises an important point and question: is this case an isolated one? Other studies of this nature have been conducted. One of them was done by Nick Davies of Cardiff University (in research for his book *Flat Earth News* from 2008). The origins of some 2000 UK news stories from five newspapers were surveyed by Davies and his team.

- 12 per cent of stories were wholly composed of material researched by reporters;
- 8 per cent of stories were of uncertain origin;
- 80 per cent of stories were found to be wholly, mainly or partially written from second hand material, provided by news agencies or the PR industry;
- 12 per cent of news stories had evidence of the facts being thoroughly checked.[3]

These studies show that there is a likelihood that the poor standards of journalism are not isolated cases, which paints a worrying picture in terms of the role being played by mass media in society. One line of argument exists that if there is at least some access to good quality information, and blanket coverage of poor information does not exist, the public should still be able to make well-informed decisions. (Gripsrud 2002: 23–24) However, this line of thinking implies that the audience in question possesses a sufficient degree of media literacy to know when the quality of news is poor and where to look for alternative (good quality) sources.

The use and reliance on information provide by PR agencies and other sources that have a vested interest in releasing that information is not the only issue regarding the mass media and news sources. There is an increasing tendency to rely on the use of a narrow group of pundits in order to generate opinions. However, in doing this the effect is that mass media tends to generate more opinions than facts. Jeri Karcey, a Republican from Ashland (Oregon) characterised the problem further down the news production track. 'It is never what they are saying that is the problem. It is what they are not saying. That is where the lack of balance comes in. It is distortion by omission.'[4] Thus the issue of censorship through omitting alternative views and information may also be a problem, although a less obvious one to an external observer.

Politics and mass media in the contemporary age

One of the basic requirements of a journalist is to identify their source in a story, whereby credibility is lent. It helps the media consumer to judge and verify the veracity of the story in question. To not identify the source, the journalist is asking the media consumer to surrender their trust in the journalist and the media outlet. This does not get around the basic question of the necessity for transparency and accountability for what is being offered by the journalist and media outlet.

Information is the lifeblood of politics, and rhetoric is the medium that links politics to society. What is of interest is the role and intention of the rhetoric used in the process. An article that appeared in the *Telegraph* summed up the presumed state of affairs.

> One need not be versed in Demosthenes or Cicero to understand that politics is a rhetorical art. Long before Dr Goebbels, or his modern descendants in the trade of spin doctor, politicians were using words to conceal, rather than to amplify, reality.[5]

In addition to using deception as part of the everyday political 'trade', tougher times call for tougher measures. Simon Heffer notes in his article that 'history also shows that the worse things are, the more politicians rely on distortion to get through.'[6] Thus political use of rhetoric that spreads distortion or deception is used for either avoiding negative consequences or to promote a policy that would likely prove to be unpopular.

Media can also be used by political forces to bring about change, especially in a foreign setting. In the period of the late Bush administration and continued by the Obama administration is the use of New Communication Technology (NCT). The internet and other forms of NCTs constitute the forefront of the United States' public diplomacy programme. There is heavy use and reliance on such social media and internet based information to bring about changes in perception and opinion in the targeted audience. The programme is based in the State Department and is called *Public Diplomacy 2.0*. James Glassman, the former Undersecretary of State for Public Diplomacy stated the motivations for the US to engage. 'Anyway, we Americans believe in the marketplace of ideas. Our idea was to use technology and social media to promote a conversation in which our views would be aired.'[7]

There are a number of governments around the world seeking to control internet based content and conversation. This is extremely difficult to achieve given the current level of technology and access in developed countries. Yet to a greater or lesser extent, the desire to maintain control is still strong. Jared Cohen described the approach taken in *Public Diplomacy 2.0* and how it differs from convention.

> There is a fear that if we can't control the message, then we are giving the enemy more space to exploit internet tools and propagate their message. [...] realise that the 21st century is a terrible time to be a control freak and to understand that maybe we can't control the message but we can influence it. Technology is not the answer, it is a tool and there is always a risk that comes along with using it.[8]

Therefore the policy of using NCT and social media as a means of, if not toppling, at least influencing a regime did not die with the Bush administration and its notion of *Transplanted Democracy*. In carrying out such a programme a government requires a 'noble' cause for its domestic audience (for a sense of legitimacy) and a foreign target audience with access to the internet (to facilitate the *Public Diplomacy 2.0* programme) that can be mobilised.

Mixing politics, business and journalism

Concern over the decline in the standards of journalism has reached the point in the European Union (EU) when the European Federation of Journalists (representing unions in 24 countries) has called for the EU to back journalism as a 'public good.' Arne König, the President of the European Federation of Journalists (EFJ) characterised the 'spiral of decline' as being due to economic factors. He sees the decline as being a significant threat. "A toxic mix of editorial cuts, precarious working conditions and unethical journalism has created a spiral of decline for media and democracy in Europe." The hardest hit sectors of journalism due to the economic hard times are editing, investigative and specialist news reporting. The union has gone as far as to call for protection and funding from the EU, putting part of the blame with policy makers. Secretary General of the EFJ stated that "EU policy makers have not done enough to protect standards, to protect ethical journalism."[9] However, this raises a number of questions about the relationship between the state and the mass media when public funding of private business is proposed. Not the least of which is editorial independence of the mass media versus journalistic transparency and accountability to the European taxpayer.

Some two years prior to this event, on 3 October 2008 the Council of Europe passed Resolution 1636 on indicators for media in a democracy. Resolution 1636 puts a focus on the role of freedom of information and expression in the media being a crucial element for democracy. It is stated in 1636 that "public participation in the democratic decision-making process requires that the public is well-informed and has the possibility of freely discussing different opinions." There is a list of some 27 basic principles in the document. The third principle states that "media ownership and economic influence over media must be made transparent."[10]

Within the traditions of the Western Liberal Press theory is the idea of the Fourth Estate, which is meant to (ideally) be the check and balance of the executive, legislative and judicial power. However, there is a rich supply of cases that demonstrate that those checks and balances are replaced by collusion between key figures in the mass media and politics. One of the influential media figures is Roger Ailes, the head of *Fox News*, which is part of Rupert Murdoch's *News Corporation*. In an interview with *The New York Times Magazine* in 2008, President Barack Obama said that the so-called Fox Effect had cost him two to three points in the polls. In another case, a Republican candidate in the 23rd Congressional District in upstate New York withdrew after an independent candidate was endorsed by *Fox News*.[11] This demonstrates the potential of those in the mass media to use its ability to shape the political landscape, according to their particular tastes and interests.

One of the assumptions that is held is that the corporate owners of mass media assets are much more interested in money (profit making) than in ideology. However, this is not necessarily the case, especially when the long-term perspective is considered over the short-term one. Rupert Murdoch of News Corporation has supported a number of leading political figures, including Margaret Thatcher and Tony Blair, helping in shaping opinion and political ideas in Australia, United Kingdom and the United States.

Murdoch's media assets supported free market thinking, and in the past newspapers such as the *New York Post*, London *Times* and *The Australian* lost millions of dollars (US$) in supporting this position. He was once attributed to having said that those in the media business are "ruled by ideas." *The Weekly Standard*, like its owner Rupert Murdoch, was a strong supporter of President G. W. Bush and the 2003 invasion of Iraq. The magazine received an annual subsidy of US$1 million per year (corporation revenue was US$32 billion), and Murdoch's speech writer, Bill McGurn was also Bush's chief speech writer.[12] This situation demonstrates that a union between politics, business and media is not only feasible, but a reality.

News gathering and production in the internet age

A Project for Excellence in Journalism study by the Pew Research Centre[13] showed a gulf in the news agenda between traditional and social media. Social media sites have a short attention span when it comes to news stories. It was found that 53 per cent of lead stories on blogs in any given week are not likely to be shared or discussed after three days, and the figure for Twitter is 72 per cent. Fifty-two per cent of stories drop off a social network's agenda after only 24 hours. There is also a relationship between traditional and social media, with some 99 per cent of stories appearing on blogs coming from the traditional media (such as newspapers and broadcast networks). Of the links appearing on the blogs reviewed by the study, 23 per cent were the BBC, 21 per cent CNN, and 16 per cent *Washington Post*. Twitter is an exception in that 50 per cent go to traditional news organisations (as opposed to the norm of 80 per cent) and 40 per cent to web-only news sites.[14] Thus there seems to be somewhat of a mutual relationship between the traditional media and the social media. But where is this leading the news gathering and making process?

A survey in 2010 found that 92 per cent of Americans get their daily news from multiple sources. The Project for Excellence in Journalism report rated the internet as the third most popular news medium. Local and national television topped the list, newspapers and radio broadcasts trailed the internet. Some 59 per cent of respondents get their news from both online and offline sources. Only 7 per cent relied solely on either the internet or local television as their news source. Interestingly enough, some 69 per cent of respondents consider it their social or civic obligation to get the news. This survey also revealed attitudes towards news organisations. 63 per cent consider that news organisations do a good job covering subjects that matter. However, 72 per cent think that news sources today are biased in their coverage.[15]

'Mainstream' or 'traditional' journalism has been gradually shifting to using social networking sites on the internet more and more in their daily business, partly due to the reasons mentioned in the previous section. Articles on this subject are becoming more common, and reveal a distinct trend. Two recent surveys, one carried out in the United States and the other in Canada, among journalists give an idea of the level of reliance and use of social networking sites.

In 2009 *PR Week/PR Newswire Media* conducted an online survey of 2174 journalists, bloggers and public relations professionals in Canada and the United States. Thirty-seven per cent of journalists contribute to *Twitter* and 39 per cent produce content for a blog as part of their expanded duties. Social networking sites are being used by journalists to find story ideas. Sarah Skerik the Vice-President for Distribution Services at *PR Newswire* stated that "journalists are doing more with less. They seem to be acting more aggressively about finding their stories, digging a bit deeper for story angles."

- 24 per cent state that they consider sites such as *Facebook* and *Twitter* as an important way to connect with experts (this figure was 13 per cent in 2009);
- 46 per cent of journalists say that they sometimes use blogs for research;
- 33 per cent report using social networks for research (this figure was 24 per cent in 2009);
- 43 per cent of journalists have been pitched to through social networks by the PR industry (compared with 31 per cent in 2009);
- 59 per cent of journalists are writing a blog, either professionally or personally, 31 per cent are writing a blog for their traditional media outlet (this figure was 28 per cent in 2009).[16]

The Executive Editor of *PR Week*, Erica Iacono attributed the changes to "heavier workloads, shorter deadlines, and increased competition [which] are causing journalists to seek out new sources of information to help them get their jobs done, including social networks."[17] Another survey was conducted in the United States among a sample of 371 US journalists and editors by Cision (a PR company) and the Masters Degree Programme in Strategic Public Relations at George Washington University.

- 89 per cent of respondents use blogs in their research;
- 65 per cent turn to social networks;
- 55 per cent use micro-blogging sites as part of their research;
- 61 per cent turn to Wikipedia;
- 96 per cent refer to corporate websites for their research;
- 72 per cent of newspaper and on-line journalists use social networking sites for significant on-line research;

- 84 per cent thought that news delivered by social media was less reliable than that distributed by traditional media;
- 44 per cent state that they depend upon PR professionals for "interviews and access to sources and experts";
- 23 per cent rely upon PR professionals for "answers to questions and targeted information";
- 17 per cent rely on PR professionals for "perspective, information in context, and background information".[18]

These figures reveal a number of important and interesting points. Firstly, there is the great importance of social media and networks in gathering and finding news stories. Next is the point that although journalists understand that information derived from 'non-traditional' media is less credible, they use it anyway. The final point to be raised is the issue of the reliance on PR professionals (and corporate websites) in researching their stories, in spite of a highly likely element of bias in the information that they receive (depending on the interests of the PR firm). When mass media attach themselves in such a manner to PR, the result is that it inevitably decreases the quality of the information produced. Any notion of objectivity and truth is lost in the process.

Media outlets are beginning to position themselves in order to adapt to the new age of news gathering and production. Among the outlets that have announced structural and procedural changes designed to evolve to the new news environment is *AOL*. In December 2009 *AOL* launched *Seed.com*, which is aimed at grooming freelance writers to cover a diverse range of subjects and interests. Saul Hansell, Programming Director at *Seed* said that "*AOL* is repositioning itself as a news and information company."[19] The motivation for using this particular model of operation seems to be its cost effective means (as opposed to the establishment of an off-line/traditional media operation) of entering the news business.

Another media outlet to adapt to the internet news environment is *Sky News*. They are installing Twitter software on the computers of their journalists in order to encourage and enable greater use of social media in newsgathering and reporting. Julian March, the Executive Producer of *Sky News* summed up the change in philosophy and approach when it came to using social media. "The big change for us in 2010 is evolving how social media plays a role in our journalism. We no longer *ghettoise* it to one person, but are in the process of embedding throughout the whole team."[20] The term used by the *Sky News* executive, *ghettoise*, is as interesting as it is revealing of the old attitude towards social media, and the change that has not taken long to come about.

Public opinion and war

All of the different subjects that constitute the news that we see, read and listen to are not equal. Some news stories hold a greater news value than others, and draw the attention of the mass media. One common trait of those 'newsworthy' stories is that they contain an element of perceived deviancy in them – crime, sex, violence and war for example. They all contain the human element plus the element of excitement (through the association of deviancy). Therefore politicians are very aware of the likelihood of an event that contains war to draw a great deal of mass media attention with high audience consumption.

Modern conflict is determined more and more through political considerations and goals rather than by pure military means. Therefore the case can arise where a battle is won militarily, but the war is ultimately lost politically. In the wake of the Vietnam War, the US military firmly laid the blame for the humiliating defeat at the feet of the mass media. They were blamed for sapping the public's will to fight and support their soldiers. However, by the 21st century there had been a re-think of this presumed reason for the defeat. This time the blame shifted to the role played by US officials and politicians. It was said that they did not show and maintain enough perception of faith that the war could be won. And that this doubt was passed on to the public. Therefore the new wars required public officials and politicians to maintain an upbeat assessment of progress and events, to convey a sense that the war is winnable.

The role played by mass media and journalists in society has been a hotly debated topic for some time. One side of the story, which assumes a powerful and influential mass media, posits that they protect public interest and take an oppositional stance to the government (Edwards 2001). Others are more cynical concerning the role of mass media in society, where journalists and the mass media do not function as a check and balance (either as a result of passivity or collusion with the authorities) in the traditions set out in the notion of the Fourth Estate (Louw 2010; Herman & Chomsky 2002).

> The mass media serve as a system for communicating messages and symbols to the general populace. It is their function to amuse, entertain, and inform, and to inculcate individuals with the values, beliefs, and codes of behaviour that will integrate them into the institutional structures of the larger society. In a world of concentrated wealth and major conflicts of class interest, to fulfil this role requires systematic propaganda (Herman & Chomsky 2002: 1).

Even in the established democracies of the world, such as the United Kingdom and the United States, the issue of the concentration of mass media ownership into fewer and fewer hands ensures that less pluralism is heard in media. Additionally, a close relationship can form between media owners and governments that can further erode any public watchdog functions of the mass media (Goldberg 2003; McNair 2004; Herman & Chomsky 2002). Therefore there is the possible scenario that mass media may knowingly cooperate with authorities, and form some kind of symbiotic relationship.

There is also the possibility that mass media may unknowingly resist influence from external agencies or at least offer resistance to influence from external agencies (such as political parties, organisations and PR agencies) that seek to influence the narrative. Leading up to war, and during war, is a period of high political stakes and tension. Therefore mass media content is crucial in getting the 'right' image conveyed.

> There is no doubt that the activities of the public relations firm Hill and Knowlton during the Gulf War (1990-1) helped the Bush administration to secure a congressional majority for military intervention in Kuwait and Iraq. Although the resulting conflict may have been a 'just war', insofar as any war can be just, it is clear with hindsight that 'black propaganda' and disinformation were important tools used by the politico-military establishment and by the public relations companies in the context of the Gulf conflict, under contract from interested parties, to secure mass support for military actions which might otherwise have been unsympathetically received (McNair 2004: 158).

The current structure and operating procedures of news organisations make them susceptible to manipulation from actors interested in influencing the news content (in order to affect the opinions and behaviour of an audience as a means of meeting organisational objectives). News organisations are streamlined in terms of their staffing, the advent of the 24-hours-a-day and seven-days-a-week news cycle places pressure on time and staff. The economics of the news media means that there are fewer journalists, but those fewer journalists are working more intensively. These pressures, combined with the issue of deadlines, and competition between the different news media outlets to get the story out first, means they are more susceptible to accepting material from external agencies such as PR agencies and other organisations with a vested interest.

In October 2008 with the passing of Resolution 1636, by the Council of Europe, there was now a potential 'threat' to journalists placing 'bought' news content in to their work. Basic principle 26 states clearly that journalists should "disclose to their viewers or readers any political or financial interests as well as any collaboration with state bodies such as embedded military journalism."[21] Thus there is rightly a significant concern about undisclosed or hidden agenda being embedded in the news, and possible effects that this may have on the audience. However, it is not always only hidden backers and intentions that are the cause for concern. There are some trends that risk undermining the news and its value through trivialisation.

Infotainment and its rise has been one of the significant elements to affect the quality of the news, where news is viewed as being something that should be entertaining, rather than informative (which could be construed as being boring by decision makers in the mass media sphere). One of the fundamental problems for the audience in this particular stylistic approach to news production is that it makes the content very descriptive and there is a distinct lack of analysis. Therefore the value of the information neglects the basic issues and people that lie behind and around the event. There are no answers to the what, how and why questions relating to the war as the information is a superficial presentation of the ('newsworthy') present.

Daya Thussu notes that the demands of the 24 hour news cycle mean that journalists find it hard to gain sufficient material to fill the airtime. He notes that in the absence of a flow of information, journalists tend to work on rumour, to manufacture reports and use unattributed sources. Using the 9/11 case, Thussu states that TV networks resorted to speculation and rumours rather than accurate reporting. Therefore there is a rush to use any new information first, even if it is at best, remotely connected with events (Thussu 2009: 114). These observed operating procedures used by journalists are not conducive to providing their audience with good quality information on which to base solid decisions, at a point in time when such decisions are necessary.

Good news in the GWOT

George Creel, the civilian director of the Committee for Public Information, a government agency that has been credited with helping to bring the United States into the First World War in 1917 once stated: "people do not live by bread alone; they mostly live by catch phrases." (Ewen 1996: 112) This implies an ability to drive the thoughts and behaviour of man by a relatively 'shallow' process of perception and emotion. Within the context of the contemporary ongoing conflicts, this is most evident when viewed through the catch-phrase 'war on terrorism.' It is intended to convey not only a sense of urgency, but also a sense of legitimacy.

To deliver this catch-phrase, and make sure that it reaches a large enough audience for it to have a noticeable effect on public opinion requires the aid of a mass medium. An embedded journalist in Afghanistan reflected upon a combat experience he had, and the role of combat in the wider sense through its impact upon the psyche of man.

> So raw and instantaneous, combat inspires introspection. The premise that war exposes the essential nature of people is hard to dispute, once you have witnessed it. Centuries of literature attest to its magnetism. Combat is the most elemental act, and the most intricate. For all of its spectacular horrors, it will never lack an audience.[22]

There is no doubting that combat makes a very newsworthy story, which is bound to attract interest due to the dimensions of human interest and drama that is part and parcel of it. The subject of war is a controversial one to cover and has the effect of evoking strong emotions, although for different reasons in different audiences, which makes the issue of objective coverage not only difficult from a practical point of view, but also from a point of view of psychological objectivity. Both the news maker and news consumer are affected by these factors. This is compounded when the conflict is ongoing.

PR and massaging the war effort

Wars tend to be perceived along two lines or stages in terms of ethics. This also has an effect on the type of communications from parties with an interest in a conflict, whether it is emerging or actual. The first line or stage is before a war or conflict has broken out, the focus is on *Jus ad Bellum* or the 'right' to wage war. Communications around this concept are aimed at trying to establish the perception of just and reasonable grounds to begin a war. The other aspect to be aware of is *Jus ad Bello*, which occurs after the shooting starts and is related to creating the perception of a conflict being conducted ethically and justly. Therefore communications here are focused upon conveying the notions of justice and righteousness by the 'good' side and the sense of evil and inhumanity of the identified 'bad' side.

The events of 9/11 in the United States, and the fear that this generated among the American public, provided an opportunity for this to be exploited for the purpose of laying the foundations for *Jus ad Bellum*. Evidence of this is suggested by two non-profit journalism organisations that conducted a two-year study from the 9/11 attacks until the US-led invasion of Iraq in 2003.[23] Speeches, interviews, briefings, government reports and other public announcements by President Bush and his administration officials were searched for references to weapons of mass destruction (WMDs) and links of the Saddam Hussein regime in Iraq to terrorism. The results of the study were both revealing and somewhat disturbing (owing to the hint of public manipulation).

- A total of 935 false or misleading statements were counted;
- On at least 532 occasions it was stated that Iraq had WMDs or was trying to produce/obtain them or had links to terrorism;
- The holder of the most false statements was Bush with 259, 231 concerned WMDs and 28 about Iraqi links to Al Qaeda;
- Collin Powell was the next, with 244 false statements on WMDs and 10 on links between Iraq and Al Qaeda.

The study commented on the nature, meaning and significance of these figures in a wider context. Such a situation has consequences, both in terms of the standards of journalism, but also hinting at possible effects that this could have on the public.

> The cumulative effect of these false statements – amplified by thousands of news stories and broadcasts – was massive, with the media coverage creating an almost impenetrable din for the critical months in the run-up to war. [...] Some journalists – indeed, even some news organisations – have since acknowledged that their coverage during those pre-war months was far too deferential and uncritical. These mea culpas not withstanding, much of the wall-to-wall media coverage provided additional 'independent' validation of the Bush administration's false statements about Iraq.[24]

False statements that were given on such a systematic basis and in such overwhelming numbers hint at the intention to create a perceived legitimate basis for *Jus ad Bellum*. The state of the mass media as a result of the 'new' system of news gathering and production, plus the psychological factor of fear in society generated from the 9/11 attacks perhaps contributed to the mass media failing in their duty as the Fourth Estate. This may also account for the differences in public opinion between the publics in the United States and Europe. The European publics did not have a large scale terrorist attack fresh on their minds.

There has also been evidence of communications aimed at shaping public perception after the GWOT was underway and its sense of legitimacy getting eroded. Periodically the narratives and key messages of the campaign need to be renewed after the older ones become obsolete and lose their power to exert any effect on perception and behaviour in the target audiences. PR and branding has been used in both the Iraq and Afghanistan campaigns.

The brand is an important and highly symbolic aspect of an object that is intended to shape the way the branded object is perceived by a target audience. February 2010 saw an example of a rebranded operation, when Secretary of Defense Bob Gates officially requested that US Central Command change the code name of the Iraq operation from *Operation Iraqi Freedom* to *Operation New Dawn*.[25] One of the symbolic implications of the name change is that it is losing the American connection, with a withdrawal of US combat forces in 2011 (at this stage). It implies that the job is done and that a sense of 'normality' has been restored to Iraq. This painted picture belies the realities of daily life in Iraq, where bombings are still taking a heavy toll on civilians.

In terms of tactics there is some continuity in use of rhetoric and perception to try and influence how the GWOT is understood. This includes manipulating and changing details down to the very words we use to describe actors and events in the conflict.

> It is not the first time the Obama administration, like the Bush White House before it, sought to beautify its military endeavours through facelifts and marketing appeals. Last March it announced that it was discontinuing the tarnished term *enemy combatant* to describe those prisoners captured as part of the *war on terror* (while reserving the right to detain them indefinitely without trial). Soon thereafter it was reported that speechwriters were being asked to scrap the troublesome phrase *war on terror* altogether in favour of a more neutral, blandly technical *Overseas Contingency Operation*.[26]

By introducing a specific vocabulary it is hoped to constrict the latitude with which we perceive and understand actors and events occurring in society and the wider world. It is not only the international forces engaged in the war against terrorism that communicate to various publics in an attempt to influence their thoughts and behaviour. A glossy magazine has appeared in Afghanistan called *Al-Samoud* (meaning 'Resistance' or 'Stay Put!'), which appears in Arabic, Pashtu and Dari. It is intended to fill a niche where it gives a view that diverges from the Western view and from the Afghan media (which it claims is controlled by the West).

There is a substantial network of mass media assets belonging to the Taliban in Afghanistan, where the choice of words and symbolism is equally as important as in the case of the examples given from the coalition forces communications.

> *Al-Samoud* and the Taliban's three other magazines in Pashto and Dari – the bi-monthly *Morchel* (*Trench*), *Saraq* (*Flame*) and *Shahamak* (*Dignity*) – are obviously produced on modern presses, although Abu Ahmed will not reveal their location. I suspect they are in Pakistan and receive a sharp look by way of reply. But they reveal two new characteristics: an almost obsessive attention to detail, and the new name of the Taliban. The group now calls itself the *Islamic Emirate*. That's the original name of the country the Taliban governed until 2001, and its readoption is an attempt to free itself from the thieves and mafiosi in Afghanistan who call themselves *Taliban* but who have nothing to do with Islam or hostility to the Western forces in the country. *Al-Samoud* describes itself as 'the Islamic monthly magazine published by the media centre of the *Islamic Emirate of Afghanistan*'. The Taliban distribute it across the Arab Gulf.[27]

The names of the various magazines are highly symbolic, which mimics in some ways the Western approach. These specific words, together with their meanings that resonate in their target audience(s), attract attention and from that, possibly influence. An interesting additional aspect is the rebranding of the image, from *Taliban* to *Islamic Emirate* in order to bypass any negative associations with the first brand name. One of the possible problems encountered by producing propaganda in written form is the low rate of literacy among the Afghan population.

On the internet *Shariah radio* is also part of the organisation's mass media assets. It takes a direct and populist approach to issues that resonate with the local Afghan population. Abu Ahmed, one of the creators of the Taliban effort stated that "most of our websites are run by professionals. That's why the Americans have tried to block them so many times, using different *gates* in Afghanistan and other areas – but we have been able to unblock them every time."[28]

There seems to be a professional approach and an awareness of good news production standards. An emphasis was placed, for instance, on waiting to publish information before it was independently confirmed. There is an editorial board named by *Al-Samoud*. The propaganda wing of the Taliban, which is headed by Abdul Hai Mutmain from Zabul, has given itself the title of the *Information and Cultural Department*.[29] The management style and practices described in the interview are fashioned very much upon the ideal model of journalistic style and news production practices employed in a liberal model of journalism. They have learned to adapt and cater for the target audience that they are trying to reach, a focus seems to be on the rural Afghan population, although there are plans to touch a much wider audience.

Even if news and journalistic practices do happen to be good (in a theoretical and practical sense) and ethical that does not necessarily automatically bestow balance upon the resulting news product. In a talk at Southern Oregon University in 2009, Amy Goodman the host of *Democracy Now* criticised print and TV media in the US for failing to provide the public with balanced and contextual coverage of critical issues being faced by the American public, including Iraq and Afghanistan. To illustrate her point, Goodman stated that as the US was poised to invade Iraq only three of 400 commentators in TV news programmes and newspapers were in the anti-war camp (according to a count by *Fairness and Accuracy in Reporting*).[30]

Coalition force messaging in and on Afghanistan

The former Commander of ISAF forces General Stanley McChrystal in an interview in *The New York Times* stated that "this is a war of perceptions [...] This is not a physical war in terms of how many people you kill or how much ground you capture, how many bridges you blow up. This is all in the minds of the participants."[31] In the current 24/7 news age the term participants takes on a different meaning. There can be considered to be two broad categories, *physical participants* – combatants and bystanders in the actual field of conflict (where the fighting and violence physically occurs). The other can be termed *remote participants*, those people remote from the battlefield but connected to and following events through the mass media.

The military actors have recently begun to understand some of the shortcomings in their strategic communications, which is related to messages having an effect upon the publics' expectations. Therefore a new approach to expectation management is needed to more carefully 'guide' what is expected. "In so doing, we need to be careful that we do not continue to over promise and under deliver across the lines of operation."[32] This strategy may herald some changes from earlier messages that implied 'easy', relatively 'painless' and quick military victories.

Making progress and keeping the faith in Afghanistan

There are two specific facets concerning the public and their perception that needs to be addressed with communications from political and military actors engaged in the Afghan conflict. One of the measures that needs to be shown in order to try and keep public support for a military operation is that some sort of progress in a conflict is demonstrated or at least perceived. If this is not attempted, the public may assume that since a war is not being won, it must be in the process of being lost. This can be extremely problematic in an insurgency or terrorism operation, where there can be periods of lull, and hence there is no sign of progress either way.

A second perception that is deemed to be necessary to address was derived from the process of the 'post-mortem' on the United States' eventual loss in the Vietnam War after their withdrawal in 1972. The US military laid the blame for their loss on the mass media, specifically that their reporting eroded public confidence and support in the war owing to the deluge of 'negative' images. However, the G. W. Bush administration revisited the Vietnam War experience and arrived at a different finding. The conclusion was that it was not mass media that were to blame, but the officials. The officials did not show enough 'sincere' belief that the Vietnam War was winnable and the American public 'caught' the effect and lost confidence too. Therefore, officials needed to demonstrate more confidence publicly that a war can be won in order to keep public support.

In late September 2009, the Secretary General of NATO Anders Fogh Rasmussen summed up the situation in Afghanistan. "We are winning. [...] The situation is serious, but success is achievable."[33] The manner in which this short statement is posed demonstrates a PR communication tactic that is used when a communicator is addressing an audience that is potentially educated and/or not in agreement with the sender's point of view (or of their organisation's perspective).

The Chief of General Staff of the Australian Defence Forces, Air Chief Marshall Angus Houston was much more upbeat on the assessment of the future. He stated, like the NATO head, that the war was being slowly won. But then went as far as to claim that allied troops may "break the back of the insurgency" in 2010. "It is a very focussed campaign. I think you will see a lot of action in the south in the coming weeks. I think that as we could go forward things are looking better than they have."[34] This statement was taken without question, in spite of a less than impressive eight-year long track record in military engagement in Afghanistan. The words were simply taken at face value and no alternative or counter viewpoint was offered. Houston's comments came shortly before the much heralded offensive against the Taliban in the Helmand province in Southern Afghanistan.

At the House Armed Services Committee hearing in Washington DC in May 2010 the progress of the new counter-insurgency strategy announced by President Obama in December 2009 was briefed by Michele Flournoy, the Undersecretary of Defence for Policy. "We are on the right road for the first time in a long time in Afghanistan. I would argue for the first time, we finally have the right mission, the right strategy, the right leadership team in place."[35] The plan to introduce an additional 30,000 troops to Afghanistan was modelled upon the Iraqi *Surge* experience during the Bush presidency. An attempt has been made to try and transfer the presumed aspects of success from the previous experience in Iraq to the present situation in Afghanistan.

General Stanley McChrystal tried to paint the picture of the war in Afghanistan as being at the point where the tide was turning in favour of the international and Afghan government forces. "I think I would be prepared to say nobody is winning, at this point. Where the insurgents, I think, felt that they had a momentum a year ago, felt that they were making clear progress, I think that's stopped."[36] There is no challenge to McChrystal's opinion in the form of either an alternative point of view or a question. For instance to pose the question, how were the Taliban able to gain the ascendency over the ISAF forces when they are outgunned and without any air power?

Sometimes it is possible to introduce a new factor into an existing scenario in order to create the perception of a more positive prognosis of the situation. Additional factors surrounding the 'discovery' may be ignored, which may be difficult to realise in the environment in which it is located. An announcement was made that untapped mineral deposits worth US$1 trillion were discovered in Afghanistan, which has been described as being an opportunity for both Washington DC and Kabul. Patrick Doherty, Director of the *Smart Strategy Initiative* at the *New America Foundation* went as far as to say that this discovery had the potential to "change the narrative from counterinsurgency to locally controlled sustainable development."[37]

This tactic seems to be offering a *Red Herring* to the public, which can be partly seen in the attempt to try and change the Afghan narrative. A possible perception here is that the insurgency is going to 'disappear'. The question being, why should it? The same basic conditions remain in place. Another point is the nature of this 'discovery' how can this all of a sudden be found out only now? A final point to ponder upon, if these deposits do in fact exist, how is it to be extracted in a safe and fair manner? These basic questions are seemingly not being asked in the mass media.

The messages sent in this category are quite vague in terms of specifics, rather they rely on the perceived credibility of the sender and the promise that things are going in the right direction. Officials are keeping a brave face on the situation and expressing publicly their belief in a final victory in Afghanistan. Origins of this tactic coming from the Bush administration's rethink on the cause of defeat in the Vietnam War. Mass media, with the exception of some exposes on excesses of *jus in bello* (such as Abu Graib and the Pentagon Pundit Scandal) there has been little in the way of challenge to the official narrative.

Expectation management in Afghanistan

What a public expects in terms of why and how a war is fought is linked to their perception of what may be a remote event (physically remote from their experience). This is in turn influenced by the narratives provided by the responsible political and military actors. An early approach in shaping public expectations for what was to come was to portray the upcoming war as being one sided and legitimate, and would be over quickly. Afghanistan, unlike Iraq, was perceived as being a legitimate war on the heels of the 9/11 events.

However, although the initial fighting phase seemed to go well and the Taliban were removed from power, and attention was shifted to events in Iraq, the conflict was not over. Thus the situation arose that those early 'promises' or constructed expectations that were created through the use of directed communications could not be fulfilled. This particular problem was identified in the *Commander's Initial Assessment* (Commander's Initial Assessment, Headquarters, ISAF, Kabul, Afghanistan, 30 August 2009), and the need to not raise target audience expectations.

A much more careful and nuanced approach to managing the expectations of the target audience(s) and how long the fighting would continue in Afghanistan was undertaken. One of the means of helping to ensure expectations cannot be met is to make progress contingent or to use the well used narrative – things shall get worse before they get better. Flournoy used this tactic with the House Armed Services Committee. "Inevitably we'll face challenges, possibly setbacks, even as we achieve success. [...] We need to recognize that things may get harder before they get better."[38]

Many of the key political and military actors involved with operations in Afghanistan have made reference to and used the narrative 'there is still hardship ahead'.

- General David Petraeus – "as was the case in Iraq, the reality in Afghanistan is that everything is hard, and it is hard all the time. [...] There is no desire, in fact there is no ability to try and turn Afghanistan into Switzerland any time in the next few years."[39]
- US Secretary of Defense Robert Gates – "there is no doubt that there are positive developments going on, but I would say that it is very early yet. [...] some very hard fighting, very hard days ahead [...]. I think more needs to be done."[40]
- President Barack Obama – "What I've tried to emphasize is the fact that there is going to be some hard fighting over the next several months. [...] There is no denying the progress. Nor, however, can we deny the very serious challenges still facing Afghanistan."[41]
- Marine Major General Richard Mills warned of "tough fighting" as the war enters its *critical* year (2010), and that "I think we have some sacrifices that we are going to have to make. [...] What you have to do in this area of the world is to manage expectations. Make sure people know what the progress is."[42]

There are a number of different messages being entered into the information space by political and military actors. Those messages need to differ from the overly positive messages that were sent in the early stages of the conflict, owing to the fact that there has been information concerning negative aspects and sides to the war in Afghanistan. Managing expectations in this instance refers to ensuring that the target publics are not permitted to grow to an unrealisable state. As such, any hinted sign of progress is framed within the narrative that there is still much hard work to be done. These messages are let into the media sphere in an essentially unchallenged manner by those in the news production cycle.

Timeline or no timeline?

The public of a nation engaged in a military conflict has an expectation about the nature of wars. If there is a beginning to a war, so should there be an end. Wars are not open ended affairs without any foreseeable finish. Therefore political and military authorities can face growing public opposition and a demand for withdrawal when there is no end in sight and casualties are mounting among the troops deployed. Thus a rhetorical balance is attempted that seeks to imply a withdrawal is coming, but in order not to panic the government and country being assisted that there shall be a rush to leave them. Therefore target audiences with conflicting agenda need to be simultaneously addressed.

Arguments used in order to necessitate the presence of troops can come in a number of different plausible excuses and slogans.

- Anders Fogh Rasmussen stated that troops would remain in Afghanistan "as long as it takes to finish the job".
- General David Richards (British Chief of the General Staff) warned that "failure would have a catalytic effect on militant Islam around the world and region. […] Even if only a few of those weapons (nuclear) fell into their hands, believe me they would use them. The recent airliner plot reminded us that there are people out there who would happily blow us all up."[43]
- General David Petraeus stated that "I thought from the start that Afghanistan would be the longest campaign in the *Long War* (against terrorism)."[44] "It is important that July 2011 be seen for what it is: The date when a process begins, based on conditions – not the date when the US heads for the exits."[45]
- President Obama tried to reassure that "we are not suddenly as of July 2011 finished with Afghanistan. After July 2011 we are still going to have an interest in making sure that Afghanistan is secure, that economic development is taking place, that good governance is being promoted."[46]
- Major General Mills cautioned that "there is a job to be done here and it takes time to do it. [The Afghans are] very, very concerned that we may leave them prematurely."[47]
- Robert Gates disparaged the idea of withdrawal, saying that "the notion of timelines and exit strategies and so on, frankly, I think would all be a strategic mistake. The reality is, failure in Afghanistan would be a huge setback for the United States. […] Taliban and al Qaeda, as far as they are concerned, defeated one superpower. For them to defeat a second, I think, would have catastrophic consequences in terms of energising the extremist movement, al Qaeda recruitment, operations, fundraising, and so on. I think it would be a huge setback for the United States."[48]

There is increasing public demand for the withdrawal of foreign troops from Afghanistan, which is exacerbated by other Western countries taking their troops home and the increasing losses of dead and wounded military personnel. This means alluding to the promise of eventual withdrawal, but at the same time make it appear conditional so as to not overly concern the Afghan government. The selection of quotes from key political and military actors reveals that there is an understanding on their part of this dilemma in balancing the opposing goals of different pressure groups. There is also an attempt to use the elements of risk, uncertainty and fear in order to 'buy' some more time. Timelines as a consequence become a critical feature in communications, from a number of different perspectives of parties with vested interests.

Conclusion

Decisions are only as good as the information on which you base them. Bad or misleading information is likely to lead to unsuitable decisions, insofar as they are based upon a perception that does not match reality. A number of different deficiencies in the good practice of journalism and news production have been highlighted. The question is, Is the flow-on effect to the public and their ability to make good and informed decisions that are needed in a healthy and active democratic environment, when the information they receive is either incomplete or distorted?

Certainly in terms of motivation and reasons, it can be understood why political and military actors are tempted to engage in an information campaign that is deceptive and/or manipulative. One of the leading reasons for this is that the conclusion of armed conflicts are determined more by political than military factors. Thus it is a possible scenario to win the various battles militarily, but to ultimately lose the war politically. Therefore it is not only a matter of directing and influencing the actors that are directly involved in the conflict, but those who participate indirectly through consuming news through mass media channels. News management should be seen within the wider picture, where it forms a part of the communication management effort, in order to try and channel the means of information and communication towards a desired image and perception.

The *Commander's Initial Assessment* (of Afghanistan) from 30 August 2009 touched upon the issue of the state of strategic communications. Its background painted a very dismal picture of the state of coalition communications compared to the efforts of the insurgents.

> To date, the insurgents (INS) have undermined the credibility of ISAF, the international community (IC), and Government of the Islamic Republic of Afghanistan (GIRoA) through effective use of the information environment, albeit without a commensurate increase in their own credibility. Whilst this is a critical problem for ISAF, the consequences for GIRoA are even starker. GIRoA and IC need to wrest the information initiative from the INS.[49]

A point missed by the assessment is that the insurgents do not necessarily need to prove their credibility when the ISAF and Afghani Government have significant legitimacy and credibility problems among the Afghan public and segments of international publics. As suggested in the report, the insurgents are more adaptive to the political and information environment. On the surface it isn't complicated to understand how this has come to be. Partly, the answer may be related to the short-term approach taken by the international forces, which is tied to the influence of politics and the outcome of armed conflict. Politics and policy in the present age is the art of compromise rather than applying the best solution to the identified problem.

Mass media and the ability to communicate the key messages to the desired target audiences, together with the influence and intended effect become crucial.

Mass media have gradually lost their adversarial role in favour of a more symbiotic relationship. In times of war a number of studies have found that mass media tend to support a government rather than challenge them.

Political and military actors seem to have remarkable success in getting their sound bites in with little to no resistance. This is likely to be related to the 'new' style of news production and management, and the growing reliance of journalists on already produced texts, regardless of possible vested interests embedded in that information. Therefore when those narratives do enter the information sphere via mass media there is no alternative view offered nor is the material challenged.

In the symbiotic relationship between mass media and authorities, both sides stand to win. Journalists get access to key sources, and a human-interest story that contains drama and excitement. Authorities get to have their key narratives delivered, without challenge or distortion. The stakes are high, and there is a need to try and keep an upbeat image (as much as can be credible) in order to try and maintain public support in an existing conflict or to build the case for a future 'legitimate' conflict (as was the case with Iraq). Therefore much relies on the ability of the sender to reach the desired target audience with a message that resonates with them, in order to influence their thoughts and responses.

The primary means of manipulation is the presentation of one side of the story or just a scant account (at best) of alternative views. It can be said that messaging effectiveness relies on the use of omission and to trying to communicate first with overwhelming saturation coverage. In the contemporary age and development of New Communication Technology, it is an almost impossible task to have an effective regime of censorship. Therefore winning the information war requires an actor to dominate the information space with their messages (both in terms of quantity and quality).

By using material produced by PR agencies and authorities, the quality of journalism is reduced considerably. Journalism is a creative enterprise as opposed to PR, which is an informational technology. The elements and notions of truth and objectivity are subsequently lost in news production, thus depriving the public of reliable and accurate information on which to base their beliefs and decisions on events occurring in and affecting their society.

Notes

1 Miller, J., *News Sites Funded by Think Tanks take Root*, Associated Press in The Daily Herald, http://www.dailyherald.com/story/?id=372982&src=109, 13 April 2010 (accessed 16 April 2010)

2 Townend, J., *More Than Half Australian Newspaper Content is PR-led, Says Six Month Study*, Journalism.co.uk, https://www.journalism.co.uk/news/more-than-half-australian-newspaper-content-is-pr-led-says-six-month-study/s2/a537932/, 16 March 2010 (accessed 23 March 2010)To see the study go to: https://www.crikey.com.au/spinning-the-media/

3 Davies, N., *Our Media Have Become Mass Producers of Distortion*, The Guardian, https://www.theguardian.com/commentisfree/2008/feb/04/comment.pressand publishing, 4 February 2008 (accessed 13 March 2017)

4 Achen, P., *Goodman Calls for More Thorough Journalism: Author, TV and Radio Host Laments Skewed Media Coverage of Health-Care and US Involved Wars*, The Mail Tribune, http://www.mailtribune.com/apps/pbcs.dll/article?AID=/20091123/NEWS/911230319, 23 November 2009 (accessed 27 November 2009)

5 Heffer, S., *The New Politics is as Obsessed With Propaganda as the old was*, Telegraph, http://www.telegraph.co.uk/comment/columnists/simonheffer/7795052/The-new-politics-is-as-obsessed-with-propaganda-as-the-old-was.html, 1 June 2010 (accessed 2 June 2010)

6 Ibid.

7 Buxbaum, P. A., *Public Diplomacy 2.0*, ISN Security Watch, http://www.isn.ethz.ch/isn/Current-Affairs/Security-Watch/Detail/?id=115247&lng=en, 22 April 2010 (accessed 22 April 2010)

8 Jared Cohen serves on Hillary Clinton's policy planning staff, and advises her on the role that technology can play in realising foreign policy goals.Ibid.

9 Phillips, L., *European Reporters' Unions Want EU to Back Journalism as 'Public Good'*, EU Observer, https://euobserver.com/economic/29899, 20 April 2010 (accessed 21 April 2010)

10 *Council of Europe Passes Resolution on Indicators for Media in a Democracy*, Press Release, Article 19 in IFEX, http://www.ifex.org/international/2008/10/09/council_of_europe_passes_resolution/, 9 October 2008 (accessed 12 October 2008)

11 Carr, D. & Arango, T., *A Fox Chief at the Pinnacle of Media and Politics*, The New York Times, http://www.nytimes.com/2010/01/10/business/media/10ailes.html?ref=roger_e_ailes, 9 January 2010 (accessed 18 January 2010)Ailes was a political strategist for the Republican Party, including for Richard Nixon in 1968.

12 McKnight, D., *Philosophy Papers*, The Sydney Morning Herald, www.smh.com.au/articles/2008/11/07/1225561136700.html, 8 November 2008 (accessed 20 November 2008)

13 (The 'New Media, Old Media' report https://www.journalism.co.uk/news/pew-study-shows-gap-in-news-agenda-between-traditional-and-social-media/s2/a538842/)

14 Oliver, L., *Pew Study Shows a Gap in News Agenda Between Traditional and Social Media*, Journalism.co.uk, https://www.journalism.co.uk/news/pew-study-shows-gap-in-news-agenda-between-traditional-and-social-media/s2/a538842/ 25 May 2010 (accessed 26 May 2010)

15 Ngo, D., *Internet Changes News Consumption Landscape*, CNET News, http://news.cnet.com/8301-1023_3-10460854-93.html, 1 March 2010 (accessed 1 March 2010)

16 1) Sachoff, M., *More Journalists Using Facebook and Twitter: Journalists Relying on Social Media for Stories*, WebProNews, http://www.webpronews.com/more-reporters-using-facebook-and-twitter-for-story-research-2010-01/, 5 April 2010 (accessed 7 April 2010)Zhu, H., *Journalists Increasingly Turn to PR, Social Networks: Study*, The Epoch Times, http://www.theepochtimes.com/n2/content/view/33055/, 8 April 2010 (accessed 9 April 2010)

17 Ibid.

18 1) Oliver, L., *Journalists use of Social Media for Newsgathering has Reached Tipping Point*, Journalism.co.uk, www.journalism.co.uk/2/articles/537316.php, 22 January 2010 (accessed 25 January 2010)2) *Most Journalists use Social Media such as Twitter and Facebook as a Source*, The Guardian, http://www.guardian.co.uk/media/pda/2010/feb/15/journalists-social-music-twitter-facebook, 15 February 2010 (accessed 16 February 2010)

19 Chapman, G., *AOL Plants Seed for Internet Age News Operation*, Google.com, http://www.google.com/hostednews/afp/article/ALeqM5iNFeCi9ltJnZFBCKUUk7gHZ9KN4w, 16 March 2010 (accessed 23 March 2010)

20 Oliver, L., *New Tools for Sky Journalists as Social Media Strategy Moves from One to Many*, Journalism.co.uk, www.journalism.co.uk/2/articles/537082.php, 7 January 2010 (accessed 18 January 2010)

21 *Council of Europe Passes Resolution on Indicators for Media in a Democracy*, Press Release, Article 19 in IFEX, http://www.ifex.org/international/2008/10/09/council_of_europe_passes_resolution/, 9 October 2008 (accessed 12 October 2008)

22 Torchia, C., *Journalist in War Faces Troubling Questions*, Associated Press, in The Seattle Times, http://seattletimes.nwsource.com/html/nationworld/2011632195_apasafghanistanjournalistunderfire.html, 17 April 2010 (accessed 19 April 2010)

23 The two organisations are the Centre for Public Integrity (www.publicintegrity.org/default.aspx) and the Fund for Independence in Journalism (www.tfij.org).

24 Daniel, D. K., *Study: False Statements Preceded War*, Associated Press in the Huffington Post, http://www.huffingtonpost.com/2008/01/23/study-false-statements-pr_n_82764.html, 23 January 2008 (accessed 24 January 2008)To read the report see - http://projects.publicintegrity.org/WarCard/.

25 Segura, L., *Obama's Pentagon Rebrands Iraq War, Rolls Out PR Offensive in Afghanistan*, Alternet, http://www.alternet.org/world/145743/obama%27s_pentagon_rebrands_iraq_war,_rolls_out_pr_offensive_in_afghanistan, 20 February 2010 (accessed 1 March 2010)

26 Segura, L., *Obama's Pentagon Rebrands Iraq War, Rolls Out PR Offensive in Afghanistan*, Alternet, http://www.alternet.org/world/145743/obama%27s_pentagon_rebrands_iraq_war,_rolls_out_pr_offensive_in_afghanistan, 20 February 2010 (accessed 1 March 2010)

27 Fisk, R., *Glossy new Front in Battle for Hearts and Minds*, The Independent, http://www.independent.co.uk/opinion/commentators/fisk/robert-fisk-glossy-new-front-in-battle-for-hearts-and-minds-1934020.html, 2 April 2010 (accessed 7 April 2010)

28 Ibid.

29 Ibid.

30 Achen, P., *Goodman Calls for More Thorough Journalism: Author, TV and Radio Host Laments Skewed Media Coverage of Health-Care and US Involved Wars*, The Mail Tribune, http://www.mailtribune.com/apps/pbcs.dll/article?AID=/20091123/NEWS/911230319, 23 November 2009 (accessed 27 November 2009)

31 Segura, L., *Obama's Pentagon Rebrands Iraq War, Rolls Out PR Offensive in Afghanistan*, Alternet, http://www.alternet.org/world/145743/obama%27s_pentagon_rebrands_iraq_war,_rolls_out_pr_offensive_in_afghanistan, 20 February 2010 (accessed 1 March 2010)

32 Commander's Initial Assessment, Headquarters, ISAF, Kabul, Afghanistan, 30 August 2009, p. D-1

33 *NATO Head on Afghanistan: 'We're Winning'*, NPR, http://www.npr.org/templates/story/story.php?storyId=113241784, 26 September 2009 (accessed 28 September 2009)

34 *NATO Forces Slowly Winning Afghan War*, Big Pond News, http://bigpondnews.com/articles/World/2010/02/10/NATO_forces_slowly_winning_Afghan_war_427167.html, 10 February 2010 (accessed 11 February 2010)

35 US Gives Upbeat View on Afghan Mission, UPI.com, http://www.upi.com/Top_News/Special/2010/05/06/US-gives-upbeat-view-on-Afghan-mission/UPI-46171273163829/, 6 May 2010 (10 May 2010)

36 *McChrystal Sees Progress, but 'Nobody is Winning' Afghan War Yet*, Fox News, http://www.foxnews.com/politics/2010/05/14/mcchrystal-sees-progress-winning-afghan-war/, 14 May 2010 (accessed 17 May 2010)

37 Doherty, P., *Afghan Minerals Could Turn War's Tide*, CNN.com, http://edition.cnn.com/2010/OPINION/06/15/doherty.afghan.minerals/index.html?iref=allsearch, 15 June 2010 (accessed 16 June 2010)The Smart Strategy Initiative (http://smartstrategy.newamerica.net/home) claims to "provoke a new discourse across the United States and world capitals on three topics: the central challenge facing the United States and the great powers in the first half of the 21st century; the nature and function of grand strategy in today's constitutional democracy and market economy; and, finally, the contours of a new grand strategy capable of forging a prosperous, secure and sustainable future for the American Experiment and the community of nations."

38 US Gives Upbeat View on Afghan Mission, UPI.com, http://www.upi.com/ Top_News/Special/2010/05/06/US-gives-upbeat-view-on-Afghan-mission/UPI-46171273163829/, 6 May 2010 (10 May 2010)

39 Bronskill, J., Tough Fighting Lies Ahead in Afghan War, says Senior US General, The Canadian Press, www.canadaeast.com/rss/article/973321, 4 March 2010 (accessed 5 March 2010)

40 *Gates Says More Tough Battles Ahead in Afghan War*, Space War, http://www. spacewar.com/reports/Gates_says_more_tough_battles_ahead_in_Afghan_war_999. html, 8 March 2010 (accessed 10 March 2010)

41 Gearan, A., *Obama: Afghan War will Worsen Before it Improves*, AP in Fox News, http://www.foxnews.com/politics/2010/05/13/obama-afghan-war-worsen-improves/, 13 May 2010 (accessed 14 May 2010)

42 Perry, T., *Marine Official Says There is More 'Tough Fighting' Ahead in Afghanistan*, Los Angeles Times, http://www.latimes.com/news/custom/topofthetimes/callocal/la-me-marine-general-20100516,0,4776030.story, 16 May 2010 (accessed 17 May 2010)

43 NATO Chief: Afghan War is Winnable, Gulf Times, http://www.gulf-times.com/site/topics/article.asp?cu_no=2&item_no=318240&version=1&template_id=41&parent_id=23, 4 October 2009 (accessed 5 October 2009)

44 Petraeus Sees Long Afghan Campaign, UPI.com, http://www.upi.com/Top_News/US/2010/01/21/Petraeus-sees-long-Afghan-campaign/UPI-67211264108033/, 21 January 2010 (accessed 22 January 2010)

45 McMichael, W. H., *Petraeus Reaffirms 2011 OEF Pullout Conditional*, Navy Times, http://www.navytimes.com/news/2010/06/military_afghanistan_withdrawal_061610w/, 16 June 2010 (accessed 17 June 2010)

46 Gearan, A., *Obama: Afghan War will Worsen Before it Improves*, AP in Fox News, http://www.foxnews.com/politics/2010/05/13/obama-afghan-war-worsen-improves/, 13 May 2010 (accessed 14 May 2010)

47 Perry, T., *Marine Official Says There is More 'Tough Fighting' Ahead in Afghanistan*, Los Angeles Times, http://www.latimes.com/news/custom/topofthetimes/callocal/la-me-marine-general-20100516,0,4776030.story, 16 May 2010 (accessed 17 May 2010)

48 *Gates Wary of Timeline for Afghanistan*, Telegram.com, www.telegram.com, 27 September 2009 (accessed 28 September 2009)

49 Commander's Initial Assessment, Headquarters, ISAF, Kabul, Afghanistan, 30 August 2009, p. D-1

Bibliography

Allan, S., *News Culture*, Buckingham: Open University Press, 2001

Edwards, L., *Mediapolitik: How the Mass Media Have Transformed World Politics*, Washington D.C.: The Catholic University of America Press, 2001

Ewen, S., *PR! A Social History of Spin*, New York: Basic Books, 1996

Goldberg, B., *Bias: A CBS Insider Exposes How the Media Distort the News*, Washington D.C.: Perennial, 2003

Gripsrud, J., *Understanding Media Culture*, London: Arnold, 2002

Herman, E. S. & Chomsky, N., *Manufacturing Consent: The Political Economy of Mass Media*, New York: Pantheon Books, 2002

Ignatieff, M., *The Lesser Evil: Political Ethics in an Age of Terror*, Edinburgh: Edinburgh University Press, 2005

Leavy, P., *Iconic Events: Media, Politics, and Power in Retelling History*, Lanham (MD): Lexington Books, 2007

Louw, E., *The Media and Political Process*, 2nd Edition, London: Sage, 2010

McNair, B., *An Introduction to Political Communication*, 4th Edition, London: Routledge, 2007

McNair, B., *The Sociology of Journalism*, London: Arnold, 2004

Payne, K., The Media as an Instrument of War, *Parameters*, Spring 2005, pp. 81–93

Robinson, P., The CNN Effect: Can the News Media Drive Foreign Policy?, *Review of International Studies*, 25(2), 1999, pp. 301–309

Seaton, J., *Carnage and the Media: The Making and Breaking of News about Violence*, London: Allen Lane, 2005

Thussu, D. K., *News as Entertainment: The Rise of Global Infotainment*, London: Sage, 2009

Tuman, J. S., *Communicating Terror: The Rhetorical Dimensions of Terrorism*, 2nd Edition, Thousand Oaks: Sage, 2010

Zelizer, B. & Allan, S. (eds), *Journalism After September 11*, London: Routledge, 2002

3   Hybrid warfare, lawfare, informational warfare

The wars of the future

Iulian Chifu

The 21st century has come with challenges to the very nature of international relations and with huge threats to security. And it has come with new forms of conflict presented to us by entities and states using new types of wars. The 4GW (fourth generation war) is the general approach to these new types of conflicts, characterised by a blurring of the lines between war and politics, combatants and civilians. Carl von Clausewitz spoke about war as a continuation of politics with different means (Clausewitz 2007). Fourth generation war makes a concrete passage to this reality, with the fusion between the two principles of politics and war.

In this context, we have witnessed the emergence of hybrid war – a combination of conventional, irregular, economic, energy, cyber, plus informational, identity and proxy war, all being combined in a very tricky and unstable form, with a limited and, at the same time, unrestricted war, in the sense of deployment of capacities of all kinds, without rules: criminal capabilities with economic, informational ones, propaganda and irregular proxy war, insurrection, insurgency and terrorism in the same theatre where, according to the Machiavelli's realistic approach, *tous les coups sont bons*!

It is definitely the case that old rules of engagement and laws of war have not been updated to guide this new form of hybrid war. On the contrary, the use of non-registered and non-assumed soldiers and the invention of the 'little green men' introduced the instruments necessary to make use of the gaps in international legislation, a position that also aids the avoidance of responsibility. This is the new type of war, the legal warfare or lawfare, speculating international legislation in order to take advantage of your capabilities and dominant position for national advantages.

Last but not least, a component of a hybrid war is the informational war, creating alternative false realities and spreading them by using free speech and the free communication of ideas. It deals with perverting reality and truth, twisting it by using a combination of facts, syllogisms, sophisms, propaganda, interpretation and numerous lies. These are all used to create an alternative reality that leads the targeted population to a pre-designed model or way of seeing things, at the same time in a combination with psychological operations, misinformation and propaganda.

The present article represents an overview, a first charted analysis on the evolution of 21st century conflicts, and our original contribution to the debate of modern warfare, the evolution of those concepts and, especially, the way that those concepts are applied in practice, on the ground, in real combat.

Fourth Generation War – 4GW

At the end of the Cold War, William Lind (Lind et al. 1989: 22–26) brought us the idea of the periodisation of modern type of conflicts and introduced the term 'generations' for the different ways of making war. This type of division is proposed, in accordance with the evolution of warfare tactics and the technology of weaponry. Lind presented the development of warfare in the modern era in three distinct generations of the traditional inter-state confrontation with numerous armies and different tactics, and, later, added the fourth generation.

The last category was an equivalent to a return to decentralised forms of warfare, blurring the lines between war and politics, combatants and civilians, due to nation states' loss of their near-monopoly on combat forces, prompting a return of models of conflict common in pre-modern times (Lind et al. 1989: 22–26).

Lind accepted at that time the idea that organised combat operations are no longer reserved for the state, which no longer has a monopoly on violence, that technology used for all types of weapons is available on the black market as soon as any weapon is produced, and that inventive tactics result even from the merging of traditional fighters and modern technology.

His work was published in 2004. Some characteristics of this fourth-generation war were the result of numerous findings garnered from experiences on the ground. First, the main difference between the wars of the fourth-generation and the previous ones is that we are talking mostly about ad hoc warriors and moral conflict. The motifs behind this evolution are outcomes of the globalisation of power, technology, access to techniques and tactics or, should this be the case, a technological integration of the world.

At the same time, the loss of the nation state's monopoly on violence was concomitant with the rise of cultural, ethnic, and religious conflict, involving groups far less equipped, but much more inventive and creative in using the modern technology they possess in a way neither creators of the technology, nor strategists nor even the soldiers use it in regular armies. And since we mentioned tactics, they refer to undermining enemy's strengths within its ranks and not avoiding them. At the same time, they suppose exploiting the enemy's weaknesses and vulnerabilities on the field by using all the means available, namely asymmetric operations, with weapons and techniques that differ substantially from the opponents'.[1]

Fourth generation warfare is a reflection for confrontation of societies within the nation states, rather than armies, fighting using psy-ops, the psychological operations, including terrorism tactics and harsh insurgency activities that extensively use terror against the civilians of the society and, certainly, using the enemy's strengths against it. The latter takes advantage of the inertia of the state decision-making systems, low capacity of movement on the field, difficulties of deploying in urban areas and populated environments, and the low level of flexibility when it comes to irregular warfare and human shield tactics.

Even though this 4GW is not new, some changes in international relations and the security environment are clearly placing it in this post-Cold War era and even in the post-9/11 era, where terrorism has become more visible and has access to better tools, challenging the world order and the primacy of the state. There are important differences to how it is applied today. These include:

- The existence of modern technologies and economic integration has enabled global operations.
- The decline of nation state warfare has forced all open conflict into 4GW, especially when it deals with confronting an enemy with higher capabilities and resources, in an asymmetrical manner.
- The emergence of small viable groups and variety of reasons for conflict permits polarisation on different grounds, and complicates the complex task of solving each and every dispute that generated the conflict at the end of the combat operations.
- The existence of democratic open societies and economies provides a space with enough vulnerabilities, including the presence of 'the enemy inside the gates', with no front line and no limit in the rules of engagement, involving civilians becoming overnight fighters and being versatile enough to switch between these statuses several times per day.
- The new technologies are more or less globally available and this leads to an increased effectiveness of small groups in fights against regular armies or police special units in crowded spaces.
- Media access offers the possibility of manipulation and promoting a particular vision and perception of facts.
- International networks and social media are providing across the world new means of communication used for spreading organised structures, improving technology and gaining access to information that improves the groups' capacity to learn, survive, and act in a confrontation.[2]

In the end, there are four basic principles of the 4GW:

- Missions and operations are undertaken in small groups of fighters, acting in any place where the enemy lies or acts, in the entire society.
- There is flexibility and capacity to fight with a high degree of autonomy, without huge centralised logistics, with a high level of mobility and space to move and act.
- The capacity of manoeuvre is much more important than firepower in modern confrontations. This aspect ensures superiority in the field.
- Destroying the enemy from within. Its centre of power, credibility and strength are targets for attacks and dictate the way combat is addressed.

Hybrid war

The introduction of the theoretical approach to 4GW offers us the possibility of analysing the sources of inspiration for the hybrid war concept. An emphasis on this concept and its developments, including the very recent ones, is worth it because it represents the source of inspiration for strategists and planners in order to create advantages for small groups and little armies confronting huge military mechanisms and powers. And, in our opinion, that's the direction in which future wars are heading.

It is also important for the analysis of the examples on the ground that inspired those evolutions. This could help us find out how these theoretical approaches have been developed, sometimes naturally, through the empirical study of the adaptation of the strategies to the evolution of tactics and technology and sometimes we realise that we have witnessed the thorough application, in a planned manner, of the type of military engagement conceived in advance in a laboratory.

The primary theoretical source of hybrid warfare is a Chinese book: *Unrestricted War* by col. Qiao Liang and col. Wang Xiangsui, a book published in 1999 at the PLA Literature and Arts Publishing House.[3] The book coalesces the innovative thinking and finding ways of fighting against whatever adversaries and capabilities are in front of you.[4] And this is the first characteristic of the hybrid war, a war without any rules or restrictions. The hybrid war is unrestricted and unlimited in that sense.

The main idea of the Chinese authors was that unrestricted war means multiple attacks on the social, economic and political system of the opponent, together with asymmetric attacks in an irregular military warfare context, planned in a specific rhythm and synchronicity, in order to achieve the goal of weakening the adversary. The unrestricted war "ignores and transcends the limits of the battle field and what doesn't represent the battle field, between what is and is not a weapon, between military staff and civilians, between state and non-state actors" (Metz 2014). The scope of unrestricted war is to grant equal chances to the weakest party in a conflict.

Theorisation of hybrid war has extended to the point where some scholars portray hybrid war as a strategy a belligerent uses to promote its political goals by engaging military force subversively, rather than hybrid war as a new form of conflict. Seen as an irregular type of warfare, hybrid war is thus meant to show and exploit the target's vulnerabilities, but with a decreased military confrontation. As it mixes both regular and irregular military means, hybrid warfare heads to complementary results. The irregular component encompasses various tactics such as propaganda, espionage, agitation, criminal disorder, the creation of a 'fifth column', inserting unmarked soldiers or frontier skirmishes (Lanoszka 2016: 178–179).

While the content of the concept is there, the real use of the name of hybrid war appeared first in the thesis of William J. Nemeth, *Future War and Chechnya: A Case for Hybrid Warfare* (Nemeth 2002). Nemeth's thesis is that countries are under siege from the violence of the decomposing states, the new unstable entities, with a high degree of violence inside those societies, with anarchic communities where traditional norms and rules are mixed with laws, norms and modern socio-political constructs. This situation being combined with modern technology creates this hybrid society. The basic result comes from the fact that this mix of traditional and modern components leads to a special kind of creativity and innovation when it comes to the way people from the proto-state use of modern technology and weapons, and this manner of thinking creates surprises and tactics able to overcome the difference of power between the two armies.

Hybrid warfare is nonetheless an old strategic concept, reminiscent of compound warfare, which consisted of a regular force increasing its operations with irregular means. History has been witness to a plethora of such moments, starting from the Peninsular War, when the Duke of Wellington dislodged the French from Spain with conventional means against Napoleon's military leaders, while he used guerrillas against the French, to the more recent strategies of Israel fighting Hezbollah by deploying irregular fighters adapting to operations without being dependent on centralized command and control (Wilkie 2009: 15).

But the hybrid war is also a limited war, in the sense that the parties involved choose, via mutual acceptance, due to its toll on image and symbolic capital, not to involve all their capabilities in this combat, but only a limited part of them, in order to solve their dispute. Lawrence Freedman noticed limited nature of the hybrid war (Freedman 2014–2015: 7–38).

The concept comes from the time of the Cold War, and the Mutual Assured Destruction (MAD) which forced the US and USSR to solve their disputes through intermediaries and proxies and to avoid sitting one in front to the other, in order not to escalate and reach the level of conflict where using nuclear weapons was necessary, therefore destroying the planet. Freedman underlines the characteristics of the hybrid war that fit into the definition of the limited war: avoiding escalation above a certain threshold convened directly or inexplicitly by the parties, avoiding a long war to limit its operations in time, limiting the area of the operations and avoiding the expansion of the combat outside of the established area, and limiting the intensity of the combat.

The concept was not build on empty ground, since 4GW already prepared the appearance of the hybrid war. The content of the concept has been defined by the Chinese colonels as unrestricted war. The name is due to William Nemeth and Lawrence Freedman contributing the component of limited war to refine the concept, however the parents of the concept of hybrid war, as we know it now, are James Mattis and Frank Hoffman (Mattis & Hoffman 2005: 2).

The essence of the definition resulted in thinking like the enemy of the US and identifying niche solutions that can be used to fight a superpower: modern technological combinations and unusual tactics used by opponents in order to achieve strategic advantages (Mattis & Hoffman 2005: 4).

Israel has been prominent in engaging a similar strategy during the second Lebanon War, a fruitful example of challenges of the hybrid warfare. The Israeli Defence Forces then plunged into a multifaceted conflict between states and armed groups, with multiple forms of combat used simultaneously like conventional manoeuvre warfare, irregular tactics, informational war, terrorist acts, criminal disorder, as exemplified by testimonies of Israeli officers, and epitomised by William Fleser (Fleser 2010: 11).

Concomitantly, the Russian Federation has been a prolific long-term example of promoting hybrid methods, especially in Ukraine starting in late 2013 and the beginning of 2014. First some generalist features rely on '*Po Zakonu*'', meaning 'in accordance with law', and translate into actions which have the appearance of legality: the 'authorization' of the Russian army to operate in Ukraine, the so-called referendum in Crimea, Russian passports freely distributed in Crimea; secondly, the military show of force and readiness, and snap inspections. In third place, in order to avoid inviting foreign observers as required by the Vienna document, the Russian Ministry of Defence announced 'intensive combat training in spring and summer' near the border with Ukraine, while insisting that no joint manoeuvres were performed, in order to restrict observers. Moreover, the 'little green men', also referred to as 'polite people' in Vladimir Putin's words, were apparently acting as 'local security forces' or unidentified forces in Crimea. This tactic included the psychological warfare component, as well. Another element involved taking advantage of local tensions and local militias, an operation famously labelled by Russian officials as a manner "to protect the Russians abroad" (Reisinger & Golts 2014: 3–4).

Therefore, the hybrid war is fundamentally an irregular war, according to Mathis and Hoffman, using instruments like terrorism, guerrilla tactics, criminal actions, cyber operations, information attacks, in a planned combination that could affect the security interests of the state. Its impact targets different fields that are transformed in strategic ones, like those of the information operations made with the support of friendly media. The objective is to alter and transform the will and support of the target state's population for the engagement.

We also propose an approach to the concept of hybrid war: a combination of conventional, irregular, economic, energy, cyber, plus informational, identity and proxy war, all being combined in a very tricky and unstable form, with a limited and, at the same time, unrestricted war, in the sense of deployment of capacities of all kind, without observing any rules. Criminal capabilities with economic, informational ones, propaganda and irregular proxy war, insurrection, insurgency and terrorism could be deployed in the same domain in order to achieve a specific objective. The display follows Machiavelli's realistic approach where *tous les coups sont bons*!

Another characteristic which we introduce refers to the fact that hybrid war is not only introduced by insurgent groups and small, weak armies, but by all actors, even powerful states, with incredibly well-prepared, trained and equipped armies, who use this form of engagement in order to dissimulate involvement, to avoid costs and to have access to credible denial. This allows them to avoid recognising the involvement of their own regular forces and usage of Special Forces, civilians or military regulars in uniforms without distinctive signs. All these being considered, we reached the other component of the hybrid war, a distinct way of planning and conducting conflicts: legal warfare or lawfare.

Lawfare

The concept of International Law Legal Warfare or lawfare first appeared in the 1975 article 'Whither Goeth the Law – Humanity or Barbarity' by John Carlson and Neville Yeomans in reference to the peaceful resolution of conflicts.[5] But also the book *Unrestricted Warfare* addressed this concept as a part of unrestricted war. In this case, lawfare meant the use of law and judicial processes as an instrument of warfare, a strategy of using (or misusing) the law in place of, or in addition to, traditional military strategies to achieve military objectives.

In this field of debate, lawfare becomes 'positive' when it is about the legitimate use of law to achieve military objectives, in a way which is in full observance with the spirit of the rule of law. 'Negative lawfare' could be defined as the misuse of the law to achieve military objectives, the practice of manipulating judicial processes to undercut military objectives of other states, the use of law to prevent or hinder a nation or non-state actor from carrying out legitimate military operations.[6] It is also about 'offensive lawfare' designed to include efforts to deny enemy forces sanctuary, to blunt their abuse of courts, and to use both foreign and domestic courts to better support the national security strategy (Holzer 2012).

The idea of lawfare was first developed and explored by the US Air Force Colonel Charles J. Dunlap, Jr. (Dunlap 2001 2008), who defined it as "a strategy of using – or misusing – law as a substitute for traditional military means to achieve an operational objective". This is rather a 'neutral' concept and is designed in order to assist militaries in the conflict areas in order to avoid any legal consequences, but also to make sense of the fact that planning any military operation should take into consideration the legal aspects and the possibility of using law to support the legitimacy of military and special operations, as well as to block them or to sabotage the legitimacy of a cause, in the case of enemy operations, thus creating problems with the polarisation and public support for a war. By reclaiming a neutral conception of lawfare, Melissa Waters argues that two conceptions of lawfare coexist within this paradigm. The first one refers to use of law and legal processes as an instrument or weapon of war, while the second makes reference to what Wouter Werner called a 'reflexive lawfare', consisting of using the term to discredit an opponent's reliance on law and legal procedure (Waters 2010: 329).

Later, the evolution of lawfare as a concept leaned more towards the misuse of the law and using trials in order to undermine military operations or their legitimacy. It is not about the legitimate defence of human rights, but more about abuses. At the same time, it also supposed achieving a planned military objective using legal means by different actors. In this area, we can give the example of the politicisation and use of legal means in politics domestically in order to undermine military objectives[7] or important studies discussing the misuse of the legal grounds and treaties, used by some actors in order to accommodate or to fit inside the existing legal framework their actions, operations and wars designed to achieve their own interests and military objectives (Bartman 2009).

"The Soviet Union and the Russian Federation practiced manipulation or exploitation of the international legal system to supplement military and political objectives, or lawfare, via the definition of aggression and aggressive war, from 1933 through 1999" concluded Christi Scott Bartman (2009: 181) in a thesis discussing aspects of aggression and intervention. The twisted reading, understanding and misinterpretation of international law were used by the Soviet Union and Russia in order to obtain some legal grounds and legitimacy for its military operations and wars.

Invoking self-defence has been extensively engaged by Russia in Ukraine's case, when Russia invaded Crimea. However, the issue of proofs is problematic. There were no reports that the Russian fleet in Crimea were subjected to violent acts from Ukrainian authorities before President Putin authorized the deployment of forces in Crimea. The challenge of legality and legitimacy continues to be an issue of dispute between academics with regards to the right to invoke the concept of armed attack for the protection of nationals in another state. However, Russia failed to provide evidence on how the Russian citizens had been endangered on 23 February 2014 in Ukraine. A similar pattern was enacted by Russia in Georgia in 2008, as it invoked the right to protect its nationals. Scholars Randelzhofer and Nolte deny the very existence of such right, because it brings upon the risk of "blurring the contours of self-defence".[8] As Daniel Wisehart assesses, the Russian use of force in Crimea was illegal under international law, humanitarian intervention was doubtful, as Russia has not even invoked it; besides, humanitarian intervention would not be applicable because there would have to have been committed crimes against humanity or genocide.[9]

The neoconservative-sponsored group called 'The Lawfare Project'[10] (Scharf & Andersen 2010: 2) used the definition of lawfare in the sense of "manipulation of international law and legal proceedings to make claims against the state, especially in areas related to national security". Examples of lawfare would be the case brought to the International Court of Justice on the legality of Israel's security barrier, human rights cases sponsored by organizations sympathetic to the Palestinian cause and litigation in support of terrorist detainees.[11]

Michael Newton signalises a challenge brought by Additional Protocol I (Geneva Conventions) and how nations should pay attention in opposing efforts to create or reinforce the legal framework that can become tactically irrelevant on modern battlefields (Newton 2010: 267).

In Israel's case, Newton exemplifies the famous Goldstone Report referring to Gaza Strip (2008–2009) that is relevant in showing how sometimes it may be inappropriate to impose human rights in the middle of conflicts that can provide illegitimate lawfare, and that may express a "pernicious expansion of international common law in a manner that would dramatically undermine military operations" (Newton 2010: 271).

I think that the recent developments in Crimea and Eastern Ukraine, the Islamic State activities in Iraq and Syria, the construction of artificial islands by China and its actions in the South and South-East China Sea, the developments in technology and cyber space are all enriching the concept of lawfare.

We propose that the concept of lawfare should also include a component related to the speculation and abuse of the international law loopholes and lack of legislation in order to use military instruments or to achieve military and strategic objectives through those means. This includes the premeditation and strategic planning needed for achieving those goals. It is not a random action, nor is it one that just takes advantage of the opportunities available due to the vulnerabilities of the target country that are present at a certain moment.

A counter-measure to exploiting lawfare against one state is the decision of the US administration to oppose its participation in the International Criminal Court, because of the concerns that actors' hostile to US might start trials against American leaders or soldiers. The US administration feared in fact that the standard criminal trials of Al-Qaeda suspected terrorists could be manipulated by the defence and that the prosecutors could be placed in a position to opt between revealing sensitive US intelligence information or setting terrorists free (Kittrie 2010: 399).

Examples of lawfare are globally omnipresent: creating the new form of war, hybrid war, with the use of non-registered and non-assumed soldiers, the invention of the 'little green men' as a military force and an instrument for avoiding responsibility, both for an aggression and regarding the rights of those soldiers and their families; taking advantage and using the gaps of international legislation in order to take advantage of the capabilities and dominant position for national advantages in cyberwar and energy driven aggressive actions, since it is not sanctioned yet as an aggression by the international law; creating artificial islands on the sea in order to increase offshore rights as well as create new strategic strongholds, including by using natural grounds and using the appearance of natural development of those artificial islands (as China has done, see p. XX); and, last but not least, the case of groups of adventurers that want to establish and have, by buying or taking by force, their own state on the territory of weak states, and use lawfare to control territories of states that have weak and unprepared armies.

Informational war

Another component of the hybrid war is the informational war. Nicholas O'Shaughnessy reproduces an epitomised history on how informational war has been engaged in since ancient times, from Napoleon and Frederick the Great, and then to the 20th century, which represented the 'propaganda century'. The process of expanding and developing the informational type of warfare was concomitant to the technical evolution of communication. Hitler's rise and sophisticated propaganda, a subdivision of informational war, was completed by the Russian informational warfare, mainly focused on spetspropaganda – firstly taught as subject at Russian Military Institute of Foreign Languages in 1942 and meaning a combination between agitation and propaganda – and on dezinformatsiya (disinformation). These pillars became the features of the Cold War (Lucas & Pomeranzev 2016: 2–6).

A summary of the evolution of modern Russian informational war includes elements of fake and forgeries, reflexive control and active measures. The active measures became essential in influencing the policies of another government, undermining confidence in its own leaders and institutions, disrupting that country's relations with other nations, discrediting and weakening governmental and nongovernmental opponents. (Lucas & Pomeranzev 2016: 7)

Valery Gerasimov, the Chief of the General Staff of the Armed Forces of Russia brought a fresh approach on informational war in 2013, when he described it as instrumental for achieving political and military goals, through "indirect and asymmetric methods" outside conventional military intervention. (Polyakova et al. 2016: 3)

Concerning informational warfare, the debate is far more complicated because the definition has to be nuanced and adapted through a family of actions, legitimate and legal, as well as illegitimate and profoundly illegal. On one hand, there is the expression of fundamental human right of opinion, free thinking and free circulation of ideas, as well as the democratic principles of the freedom of speech. Then, we have the legal use of communication and PR, but also immoral and illegitimate polit-technology and agit-propaganda (Simons 2010). Last but not least, in the same family we can find the illegal use of components of psychological operations and informational war.

Informational war, according to our own definition of the concept, signifies creating alternative realities by perverting the truth based on data, facts and concrete arguments and twisting it by using a combination of facts, syllogisms, sophisms, propaganda, interpretation and a lot of lies. The alternative reality perverts the perception of the targeted population employing a combination of psy-ops – psychological operations, misinformation and propaganda which use basic beliefs, feelings and created images in order to lead the public to a predesigned perception. At the end of the day, since the public already has an opinion, its perception has taken the place of the reality (Stern 1999) and whatever argument and proof of the truth would face that opinion, the blockage of the perception has already been established.

This strategy perfectly coalesced with Russia's strategy on Ukraine. NATO StratCom Centre of Excellence offers extensive research on how asymmetric and information activities were instrumented in order to achieve political and military goals in Ukraine, by deception, information and psychological operations, social media, English- and Russian-language satellite TV-based propaganda and older Soviet-style techniques such as 'active measures' and #reflexive control', especially in Crimea. The main component has been founded on the Russian perception of the world, meaning Russia, Ukraine and Belarus being the three pillars of the Slavic Orthodox civilisation jointly sharing history, values, culture and recognised Russian supremacy (Bērziņš et al. 2014: 6–7).

The Russian informational strategy galvanised a network-flow model, representing the 'unvirtuous circle' of Russian influence, aiming to gain influence over state institutions, bodies, economy, achieving power to shape others' national decisions, a method in which corruption became a "lubricant on which the system operates". Russia's influence in Central and Eastern Europe has mainly followed two pathways in Vladimir Putin's third mandate – manipulating one country by dominating or abusing strategic sectors of economy, which is translated into economic capture. The second one refers to cultivating political relationships with autocrats, nationalists, populists, Euroskeptics and Russian sympathisers, thus achieving the political capture of another state (Conley et al. 2016: 1–2).

As Edward Lucas and Ben Nimmo demonstrate with concrete examples, the Russian doctrine of informational warfare is monolithic, while its implementation is segmented. In the Baltic states, the Russian-owned media outlets continue to exploit fears of US abandonment of their own country, while stimulating Soviet nostalgia. In Romania, the informational type of war seeks to erode public faith in democratic institutions and consolidate the impression that EU accession was a failure. Concomitantly, in the Czech Republic and Slovakia, the Russian strategy focuses on local environmental and anti-war themes to bring a negative perspective on Western energy politics and the US/NATO security reassurances (Lucas & Nimmo 2015: 3).

In a world where information quickly reaches a large amount of people in real time, via television, internet and social media, the perception of a specific event is easily formed, derailed, twisted and imposed. Presenting the truth later would have a limited impact on the large-scale opinion due to the lack of critical thinking of the majority of the general population, as well as the conservative approach in accepting its own mistakes at a large scale and the ease associated with the use of the explanation already internalised by an average person, especially in a community that has developed a conformism and has its own description, perception and 'truth'.

Notes

1 *4GW - FOURTH GENERATION WARFARE*, in Global Guerrillas, Networked tribes, system disruption and the emerging bazaar of violence. A blog about the future of conflict, http://globalguerrillas.typepad.com/globalguerrillas/2004/05/4gw_fourth_gene. html, 8 May 2004 (accessed 15 March 2015).
2 Ibid.
3 There is no official English translation of the book available, but there are many references and samizdat, as well as partial translations of the book. We use as reference James Perry, *Aerospace Power Journal*, Summer 2000.
4 "The venue for publication and the laudatory reviews of the book in official publications suggested that Unrestricted Warfare enjoyed the support of some elements of the PLA leadership. The Western press quoted various sensational passages from the book and described it in terms that verged on hyperbole. The book was not a blueprint for a "dirty war" against the West, but a call for innovative thinking on future warfare", said James Perry.
5 Harriette Hill, *Lawfare and the International Criminal Court: Questions and Answers,* January 14, 2008, United Nations Association of the United States of America, www. amicc.org.
6 Ibid.
7 See the Brooke Goldstein speech *International and Domestic Legal Recourses: Responding to Lawfare and the Goldstone Report*, at Fordham Law School on Lawfare & Combating the Goldstone Report, 27 April 2010.
8 Daniel Wisehart, *The crisis in Ukraine and the Prohibition of the use of force: a legal basis for Russia's intervention?* Blog of the *European Journal of International Law,* http://www.ejiltalk.org/the-crisis-in-ukraine-and-the-prohibition-of-the-use-of-force-a-legal-basis-for-russias-intervention/, March 2014 (accessed 23 July 2016). Georg

Nolte, Albrecht Randelzhofer, Ch. VII Action with Respect to Threats to the Peace Breaches of the Peace, and Acts of Aggression, Article 51, in The Charter of the United Nations A Commentary, Volume II, 3rd Edition, edited by Bruno Simma, Daniel-Erasmus Khan, Georg Nolte, Andreas Paulus, Nikolai Wessenforf.

9 Ibid., p.5.

10 The Lawfare Project is a New York-based organisation devoted to exposing alleged abuses of the international legal system. *About Us*, The Lawfare Project (accessed 16 December 2010), http://www.thelawfareproject.org/about. When references are made to the hijacking of the term, the Lawfare Project is usually the chief culprit. The Lawfare Project defines their goal as analysing *lawfare* as it used (via the Western legal system), nationally and internationally, to: (1) Thwart and punish free speech about issues of national security and public concern, (2) De-legitimise the sovereignty of democratic states, and (3) Frustrate and hinder the ability of democracies to defend themselves against terrorism. The primary goals of the Lawfare Project are: (i) To raise awareness about the phenomenon (and specific instances) of lawfare assuring the subject matter receive the credibility and immediacy that it warrants, (ii) facilitate (legal and non-legal) responses to the perversion and misapplication of international & national human rights law, (iii) identify and mobilise human and institutional resources, and (iv) bring diverse and interested parties together in a common forum to discuss the threat. Reference from Michael Scharf & Elizabeth Andersen, *Is Lawfare worth defining? Report of the Cleveland Experts Meeting*, September, 11, 2010, p. 2, at http://law.case.edu/journals/JIL/Documents/43_Lawfare_Report.pdf.

11 *What is Lawfare?*, The Lawfare Project, Dec. 16, 2010, http://www.thelawfareproject. org quoted by Michael Scharf & Elizabeth Andersen.

Bibliography

Bartman, C. S., *Lawfare: Use of the Definition of Aggressive War by Soviet and Russian Governments*, dissertation for the title of Doctor of Philosophy, Bowling Green State University, August 2009

Bērziņš, J., Jaeski, A., Laity, M., Maliukevicius, N., Navys, A., Osborne, G., Pszczel, R. & Tatham, S., *Analysis of Russia's Information Campaign against Ukraine*, Riga: NATO StratCom Centre of Excellence, 2014

Clausewitz, v C., *Despre război*, Bucharest: Antet Publishing House, 2007

Conley, H. A., Mina, J., Stefanov, R. & Vladimirov, M., *The Kremlin Playbook. Understanding Russian Influence in Central and Eastern Europe,* CSIS, Washington, October 2016

Dunlap, C. J. Jr., *Law and Military Interventions: Preserving Humanitarian Values in 21st Conflicts,* Humanitarian Challenges in Military Intervention Conference, Carr Centre for Human Rights Policy, Kennedy School of Government, Harvard University Washington D.C., 29 November 2001

Dunlap, C. J. Jr., *Lawfare Today: A Perspective*, speech presented to the American Bar Association's 17th Annual Review of the Field of National Security Law Conference, 16 November 2007, *Yale Journal of International Affairs*, Winter 2008

Fleser, W., *Preparing for Hybrid Threats. Improving Force Preparation for Irregular Warfare,* GlobalSecurity.org, CALL Newsletter 11-34: Irregular Warfare – A SOF Perspective Newsletter, June 2011, Fort Leavenworth, KS: Centre for Army Lessons Learned

Freedman, L., Ukraine and the Art of Limited War, *Survival*, (56)6, December 2014 – January 2015

Holzer, M. W., *Offensive Lawfare and the Current Conflict, National Security Journal*, Harvard Law School, 10 April 2012

Kittrie, F. O., Lawfare and US National Security, *Case Western Reserve Journal of International Law*, (43) I, 2010

Lanoszka, A., Russian hybrid warfare and extended deterrence in Eastern Europe, *International Affairs*, 92: 1, 2016

Lind, W. S., Nightengale, K., Schmitt, J. F., Sutton J. W. & Wilson, I. G., The Changing Face of War: Into the Fourth Generation, *Quantico: Marine Corps Gazette*, October 1989

Lucas, E. & Pomeranzev, P., *Winning the Information War. Techniques and Counter-strategies to Russian Propaganda in Central and Eastern Europe*, Washington, DC: CEPA's Information Warfare Project in Partnership with Legatum Institute, August 2016

Lucas, E., & Nimmo, B., *Information Warfare: What is it and how to win it?*, CEPA Infowar Paper No 1, November 2015

Mattis, J. N. & Hoffman, G. F., Future Warfare: The Rise of Hybrid Wars, *U.S. Naval Institute, Proceedings Magazine*, November 2005

Metz, S., *Strategic horizons: In Ukraine, Russia Reveals Its Mastery of Unrestricted Warfare*, Brooklyn, NY: World Politics Review, 16 April 2014

Nemeth, J. W., *Future War and Chechnya: A Case for Hybrid Warfare* (Monterrey CA: Naval Postgraduate School, June 2002), Thesis for the degree of Master of Arts in National Security Affairs

Newton, M. A., Illustrating Illegitimate Lawfare – 43, *Case Western Reserve Journal of International Law* 255, 2010

Polyakova, A., Laruelle, M., Meister, S. & Barnett, N., *The Kremlin's Trojan Horses*, Washington DC: Atlantic Council, November 2016

Reisinger, H. & Golts, A., *Russia's Hybrid Warfare. Waging War below the Radar of Traditional Collective Defence*, Research Paper, Rome: Research Division – NATO Defence Collage, No. 105, November 2014

Scharf, M. & Andersen, E., *Is Lawfare worth defining? Report of the Cleveland Experts Meeting*, 11 September 2010, http://law.case.edu/journals/JIL/Documents/43_Lawfare_Report.pdf.

Simons, G., *Mass media and Modern Warfare*, Ashgate, 2010.

Stern, E., *Crisis Decision Making. A Cognitive Institutional Approach*, Dept. of Political Science, University of Stockholm, 1999

Waters, M. A., "Lawfare" in the War on Terrorism: A Reclamation Project, *Case Western Reserve Journal of International Law*; 43, ½; 2010

Wilkie, P., Hybrid Warfare. Something old, not something new, Alabama: *Air & Space Power Journal*, Winter 2009, (23)4

4 Hybrid Warfare

Comparative view, ISIL versus 'Little Green Men'

Iulian Chifu and Gabriel Anghel

The hybrid war, a concept which appeared during the last decade, has developed explosively during the last two years and caught everyone's attention, including the attention of the NATO strategists, ending up on the planners' blueprints for finding counteraction instruments. This concept's innovation consists of the fact that it is simultaneously synonymous with the *limited war* and the *total war*, a truly major achievement for a form of complex conflict which includes classical military operations and is synonymous with two obvious logical antonyms.

Nevertheless, things are not that innovative, since from the collocation *limited war* the hybrid war took over the part which talks about the fact that we are not dealing with a large scale confrontation, using all military potential and all types of military force, while, from *total war*, it preserved two components, the fact that there are no engagement laws, so the war/conflict has no laws, also, all the components that are useful to the conflict are to be engaged, not only the military dimension, or in any case, not only the classical military dimension.

Therefore, the hybrid war is an attractive concept, with a vast form of application in reality. Furthermore, if we analyse the elements and conceptual roots and the practical use of this concept, we can identify the theoretical sources in totally different geographical regions than the area where we find it applied on the field. Hence the interest towards what could or has already become the defining type of conflict for the 21st century.

We try, in this chapter, to put some order in the concept and to present a relatively exhaustive image of the concept/relevance and the reality/significance in the hybrid war, presenting, at the same time, two distinct special cases that can be brought under the cloak of the hybrid war: the case of the Islamic State and Ukrainian hybrid war, with both its elements of implementation in Crimea and in Eastern Ukraine.

Theoretical sources for hybrid war

The primary source for hybrid war/conflict is difficult to determine. What we can say is that there is an idea that evolved in this direction simultaneously from many different military schools. Thus, the oldest reference to the theoretical area and content comes from China. Two Chinese colonels initiated the *total war* concept, practically containing every available instrument that was necessary in a defined, dynamic and complex combat zone, beyond special and military.

The book itself has a remarkable history. Thus, Col. Qiao Liang and Col. Wang Xiangsui published the book in February 1999, at the PLA Literature and Arts Publishing House, with the title *War Beyond Limits,* translated into *Unrestricted Warfare,* in the universal literature. The first reference to the book in the USA belongs to James Perry and published in Aerospace Power Journal,[1] in the summer of 2000. The book received laudatory reviews and Perry calls it '*a call for innovative thinking on future warfare*, rejecting the *blueprint for a dirty war* against the West label.[2] In 2003 an official French translation was published that followed a 1999 anonymous English translation. This English translation was disseminated on the internet at the same time as another version by an unknown panama publisher. This panama publisher was distributed in SAMIZDAT form and it had a bellicose approach not intended by the original authors.[3]

The main approach of the Chinese authors is the use, within irregular warfare, of multiple attacks on the social, economic and political systems of the opponent, at the same time as asymmetric, diverse and simultaneous or planned with a certain synchronicity of attacks. Unrestricted warfare (or the *war beyond limits*) "ignores and transcends the boundaries between the battlefields, between what is a weapon and what is not, between soldier and non-combatant, between state and non-state or sur-state" (Metz 2014). The purpose is to ensure equal chances for a weaker actor in a conflict.

The unspoken side effect of unrestricted warfare, in which Russia added not taking responsibility in Eastern Ukraine, is that we can't talk about respecting the laws of war and those of Geneva Convention regarding prisoners of war, there is no set of instruments regarding war crimes, more than that, there is no responsibility of the author of those crimes. Practically speaking, all normative frameworks in wartime are called off and by not admitting to the aggression, normative commitment in the matter is evaded.

If in Eastern Ukraine we can talk about war crimes, extrajudicial executions or political assassinations (for example the case of the local councillor tortured, executed and abandoned in a river), in the case of Islamic State, which we would like to analyse in the same context, we can find the ingredients of terrorism, namely horrible executions, beheadings, people burned alive in cages, all filmed – as part of psychological warfare – but also 'black widows' and suicide bombers, instruments borrowed from the mother organisation by this Al-Qaeda 2.0.

Nemeth and the unrestricted warfare

An important theoretical framework appeared in the United States as early as 2002, when William J. Nemeth, published his thesis at the Naval Postgraduate School Monterey, California with the title 'Future war and Chechnya: a case for hybrid warfare'. Here we find, for the first time, the term of hybrid warfare applied to this concept (Nemeth 2002).

In his thesis, Nemeth advocates that modern states are increasingly challenged by the violence created through the devolution of states and through new unstable entities, which are highly violent, with anarchist societies where traditional norms and rules mix with laws and norms from modern socio-political constructions and with modern technology as well, resulting a mixed society, or 'hybrid' society, as he calls it. His thesis describes rules and instruments for this type of society, a hypothetical society called "hybrid society", studying the interference between modern and pre-state or proto-state societies and the impact, namely the innovation and the adaptation of the modern technology to the needs and habit of mind of such a society, especially when it comes to military forces.

The frame of reference is Chechen society after the dissolution of the Soviet Union and the desire for independence of the nations or the ethnic groups within the Russian Federation. In Nemeth's thesis, the 'hybrid' fusion between religion, society and modernisation, namely technology in the hybrid society results in the postulation of hybrid war/conflict. In his thesis there are recommendations for the modern armed forces about how they should adjust in order to successfully counteract this type of hybrid conflict.

Nemeth's thesis explicitly contains elements of society and state aspirations which were linked, nevertheless, to the military component of this society, which was built on tradition and religion and based on a solid military component. He uses the "component inside society", referring to intrinsic rules and pre-state and proto-state adjustment to technology and context, insisting on the hybrid war components, in the sense of hybrid instruments and several fields of approaching such conflict.

The thesis is extremely interesting and is worth another reading, because it approaches the analysis of society's organisation on the eventuality of war, war preparations, structure, leadership, training, but it also includes elements of types of weapons, new tactics, including psychological operations and information operations as indispensable and universal components that we find in the hybrid war today. The Chechens' operational weakness was their incapacity to hold sustained and durable campaigns, wherefore the military component in Chechnya remained just an insurgency, while in Eastern Ukraine, the Chechen pattern which we believe was used by the Russian Federation, was improved by its capacity to overcome those limitations.

Other theoretical approaches

Being a concept which in the last few years has more and more attracted the attention of specialists in the international security field, a relatively large space has been assigned to *hybrid warfare*. Thus, we can find a few interesting writings on this topic in the specialised literature. In many of these, the authors approach the hybrid war in a theoretical way in their attempts to understand and explain this concept. In his paper entitled 'Hybrid Warfare. Something Old, Not Something New', Robert Wilkie gives a comprehensive definition of the concept, with hybrid warfare being explained as a "conflict in which states and non-states actors exploit all modes of war simultaneously by using advanced conventional weapons, irregular tactics, and disruptive technologies or criminality to destabilize an existing order" (Wilkie 2009: 14).

In another paper, 'Preparing for Hybrid Threats', William Fleser brings into discussion a document issued by the Department of Defense in 2010, *Quadrennial Defense Review*, which recognises the increased complexity of war; the fact that today's adversary may engage in 'hybrid approaches'; and the fact that they may use terror as a tactic, as an operational concept or as a strategic gambit (Fleser 2011: 23).

We cannot approach the subject of hybrid warfare without mentioning the threats it generates. In his paper, Timothy B. McCulloh, explains the hybrid threat as being uniquely focused on organisational capability and generally attempting to gain an asymmetrical advantage over purely conventional opponents within a specific environment. Also, the author indicates the relevance of a hybrid threat in a time of emerging non-state actors and changing state actor dynamics in the Middle East, Africa, and the Pacific.[4]

Practising the unnamed-unassumed hybrid warfare

When it comes to using hybrid warfare tactics and instruments on the field, these elements have been around for some time. Thus, in Somalia, the insurgents have innovatively used weapons that were destined for other purposes, such as using reactive projectiles against buildings, troops and helicopters. This is a product of societies' and pre-state armies' adjustment to modern technology, a tactic that was also used by the Chechens, even though they had no knowledge of its use and the way it was used in Somalia.

As for the psychological and information operations, they were of great success, that went as far as far as receiving the Western support for Russia's position. The West was persuaded by the narrative and reacted not only by responding to Moscow's demand, but also by cancelling its usual openness in accepting, hearing and listening to information concerning the Chechens' position, specifically, their willingness to go forward, deeper, towards the clash and dissolution of the Russian Federation, a moment which, the Chechen insurgency, never overcame. Hence, the subsequent employment of armed resistance and embracing of terrorist tactics by Chechnya.

If China was the one who set the theoretical framework for the 'unlimited war', Iran was the state which acted according to the norms of the hybrid war, acting on numerous dimensions and skilfully using a variety of organisations and entities, which combine illegal activities, smuggling, illegal arms trade and all areas of crime, organised to finance activities, terrorism, insurgency, dissimulation and, most of all, unassuming paternity.

And so, if there was a source for these tactics of using unissued instruments, Iran could be considered the first state that ever staged this type of hybrid warfare, Without defining the concept theoretically and without giving it the name of hybrid warfare (although we must admit that it is possible that our limited access to the Iranian strategies and tactics, to documents and classified theoretical works could be the reason why Iran is not considered its founder). Iran has the advantage of a good knowledge of the American establishment. Especially after the War in Iraq, 2003, Iran was sure, even without concrete proofs and substantial evidences, that it was impossible to obtain political support in order to counteract these actions, even though it concerns the vital interests of the USA (Metz 2014).

Lawrence Freedman: About hybrid warfare as a limited war

As I mentioned before, hybrid war has the trait of being an 'unlimited warfare' and a 'limited war' at the same time. Lawrence Freedman, a War Studies Professor at King's College London, was the one who made that connection, directly referring to the war in Ukraine (Freedman 2014–2015: 7-38).[5] He states that, although it was supposed to be a limited war and hybrid warfare, Russia missed that target in Eastern Ukraine and this additionally affected that 'credible denial' – the credibility of denying its presence on the field, initially maintained over the perspective of assuming this conflict as an interstate one, or its direct implication.

The features of the war in the Eastern Ukraine (which was treated by Freedman as being a completely separate matter from the situation in Crimea – which can raise questions about his methodology, since, in Crimea, as we will find, there was an assumed action, too obvious to be dissimulated, which brings additional disclosure elements into the next operation) would be:

- Russia's poor handling of the war, in the way that it never achieved or secured fundamental interests without amplifying the conflict;
- afterwards, the sharp deterioration in relations between Russia and the West, and continuing unsettled violence within Ukraine;
- finally, the implication of the Russian Federation was necessarily made more direct and overt, because the irregular forces were unable to defend the front lines and control the conflict until a peace plan was made – see the September 5th 2014 situation, before the Minsk Agreement.

The Russian 'mediators' lacked the capacity accomplish their expected objectives in eastern Ukraine, therefore it became necessary to introduce massive Russian forces, thus changing the paradigm of the war from one concerned with an internal insurgency sponsored from the outside, into a direct interstate limited war between Russia and Ukraine (Freedman 2014–2015: 7).

The hybrid war pattern for the Eastern Ukraine comes, according to Freedman, from the war in Lebanon, 2006, where Israeli troops were surprised by the combination of guerrilla and conventional tactics adopted by Hezbollah, the Lebanese pro-Iranian militia.[6] Freedman defines, for the first time, the hybrid war as a combination which uses a mix of different forces, covering all types of operations, from terrorism, insurgency, to regular warfare, all implemented through extensive use of Information Operations.

The irregular war/conflict component or the regular-irregular warfare combination form doesn't cover hybrid war, since the tactics extend beyond war operations and are more likely to use instruments used in tactics by a less prepared force. Thus, the hybrid war is not a simple combination between regular and irregular warfare, in a certain proportion, but has more ingredients.

Why should the hybrid war be a form of contemporary limited war?

The limited war is a conflict in which the belligerents choose not to fight at full capacity, but they limit it so that it won't escalate, extend in time, space or intensity. A war in which the limits are set by resources and geography or a state limits its forces when fighting a weaker opponent is not a limited war. It's a decision that both parties decide to embrace and accept. The opposite concept is that of a *total war,* during which all parties use all capabilities at their disposal in order to eliminate their enemy and to achieve their objectives.

The Cold War and reaching the level of nuclear arsenal that would guarantee the Mutually Assured Destruction made the idea of a limited war gain ground. The solving formula was not achieving victory in war, but a special agreement, a mutual assumption of a *status quo* situation. The big issue with such a system is that the 'sandwich tactic',[7] should never be applied, for example, the enemy generates repeated conflicts in different areas, which end in a limited format and restabilises the situation so that through overlapping different gains, the result is an achievement of the enemy's objective, or through the wish of the one being attacked not to further escalade any conflict. So, the inexact and *sine die* approach to this tactic can lead to a real defeat and capitulation through accumulation of victories.

Freedman talks about the 'salami-slicers' (Freedman 2014–2015: 9), meaning that each slice would appear not to be worth a major conflict, with relevant objectives and would be easily preserved, frozen into a certain situation, based on limited war tactics, but, cumulatively, the successive slices would eventually turn into the whole, which becomes a major problem that would require a much stronger reaction.

With regard to Russia, the idea of recomposing the 'salami' from the 'slices' started in frozen conflicts, then in Georgia, Crimea and the Eastern Ukraine, could be a warning formula stating that European and American authorities face a significant threat. However, changing the attitude line and the coagulation line of public support would be difficult to accomplish at this stage, specifically because the alert wasn't issued at the first 'slice', in regard to recomposing the ensemble, i.e. the 'salami'.

It is hard to accept the ideology that was the basis for the action of the one who generated the 'slicing', namely the small steps action as it is called today, and also the information warfare counteraction which discourages the current war formula polarisation, taking advantage of the lack of appetency, training and capabilities necessary for a direct and assumed conflict with Russia. In the public opinion, Russia is not a virtually defined by the negative terms of the Cold War opponent anymore, but a partner, difficult indeed, but one who is inoffensive. Reputation, credibility and pride seem to have become obsolete or at least they have less power in the western fractionalised societies. Small steps tactics seem to have turned out well here.

Escalation theorists, like Herman Kahn (Khan 1965), explained why the Occident resisted the impulse of an intervention at every step, reaching the final formula, which marked a real gain in favour of the then Soviet Union. We are talking about the idea of not losing control over the escalation, which would lead to the beginning of a total war, namely a nuclear war. The game of 'escalation dominance' depends on each of the opponents' inclination to accept escalation and the later difficulty of going back to calmer phases, without getting to an intense direct and total war situation, with all ammunition at disposal, until the complete destruction of the enemy is achieved. The West and the liberal approach to security through interdependency excludes, not only the instruments of war, but also the acceptability of a minimal risk of approaching escalation, thus Russia dominates the West at this level beyond debate.

We have seen why, from Russia's point of view, this was a limited war, a hybrid war. Russia turns to its advantage the possibility of anonymity and repellence of the formal, juridical, responsibility assignment in the Eastern Ukraine. Ukraine itself had major problems in approaching the war with all means: firstly defining the action as an 'anti-terrorism operation', the terrorists being paramilitary structures of the 'people's republics', but later, the use of military force in counteracting similar capabilities introduced in the theatre of operations unveiled a low level of training, Russian advance and control, lack of ammunition, capabilities and unity of command.

Nevertheless, Freedman states that the poor handling of the limited war and the hybrid war, the incapacity to control various types of forces on the field, brought in by the Russia, the rivalries between them, imposed assumed real coordination on the field and also introducing new forces and means on the field. All this and the large number of dead and wounded made the 'limited' approach and the hybrid war used a failure, leaving a situation where more sophisticated instruments were required.

The distillation is that, "*in disputes over territory, the most effective forms of control involve regular armed forces and superior firepower*" (Freedman 2014–2015: 17). However, the physical occupation of a territory doesn't also ensure the functioning of the economy and the society, which is necessary to enter the more sophisticated institutional construction of a state building phase.

Theorising the concept of hybrid warfare: James Mattis and Frank Hoffman

Then again, if we were to nominate the hybrid war "fathers", they would be James Mattis and Frank Hoffman. In 2005, when *Future Warfare: The Rise of Hybrid Wars Proceedings* was issued, James Mattis, who was to be commander of United States Central Command and of Unites States Joint Forces Command, was, at that time, General Lieutenant, commander of the Marine Corps Combat Development Command, Quantico Virginia, and Frank Hoffman was a Lieutenant

Colonel (Ret.) and was working as a Research Fellow at the Centre for Emerging Threats and Opportunities, in the same location.

According to Mattis, the conflicts in Afghanistan and Iraq influenced the balance of American strategic thinking, which now takes into consideration retaliation methods when facing a large variety of threats against the US interests. Nevertheless, conventional threats will never completely fade, and Mattis believes that the American military forces must maintain superiority in this area, in order to always be prepared to handle a major war of high intensity.

The superiority of American military capacities leads the US-concentrated strategic efforts by its opponents towards identifying niche solutions, materialised through technological variations and unusual tactics, with the purpose of obtaining some strategic advantages. This is, in fact, the hybrid threat that generates the hybrid war (Freedman 2014–2015: 2).

The hybrid war is a fundamentally irregular one, which uses instruments such as terrorism, guerrilla tactics, and criminality, informational and cybernetic attacks and through these instruments in combination, the state actor's security interests can be more easily affected. It has great impact on several areas, giving them strategic importance, through informal operations and with the support of favourable mass-media, all with the purpose of the will to support action, to fight, to go to war of the people in the targeted state.

Thus, according to Mattis and Hoffman, Americans have to simultaneously face all types of threats, to be able to successfully operate against all types of enemies, within complex conflicts and in every possible environment. This is, in the authors' opinion, the essence of the hybrid war (Mattis & Hoffman 2005: 2).

Thereby, the hybrid war, which is not a recent invention, is not simply guerrilla warfare waged by a strong state. It can incorporate the features of guerrilla warfare, but some aspects of it do not have to be present. One example in this respect is the fact that the hybrid warfare doesn't preclude the use of heavy weaponry.[8]

Frank Hoffman highlights the impressive adaptability of some possible opponents, as they innovatively developed and used asymmetrical capabilities and methods (Nemeth was the first to make this observation, as previously shown). As a consequence, we will not be able to sort future conflicts into regular or irregular, since the most dangerous opponents will seek to combine a multitude of means and capabilities into a complex blend, making the uncertainty of defining methods a constant.

The challenge will not come from a state that chooses a certain approach, but from states or groups with no affiliation to states which chose, from the whole arsenal, technologies and tactics that are strategically advantageous to their geography and culture (Hoffman 2007: 27), again, an element identified by Nemeth.

From these premises and foundations, the hybrid war has been theorised and analysed throughout the last decade in the USA and it is found in various programmatic documents:

- the main document governing the joint operations of US forces (2009), emphasising 'as often in the past, future conflicts will appear as hybrids comprising diverse, dynamic, and simultaneous combinations of organizations, technologies, and techniques that defy categorization';[9]

- the Training Circular of the US Department of the Army (2010) hybrid threat is represented by 'the diverse and dynamic combination of regular forces, irregular forces, criminal elements, or a combination of these forces and elements all unified to achieve mutually benefitting effects';[10]
- the 2011 United States doctrine, 'A hybrid threat (HT) is defined as the diverse and dynamic combination of regular forces, irregular forces, and/ or criminal elements or a mix of these forces, unified to achieve mutually benefitting effects".[11]

In another paper, entitled 'Hybrid Warfare and Challenges', Frank Hoffman mentions the fact that many military analysts have suggested that future conflict will be *multi-modal* and *multi-variant,* so they are calling for greater attention to more blurring and blending of war forms in combinations of increasing frequency and lethality, a construction described, Hoffman specifies, as hybrid warfare (Hoffman 2009: 35).

Hybrid warfare in theoretical documents and Russia's campaign in Ukraine

During the past 20 years, Moscow was permanently concerned with bringing its society under a single authority and has developed a strategy to become a regional if not a global leader/superpower once again. In order to achieve this it used levers such as foreign affairs, natural resources and military means. Russia interfered with the internal politics of former Soviet countries, particularly Ukraine, aiming to bring them back into Russia's sphere of influence, primarily by compromising their European and Euro-Atlantic aspirations.

Practically, strategy-building was undertaken mostly by using non-military means (political, economic, social and informational) in order to generate strategic effects, in order to destabilise actions and espionage, alter perceptions and mentalities, construct legitimacy for future actions, divide and undermine local, regional and national authorities and entities, create alternative administrative structures or use existing ones, and increase social tensions and dissatisfaction with the local authorities. It is beyond doubt that Russia's recent actions can be regarded as part of hybrid warfare. They are a mix of military and non-military, conventional and irregular components, none of them new, a combination and orchestration of different actions meant to create a surprise effect and ambiguity, making an adequate reaction extremely difficult (Reisinger & Golts 2014: 3).

In terms of doctrine, as a result of deficiencies in the operational area revealed during the Russian-Georgian war in the summer of 2008 and other such conflicts in other areas, Moscow leadership decided to transform and modernise the Russian military trough, an in-depth reform which will continue until 2020.[12] Afterward, the Russian Federation used the conclusions of the operational experiences of US and NATO, especially those regarding nonconventional elements, such as the cybernetic field, intelligence, gathering information or usage of armed forces for special operations.

In its military actions in Ukraine, Russia enforced its own foreign policy and national security agenda, and militarily used the 2010 doctrine. This did not prevent the Moscow leadership from continuing the structural reforms and on December 26, 2014, adopted a new military doctrine,[13] which identified the development and expansion of NATO military capabilities, especially those in the proximity of its frontiers, as the main external threat.

Since the hybrid war emerged, spread and proved viable and practical in Eastern Ukraine, let us look at what the theoretical basis of the concept is in Russia, as well. The last military doctrine of the Russian Federation that was issued as a public document in December 2014 theorises the action in Eastern Ukraine,[14] stating that "modern warfare is a complex usage of military force and political, economic, information, and other non-military means, accomplished through the extensive exploitation of the potential of popular protest and special operations forces".[15] Here we find the content of the hybrid war concept in a public document, in a Russian military document.

But how was it applied practically on the field and which are the main traits of the hybrid war led by the Russian Federation in Ukraine? Obviously, we have two distinct components or forms of implementation, one in Crimea and another in Eastern Ukraine, which 'slipped', as Freedman remarked, toward an inter-state regular war, after September 2014.

First, we should write a chronicle of a failed war, namely the Novorossiya project failure. Right before leaving the Ukrainian president's chair, fleeing from Kiev, although he had an agreement guaranteed by the EU mediators, Yanukovych intended to build Novorossiya after a Taiwanese model (Chifu 2014).

In Donetsk, the 'Congress of deputies of all levels'" was organised, namely a reunion of all deputies of the village, town, city, district and regional councils in South-Eastern Ukraine, all the way to Odessa, to vote upon separation from Ukraine and proclaim sovereignty of Novorossiya. Yanukovych had even signed a decree, moving the capital to Sevastopol, where he was to take refuge, taking over the legitimacy of state succession on treaties. It was, nonetheless, a failure.

The deputies did not vote the expected documents. They didn't even proclaim sovereignty of Novorossiya. Even participation was less than expected. So, the Party of Regions and the Russian minority in the Eastern Ukraine could not be a base for Yanukovych's new state and the resuscitation of the Novorossiya project. On the contrary, it proved that the Russian propaganda encountered major barriers in the region and, mostly, that the assumption about the Russians in Ukraine wanting to live in Putin's Russia was wrong.

And Moscow experienced that reality immediately, when it tried to make up for this failure through public protests in Eastern Ukraine. Russian 'tourists' sent to fan the flame and create a critical mass of genuine separatism, didn't manage to instigate the locals, the 'local' protest movement 'wasn't set ablaze', didn't 'roll', but on the contrary, then the Russians living in Ukraine started a fight and chased the Russian provocateurs, claiming that that 'they stole Crimea'. This was the starting point that demanded using a hybrid war approach, but it also represented the failure to have a limited war, beyond Freedman's argument that territorial dispute requires regular armed forces, logistics, military hierarchy assumed by a state (Freedman 2014–2015).

Getting back to 'successful' hybrid conflicts, particular differences and nuances are mandatory. We shall start with the Crimea case, where comparative advantages were used: official presence of the Russian troops in the region, underground control and logistics of the Ukrainian troops, introducing the 'little green men' – Russian paramilitary troops in impeccable, new uniforms (which made it difficult to deny the subordination to the Russian army of their soldiers, going by the name of 'self-defence people's militia'), direct involvement in blocking Ukrainian units, elimination of those who wouldn't switch sides, Russian people's support and that of Russophile Ukrainians from the peninsula.

In spite of these major advantages: the taking over of power and organising a referendum at gunpoint, only 15% of the population went to vote, out of which only 50% voted for reuniting with Russia, according to official data in the diplomatic environment in Kiev, which quoted news from the Russian media, but was immediately erased.[16]

Besides, not even the leaders who were appointed to ensure an apparent local representation and to take over power in Crimea were part of the local elite, but, more likely soldiers of fortune and common criminals, coordinated by Moscow.[17]

Regardless of the numbers, a sure fact is that Crimea embraced reuniting with Russia without major protests and this while the pro-Russian option – more likely autonomist than separatist, especially the option of reuniting with Russia – was already important there.

President Vladimir Putin has publicly admitted the presence of the 'little green men' in Crimea[18] and their special mission on Ukrainian territory. But many ingredients were needed to obtain an almost immediate surrender of Crimea without a hard reaction (except that of the Crimean Tatars) against the annexation of the self-governing republic in Ukraine.

The Crimean question has two dimensions: one that constitutes motivation, the 'unconstitutional' change of regime and governing in Kiev, and another that represents motive, the existence of a naval base in Sevastopol and the tendency to reopen the discussion over maintaining it, then, the tendency to migrate towards the EU and NATO, renouncing Ukraine's non-aligned status. All that was left to do was to immediately orchestrate, under occupation, the firm 'rejection of the idea of integration within the EU and NATO'[19] from the population.

Moscow immediately took advantage of the situation, as Sergey Markedonov, one of the most important military analysts in the region and in the North Caucasus, tells us. But what no one manages to explain, though, is why Russia wasn't capable pf playing a more subtle game, like supporting the *de facto* independence of Crimea without recognising it, like in Transdniester, or unilaterally recognising its independence and by signing an intergovernmental treaty acknowledging Russian presence and 'common defence' in the region, like in South Ossetia and Abkhazia.[20]

Crimea provides 80% of the infrastructure for one of the most important Russian fleets, the one in the Black Sea, the only one that provides access to warm seas. That's why in the case of a possible threat of losing this facility or 'seeing NATO troops in Sevastopol', Putin decided to cut the Gordian Knot with one blow and contain potential danger. Moreover, any kind of military clash that would have taken place in Crimea against Russian troops stationed there, would have engaged the Black Sea Fleet and would have led to the same outcome, but with more casualties. As Russia lacked trust in the new Kiev government, before the election, the step had already been made.

Hybrid warfare succeeded without a single shot fired, also due to, as we can see today, despite rigged participation and results in the so-called referendum, the majority of the Crimean population, accepting, if not supporting, the annexation of the territory. In this situation, the mass defection of Ukrainian troops was of substantial importance (armed forces, secret service members), as it was the defection of the vice-admiral of the Ukrainian fleet, Denis Berezovzky, and the Speaker of the Crimean Parliament, Vladimir Konstantinov, 'something that never occurred in Donbas', which explains the failure of Novorossiya",[21] according to Sergey Markedonov.

Once the Crimea integration process started, Moscow sought the gathering of a critical mass of protesters supporting federalisation in Eastern Ukraine, who would force the Kiev leadership to amend the constitution in that sense. The lack of or the weak reaction of the Russian minority probably determined the Russian leadership to resort to infiltrating special groups with units trained in destabilisation. Simultaneously, Russia kept an important military force at the eastern borders of Ukraine in order to exert further pressure on the Kiev leadership and to discourage any military action by the Ukrainian authorities against the pro-Russian separatists.

In Eastern Ukraine, as we have seen, 'the spontaneous revolution' against the Kiev regime 'wasn't set ablaze', even though it was actively inspired by the local politicians close to Viktor Yanukovich or members of the government or of the former president himself. This is why Vladimir Putin ignored him and didn't join him in the press conference in Kremlin, sent him to a press conference in Rostov-on-Don and then recognised the elections and the new government.

We can assume that the Russian nonconventional forces (FSB, GRU or Special Forces) acted in Ukraine long before the break out of military operations and takeover of the institutional buildings, by creating and encouraging pro-Russian feelings and anti-Ukrainian reactions, even before identifying potential recruits for the irregular troops. In the case of Eastern Ukraine presenting irrefutable evidence for the involvement of these troops is hard to accomplish, which may constitute an important element of hybrid approach. They could be identified only based on behaviour analysis, individual habits, discipline and equipment.

Simultaneously, irregular forces offered Russia the perfect cover and an efficient method of acting covertly, while still being able to deny any accusation. Their utility and low operating costs make these forces very attractive. Another advantage of irregular troops recruited from the Russian minority, dissident political groups, criminal elements and other ethnic groups from Ukraine is that they are indigenous and therefore have a more profound understanding of the operational environment. Irregulars are not easily detectable when they are not conducting operations. Even though their primary motivation is financial gain, they are efficient as subversion agents and as a way of distracting focus from other actions, in this case, plausible deniability by the Russian Federation.

Now, the hybrid war became more clear with other instruments introduced to the region, with volunteers, with Cossacks, mercenaries, Chechens, paramilitaries, released convicts from local prisons and whoever else could be trained from former local personnel trained ahead in training camps, or locally, during the conflict (Chifu 2014).

This is why here we find new leaders, clashes between groups and all control on the field was lost, hence the need to bring in, after September 2014, some regular troops, 'Russian soldiers on leave' or 'Russian soldiers, lost beyond borders, in Eastern Ukraine'. This turned, from a classic war, into an interstate war, as Freedman stated (Freedman 2014–2015).

Another observation, taking into account what we have learned and the perspective elements that affected the evolution of conflict in Eastern Ukraine: the information war that was required to change people's options, acted and catalysed options, but proved not to be sufficient or convincing enough to determine territorial rupture and the desire to reunite with Russia of the targeted population.

Even in the areas inhabited mainly by Russian ethnics, the information war didn't have much impact in getting total support for Russian troop military actions and for reuniting with Russia, neither in Eastern Ukraine, or Odessa, which shows that the evolution and reprise of the attack demands an upgrading of the plans, recommencing informational warfare, influence, psychological actions, obtaining support from population majority, before launching any military aggression or turbulences further into the heart of Ukraine. Otherwise the Russian troops or the volunteer proxies, brought in the theatre should be more numerous and act as in an occupied territory, with hostile locals, and the appearance of an existing separatist local movement could not be shown.

Overall, the actions undertaken by the Russian Federation in Ukraine have proven to be backed by well-developed military thinking, based on traditional elements combined with new approaches of deployment and modern warfare, with the scale leaning towards nonconventional tactics that deliver the strategic goals. Russia adapted military art and thinking, developed a flexible system for projecting a military force outside its borders while maintaining operational conventional and nuclear power as both a deterrent and a tactical support system for supporting and protection of conventional and unconventional operations.

Islamic State in Iraq, a hybrid war? Nuances, mutual traits and particular differences

To talk about the war led in Iraq and Syria by Baghdadi's Islamic State,[22] with the impact it had over development of the groups that embraced terrorism all around the Middle East and Northern Africa and even in Europe and North Caucasus, would a mistake. Nonetheless, if we were to cut out some particular elements, we will find that IS's (former Al Qaeda in Iraq, former Islamic State in Iraq, former Islamic State in Iraq and Syria, former Islamic State in Iraq and the Levant[23]) action comes from the same family of instruments of action as the ones in Eastern Ukraine, combining the elements of hybrid warfare even better than 'pro-Russian separatists' in Eastern Ukraine.

Islamic State[24] (IS) considerably expanded its area of operations and influence in the second half of 2014, through a strategy that combined conventional forms of combat specific to terrorist groups, brutal and well-coordinated, with unconventional actions specific to organised crime (robberies, arms trafficking, kidnapping people for reward) mixed with sustained propaganda designed to attract new followers, but also to fuel sectarian tensions amid political and security weaknesses in operation controlled areas of Iraq and Syria.

Since 2010 IS has constantly evolved as a terrorist group, led by Al Qaeda leaders to become a 'real army', whose overall strategy to strengthen and expand the Caliphate 'was fundamentally based on its military superiority capable to take control of territories and towns of modern states'.[25]

Even though, in terms of organisation/structure and ideals, IS is, and will remain, a terrorist organisation, its expansion and pursued strategic objectives are more advanced given the fact that they try to build and secure a 'state' based on fundamental Islamic principles in the territories of eastern Syria and western Iraq.

So far, it seems that this strategy has worked considering the increasing number of followers (including those in other regions of the globe) and the fact that it attracts a significant number of foreign fighters of various nationalities. Additionally, the strategy allowed benefits in the form of substantial financial resources.

From a military perspective, the group demonstrated similar abilities to those of the conventional structures of light infantry, supported by artillery, and Special Forces, trained and prepared to fight concealed among the local population. Due to these considerations IS cannot be considered and treated only as a terrorist group, but rather should be perceived and analysed as a real hybrid threat (Anghel & Ioniță 2015).

This claim of being a hybrid threat and not only a terrorist organisation (see previous paragraph) can be motivated and supported by the hybrid character of IS's actions, the mode of operation (which includes actions of conventional military tactics combined with asymmetric attacks) and terrorist-insurgent tactics executed by small groups, benefiting from enhanced mobility. Furthermore, flexibility and adaptability allows the execution of operations similar to those carried out by conventional formations – with large numbers and broad openings, which have multi-purpose objectives, and also allows the execution of actions consisting of a small number of fighters, with precise high value objectives (Anghel & Ioniță 2015).

With high mobility and resorting to deception techniques, IS achieved in many cases local numerical superiority, even if the forces participating in the operation were lower compared to those of their opponent. After such operations, armed elements at a level of tens to hundred, succeeded in occupying successive positions held by Iraqi or Kurdish forces.[26]

Also IS fighters demonstrated mastery in misleading tactics. Such tactics have been used frequently to avoid areas with strong defences, but also were implemented to divert the attention of opposing forces from the main target and redirect it to a secondary or false one.

The unconventional nature of the hybrid approach is the most visible characteristic, and it includes also terrorist actions (of an unimaginable cruelty that generate terror among the population or security forces) and specific actions of organised crime that are used as a primary source for obtaining funds to support combat actions, recruitment, training and management of the conquered territories.

Despite enjoying a significant arsenal of weapons and modern weapons systems, the terrorist organisation remained faithful to 'traditional' methods – attacks with explosive devices. Thus, many of the attacks on targets were initiated by car bomb attacks (suicide or detonated remotely) and/or suicide bombers, in order to cause a large number of casualties.

The novelty, which stresses the hybrid nature of the conflict caused by the IS, is represented by the process of governance, namely the administration of the occupied territories. Thus the challenge that IS faces is the successful governance and control of the territories and their direct rule. Other problems are the difficulties that emerge from identifying personnel that are both loyal and qualified for ruling the newly acquired areas, given that a large part of the population has already left the territory occupied by terrorists. For them, loyalty seems to be more important than the act of governance in itself, however only good governance and management of territories can ensure the sustainability of the so-called State.[27]

For the administration of the territories, IS developed a bureaucratic structure similar to the military one, based on the delegation of responsibilities and transmission of orders under the leadership chain. The system allows local governors a certain degree of autonomy, given that they are often replaced, presumably to ensure consistency of the administration or to avoid the emergence of independent local powers.[28] The governors have power over an administrative structure and a structure responsible for providing essential public services.[29]

The distinctive trait is the use of terrorism on a large scale, an element which doesn't appear in Eastern Ukraine where war crimes, plunder, terror, extrajudicial executions were committed, but not terrorist acts such as beheading, burning the opponents alive in front of video cameras, nor the use of suicide bombers.

Yet, here we find the creation of the illusion of following the radical Islam and Jihad ideology (although its members, especially the 'militants' around the world are not as religious as Bin Laden's Al Qaeda), just like in Eastern Ukraine where the 'protecting all Russians abroad' ideology was invoked and it animated volunteers from Russia to act in Eastern Ukraine.

In both cases 'mercenaries' and 'soldiers of fortune' were used, all paid and not subordinated to the ideological cause that was being promoted. It is true that volunteers from all over the world joined IS, most of them religionist zealots, who really desired to protect the cause of Islam, while in Eastern Ukraine, the ideological background didn't exist and the combatants were, almost exclusively, from inside Federation.

In the case of the Islamic State there are no known real, state-like, visible sponsors who are obvious in the case of Eastern Ukraine, where the role of sponsor is played by Russia which stands to gain territory and geopolitical advantages.

Psychological and information warfare are elements of both conflicts such as using high-tech weapons received or bought, appropriated from Ukrainian or Iraqi military units, in both cases. Also, the fact of using different instruments, from crimes – bank robbery, thievery, mugging etc. – to insurgency, non-conventional warfare and non-conventional confrontations is common, except for the terrorism.

The absence of popular support is obvious as well. In one case, the depopulation took place through crimes, robbery, rape and by killing the resistance – especially in Slaviansk and Kramatorsk. In the other case, the ideology of defence of Sunnite interests migrated towards the ambition of state-building and imposing a way of living that led to mass murder of thousands in the region.

The Islamic State has widely used Sunny soldiers and generals cleansed by the de-Bathification[30] of Al Maliki,[31] people with extraordinary military and intelligence capacities, recruited and paid by the organisation without having any inclination towards the religious ideology. In Eastern Ukraine, the recruitments envisaged personnel with military training from Russia but also Ukrainian military who had taken part in the Afghanistan war and had been trained in the Soviet Army. The Chechen group was preferred due to the experience it had gained during the guerrilla warfare in the hybrid war against Russia.[32]

In both cases we are dealing with a group that wanted to build a state and took advantage of the structural weaknesses of weak states – Syria and especially Iraq in the case of the Islamic State and Ukraine in the case of the Russian-pro-Russian breakaways. Moreover, in both cases, they acquired weapons from occupied military barracks (or from the requisites of the sponsor state), took over financial resources from the banks in the occupied region and from the population and used the resources and economic facilities from the regions – oil refineries (for the Islamic State), coal in Eastern Ukraine, and in the end created a new state that took over so-called state offices.

As Ukraine is in Europe there was a need to set the scene for 'referendums' that confine the separation, a useless thing in the Syrian and Iraqi deserts. This is where the similarities stop because the interests of the two sides in the two cases are distinct as well as their objectives as are the instruments used to counteract them. In Iraq and Syria, the Islamic State is fought through air strikes and training of the local army, the Kurdish Peshmerga and the Iraqi troops, local tribal troops, while in Eastern Ukraine, air strikes are useless, the force ratio tilting in the favour of the insurgent forces armed by Russia and backed by Russian troops.

In regard to arming the local population the approaches are also distinct: even if there are cases of defection in the case of the Islamic State the Iraqi troops can be armed because the organisation lacks a direct supplier of modern weapons. while in Ukraine, admitting there is enough time to arm the Ukrainian army, whatever weaponry the Ukrainian troops would receive they can always be outmatched by the capabilities Russia can bring to the field. Moreover, it remains open to debate if we are dealing with a proxy war in Iraq as there is no state that has claimed responsibility of the actions of ISIS while in Ukraine the instigator is obvious as well as the proxy war.

Beyond the obvious differences, the Islamic State bears a hybrid war in a similar way as the pro-Russian or insurgent forces but in the second case the war transformed more and more into an inter-state war. If in Iraq the fighters can suddenly disappear, they can melt away amidst the population, covered by the locals that remain in the Islamic State controlled regions, in Eastern Ukraine we are dealing with an occupation zone, which the locals have abandoned in a similar manner as South Ossetia, Abkhazia and Transdniester but not as in Crimea, where we had a perfect hybrid war, more or like a blitzkrieg, that benefited from advantages of Russian presence.

The problem of foreign fighters.[33] The future source of hybrid warriors in the West?

The way that we've witnessed the creation of the hybrid wars in Crimea, Eastern Ukraine and Syria-Iraq, we can realize that differences are there, experiences have particularities but communalities are obvious. For a hybrid war to succeed there's a need for an internal support in the area where it is going to be developed, a sustained and enduring informational warfare and civilians from the targeted area trained in advance by the aggressor and willing to fight in this hybrid war.

In Crimea, it was a proper hybrid war, with Russian Special Forces disguised as little green men[34] supported a small group of local adventurers succeed in taking over the peninsula from Ukraine basically without a gun being fired, since the Ukrainian military units were blocked and the locals received orders not to fire against the civilians under any circumstances.

In the case of Eastern Ukraine, the little green men were not enough on their own. Information warfare played an important role as well as previously prepared paramilitaries on the ground, support from a section of the public and the presence of volunteers and mercenaries as well as military equipment and military troops coming from Russia. After Debaltseve, regular Russian Military forces were obliged to step in and take over the fight in order to avoid the collapse of the so-called Popular republics. Numerous proofs of this constant Russian presence are there, in spite of the deniability still maintained by Moscow, even at the expense of the credibility of the Ministry of Foreign Affairs and of a number of very obvious lies.[35] In Syria, Russia had the same approach with mercenaries, special forces and volunteers on the ground in spite of the fact that the same denial was maintained for the ground presence.[36]

In the West, the IS information war could be considered that of the propaganda and dark web, recruiting and PR for Daesh and other terrorist organisations. The support on the ground was reduced to the level of the radicalised local citizens and some enclaves of criminality, trafficking of all kinds, radicalisation and terrorism, revealed in some countries like France and Belgium after the terrorist attacks in 2015–2016. But the fighters that could take the role of the armed force for a hybrid internal war are the foreign fighters. That's why, for early warning purposes and practical motifs, we want to present the most common aspects of this new threat: the enemy inside the gates of the Western world. Together with the free movement of European citizens inside the Schengen space, a weakness in one country is the weakness of the whole EU and no European state is free from the threat of terrorist attacks and hybrid wars of that kind.[37]

The problem of foreign fighters is intertwined with a lot of other issues like those of the returnees, of the Jihadi brides, radicalisation and converts, the lone wolves and the social mechanisms of integration and multiculturalism in Western societies. It is also very difficult to address foreign fighters' policies without discussing the links between terrorism and Islam, refugees, migrants and returnees as well as terrorism. So that gives us a complex object where research has been undertaken but a lot of change comes with the new evolutions of terrorist activities, where Daesh-ISIS, the so-called Islamic State has made steps ahead of the old classic Al Qaeda.

Moving to policies, some are global, a few require a European touch since the freedom of movement of people and goods happens at a European level, and in some cases individual national policies are making the difference. Discussing the enclavisation of the second-third generation of refugees or former oversea citizens after decolonisation, integration policies and multiculturalism are as important as small arms control, explosives and precursors of IED survey and exchange of intelligence in all anti-terrorist and counter terrorist activities, from finance to recruitment and Internet propaganda.

The problem of foreign fighters is more far reaching than that of a simple issue related to mercenaries. In the second case it is about a job or an occupation where the only problem would be the fact that some citizens of one country acquire skills of military fighting, strategies and tactics as well as the ability to produce and work with explosive and weapons, where their primary motivation is linked to money. In the first case, we are talking about skills to make improvised explosive devices (IED), to improvise weapons and to conduct a war in a difficult environment, but also to survive in difficult environments, based on heavy ideological and religious motivations. At the same time, foreign fighters in terrorist environments, from the first or the second category alike, do embrace the jihadi ideology and terrorist propaganda, as well as some of them participating directly in terrorist activities and of all of them in the day to day life in terrorist and jihadi camps.

A clear and correct definition of the solution would require an excellent definition of the problem and of the related issues. And this is maybe the most important and challenging part for the authorities dealing with this problem. First one has to identify the enemy or at least the most persistent and present enemy, Al Qaeda and Daesh-ISIS, the so-called Islamic state, with the differences between the two organisations.

Then it is about the fact that foreign fighters are a topic that should be treated together with that of the returnees and of the Jihadi Brides, who are also western citizens, moving to live together with the terrorists and the foreign fighters in warzones.[38] The issue of "the enemy inside the gates" or "the enemy within the walls" is about radicalised persons in the West and Europe, about converts (non-Muslims converting to Islam) their recruitment, radicalisation and use, and conditioning of "lone wolves" directly from the heart of Europe. Even an important part of the foreign fighters in Syria and Iraq come from the West. And the source of those recruited, as the way the recruitment is done, is of tremendous importance for heaving the clear definition of the problem we are dealing with, labelled as 'foreign fighters'.

Then it is not only about one of our co-citizens travelling in terrorist-held warzones, it's also about the fact that a country could be a source of foreign fighters, transit area for such fighters or returnees, or jihadi brides, or it could be a country of destination for such fighters, upon their return. And recruitment or radicalisation could happen in third-party countries as well, as the return or missions of such fighters could target EU countries other than that of their own country of origin or residence.

An important debate to be had is about the link between foreign fighters and refugees or migrants and terrorism. Another link to be explored is that of the relation between Islam and terrorism. And the most important case to contradict the oversimplification of such a problem is that of Saudi Arabia, the country accused, not always without merit, of providing via foundations, donors or even secret services, the resources needed for recruiting foreign fighters.

Last but not least, this complex problem has to be translated into public policies at an international and European level, and also at the national level. There's a lot of experience in that area, but a lot more to investigate, to research and to explore in search of solutions for this complicated issue. For sure, I could not avoid presenting here the Romanian case in identifying and coping with the issue of foreign fighters. Findings and recommendations from the new Global European Security Strategy, the Mogherini papers, is also present in our presentation and assessment.

Foreign fighters

Foreign fighters represent a concept generally designating the people from other countries involved on one side in a conflict, that is not their native or residence country. More specifically, in current and journalistic wording, but also in the general public perception, foreign fighters are designated European nationals who participate in wars involving terrorist organisations, especially in Syria and Iraq. In a strictly scientific context, foreign fighters can be differentiated according to their motivations:

- first, we are talking about mercenaries or soldiers of fortune, if the motivation is money or adventure;
- then, we have the persons estranged from the society where they are living, subject to criminal charges or already serving in prison in their countries, those with a low level of integration and feeling hugely discontented with their position in society, without possibilities or skills to achieve a better situation or without any aspiration in the Western world they are living in;
- and third, the most dangerous, those with an ideological motivation to go and fight in a war that does not involve their country.

There is no strict separation between these different categories since entering the theatre of war or the space governed by an international terrorist organisation, even the mercenaries or adventurers, not talking about those estranged from their societies of origin, can fall into the ideological motivations of the terrorist organisation, converting to radical jihadi Islam or embracing jihadism. These changes could begin at home or in the process of radicalisation and during the process of recruitment in the fighters' countries of origin, directly, through friends or relatives or via the Internet. But since the other motivations are not leading directly to people turning into terrorists, the ideologically motivated foreign fighter is the one ready to attack his/her own co-citizens once he/she returns home (Carter et al. 2014: 9–10).

Different motivations behind their recruitment give us hints on the methods that can be used for de-radicalising and reintegrating foreign fighters. Just hints, not certainties. Every group should be addressed properly, with due nuance, but since there is a thin line between returnees that left with a certain motivation, it is a case-by-case approach that is needed. Moreover, a part of the returnees are themselves subject to the shock of the life found in those spaces, the war, the unexpected difficulties, because there are huge differences between the patriotic or greatness of the messages that are used to recruit, the expectations and even stories about this life in such conflict areas, and the real thing, the real life the adventurers are discovering there. After such an experience, they often need specialised help to reintegrate in the society and many of them are victims of the stories told by the recruiters.[39]

But let's not forget that it is very complicated to find and realise who is a foreign fighter or not, who is a returnee, and how to act, if those persons are not looking for support and psychological help to reintegrate and de-radicalise. Usually, nobody notifies the embassy of the country where they are travelling and none of them say when they are leaving the country of origin or residence with a destination that is a conflict area. Moreover, the trip there includes several detours, via different countries, in order to hide their final destination. The same is true for the purpose of such visits in a conflict environment. One could use the need to visit the family, to liquidate some businesses or to bring some goods in the country of origin as an explanation of why they are going to such an environment. Finding out if a person wants to travel to conflict areas and if they have a legitimate motivation other than joining the fight is very difficult, and requires a lot of instruments, information and intelligence.[40]

The general definition of the foreign fighters motivated by the ideology offers the possibility of looking at not only to this subject, radicalisation and jihadism as an ideology, but also to some other ideologies. It is the case of the Russian ideology of exceptionalism, of a special right to defend "Russians, Russian speaking and Compatriots all over the world", the concept wide spread in the post-Soviet space of a Russian World[41] or even the Slavic brotherhood, that brought in Donbas fighters from the former Yugoslavia, especially Serbs, but also Croats, Slovaks, Czechs, on the separatist pro-Russian side, in Ukraine, as well as citizens from the Republic of Moldova or other post-soviet origins. It is true that on the other camp we also had Chechens and other northern Caucasians fighting against Russians. The figures are showing generally a spread between camps for almost all the nations in Eastern Ukraine more than is the case in Syria and Iraq with the ISIL.

Here we do have two different meanings. The first is the Ukrainian official designation of the separatist 'popular republics' of Donetsk and Luhansk – DNR and LNR – as terrorist organisations, a context that is the basis for the definition of the ATO – Anti terrorist Operation in Donbas. But this is a political motivation rather than one with a solid theoretical base. On the other hand, returnees from such a theatre of operations acquired military skills and are subject to Russian ideological propaganda and conditioning that can introduce high level risks for the country of origin. I would be inclined to include those returning from Donbas to their home countries, especially in the post-soviet space, as foreign fighters who are ideologically motivated if they are subjected to Russian imperialistic ideology or the variations produced by Moscow – neo-Eurasianism (Dugin), as well as Putinism (sovereign democracy, "vertical of power", defence of the Russians, Russian speakers and compatriots, special right on the territories inhabited by Russians in other post-soviet countries, limited sovereignty of the post-soviet states based on a self proclaimed right to avoid the threat of NATO and EU moving closer to the Russian borders).

Even if they are not proper foreign fighters, citizens from the European countries travelling to conflict areas, especially under a terrorist organisation control, could be also used in activities linked to the needs of the terrorist organisation other than the direct fight: they could be used for their IT or communication skills, some of them in propaganda activities, in other technical activities or in support operations. They are as dangerous as the other returnees once they can propagate the jihadist ideology, recruit for the jihadists or organise, participate or support a terrorist attack at home. They are in the same risk category as the proper foreign fighter.

In some cases even those attempting to travel to a terrorist theatre are dangerous and should be associated with the phenomenon and the risks generated by the foreign fighters since the residence state or their families are the ones preventing them from joining the Jihad in the Middle East. They are the most inclined to replace this activity of fighting in a conflict area that they were prevented from achieving, with other activities just as useful for the terrorist organisation they wanted to support, just by staying in their native or residential country in order to recruit others, plan, support or participate in terrorist operations.

In all those cases, the identification of a foreign fighter[42] could be very difficult since a lot of them are trying to hide their travels in those regions by using alternative routes or presenting different motivations for any travel. At the same time, their journey to join the terrorist war is making them travel through different European countries and those trips to and from terrorist combat areas are amplifying the risks even for the countries that are not of origin for the foreign fighters, neither the destination of returnees. Moreover, some foreign fighters move from one theatre of operations to another, and could also move from one activity to another, and that flexibility is also challenging in establishing ways of addressing and qualifying the level of risk that such a person represents.

Returnees

The returnees are the persons that went into at least one of the theatres of terrorist operations and returned to their countries of origin or residence. They could come back after several trips in a terrorist controlled space, or change several such theatres before returning home. They could also go to a different EU country, considering the free movement of people within Europe and the possibility of becoming resident in a different EU country from the one of origin.[43]

On the other hand, returnees are not automatically persons that could be charged with or accused of any criminal activity or terrorism. The legislation in different countries is beginning more and more to sanction those travelling in conflict areas and fighting or financing, or recruiting, or supporting in any kind a terrorist organisation. This is just complicating the survey of such persons since they tend to cover their trips in such regions under very credible motivations. But the fact is that they represent a high risk for the country of origin as well as for those which such a person is crossing on its way to and from a terrorist theatre of operations.

The majority of the returnees are coming back from the theatre of operations very quickly due to a high level of disappointment. They are the victims of the recruiters and of the propaganda that pushed them to take such a risk. They are not ideologically motivated and the original heroic images and stories presented to them are far removed from what they find on the ground, where famine, poor training and huge misery are being offered to them instead of a glorious goal that prompted their journey. They are psychologically affected and their capacity or reintegrating in the origin societies is even lower than before leaving. This category of foreign fighters should be treated as any ill person.

But a quick return is not only a sign of disappointment. Some foreign fighters with a strong ideological motivation are sent back home to recruit new people or find financial support for the organisation, or even for preparing and supporting a terrorist act. In some cases, their communication with any terrorist organisation is lacking since they decide themselves to act independently and became *lone wolves* or are doing the recruiting themselves among relatives and friends for a terrorist operation in the respective country.

Jihadi brides

There is a special category that may or may not be included under the over arching label of foreign fighters. It all depends on the interpretation. Here we are talking about women involved in conflict areas, woman that are recruited in the same way, using several types of instruments.[44] Some methods of recruitment are the same as those used in the case of foreign fighters: the promise of an adventure, fighting on the field, or a promise to belong to a community, a solution to identity issues. But in the particular case of women, or even young ladies, adolescents, a new way of attracting them is the promise of becoming futures wives of the fighters. So, in addition to the usual three motivations that we could identify in the case of foreign fighters – mercenaries for money and adventure, integration in a new society and a new beginning for unintegrated persons and support for the jihad ideology – there is an extra one, becoming the wife of a foreign fighter.

As usual, the promise and PR do not match at all with the reality of being a jihadi wife. First, in spite of some photos of women with a Kalashnikov in the middle of foreign fighters, the women are not really involved in fighting if it is not about suicide bombers. Second, the new promised society to where the foreign fighters and the women are travelling is completely different than the one advertised on websites or by recruiters. And third, the most important, it is not about becoming a wife of a foreign fighter of her choice, but more about becoming wife of a foreign fighter decided by ISIS or even becoming sexual slaves for the fighters.

The liberty they enjoy at home and the one expected in the conflict zones are far from the reality of the complete limitation of the rights, of the freedom of action and no decision belongs to the lady arrived in conflict areas, but to her owner, either husband or ruler of the group of young jihadi brides. And coming to the rules of Sharia, limiting drastically their freedoms and movements is the best case. The worst is serving as a sexual object for the foreign fighters and locals without limits.[45]

After the 'husband' or allocated man dies, it can happen that the young wife will join the ranks of the black widows. Black widows are former wives or sisters of a fighter, usually local fighter, but also those of the dead foreign fighters, who are often used as suicide bombers, in order to take revenge on the death of their husbands, using the advantages of being a woman in a Muslim country, since nobody is attempting to control their body. But the fall in the condition of a suicide bomber could happen even if it is about the sexual slaves without a proper or designated "husband": they are conditioned and sent to blow themselves up in key places, at the request of the jihadist leaders and planners.

We are talking, according to the general figures, about some 550 young ladies until mid 2015, some younger than 18 years old, travelling on their own to Syria and Iraq due to local recruitment in the West or as a result of a conversation on the Internet. The life that was promised is not that of famine, reclusion and prison that they are obliged to follow. At the same time, their state of origin is putting them on the list of foreign fighters and that means either being charged upon return, or, at the very least, being surveilled. If they stay, ISIL is ruling their life and in the real and proper sense, sometimes until death.[46]

This category is the most exposed and fragile one, and certainly the persons included here are the victims, from the recruitment period until their eventual return home. The capacity of reintegrating such a person in the society is very limited and the trauma they have experienced has an important effect. Moreover, if they are not directly embracing the jihadi ideology, the life in the conflict area and their position as slaves can play an important role in conditioning their actions, once they have returned home. It is very easy for the people involved in their prisoner life in the conflict area to obtain from them the support for terrorist activities or oblige them to be a part of the terrorist attack.

In numbers, the foreign fighters in Syria and Iraq

If we want to appreciate the number and the impact of foreign fighters, we face a very difficult challenge. How do we find reliable figures for those involved in such activities? In this paper we considered a combination of data from the International Centre for the Study of Radicalization, Brookings Institution, EU figures – from documents prepared for JHA Council or for the EEAS – and the European External Action Service.

The figures in 2015 were the following: about 3790 persons from the former Eastern Bloc, 1160 from Asia and Pacific region, 5200 from the Middle East, 5800 from Africa, 5480 from Western Europe and 230 from Northern America (the US and Canada). We are talking about 20000 confirmed until mid 2015, from the beginning of the conflict in Syria and Iraq only, including dead persons and returnees.

In Europe, France was leading in 2015 with 1500, followed by Great Britain with 700, Germany at 680 and Belgium at 650. In the former Eastern Bloc: Russia had 1500, Uzbekistan 500, Bosnia 380 and Kosovo 220. One hundred and thirty have been identified in the US and 100 in Canada; in the Middle East: Saudi Arabia had 2500, Jordan 1500, Lebanon 900; in Africa: Tunisia had 3000, Morocco 1500 and Libya 600; while 500 were from Pakistan, 300 from China and 350 from Australia.

For 2016, the figures are: 14072 from Asia, 9607 from Africa, 5997 from Europe, 330 from North America, 195 from Oceania and 76 from South America. The foreign fighters joining the terrorist groups in Syria and Iraq are from at least 86 countries.

The top 10 nationalities of foreign fighters in Iraq and Syria are the following: Tunisia with 6500 fighters; Saudi Arabia with 2500; Russia with 2400; Jordan with 2250; Turkey with 2100 fighters; France with 1700; Morocco with 1350; Lebanon with 900; Egypt with 800 and Germany with 760 fighters.[47]

Knowing the enemy: Al Qaeda and Daesh

We used to consider Al Qaeda as the main threat to our societies, I mean terrorist threat. After 9/11, researchers' full attention focused on how Al Qaeda was developed, how it acts and how somebody would ever join the ranks of Al Qaeda (Chifu et al. 2012; Speckhard 2006). But little by little, the Al Qaeda threat was more that of the external terrorist attack than creating the enemy inside the gates, in our own territory, or attracting foreign fighters in terrorist theatres of operations.

However, the shift to ISIL-Daesh didn't happen overnight but with an important change of generation. This so-call 'Al Qaeda 2.0' or 'Al Qaeda Reloaded' proved to be of a completely different substance than the original Al Qaeda that inspired Al Qaeda in Iraq, than Daesh, self proclaimed as Islamic State, the ISIS (Islamic State in Iraq and Syria) or ISIL (Islamic State in Syria Al Sham or Islamic State in Syria and Levant). The very essence of the core beliefs and substance of the new organisation proved to be different. The basic paradigm and *modus operandi* changed.

If we are looking at the ideology, the basics are there: Islamic Jihad, imposing Islam in the world, using terror to achieve it, and interested in challenging and attacking the West. The differences between them are apparent when it comes to their tactics: Al Qaeda first wishes to spread the global Jihad, and then to declare the Caliphate. In contrast, Daesh-IS wants to create the Islamic State in a territory, declare the Caliphate, then spread the Islamic Jihad all over the world. It is true that this competition led to the change in the concept of Al Qaeda in 2016, when its Syrian branch, Jabhat al Nusra, was instructed to declare its own Caliphate in North-Eastern Syria, in a region on the borders of the Mediterranean Sea and near the Allawi triangle supported by the Russian troops.

If we compare their actions, Daesh-IS is about indiscriminate violence, terror at its highest level, including against the local Sunni citizens, but even against its own operatives who failed. Even Al Qaeda considers IS to use an extreme level of violence and terror.[48] Moreover, the relation to Islam, to the religion, beliefs and practice is extremely different. Osama bin Laden was a real believer and he requested from all his followers to respect Islam and to be fervent believers, which they were.

In the case of Daesh, due to the way it was formed, including by attracting the Bathist military and intelligence officers from Saddam's Army, it is more secular, as well as the attraction of foreign fighters, representing around 50% of Daesh's troops,[49] the spread of drugs, alcohol in those ranks was high, as well as was and is gambling. It is the same with the respect for women. The local ones are treated with more respect and taken first as wives, then used as sexual toys, but only for the fighter designated as their husband. In the case of Western Jihadi Brides, sex outside marriage and the use of the women brought from the West was far more widespread, without a proper wedding to a fighter first. So the perceptions of the Quran were far less respected in the Daesh-IS territory and administration, especially among the foreign fighters. The perception and application of the Quran is main difference between Daesh-IS and Al Qaeda, an organisation formed of real Muslim believers.

Then, the Al Qaeda ideology was more inclined to counter the West, challenging the former colonial order, as well as using the Palestinian cause in order to explain their hatred towards the West. The presence of Western Crusaders colonists on the holy lands of Islam is another part of their ideology, while the need to regain the position that the Islamic Word deserves, that has been denied to it due to the spoiling of resources by the Western companies, via colonisation, is another rationale in Al Qaeda's beliefs. Al Qaeda refers to important ideologues (Abdullah Azzam, Anwar Al-Awlaki).[50] Daesh-IS were not interested in their ideas, who moved first and more pragmatically to declaring and building the Caliphate, then to defend it with foreign fighters from the West, and finally to propose that everybody should work according the norms imposed by the Prophet (except the leaders of the movement and the foreign fighters, who can drink, smoke and gamble in a Westerner style and this behaviour is tolerated). The ideology was far less important, and it was replaced by the sectarian rivalry and even a sectarian Sunni-Shia War. Daesh-IS has claimed to be the protector of the Sunni population minority in Iraq, discriminated against after the fall of Saddam Hussein, and the Sunni majority in Syria, ruled by the Allawi of Bashar al-Assad. Those were the grounds for collecting money and fighters, as well: Al Qaeda for fighting the West, Daesh-IS for defending the Sunnis in the Middle East. The idea of fighting the West is not proper to the original Daesh/IS ideology. It appeared in time as a purpose once some Al Qaeda franchises were accepted, more particular the ones in the MENA (Middle East Northern Africa) region, former colonies of the Western European states. Another important difference comes from the evolution of technology. Daesh-IS became master at using social media and making online propaganda for recruiting foreign fighters inside Western societies and local radicalised jihadists. As a result, in Al Qaeda we see foreign fighters from Muslim countries in the MENA, all of them Muslims and fervent believers, in Daesh-IS we have a lot of Westerners, converts or Muslims who discovered the religion online, or even Christians who died even before converting to Islam.

Comparing the *modus operandi* of the two terrorist organisations, we can find differences could be found, not only from the evolution of technology since 2001. In the case of Al Qaeda, we've seen large scale attacks, well planned in advance, with important prior preparation before, with a large number of victims, attacks on symbolic targets (2001 – WTC, Pentagon), using complex methodology (WTC – crashing airplanes), with coordination and usually suicide attacks.

On the contrary, Daesh emerged in an era with a huge development of online technology. It also with important tools to counteract anti-terrorist techniques and uses sophisticated means of communication. It is inclined to carry out small scale attacks with comparatively small number of victims, which are less sophisticated, with a high degree of flexibility of the operatives involved, and with a lot of improvisation in their actions, with a lot of lone wolves or self radicalized persons that join (or not) formally their ranks, but were adopted after an attack in the West. The targets are "soft" but symbolic with no or low security (Bataclan, Brussels airport check-in area etc.), where the attackers use conventional methods and tools in a tactic of hit and run (IEDs, Kalashnikovs). They use less or no suicide bombers but with a lot of attacks that have exit strategies, and operatives that are alive after those attacks. The attacks have been coordinated, but with innovative ways and means of communication, and an extended use of the new technologies (Paris, 13 November 2015; Brussels, 22 March 2016).[51,52]

As we've seen above, the biggest difference between the two terrorist organisations is the profiles of their operatives. For Al Qaeda, generally the operatives are very religious from a young age, persons who have always lived according to Islamic principles, coming from traditional Muslim families, generally born and raised in Muslim countries, without any criminal record. Daesh-IS is made of individuals who are far less religious, even Christians, persons that started frequenting mosques as adults, that were radicalised in West – sometimes in prison, a lot of them self radicalised via Internet. Those born in Muslim families (a vast majority) are rarely very religious or traditional, and the biggest contingent of the Daesh representatives were generally born and raised in the West and are Western citizens, less integrated, with huge problems of identity and the majority with criminal backgrounds in petty crime, drug trafficking, and even some of them coming from the foreign fighters, mercenaries or adventurers that converted late, eventually, to Islam.

The strongest arguments that attract fighters for Daesh-IS's cause, either Muslims and Sunni Muslims first, mercenaries and adventurers second, but also people in the search for an identity and a community to accept them, after being marginalised and isolated in their origin Western societies, are:

- a goal and an ideal State to protect, the mythic Caliphate;
- then a goal for the Sunni, a patriotic and religious goal, defending the Sunni in Iraq and Syria from an existential threat, from discrimination and fear, with the purpose of attending the deserved positions of self governance in the new Caliphate, since they were deprived of such a role in their Iraqi and Syrian states of origin;
- fighting the Sunni and Shia in a sectarian war declared at the regional level in the Middle East, with Iran supporting Shia groups and Saudi Arabia (as well as Turkey) as main supporters of Sunni groups;
- building a state where the operatives are able to reach important positions that were refused to them in their countries of origin;
- finding a society that accepts and integrates them, a society and a community that they didn't find at home, in the West;
- beginning a new life, a fresh start, without scars from the old one;

- having the possibility of repenting and paying back their debts to a society after criminal charges and serving time in prison in their Western states of origin;
- having access to a wife and a family that they couldn't afford or couldn't find at home.

Notes

1 (Dr. James D. Perry, *Operation Allied Force. The View from Beijing,* Document Published Aerospace Power Journal - Summer 2000, http://www.au.af.mil/au/afri/aspj/airchronicles/apj/apj00/sum00/perry.htm

2 In the original Perry wrote: "The venue for publication and the laudatory reviews of the book in official publications suggested that Unrestricted Warfare enjoyed the support of some elements of the PLA leadership. The Western press quoted various sensational passages from the book and described it in terms that verged on hyperbole. The book was not a blueprint for a "dirty war" against the West but a call for innovative thinking on future warfare".

3 The English version had the subtitle "China's Master Plan to Destroy America" – and had a flaming picture of the burning World Trade Centre before collapsing, according to Wikipedia.

4 Timothy B. McCulloh, *The Inadequacy of Definition and the Utility of a Theory of Hybrid Conflict: Is the "Hybrid Threat" New?*, School for Advanced Military Studies 320 Gibson Avenue Fort Leavenworth, KS 66027-2301, 2012, file:///D:/Downloads/ADA611608.pdf, pp. 9-11 (accessed 25 February 2016).

5 A prior version from October 2014, also from the "Survival" magazine, only covers the theory of the limited war in the terms of Russia's failure to maintain anonymity or unassumed forces and the Eastern Ukraine wars' quality of being "limited".

6 He's not the only one who connects hybrid warfare in Lebanon, 2006 to the Operation Cost Lead, 2008-2009 (and to the Iranian tactics and instruction for sponsored and used organisations). David E. Johnson published, at Rand Corporation in 2011, the article *"Hard fighting. Israel in Lebanon and Gaza"* RAND MG 1085. The thesis highlights the same elements suggested by Freedman as components of hybrid warfare.

7 The tactic was presented by the Hungarian communist leader, Matias Rakotzi, who explained how the Soviet Union gained total control in Eastern Europe, despite the arrangements settled in Yalta: creating, firstly, anti-fascist regimes, secondly, eliminating the right wing ideology, one by one and then the left wing ideology, except Communist Parties. If every stage seemed non-invasive, or, ultimately, acceptable to western partners, small step tactic led to fundamental change, which could be *casus belli.*

8 Lanoszka, A., *Russian hybrid warfare and extended deterrence in Eastern Europe,* International Affairs, 92:I, 2016, http://www.alexlanoszka.com/LanoszkaIAHybrid.pdf, pp. 179 – 180 (accessed 1 June 2016).

9 Department of Defence, *Capstone Concept for Joint Operations*, Version 3, Washington D.C., January 15, 2009, p. 2.

10 U.S. Department of the Army, *Hybrid Threat*, Training Circular 7-100 (Washington DC, November 26, 2010), 1-1.

11 US Army, *Field Manual 3-0 Operations C-1* (GPO, Washington DC, February 2011).

12 Since 2008, a series of structural reforms in the defence sector were initiated, in 2009 a new National Security Strategy was published, a new Military Doctrine in 2010, and in 2012 National Security Concept of the Russian Federation.

13 www.kremlin.ru (accessed 28 December 2014).

14 *Russia dubs NATO major threat in new military doctrine*, http://mashable.com/2014/12/26/russia-military-doctrine/ (accessed 28 December 2014).

15 Ibid.

16 Roderick, P. G., *Putin's 'Human Rights Council' Accidentally Posts Real Crimean Election Results*, Forbes, http://www.forbes.com/sites/paulroderickgregory/2014/05/05/putins-human-rights-council-accidentally-posts-real-crimean-election-results-only-15-voted-for-annexation/, 5 May 2014 (accessed 25 February 2016).

17 Among them there is also Felix Chernyakhovsky, known as "Black Raven" one of the leaders of the Night Wolves, a Russian nationalist motorcycle group, which joined in the armed takeover of Crimea, in March 2014. Other persons supporting Putin with the annexation of Crimea were Belarusian citizen Vladimir Korotkevich, who had a contribution in the seizure of government buildings in Crimea; the former Afghan intelligence officer Hostai Mubarak Shah; a 26-year-old man charged with assault and an armed attack on an Orthodox church; a 60-year-old director of a nature reserve charged with embezzlement and abuse of office; Viktor Keller, convicted and sentenced to eight years imprisonment for stealing 18th-century antique jewellery from a private home and others.

18 Admitting the presence of "little green men" in Ukraine took place in the televised question-and-answer session, on April 17, 2014, when the Russian President Vladimir Putin attended the annual session of "Questions & Answers with the nation".

19 Markedonov, S., *The Crimean 'question'*, Politcom.ru, 16 January 2015.

20 Russia and South Ossetia have signed a "Border Agreement" on February 18, 2015 after Russia signed, in November 2014 a "Treaty on Alliance and Strategic Partnership" with Abkhazia, the other Georgia's breakaway region. Moscow plans to sign a similar document with South Ossetia (envisaging integration of Russia's security forces and military with South Ossetia's) so, the agreement signed on 18 February is a preliminary document.

21 Markedonov, S., *The Crimean 'question'* https://www.opendemocracy.net/od-russia/sergei-markedonov/crimean-%e2%80%98question%e2%80%99.

22 Abu Bakr al-Baghdadi or Abu Du'a, alternatively called Abu Bakr al-Baghdadi al-Husseini al-Qurashi, born as Ibrahim Awad Ibrahim al-Badri and known by his adherents as Amir al-Mu'minin or Caliph Ibrahim, is the Ameer of the Islamic extremist group, The Islamic State of Iraq and the Levant (ISIL) also known as the Islamic State. Proclaimed a Caliph by his followers, he passes for the brain of the Islamic extremist terrorist group which controls the self-proclaimed 'Caliphate' in territories in Iraq and Syria.

23 The Islamic extremist group originally known as The Islamic State of Iraq and the Levant (ISIL), known in Arabic as ad-Dawlah al-Islāmīyahfī al-'Irāq wash-Shām, resulting the acronym in the same language, Da'ish or DAESH. In most cases the name of the organisation was translated "the Islamic State of Iraq and Syria" or 'the Islamic State of Iraq and al-Sham", resulting the well known acronym ISIS. On 29 June 2014, after gaining control over a large number of cities, including Mosul and advancing towards the capital Baghdad, the group self-proclaimed a 'Caliphate' and changed its name to the Islamic State (IS).

24 Al-Dawla Al-Islamiyya fi Al-Airaqwa Al-Sham, DAESH (acronym in Arabic), Islamic State in Iraq and the Levant (ISIL). Starting 29.06.2014, the group self-proclaimed Al-Dawla Al-Islamiyya/Islamic State. The group's jihadist ideology is inspired by the Islamic Hanbali school (from which also derives the Wahhabi movement), according to http://www.wilkipedia.org (accessed 11 February 2015).

25 Lewis, J., "The Islamic State: A Counter-strategy for a Counter-State", Institute for the Study of War, http://www.understandingwar.org/sites/default/files/Lewis-Center%20of%20gravity.pdf, July 2014 (accessed 15 February 2015).

26 Most columns were made up of 10-30 light commercial vehicles, some mounted with machine guns or small anti-aircraft guns. Overall, tanks and armoured personnel

carriers were rarely used in such raids, particularly due to lack of mobility over long distances.

27 Caris, C. & Reynolds, S., *ISIS Governance in Syria*, The Institute for the Study of War, http://www.understandingwar.org/sites/default/files/ISIS_Governance.pdf, July 2014 (accessed 12 February 2015).

28 Ibid.

29 http://www.reuters.com/article/2014/09/30/us-mideast-crisis-wheat-idUSKCN0HP12J20140930 (accessed 12 February 2015).

30 The new doctrine which eliminated from the forefront former members of Saddam Hussein's regime in Baath Arab Socialist Party, Sunni Muslims who occupied almost all positions in security forces and army, well trained but replaced by new authorities.

31 Nouri al Maliki, the Shi'ite Prime Minister of Iraq who failed to follow, in his second term, a list of commitments for reconciliation and equability between ethnic groups and denominations, prompted harsh reactions from Sunni tribes.

32 Ramzan Kadvrov, who became Chechen president after his father, Akhmad Kadyrov, was assassinated, was the leader of anti-Russian guerrillas, taking over leadership of the state, turned to Islam and Wahhabism, and was the main provider of combatants in eastern Ukraine. The disparity of the image is striking, based on the pragmatism of money and favours given by Putin's Kremlin and not "defending Russians everywhere".

33 *Foreign Fighters under International Law and National Law,* Ministerie van Defensie, Versie 1, 07-12-2015, file:///D:/Downloads/PUC_21650_11_1.pdf, 9 September 2016 (accessed 15 September 2016), p. 3.

34 Ash, L., *How Russia outfoxes its enemies,* BBC News, http://www.bbc.com/news/magazine-31020283, 29 January 2015 (accessed 15 September 2016).

35 Demirjian, K., *Putin denies Russian troops are in Ukraine, decrees certain deaths secret*, The Washington Post, https://www.washingtonpost.com/world/putin-denies-russian-troops-are-in-ukraine-decrees-certain-deaths-secret/2015/05/28/9bb15092-0543-11e5-93f4-f24d4af7f97d_story.html, 28 May 2015 (accessed 15 September 2016).

36 Queen, A., *Vladimir Putin sent Russian mercenaries to 'fight in Syria and Ukraine'*, The Telegraph, http://www.telegraph.co.uk/news/2016/03/30/vladimir-putin-sent-russian-mercenaries-to-fight-in-syria-and-uk, 30 March 2016 (accessed 15 September 2016).

37 Simcox, R., *The Threat of Islamist Terrorism in Europe and How the U.S. Should Respond*, THE HERITAGE FOUNDATION, http://www.heritage.org/research/reports/2016/08/the-threat-of-islamist-terrorism-in-europe-and-how-the-us-should-respond, 1 AUGUST 2016 (accessed 15 September 2016).

38 Nabeelah Jaffer, *The secret world of Isis brides: 'U dnt hav 2 pay 4 ANYTHING if u r wife of a martyr'* The Independent, 24 June 2015, https://www.theguardian.com/world/2015/jun/24/isis-brides-secret-world-jihad-western-women-syria   (accessed 17 September 2016)

39 Holmer, G., *What to Do When Foreign Fighters Come Home,* Foreign Policy, http://foreignpolicy.com/2015/06/01/what-to-do-when-foreign-fighters-come-home-isis-islamic-state-syria-iraq/, 1 June 2015 (accessed 21 September 2016).

40 Masi, A. & Sender, H., *How Foreign Fighters Joining ISIS Travel To The Islamic State Group's 'Caliphate',* International Business Times, http://www.ibtimes.com/how-foreign-fighters-joining-isis-travel-islamic-state-groups-caliphate-1833812, 3 March 2015 (accessed 15 September 2016).

41 Jilge, W., *Russkiy Mir: "Russian World". On the genesis of a global concept and its effects on Ukraine,* German Council on Foreign Relations, https://dgap.org/en/node/28188, 3 May 2016 (accessed 15 September 2016).

42 Perring, R., *Foreign fighters seeking to join Islamic State are 'using fake passports' to enter Syria*, express.uk, http://www.express.co.uk/news/world/560320/Islamic-State-Syria-Turkey-fake-passports-militants, 25 February 2015 (accessed 25 September 2016).

43   *Final Report of the Task Force on Combating Terrorist and Foreign Fighter Travel,* Homeland Security Committee, https://homeland.house.gov/wp-content/uploads/2015/09/ TaskForceFinalReport.pdf, September 2015, pp. 13-14.

44   Baker, A., *How ISIS Is Recruiting Women From Around the World,* Time, http://time. com/3276567/how-isis-is-recruiting-women-from-around-the-world/, 6 September 2014 (accessed 25 September 2016).

45   Khan, D., *For Isis women, it's not about 'jihadi brides': it's about escape,* The Guardian, https://www.theguardian.com/world/2015/jun/21/isis-women-its-not-about-jihadi-brides-its-about-escape, 21 June 2015 (accessed 15 September 2016).

46   Weaver, M. A., *Her Majesty's Jihadists,* The New Yorker Magazine, http://www. nytimes.com/2015/04/19/magazine/her-majestys-jihadists.html?_r=0, 14 April 2015 (accessed 15 September 2016).

47   Kirk, A., *Iraq and Syria: How many foreign fighters are fighting for Isil?* The Telegraph, http://www.telegraph.co.uk/news/2016/03/29/iraq-and-syria-how-many-foreign-fighters-are-fighting-for-isil/, 24 March 2016 (accessed 27 September 2016).

48   Kurt Eichenwald, *Iraq's ISIS is Eclipsing Al-Qaeda, Especially With Young Jihadists,* Newsweek, 7 July 2014, http://europe.newsweek.com/iraqs-isis-eclipsing-al-qaeda-especially-young-jihadists-257402?rm=eu

49   The number of foreign fighters in Iraq and Syria has more than doubled since last year to at least 27,000, according to a new report by an intelligence consultancy, highlighting the global dimension of the conflict.The figures, compiled by the Soufan Group could be found in The Guardian, *Number of foreign fighters in Iraq and Syria doubles in a year, report finds,* at https://www.theguardian.com/world/2015/dec/08/isis-foreign-fighters-iraq-syria-doubles-report

50   Gunaratna, R., *Al Qaeda's Ideology,* Hudson Institute, http://www.hudson.org/ research/9777-al-qaeda-s-ideology, 19 May 2005 (accessed 15 September 2016).

51   *Paris attacks: What we know so far,* France24,http://www.france24.com/en/20151115-paris-attacks-bataclan-what-we-know-attacker-victims-arrests-belgium, 15 November 2015 (accessed 29 September 2016).

52   Rankin, J., *Islamic State claims attacks at Brussels airport and metro station,* The Guardian, https://www.theguardian.com/world/2016/mar/22/brussels-airport-explosions-heardDd, 22 March 2016 (accessed 29 September 2016).

Bibliography

Anghel, G. & Ioniță, L., "New valences of the hybrid approach in contemporary conflicts" INFOSFERA Review, no. 1, 2015

Chifu, I., *Prospective of Ukraine crisis: scenarios for a mid-long term evolution,* Bucharest: Institute of the Political Science and International Relations Publishing House, 2014

Chifu, I., Popescu, O., & Nedea, B., *Religion and Conflict radicalisation and violence in the Wider Black Sea Region,* ISPRI Publishing House, Bucharest, 2012

Carter, J. A. & Maher, S. & Neumann, P. R., *#Greenbirds: Measuring Importance and Influence in Syrian Foreign Fighter Networks,* The International Centre for the Study of Radicalisation and Political Violence, London: King's College, 2014

Fleser, W., *Preparing for Hybrid Threats. Improving Force Preparation for Irregular Warfare,* GlobalSecurity.org, CALL Newsletter 11-34: Irregular Warfare – A SOF Perspective Newsletter, June 2011, Fort Leavenworth, KS: Center for Army Lessons Learned

Freedman, L., *Ukraine and the Art of Limited War,* "Survival", vol. 56, nr.6, December 2014 – January 2015

Hoffman, G. F., *Conflict in the 21st Century: The Rise of Hybrid Wars,* Arlington – Virginia: Potomac Institute for Policy Studies, December, 2007

Hoffman, G. F., *Hybrid Warfare and Challenges,* Joint Force Quarterly, Washington DC: Institute for National Strategic Studies, National Defense University, 2009

Khan, H., *On Escalation: Metaphors and Scenarios*, New York: Praeger, 1965

Mattis, J. N. & Hoffman, G. F., *Future Warfare: The Rise of Hybrid Wars*, U.S. Naval Institute, Proceedings Magazine, November 2005

Metz, S., *Strategic horizons: In Ukraine, Russia Reveals Its Mastery of Unrestricted Warfare*, Brooklyn, NY: World Politics Review, 16 April 2014

Nemeth, W. J., *Future War and Chechnya: A Case for Hybrid Warfare* (Monterrey CA: Naval Postgraduate School, June 2002), Thesis for the degree of Master of Arts in National Security Affairs.

Reisinger, H. & Golts, A., *Russia's Hybrid Warfare. Waging War below the Radar of Traditional Collective Defence,* Research Paper, Rome: Research Division – NATO Defense Collage, No. 105, November 2014

Speckhard, A. "Understanding the Psycho-Social and Political Processes Involved in Ideological Support for Terrorism" in Mary Sharpe, *Suicide Bombers: The Psychological, Religious and Other Imperatives*, IOS Press, Amsterdam, 2006.

Wilkie, R., *Hybrid Warfare. Something Old, Not Something New,* Alabama: Air & Space Power Journal, Winter 2009

5 Lawfare

Fighting with the legal framework and reaching military objectives by using the law

Iulian Chifu

Lawfare or legal warfare, a concept and word created via two words, Law and warfare, has been developed as a component of the hybrid war and as a way of making war and developing military actions with purposes of reaching military and strategic targets in itself. As with the informational war, it has its own instrument and can be used in its own or combined with other instruments in a hybrid war.

In this chapter, we are going to pass through the origins and definitions of lawfare, its direct link with the hybrid war and the origins of this form of war – the quotations in the book *Unrestricted Warfare*, by Qiao Liang and Wang Xiangsui (Beijing: PLA Literature and Arts Publishing House, February 1999) in order to reach the very core of the concept established and made popular by Col. Charles J. Dunlap in 'Law and Military Interventions: Preserving Humanitarian Values in 21st Century Conflicts' (29 November 2001).

Positive and negative lawfare, offensive and defensive lawfare, legitimate and illegitimate warfare as well as the uses and abuses of the term are thoroughly analysed here in order to avoid confusion and excess and to have a balanced and useful definition of the term.

We will introduce our own contribution to the development of the concept, a definition that takes into consideration both the technological development and the lack of legislation or the existence of some areas where legislation could be taken advantage of via a lack of technological capabilities that are now within our reach. This new development offers us the possibility of debating examples and practical application beyond the well-known debate about the rules of the war and combat operations versus human rights and using legal means in order to distort, postpone or block military actions. 'Little green men' and the annexation of Crimea, lawfare and the laws of war and combat operations, the artificial islands and the law of the sea, as well as difficulties in fighting Daesh (the Islamic State group) and terrorist organisations due to the definition of combat fighters, are part of our assessment.

Theoretical background

Historically, what are the origins of 'lawfare'? The concept of lawfare uses a term that does not yet appear in the Oxford English Dictionary. Prior to 2001, the term was used sporadically in a variety of contexts. The term 'lawfare' first appeared in 1975 in an article entitled 'Whither Goeth the Law – Humanity or Barbarity' by John Carlson and Neville Yeomans, referring to the peaceful resolution of conflicts. This paper was first published in 1975 in *The Way Out – Radical Alternatives in Australia* (eds.) Smith, M. & Crossley, D., Melbourne: Lansdowne Press. In this paper, the authors presented a history of mediation and introduced for the first time (according to our investigation) the term 'lawfare'. In the presentation made by the authors and in their understanding "lawfare replaces warfare and the duel is with words rather than swords".[1]

In the paper there are no direct steps made towards the real concept of lawfare. It is more like a presentation that supports using the law, the capacity of peace building and creative, normative, constitutional and legal frameworks, a war can be settled through mediation and negotiations rather than by fighting and combat, since at the end of the day parties should come back to the table and establish ways out of conflict through a common understanding. But it is important to note the first use of the term in this paper.

The concept of 'International Law Warfare', the first step towards the very substance of the concept, was approached in 1999 in 'Unrestricted Warfare'[2] (Liang & Xiangsui 1999), the very first book considered to be the cornerstone of the concept of hybrid warfare (see Chapter 4 of this book). This gives us the link between the two concepts. The book mentions:

> Aside from what we have discussed above, we can point out a number of other means and methods used to fight a non-military war, some of which already exist and some of which may exist in the future. Such means and methods include psychological warfare (spreading rumours to intimidate the enemy and break down his will); smuggling warfare (throwing markets into confusion and attacking economic order); media warfare (manipulating what people see and hear in order to lead public opinion along); drug warfare (obtaining sudden and huge illicit profits by spreading disaster in other countries); network warfare (venturing out in secret and concealing one's identity in a type of warfare that is virtually impossible to guard against); technological warfare (creating monopolies by setting standards independently); fabrication warfare (presenting a counterfeit appearance of real strength before the eyes of the enemy); resources warfare (grabbing riches by plundering stores of resources); economic aid warfare (bestowing favor in the open and contriving to control matters in secret); cultural warfare (leading cultural trends along in order to assimilate those with different views); and international law warfare (seizing the earliest opportunity to set up regulations) etc. (Liang & Xiangsui 1999: 55)

But the most current reference to lawfare is that of the US Air Force Colonel Charles J Dunlap Jr. in his essay written in 2001 for Harvard's Carr Centre for Human Rights Policy at Harvard University (Dunlap 2001). Dunlap defines lawfare as "the use of law as a weapon of war" (Dunlap 2001). In subsequent developments and nuances, the concept moved to the sense of "a strategy of using – or misusing – law as a substitute for traditional military means to achieve an operational objective" (Dunlap 2008). The term proposed by Dunlap was rather neutral, but in recent years, it has been used by groups and commentators in a number of alternative senses, some very different that the original concept proposed by him.

As Jack Goldsmith noted:[3]

> To my mind the most important speaker at the conference is General Charles Dunlap, the former Deputy Judge Advocate General of the United States Air Force who is now at the Center on Law, Ethics and National Security at Duke Law School. General Dunlap is an amazing man for many reasons, not the least of which is that he is a serious intellectual who regularly published influential scholarly articles during his service in the Air Force on topics ranging from cyber security to civilian control of the military to legal ethics to targeting doctrine and more. His most influential idea, however, is "lawfare." He may not have been the first to coin the term but he certainly popularised it and was the first to analyse it seriously.

General Dunlap used the term in order to assess the debate of the 1999 Kosovo campaign about the legality of the war "out of area" of NATO (before the Strategic concept adopted in Washington which introduced this approach[4]) and "without a proper UN mandate" after the veto on the resolution due to sanction the ethnic genocide in Kosovo before the adoption of 1244 UN Resolution, considered as a post-factum approval by the international community of the actions undertaken in 1999.

Goldsmith underlines the ideas behind the lawfare, which are that of a weak adversary trying to use legal principles in order to defeat a stronger opponent or to meet military objectives:

> "Is lawfare turning warfare into unfair?" he asked, and his basic answer was "Maybe." General Dunlap defined "lawfare" as the "use of law as a weapon of war," which he described as "the newest feature of 21st century combat". The paper gave many examples of relatively weak U.S. adversaries using legal principles dishonestly and strategically to "handcuff the United States" in an effort to "exploit our values to defeat us.[5]

With this observation, once again Dunlap brings lawfare into the sphere of the hybrid warfare term, as a part of hybrid warfare or a tool for a weaker party to fight against a stronger enemy without directly facing him in a direct military clash, but by using alternative means in order to have a chance against the stronger side. And it worth mentioning this observation since it integrates lawfare into the hybrid instruments presented by Qiao Liang and Wang Xiangsui in their book, also leaving it the capacity and possibility of being used not in a hybrid complex operation but by itself, only at the legal level, with the purpose of attaining some military objectives without a shot being fired.

General Dunlap insisted on cautioning against overreaction and the importance of adherence to the law of armed conflict. As a person involved in both military and law, he was in the best position to really know the perfect combination of strategies, subtle nuances and to avoid extreme interpretations that other authors introduced to the term afterwards. He concluded that "there is disturbing evidence that the rule of law is being hijacked into just another way of fighting (lawfare), to the detriment of humanitarian values as well as the law itself" (Dunlap 2001).

Last but not least, in a somehow parallel effort, J. L. Comaroff used the term 'lawfare' in his studies regarding colonial African contexts, also in 2001. But his reference is put more in the context of what we would call 'positive lawfare' or even 'offensive lawfare' today. In his view, "lawfare (is) the effort to conquer and control indigenous peoples by the coercive use of legal means" (Comaroff 2001: 306). In his book, lawfare is described as "International Law Warfare" and is mentioned alongside several other means by which offensive action may be carried out against the enemy without using the force of arms.

Developments

Developments of the term were made after the launch of the concept by Gen. Charles Dunlap. And he was also the main source of those nuances and developments. Charles Dunlap expanded on the definition, explaining lawfare as "the exploitation of real, perceived or even orchestrated incidents of law-of-war violations being employed as an unconventional means of confronting a superior military power".[6] General Dunlap wrote many more essays about 'lawfare', and in order to rebut misinterpretations or misappropriations of his work,[7] he expanded the definition of the term to mean 'the strategy of using – or misusing – law as a substitute for traditional military means to achieve an operational objective.'[8]

This redefinition or even nuancing was needed due to the fact that meanwhile, since the introduction of the term, a number of groups used lawfare in order to criticise those who use international law and legal proceedings to make claims against the state, especially in areas related to national security. It is rather an abuse of the term since the initial intent was not to challenge the legitimate use of the law for defending each individual that considers his rights to have been disregarded, but the abuse of law and legal procedures against a legitimate and clear action in national security.

This definition has been popularised in that sense by a neo-conservative-sponsored group called The Lawfare Project.[9] When references are made to the hijacking of the term, the Lawfare Project is usually the easiest example. According to The Lawfare Project, their goal is analysing *lawfare* as it is used (via the Western legal system), nationally and internationally, to: (1) Thwart and punish free speech about issues of national security and public concern, (2) De-legitimize the sovereignty of democratic states, and (3) Frustrate and hinder the ability of democracies to defend themselves against terrorism.[10]

According to the manifesto of the site, the primary goals of the Lawfare Project are: "(i) To raise awareness about the phenomenon (and specific instances) of lawfare assuring the subject matter receive the credibility and immediacy that it warrants, (ii) facilitate (legal and non-legal) responses to the perversion and misapplication of international and national human rights law, (iii) identify and mobilize human and institutional resources, and (iv) bring diverse and interested parties together in a common forum to discuss the threat"[11] and examples in that case would be the case brought to the International Court of Justice on the legality of Israel's security barrier, human rights cases sponsored by organisations sympathetic to the Palestinian cause, and litigation in support of terrorist detainees.[12]

On the other hand, Mark Martins considers that "lawfare has also been used to describe the nefarious exploitation of international law for propaganda purposes by, for example, orchestrating civilian deaths".[13]

These developments led to debates where the very existence of or the need to define lawfare were considered irrelevant. On 10–11 September 2010, Case Western Reserve University School of Law hosted a symposium and an experts meeting to debate and answer the question: What is lawfare and how should the United States and its allies best respond to it? (Scharf & Andersen 2001) They considered that lawfare is a concept that has been misused to block the access of persons to the legal system and that it covers abuses in important places where the American military fight. At the end of the debate, the experts recognised that, however defined, with or without abuses, away from the original definition and intent of Charles Dunlap, lawfare is a potentially powerful term that reflects the importance of law in the conflicts of the 21st century.

Lawfare and the International Criminal Court (ICC)

The debate has also moved onto discussing the topic of the US joining the ICC. Being an international legal mechanism, the concerns of the Lawfare Project group went that way too, discussing with concern the capacity of the ICC to become a tool of lawfare of third parties against the US. These concerns have been addressed also by the members of the American Non-Governmental Associations Coalition for the ICC (AMICC), a program of the United Nations Association of the United States:[14]

> Aggressive legal manoeuvres alone are not enough to constitute lawfare. The use or misuse of law is only lawfare where it seeks to achieve military objectives; strategic legal moves employed to gain a political, not military, advantage are therefore not lawfare. Those engaged in lawfare should also have the requisite intent to achieve military objectives, above and beyond the intent of those using of judicial processes for civil or criminal accountability. This intention does not have to be primary, however; it may still be lawfare where prosecutions are carried out to provide justice and accountability for atrocities, but also have a secondary objective of gaining a military advantage of some kind.[15]

Because of US military strength and global presence, the US military may be a target for lawfare. According to the revision of the sense of the term of lawfare, Dunlap hinted that nations and non-state actors unable to challenge the US on the battlefield could try to undermine American military objectives through non-conventional military tactics such as lawfare. Although not a symmetrical threat, lawfare could be a potent weapon for a group or state seeking to undermine US military strategy.

The ICC is considered to potentially become such a useful tool in the hands of the weak parties that could use it unlawfully against the US. But they explain why such a step is not possible:

> The ICC could be used as an instrument of lawfare to illegitimately target US leaders and service members, and undermine American military operations and objectives. They argue that the ICC Prosecutor could exercise the Court's jurisdiction to conduct frivolous investigations and prosecutions or examine situations submitted to the Court by a State Party to harass and distract US military and political officials and personnel.[16]

The supporters of human rights and of the US joining the ICC argue that although in extreme circumstances any institution could be perverted to contradict its principles, the safeguards, checks and balances in the Rome Statute nearly ensure that the Court could not be used as an instrument of lawfare in the negative sense. The guarantees would be the fact that the jurisdiction of the ICC is limited to the prosecution of the most serious cases of the crime of genocide, crimes against humanity and war crimes, and that before the Court can investigate or prosecute alleged crimes, a State Party or the Security Council must refer the situation to the Court, or a case can be initiated by the Prosecutor, if is a subject to authorisation by the Court's Pre-Trial Chamber.

Moreover, according to the principle of complementarity, the ICC is required to defer an investigation to domestic courts unless those courts are unwilling or unable to act. So the abuse that could be made by using the ICC in lawfare against the US would mean the involvement and twisting of large numbers of people and the abuse of Court procedure in ways that would be almost impossible to conceal for long, according to the Rome Statute. And the whole debate could be moved in the categories of good and bad lawfare, or positive and negative lawfare, as we can see below.

Self-inflicted wounds in lawfare

The Lawfare Project discusses the concern about the increasing frequency with which international law was being used and abused by the opponents of the US. Specifically, there is a focus on the exploitation of real, perceived, or even orchestrated incidents of law-of-war violations being employed as an unconventional means of confronting American military power. It is possible to falsify or manipulate data to make it appear that the United States is fighting in an illegal or immoral way. In a democracy, this damages the public support of the military.

The parent of lawfare, Charles Dunlap, came back in an essay and introduced the term of self-inflicted wounds in lawfare,[17] a kind of friendly fire in terms of a military combat operation. The abuses at Abu Ghraib and Guantanamo were targeted by Gen. Dunlap, as those which "produced effects more damaging than any imposed by our enemies by force of arms". What makes it very important is that these are "self-inflicted wounds", "wholly preventable incidents where adherence to the rule law would have avoided the disastrous consequences that still plague America's war-fighting effort."[18]

The communication of the facts of war, how it is made, the manner and the treatment without proper deference of such accidents with human civilian casualties could also be a source of self-inflicted wounds turned into lawfare operations. Regarding the reports about NATO's airstrikes that are causing civilian casualties, in response to a series of queries about such deaths, a spokesman of the International Security Assistance Force (ISAF) in Afghanistan insisted that "NATO would not fire on positions if it knew there were civilians nearby."[19] If the purpose of this statement was to assuage the populations', both in Afghanistan and in NATO countries, natural concerns when civilians are killed, the statement doesn't explain the loss of lives once it is the military operations' responsibility to avoid civilian casualties and to explain how it happens when they occur.

International law forbids the direct targeting of civilians but recognises that civilians are incidentally put at risk during otherwise legitimate attacks on combatants. There's a full debate about who is and who is not combatant in very complicated environments, where the enemy has no uniform at all and is present in civilian homes. According to the law, the risk to civilians not involved in combat operations need not be excessive in relation to the concrete and direct military advantage anticipated for an operation, meaning killing terrorists and other enemy fighters who threaten both friendly forces and other civilians.

Trying to completely avoid any victim or assuming that no civilian casualties would occur "creates unnecessary and often counterproductive results. Among other things, the unrealistic and unachievable expectations produced stimulate a sense of betrayal when such casualties occur, and — despite all efforts — they will always occur in war",[20] says Dunlap. On the contrary, he blames lawfare when claiming that a type of zero tolerance to civil casualties could put civilians from a war area at peril due to the fact that terrorists or insurgents of any kind could take advantage of this situation and use gunfire, improvised explosive devices or suicide bombing in order to produce civilian victims and have the arguments to attack, using propaganda, this fact. In such a case, assuming the avoidance civilian victims could mean the opposite, exposing those civilians to remaining or escaped terrorists who can use them for propaganda purposes, risking being killed in that area so they, the terrorists, can blame the bombardment.

> Excessive civilian losses must always be avoided, it may very well be more humane approach to kill bad guys when the opportunity presents itself even

though some civilian losses may also occur", says Dunlap. On a complementary note, a paradigm of "zero tolerance" for casualties could "encourage the enemy to do exactly what we do not want them to do: surround themselves with innocent civilians so as to virtually immunize themselves from attack. It creates a sanctuary that the bad guys are not entitled to enjoy, and sends them exactly the wrong message.[21]

Positive and negative lawfare

The debate about lawfare moved into the sphere of qualifying and charting its positive and negative components. So, it was natural to arrive at nuances and ethical appreciations of those types of conduct. Lawfare is the use of law and judicial processes as an instrument of warfare, as a strategy of using (or misusing) the law instead of military actions or as a complementary instrument to traditional military actions in order to achieve military objectives. This important split in the definition between using or misusing the law creates a huge space for debates, related basically to uses and abuses of law. But the difference is not thin enough to respond to all the nuances that a reality can offer to us.

The epistemological approach about qualifying good and bad in lawfare, positive and negative lawfare (aspects or consequences being at stake), has a degree of subjectivity. It depends, in other words, on who is discussing the aspects or consequences of lawfare, so it is a matter of sides rather than the neutral approach proposed by Charles Dunlap.

And so, positive lawfare would be the use of law for protecting values, human rights and defending an accused person by using all the means at hand (even though the side effect would be to limit military activities, military actions or conducts). In contrast, negative lawfare could be defined as the misuse of the law, the abuse of provisions of the law or even twisting the sense and content of the law in order to achieve military objectives. It is the practice of manipulating judicial processes to undercut military objectives of other states, and may include any use of law to prevent or hinder a nation or non-state actor from carrying out legitimate military operations.[22]

The difference, if we want to stay neutral and avoid relative approaches of the observer of a side in the conflict, should take into consideration uses and abuses as well as keeping with the spirit of the rule of law. Trying to keep the sense of a neutral concept, we have to refer those qualifications to objective divisions with a clear ethical background. That's why a positive approach could be the prosecutions of terrorist leaders or heads of state responsible for crimes of war or genocide, if the result of such inquiries and trials is aimed at achieving a military objective – preventing assistance, undermining legitimacy, limiting individual moves, blocking a chain of command or undermining the decision-making capacity on the ground.

Studies are far more elaborated upon in the sense of negative lawfare and in those situations the military impact is obvious at several levels. First negative lawfare is about possibility of using the legal system as asymmetric means in order to tie up the resources of the opponent, a more potent actor, to shift the momentum in a military operation by stopping, delaying it, questioning the decision or the context where such an operation is developed by invoking human rights, law wars or rules and norms for protecting civilians, and changing public opinion to a given cause.

The linkage to hybrid warfare is obvious since lawfare can act on its own, but at the same time could be a part of a far more extensive and complex operation that involves facts on the ground (hybrid military operations), lawfare – challenging the reaction or operations against these actions (financing, decision, manning, arming, decision of action) in court, then using the informational warfare in order to sell your side of the story as reality based on high moral grounds and propaganda, via interpretation that takes into consideration the targeted audience able to influence once again the decision to go on.

So, negative lawfare could be at a strategic level or at a tactical level. The most visible forms of lawfare are at a strategic level, like Supreme Court complaints, *habeas corpus* lawsuits by terrorist detainees[23] and complaints to international organisations regarding the violations of the Law of Armed Conflict. US forces are then bound to investigate all abuse claims. This blocks the tactical unit by tying them up in those investigations, and puts soldiers under pressure for their actions and tactics that delay an operation, which creates more casualties and obliges the forces to take more risk. There may even be a need to replace those people in combat operations who are under investigation with extra men and technique. On the other hand, insurgents use lawfare at an operational level to seek effects against a theater or regional command, complaining and trying to block a certain tactic or procedure, or via local puppet leaders complaining about an extension of operations or about the use of certain private spaces to develop the action (Dungan 2008: 9–15).

Negative lawfare, is also about filing of frivolous lawsuits with the aim of harassing and distracting a military opponent and uncovering an opponent's military strategy through legal proceedings. Here we are not talking about the big debate mentioned previously about who is and who is not a combatant, or who is a civilian, a thin line that offers alternatives for challenging the forces claiming violations of the Law of Armed Combat.[24] The images and reports of civilian casualties (real or fake) of the attacks are part of the informational war and harm public support for troops and operations, including creating grounds for lawsuits against the militaries in operations.

These are standard operating procedures in Southern Afghanistan, for instance. Intercepted Taliban communications, captured documents and interviews with jailhouse informants, confirm it is Taliban standard operating procedure to claim abuse each time a detainee moves from one facility to another (during SOTF (special operations task forces) detention facility, medical examination, first interrogation) (Dungan 2008: 9–15).

Then, the taliban adapt to the evolution of operations. So for countering that threat, the reaction was to hire and embed representatives of the legal section in direct combat operations. For instance, a SOTF[25] judge advocate and paralegal officers are integral members of SOTF staff and advise the commander.

Those reactions are causing another problem, if a state actor or another is involved or should be involved in lawfare. Engaging in an alternative battle field that the hybrid approach offers, could provide advantages since lives and resources could be spared. If the original design of hybrid warfare and lawfare were designed for weaker actors and forces to counter highly prepared, armed, trained and stronger forces, as we have seen in hybrid warfare (Chapter 4 above), these instruments could be used by a strong state actor as well, provided that they respect the rules and norms of hybrid warfare/lawfare, or create the appearance of credible denial in using such instruments.

And yes, strong state actors should be and are involved in lawfare. First, denying themselves a field of warfare, combat and confrontation that avoids human casualties would be a miscalculation, but also it could lead to a legal responsibility of the decision maker or planner for not meeting the required objective, and strategically this could be a disadvantage if a strong state actor abstains, for moral reasons or extreme chevaleresque motifs, or even more, a quixotic approach that rejects using, expanding and developing its military planning and doctrine so as to act on this specialised and unconventional form of war. As we've seen, the US already participates in some type of lawfare, maybe more in defending itself than in an offensive manner.

Before entering the debate about offensive and defensive lawfare, where these previous considerations lead us, let us also be reminded here of another categorisation of lawfare, linked with the positive and negative categories. This approach leads us to a combination of neutral, positive or random consequences but without the intent of abusing the law and without the abuse of law, and finally to the negative and intentional lawfare operation with a required and expected result in the military field, abusing the law and forcing the moral practice and ethical aspects of normal actions in observing the rule of law.

Col. Mark W. Holzer (Holzer 2012) proposed splitting lawfare three ways: neutral, nexus and negative. The neutral approach would be lawfare as method of warfare for military objectives (as Charles Dunlap originally defined it); the nexus approach means lawfare as activities with legal nexus, undertaken during conflicts, with an direct or indirect legal component in wartime and use of legal processes during a time of war, regardless of purpose or effect;[26] and negative approach, lawfare framed as abuse of legal ideals and processes, a tool used by enemies of the US, suggesting the US should consider a defensive policy. The important part of such a vision, especially when nexus approach is involved, is that it challenges the perception that lawfare is used as a strategy of the US' enemies, suggesting a stability and civil support operations view of lawfare. It somehow conciliates the Lawfare Report and military approach and human rights and provides a far more nuanced approach to lawfare and the activity of civil society and lawyers in defending clients at trial by using all legal instruments in doing so (Holzer 2012).

Offensive and defensive lawfare

There is no evidence that lawfare has ever been used by a state actor in planning military operations. It is not the case even in the classic preparation of legal procedures in order to allow international interventions. But the hybrid interventions in Crimea and Eastern Ukraine proved to have a substantive component of lawfare in the sense of allowing credible denial of the state, Russia in those cases, avoiding direct responsibility for an offensive and aggressive action. In this sense, lawfare can be used as a separate instrument as well for reaching military and strategic objectives. But that once, you need lawyers and a proper planning in that area, not a random happening in a planning process by military staff.

This does not mean that such planning could not be made or that such a tool could not be considered when planning a military operation. It could be used by itself or together with some other instruments, including military hybrid operations or informational warfare.

There are analysts pleading for the use of lawfare, particularly in an offensive context. Col Mark Holzer argues that the US Army's operational concept of lawfare provides a framework to conceptualise 'offensive lawfare' (Holzer 2012: 9) if we are talking about the efforts to deny the enemy forces sanctuary, to blunt abuse of courts, and use US foreign and domestic policy to support national security strategy. It could also be used "to explore policies to disaggregate legal actions apparently aimed at negatively impacting US' offensive against Al-Qaeda and affiliates" (Holzer 2012: 10), when it's about countering the negative lawfare that impacts on the US's ability to fight Islamic extremists, which leads to court actions that puts the US in a defensive position, creating costs and several other negative results in terms of legitimacy, image and moral amplitude (not so high moral ground, or even moral costs) of an operation.

So there's a sense of the use of lawfare by states in a defensive manner. Defensive lawfare could be presented in different forms, when it is about to create and use lawfare for defending and recovering from the offensive lawfare of the enemy. What is still debatable is if we have cases of offensive lawfare clearly identified and used, without being supported by other tools such as hybrid or informational operations, by a state actor, for military purposes.

Defensive lawfare can be identified in several cases. Bush and Obama administrations used the law's potential as a tool for advancing military objectives but in an exclusive or at most predominantly defensive way. The cases in discussion are those already revealed in this book. The most important ones take advantage of the Western actors' reliance on international law and the importance of staying on high moral ground in order to have public support, at home and on the international stage. These references to strict principles and values are used through lawfare in order to shake the actor's public will to fight (if it appears via direct action, faked or perceived via informational warfare, that the troops are involved in actions that violate law of armed conflict or human rights) and obtaining restrictions in using military tactics or technical instruments through law suits and inquiries directly on the ground. Taliban tactics of offensive lawfare against the troops of the international coalition and Hamas tactics of the same kind against Israeli troops are the most quoted examples.

There is a large list related to the efforts to manipulate legal forums, international courts and the civil society in order to advance operational objectives traditionally achieved by military means. Those were the cases of the offensive lawfare carried out by the FARC in Columbia and being documented as an explicit tactic of Hezbollah and Hamas (the leader of Hezbollah, Hassan Nasrallah, spoke about the use of such tactics in order to defeat Israel) (Kittrie 2010: 393). Even the Mavi Marmara case[27] could be framed in the same way, with a discussion about at what level the Turkish involvement could be considered a state operation. At most, it could be a state sponsored lawfare operation, but lawfare planning of the outcome is hard to prove and difficult to accept through existing public arguments.

Another interesting case of lawfare is that of Donald Rumsfeld and General Tommy Franks who were accused by a group of Iraqis of criminal actions related to Iraq invasion. They took advantage of the Belgian legislation that has universal jurisdiction and filed in the Belgian Court their complaint in 2003,[28] at the very beginning of the Iraqi war. Rumsfeld threatened to move NATO headquarters out of Brussels (a move difficult to be labelled even as a defensive lawfare), Belgium changed universal jurisdiction law and blocked prosecutions of Rumsfeld and Franks, in a move that is clearly one of defensive lawfare.

On an equal footing, during the Bush Jr. administration, the International Criminal Tribunal for former Yugoslavia had requests to prosecute NATO officers for bombing the Serbian television headquarters and for alleged war crimes during the 1999 Kosovo campaign.[29] In those terms we can see the Bush Administration reaction of defending the US soldiers from lawfare when it opposed the US participation in the ICC, in order to avoid the hostile actors or organisations bring ICC trials of the American leaders or soldiers.[30,31]

If all of these are rather executive actions and decisions that protect officials and soldiers, then a clear defensive lawfare is the reaction of the US Administration (Bush and Obama alike) that argued in Guantanamo military tribunals and related lawsuits, that "standard criminal trials of Al-Qaeda operatives could be manipulated by defence counsel to put prosecutors choose between revealing sensitive US intelligence sources/methods or letting terrorists free". (Kittrie 2010: 403)

Orde Kittrie, is one of the authors who makes a plea for offensive lawfare. He argues that increasing the legalisation of international relations made the law a powerful alternative to traditional military means of achieving operational objectives. He also criticised the "unfortunate" predominantly defensive response to the law's potential as a tool for advancing military objectives, claiming that the US's advantage in sophisticated legal weapons has been underutilized (Kittrie 2010: 394).

> US government's response should not be limited to defensive crouch (…) – there is every reason to embrace lawfare to avoid bloody, expensive, destructive forms of warfare. Lawfare is less deadly to both combatants and bystanders than conventional war, he argues. (Kittrie 2010: 401)

Kittrie was the one trying to find niches or moments where the activity of the US authorities could be rated as offensive lawfare, even though it may have been an unplanned and unexpected type of offensive lawfare. His efforts looked towards

Iran and his only lead was to try to equate sanctions as being part of offensive lawfare – a highly debatable approach.

The most recent example of this field is Iran. Iran has been aiming to gain access to nuclear military technology and to the nuclear bomb. Tehran is facing sanctions, both economic and technological. Technology that has civilian as military uses was forbidden to be sold to Tehran, which led to a blockage in the supply of spare parts for aircraft or computers. Is this a way of targeting military capabilities? The economic sanctions, not directly, technology, maybe yes. But is that lawfare?

The discussion is if by using non-proliferation documents and international legislation in adopting the sanctions as a solution, there is a direct blockage of the access to nuclear equipment, so too military advantages that are blocked via law. And in that case, the answer would be a positive one. There's lawfare, positive lawfare, via that type of analysis and arguments. But that is not a direct lawfare, rather an indirect one.

Kittrie has even more elaborate arguments. In responding to Iran, there are far more tools to use than just sanctions: speaking, sweeteners, sanctions, sabotage, soldiers (Kittrie 2010: 403). He introduced the combination, in January 2011, of sanctions and sabotage (Struxnet computer virus) which seemed to be succeeding in slowing Iran's nuclear program. The problem is that Stuxnet has never been admitted to by the US (rather, gossips were pointing to Israel). Sabotage, by definition, would not be admitted to in public; rather, it is a covert operation with credible deniability for a state. But assuming that combination, it is still indirect lawfare or to be more precise, a hybrid operation that combines lawfare, sanctions and covert operations.

What is even more interesting is that, in offensive lawfare, there's the need to combine the lack of cyber legislation related to Iran, combined with sanctions as a form of lawfare (Kittrie 2010: 404). The sanctions against Iran via the UN Security Council, the domestic US laws, the EU laws are a salient, deliberate and creative form of lawfare.

Another argument could be the case of Libya[32] and the fact that international legislation, combined with a strong will of applying it, with a history of strong sanctions, created deterrence and help to stop proliferation of illegal nuclear weapons and terrorism. Moreover, this type of approach, combined with suitable diplomacy and negotiations could expose black market and networks for trafficking nuclear technology, as was the case with Libya and A. Q. Khan network.[33]

Lawfare is extended to positions in the UN Security Council. There's a debate that Russian and Chinese positions in the case of Iran were different and weaker than those in the other cases. As a consequence, the result is that whoever wants to challenge Iran is in a weaker position and should use more forces or split them in order to achieve their military objective, and that Iran itself is stronger. Our conclusion is that, because in the Security Council it is about negotiations and sovereign position, we cannot say that such action is lawfare. We can debate this, it is legitimate to look at those developments in such a way, but we don't agree that this is lawfare.By exploring those examples and trying to propose a form of offensive lawfare, direct offensive lawfare, where only law is used as an instrument for attaining military objectives, we can realise the limits of the concept of lawfare. And the definition here helps in drawing the thin line between what is and what is not lawfare: uses or abuses of law. Once again, here too, the limits are very nuanced and the border is somehow blurred, but the importance of the distinction between uses and abuses prevents us from not introducing into the concept of lawfare the actions of defending human rights, or defending the accused with all the means that his lawyer has at hand, legitimate, legal and non-abusive. Here, too, the principle of good faith, bona fides, plays an important role.

We can discuss if there's a case of offensive lawfare in blocking resolutions and negotiating weaker sanctions when the same actor or actors, with direct links to the spoiler of the original action in the Security Council, is/are involved in the use by Iran (or third actors) of law and legal pressure in allowing the activities under sanctions: those of foreign banks in business with Iran, the activities of the foreign energy companies, or using other litigation strategies in order to avoid any blockage for transferring military technology to Iran. Premeditation is there, but we have to prove that it is a strategy, that there is a conceived plan and that the real purpose is military. If all requirements could be proved, yes, we can say that this is an example of offensive lawfare.

What could be more debatable is rating as offensive lawfare the actions taken via diplomatic means or direct contacts after the adoption of a legal framework like the sanctions in the UN Security Council with the companies and banks in order to stop them doing business with Iran. Reputation, as a value at stake for banks and companies, is used in such a creative way in order to be sure that sanctions, which are the result of lawfare, are in place. But this is restricted to enforcing legal provisions and is not a legal base on its own, it is more about tactics and direct actions than lawfare. And it touches more on resources and money than on military objectives, even though shrinking financial resources is a way of limiting military capability development. So this is not lawfare.

But the 1 July 2010 Obama Comprehensive Iran Sanctions, Accountability and Divestment Act (CISADA) is qualified offensive lawfare. This act imposes sanctions against any foreign company that does business with Iran's energy sector, including the provision of gasoline to Iran, gasoline being an integral part of the process of producing highly enriched uranium, so the atomic bomb. The same way, but on individual bases, the inclusion by the Treasury Department, of the names of companies and banks on a US ban and sanctions list is a direct act of offensive lawfare, aimed at blocking Iran's nuclear program.[34]

Another method of offensive lawfare developed by the US against Iran includes litigations such as lawsuits against foreign suppliers of dual use items for Iran, lawsuits based on apparent personal involvement of the Iranian leaders in Hezbollah attacks, legal actions for intellectual property theft for instance when Iran nuclear program used designs stolen from the European company Urenco (A. Q. Khan) (Kittrie 2010: 418). Ideas are all around and the media proposed several ways of addressing the issue via legal instruments like actions brought before the ICC against the Iranian Minister of Defence for involvement in AMIA bombing[35] or the call for pursuing legal action against Ahmadinejad on basis for him calling for the destruction of Israel and incitement to genocide (Kittrie 2010: 419; Gerstenfeld 2005).

As we can see, the US has never used lawfare in a direct, premeditated, planned manner, and moments where such actions appeared are rather a random result and side effect of those actions and not a planned one.

Legitimate and illegitimate lawfare

Another way of nuancing and making categories of lawfare is to talk about legitimate and illegitimate lawfare. There's a fundamental difference between positive and negative lawfare, which refers to the categories of good and bad, and that of legitimate or illegitimate, which are closer to the categories of correct and generally agreed or incorrect and rejected manner of using lawfare. In the debate by Michael A. Newton. (Newton 2010: 255–277) he defines illegitimate lawfare as "what clouds the correct state of laws and customs of war, feeding undercurrent of suspicion and politicization that threatens to erode foundations of humanitarian law" (Newton 2010: 255). "Illegitimate exploitation of law permits the legal structure to be portrayed as nothing more than a mass of indeterminate subjectivity, a weapon in the moral domain of conflict with media accomplices" says Newton.

Unfortunately, his pleading moves on to the subjective part of taking sides, considering parties, we and the adversary, which sweeps away from the original neutral sense of lawfare that Charles Dunlap proposed. He claims that illegitimate lawfare is different from invoking legal process on behalf of an entity of the adversary with potentially hostile goals, because that's a fundamental difference between legal processes and lawfare (properly understood). This is related to other sides in the conflict, interested in that approach.

On the other hand, he correctly realised that the recurrent problem of evolution of warfare is the struggle to define the contours of the legal regime and to correctly communicate expectations to the audience of civilians caught in conflict, shaping expectations and perceptions of political elites (Newton 2010: 257). "Modern era-operations requires warriors educated and empowered to make decisions intertwined with legality and legitimacy (…) Illegitimate warfare can transform appropriate tactical decision-making into weapon in the moral domain of conflict in front of cameras, mistakes are thus amplifying, law is misused not to facilitate operations that minimize civilian casualties, but to create greater military parity" (Newton 2010: 259).

So illegitimate lawfare misuses or abuses the law for military purposes, but also refers to high moral ground bases, and to the media and perception of both political elites and the general public, a solid ground for legitimising any decision in democratic countries. I think that that's the best way of putting it, in order to maintain the nuances with the abovementioned positive and negative lawfare. Even though, in that case too, there's still a blurred line between the two.

Uses and abuses of the term lawfare

As we have seen above, the concept of lawfare has nuances and differences of use that could let it move to spaces where its definition can cover unexpected realities and, for sure, aspects that we would not want to qualify as legal warfare. We would not easily accept to use the term lawfare to label the actions made by a lawyer in order to defend his client, even if he is accused of terrorism, or the actions of the human rights defenders in a specific case involving the abuses of military personal beyond their job description and the regulations.

So "lawfare" is a useful term in the war on terror if it stands in a more ideologically, neutral usage of the concept, as it was introduced and developed by Major General Charles Dunlap in 2001 and 2008, than in the sense it was mentioned by President Bush's 2002 National Security Strategy (NSS). Lawfare is now at risk of losing utility and being distorted from "the use of law as a weapon of war, a strategy using or misusing law as a substitute for traditional military means to achieve operational objective" – or a pejorative, but ideologically neutral concept – "lawfare is simply another kind of weapon, one that is produced...by beating law books into swords" (Waters 2010: 327).

According to Melissa Waters, unfortunately, lawfare became an overloaded term: The *Wall Street Journal* used it as a pejorative label to discredit American Civil Liberties Union and other NGOs who questioned the Obama Administration's treatment of Guantanamo detainees, and conservative pundits said lawfare is any attempt to apply rule of law to the conduct of the war on terror (Waters 2010: 332).

Melissa Waters analyses the difference between the neutral term of lawfare introduced and maintained by Charles Dunlap and the pernicious aspect of so-called reflexive warfare used not merely to discredit terrorist suspects, but also to discredit the lawyers who assist them, and sometimes the judges. For instance, we have the case of Charles "Cully" Stimson who worked in the Bush Administration. In an interview in 2007, Stimson was dismayed that attorneys from major US law firms were representing detainees at Guantanamo. He condemns a decision by a Court of Appeal that helped free a suspected terrorist[36] and calls it a dangerous game to associate American lawyers and judges with a shadowy form of lawfare engaged by America's enemies, saying that the legitimacy of the American legal system itself is undermined. On a background of criticism, the Bush Administration distanced itself from Stimson, who resigned, a proof that the American lawyers can play a critical role in lawfare's reclamation project (Waters 2010: 334).

In September 2010, the Brookings Institution, new blog "Lawfare: Hard National Security Choices" – reintroduced lawfare connected to critical self-reflection. In this effort to conserve the nuanced and useful approach of the concept of lawfare, Jack Goldsmith noted:

> There is much to say about all of this, and we will explore the "lawfare" concept at length on this blog. But for now I want to offer two examples in which

lawfare in the "a weapon of war" sense captures an important reality that is in no way derogatory towards the rule of law.

First, there is a war of sorts going on over the content and applicability of the laws of war to terrorist activities. It is a war in which battles take place across the ocean (the United States and Europe disagree, for example, whether there can be a war against terrorist groups, and whether terrorists can be detained without trial or be tried in military commissions); between proponents and opponents of the Goldstone Report; between the ICRC and government lawyers about the meaning and applicability of "direct participation in hostilities"; and among lawyers representing alleged terrorists, government lawyers, and judges in the D.C. Circuit. All of the combatants in this "war" believe they are fighting on behalf of the international rule of law, properly understood, and all use legal argument strategically to achieve this end.

Second, it is natural, I think, to see contemporary U.S. counterinsurgency (COIN) operations as an attractive form of lawfare – especially those aspects that involve the construction of legal institutions as a tool to defeat insurgents. The latest example is the brand new Rule of Law Field Force (ROLFF) in Afghanistan, commanded by the redoubtable General Mark Martins. The basic idea of ROLFF is to revive governance and rule of law functions in the Pashtun south where the insurgency is strongest during the "hold" phase of COIN operations (i.e., just after an area has been cleared of insurgents). General Martins, his soldiers, and their Afghan partners are literally fighting to bring ordinary Afghans criminal justice capacity, dispute resolution services, and anti-corruption institutions, all with the aim of promoting the legitimacy of the Afghan government and defeating the insurgency. If that's not "using law as a weapon of war" I don't know what is. (Having said that, I am not sure General Martins would agree with my characterization of his efforts as "lawfare," but I hope to persuade him to write about ROLFF on this blog so that he can explain it to us himself).[37]

Due to this imbroglio and due to the fact that the term "lawfare", popularised first in the 2001 speech at Harvard University, delivered by Major Gen. Charles Dunlap, was used later, by various analysts, politicians and officials in a number of ways meaning something quite different from the original conception, a report is needed on what lawfare is and the strategies to prevent the misuse of the term and if US institutions are equipped to respond to it. There was even the idea to basically kill the concept and send him to the oubliette since it was creating far more harm than good (Scharf & Andersen 2001: 11–27). The debates went on regarding whether the term should be identified empirically or normatively as well as debates on if "lawfare" should be used at all, considering that it may undermine respect for the rule of law.

At the same time, if we describe the lawfare generally, there is more or less a consensus; if we describe it in detail, there is little consensus and a plethora of ways to describe it. Most recent ones are those of some experts wishing to see lawfare retaining its utility as a useful label for legal and military professionals. Some others believe the term's use in military terms lost usefulness when it began to be applied broadly. Last but not least, some are using it with a more political and intentional direction as we've seen above.

Due to this situation, the evaluation around the term arrived at the idea that lawfare is already too widespread to de-invent it and because there was deep concern that the term was hijacked by the neo-conservative-sponsored group called "The Lawfare Project", the term should be dropped. But since there was the sense that lawfare may not be "a particularly useful term" and may serve as "an invented phenomenon" used only by anti-international humanitarian law "hijackers" as intimidation, the abuses of that term were considered thoroughly in order to avoid neo-conservative scholars seizing the concept as part of a broader effort to make a case for unrestrained action by the US president in "war on terror" (Scharf & Andersen 2001: 13).

So abuses of the term are situated roughly in the misuse or manipulation of law in order to achieve operational objectives, and the exploitation of Law of Armed Conflicts for strategic/tactical purposes as well as the use of lawfare as the exploitation of the law or the wrongful manipulation of the law and legal system to achieve strategic military or political ends.

On another point of the debate is that certain ill-defined concepts might invite lawfare. An example of this is the definition of "armed conflict" under the Geneva Conventions and the definition of illegal weapons under Art 36 of Additional protocol I to the Geneva Conventions about the status of violent situations such as armed conflicts that are unclear in the sense of whether a particular weapon violated Art 36 can be subjected to results-oriented interpretations of law, as is the case of the classification of white phosphorous as an illegal weapon is misplaced because in most cases white phosphorous is lawfully used as a flare (Scharf & Andersen 2001: 22).

Our concept

We covered the whole history and debate about the concept of lawfare for two reasons: first, in order to have a clear understanding of the concept, of its limits and nuances, uses and abuses of the term in different environments; and second, because we want to be sure it stays in the framework of a balanced concept avoiding extremes and abuses, a neutral term, non-politicised and useful in the theoretical world of finding the traces of the new types of wars of the 21st century. These were also the reasons behind our efforts to use the tools of epistemology and try to offer a solid concept of lawfare correctly designed and tailored for both theoretical and practical reasons.

So, maintaining the original neutral definition of Charles Dunlap, with specific nuances, we have to add to the term of lawfare, some new lines adapting the concept to the evolution of technology over the last few years, legislation (or lack of legislation) and instruments of making war and developing conflicts, in the era that moved from chess to "Go". This is the reasoning behind our introduction of three new elements to the concept, to make it contemporary and adapted to the deeds of the conflicts of the 21st century.

First, there's a high level of development in technology, and that allows things that were inconceivable in earlier periods of history to become accessible. There is now the relatively free and infinite access to information via Internet for more or less each individual, at practically no cost. This leads the way for new instruments to be used in reality, like those of instant images becoming available online, individual newspapers accessible to everyone, and an important access for each individual in the society to their own individual "newspaper", a technological gain that is used in informational warfare.

- In addition, technology allows for new types of attacks:
- New types of attack in the cyberspace
- Capacity to build artificial islands on some natural underwater rocks, pretending they could be natural
- Extending the rights on the free sea (through using the artificial islands or through technological capacity to exploit resources in deep waters)

Developing military capabilities – either on those islands or directly on ships or platforms placed on the sea. These are neither ground dependent, nor ships, and before the technical developments this could not be achieved) Using the technological development, there's a development in the field of weapons, strategies, capacity of using the outer space for military purposes(shutting down satellites, for instance)All of these give space for developments out of a legal framework and able to be speculated as new fields of development of the confrontation lines in non-conventional and hybrid conflicts.

Our second new element is directly linked to legislation or the lack of legislation in the new fields of innovation in conflict areas. Technological developments and creative uses of existing means to conduct a conflict, the use of media as a weapon, the Internet and cyberspace, informational warfare but also civilians as combatants and humans as weapons, religion as a polarisation tool or Internet as a recruiting instrument, are all far from being in an established legal framework and this existing legal framework as well as the lack of it, offers an important space for speculation, interpretation and lawfare designed in order to take advantage of those holes and gaps.

And third, the evolutions of the instruments of warfare and conflicts are proving this very thin line between war and peace, combatant and non-combatant force, civilian and combat or military/para-military force, assumed or non-assumed responsibilities and control of some forces involved on the ground. Hybrid warfare has proven to be a possibility in creating instruments for conflicts and war with credible deniability for assuming responsibility for them, and important other instruments where it is hard to prove responsibility – cyber, informational war. The advantages and objectives relevant to the new types of war in the 21st century are not only those with a simple and pure military content and definition, but more broadly, those which are strategically important.

So, in all, we are keeping the definition of Charles Dunlap in its revised form (2008): Lawfare is "the strategy of using – or misusing – law as a substitute for traditional military means to achieve an operational objective."[38] But by operational objective we understand both military and strategic objectives – the Chinese artificial islands were of strategic importance when they were built up, becoming military capabilities after the airports and military hard weapons were installed there. Then we add "law or the lack of legislation in a field developed through technology which could be used in reaching military and strategic objectives".

> So lawfare is the strategy of using – or misusing – law or the lack of legislation in new fields developed through technological achievements as a substitute for traditional military means to achieve an operational objective, both military and strategic in substance.

Now, with that definition in hand, let us see how many of the existing developments in the nature and substance of the conflicts of the 21st century we did cover. Let us see now some examples where this definition could be used, mapping real situations:

First, there's South China – China Sea, and "nine-dash line" claim to UN (2009) for military objectives and natural resources (minerals), with arguments of alleged land features as basis for marine entitlements under international law, but mostly on historical backgrounds. So, China amplifies those land features in order to amplify legal claims, by building artificial islands on existing maritime rocks. China uses the law and force in this lawfare strategy in order to first reach strategic goals – moving China from a continental and a green water naval country to a maritime blue water military power. But afterwards, building airstrips and putting military capabilities on those islands is aimed at achieving a military goal as well.

Another example is the so-called "passportisation policy" in Abkhazia/South Ossetia. Basically, Russia used the law and legal procedures for achieving political objectives (pressure on Georgia mainly), but implicitly strategic and potential military objectives. There's a clear case of lawfare, using Chapter VII of UN Chart for invoking the right to attack another state in order to protect Russian nationals. Russia used the same type of policy – a self-assumed unilateral right of defending the Russians, Russian speakers and compatriots like in Ukraine – in the separatist regions of Georgia and Crimea. Under the pretext of defending their nationals, they forged a direct attack. From the Russian perspective, this is positive/neutral lawfare (Scharf and Andersen 2001: 17–18). From this point of view, there is a primary strategic goal with secondary objectives (or even primary if planned that way) in the military field.

A further example is the "borderisation policy", also in the field of lawfare and also concerning Russia. This policy has strategic relevance and indirect military impact. The substance of the approach is that because Abkhazia/South Ossetia are

regions under Russia's control, they can be potential lands for military exploitation by Russia because the process of slowly and randomly moving the demarcation line and establishing an unrecognised border offers important strategic
advantages to Russia. It allows gradual moving of the border and the gaining of
land under Russian control. Since each move is politically driven by any step
further towards the West, the borderisation is used as a tool for political pressure
on Georgia as well as a military deterrence instrument against NATO (Scharf and
Andersen 2001: 17–18).

Last but not least, on the same note, the so-called "Treaties of Integration" with
Abkhazia/South Ossetia signed by Russia is a way of using "international agreements" to achieve a strategic goal, political and economic pressure on Georgia,
military deterrence against Georgia/NATO and direct pressure against the East-West
transport and energy lines from the Caspian and Azerbaijan to Europe.

In all these cases, the use of legal or non-existing legal frameworks helps an
actor to obtain strategic advantages and reach strategic and military goals.

Practical applications: Reference cases

The misuse of the law to achieve strategic or military objectives, the practice
of manipulating judicial processes to undercut such objectives of other states, the
use of law to prevent or hinder a nation or non-state actor from carrying out legitimate military operations are presented here by reference cases like the use of little
green men and the interpretation of the rules of war, building the Chinese artificial
islands in order to extend maritime rights, and the lack of respect for the rights of
combat soldiers dead or wounded in Eastern Ukraine.

Little green men: Crimea annexation and Donbas aggression as lawfare focused on avoiding legal responsibility

In the devastating aftermath of World War II, the international community united
in order to prevent the use of force in international relations. The Charter of the
United Nations became the only document laying down rules for the use of force
(*jus ad bellum*). Under the Charter, war could no longer be used as an instrument
by individual nations. Instead, nations could only resort to war as a collective
security measure under Article 42 of the Charter or in self-defense under Article 51.
Any use of armed action not falling within one of these two narrow exceptions
was considered a violation of international law.[39]

In this context, Russia's deployment of military forces in Ukraine, its pressure
that eventually made the Ukrainian forces withdraw from the Crimean Peninsula
and its occupation and annexation of Crimea has been described by the international community as a violation of international law. However, Russia presented
to the Security Council and the media a series of justifications arguing that it
acted in accordance to international law. Initially, Russia argued that it acted to
defend the Russian language speakers present in Crimea.[40]

Afterwards, Russia insisted that its use of force was the result of a request for
help coming from the legitimate head of the Ukrainian State. In the end, Moscow

denied using military force in Crimea and Western Ukraine hiding behind local Ukrainian militias, saying they laid siege to and later overran Ukrainian military bases. It then added that the political annexation of Crimea was the result of a legitimate democratic referendum in which over 97 per cent of the Crimean population voted in favour of joining the Russian Federation.

The UN High Commissioner for Human Rights raised questions about the referendum in a report issued on 15 April, where he stated that there were a number of preliminary findings that suggested the use of coercion during the referendum. The Office's findings included the alleged use of torture,[41] among other violations of the International Covenant on Civil and Political Rights (ICCPR), which suggests the referendum results were manipulated. The referendum was also criticised by the United Nations. On the 1st April 2014, the UN General Assembly (UNGA) adopted a resolution requiring all UN Member States "not to recognize any alteration in the status of the Autonomous Republic of Crimea."[42]

In *jus ad bellum,* aggression is identified based on the UNGA's Definition of Aggression.[43] In this resolution, aggression is described as: "the use of armed force by a State against the sovereignty, territorial integrity or political independence of another State, or in any other manner inconsistent with the Charter of the United Nations".[44]

Concerning Russia's actions in Crimea and their relation with the United Nations Charter there are two laws that should be taken into consideration. The most important of these laws is Article 2(4) of the United Nations Charter which states that:[45] "All Members shall refrain in their international relations from the threat or use of force against the territorial integrity or political independence of any state, or in any other manner inconsistent with the Purposes of the United Nations".[46]

Additionally, Article 2(7) stipulates that: "nothing contained in the present Charter shall authorise the United Nations to intervene in matters, which are essentially within the domestic jurisdiction of any state".[47]

Given the legal background, there are a few problems resulting from Russia's actions in Crimea.

The first issue is that the Russian armed forces entered Crimea around 28 February 2014. Back then, according to most sources, there were very few or no armed confrontations. The lack of the actual engagements might make the operation not seem to be an aggression. Still, Article 2(4) provides a broad definition of force. Article 31 of the Vienna Convention stipulates that any Article should be interpreted in light of its "context … object and purpose."[48]

Thus, Article 2(4) does not allow exceptions, especially since it was stated at the Charter drafting conference that "the intention of the authors of the original text [of Article 2(4)] was to state in the broadest possible terms an absolute all-inclusive prohibition … with no loopholes."[49] The deployment of foreign soldiers on the territory of another state, no matter what uniforms – if any – they wear and if they actually use their weapons, represents a use of force and is a violation of Article 2(4).

In Crimea, the non-assumed Russian soldiers – called "the little green men" – together with up to 25,000 existing soldiers according to the Istanbul 1999 provisions of the CFE Treaty and to the bilateral agreements of maintaining the Russian Military base in Sevastopol, with the prolongation signed by President Yanukovich in Kharkov Russian-Ukrainian agreements, occupied vital sites such as airports, military bases, and communication infrastructure. This is clearly a violation of the territorial integrity of Ukraine and an attempt to sabotage the Kiev Government's control of Crimea.

It should also be noted that Russia signed, together with the US and Great Britain, then joined by the other two members of the Security Council, France and Germany, the 1994 Budapest Memorandum with the access of Ukraine to the Non Proliferation Treaty, guaranteeing the territorial integrity, sovereignty and independence of Ukraine in exchange for its nuclear disarmament, therefore committing to refrain from utilising force against Ukraine. Under no circumstances were Russia's actions in February–March 2014 in accordance with the memorandum.[50]

There is also the problem of Russia's alleged assistance given to "separatist militias" in Eastern Ukraine and Crimea. Unless, of course, the militias were Russian Special Forces that prepared the intervention of soldiers who, in turn, supervised the annexation of Crimea. Furthermore, now Russia supports the separatists in Donbass. Arming rebel groups is more a grey area in international relations, but it's far from an accepted practice. And organising overnight a so-call referendum at the point of a gun, already dubious in terms of self-determination of the so-called "people of Crimea", is nothing else than an abuse of international law and the appearance of respecting the human rights of Crimea inhabitants.

"Humanitarian assistance" can sometimes be used, and was used, to justify such actions, but apart from this condition, weapons exports to any non-state or state related entity is prohibited, and more immoral if this happens under the Red Cross or humanitarian aid. Russia itself tried to hide its involvement in illegal arms transfers to the separatists, Russian volunteers and its regular special forces in Ukraine,[51] suggesting some degree of guilt. Moreover, while weapons in Crimea or Eastern Ukraine could definitely influence the result of a referendum, especially if we take into consideration the attacks on government buildings and their contribution to the takeover of Crimea, even financial or other non-lethal support constitutes an intervention which would represent a breach of the principle of non-intervention present in Article 2(7) of the Charter.

Still, we are trying to find out if Russia committed an act of aggression, not if it merely intervened in Ukraine. The distinction comes from the Definition of Aggression that explicitly mentions in Articles 1 and 2 the use of force as part of the aggression. Therefore, Russia's actions could be described as aggression only if it offered arms to opposition forces in Crimea,[52] particularly since the militias clearly facilitated the Russian takeover of Crimea, or if there's a formal recognition that the little green men are Russian soldiers.

The laws of war: Soldiers and successors lost rights as Russian self inflicted lawfare

The clashes between the Ukrainian military and the so-call insurgents in Eastern Ukraine (a combination of local pre-trained Russian insurgents, Russian volunteers and Russian regular forces non-assumed, all equipped with Russian weapons and hard artillery) are the subject of the international humanitarian law as set out in treaties as well of the rules of customary international humanitarian law. Ukraine is a signatory of the main piece of legislation in this field, Common Article 3 to the Geneva Conventions of 1949.[53] The article establishes a set of minimum standards for all parties that are involved in a non-conventional war. The hybrid nature of the war is due to avoid responsibilities but the combatants are subject to some kind of protection according to Geneva rules of war.

All the involved parties must abide by the requirements of international humanitarian law. Specifically, each party must observe and enforce the laws of war. This applies both to the Ukrainian military and any allied faction as well as to the generally labelled "rebel groups" fighting them. One party cannot violate the principles of the humanitarian law in response to the other doing the same. The reasons behind the conflict and its nature are irrelevant when it comes to the obligation to observe humanitarian law. Any disparity in the harm caused by alleged violations of any party does not affect the standards the parties are held to.

The role of the international humanitarian law is also to provide a minimum level of protection to civilians and other non-combatants in armed conflict. It focuses on the means and methods of warfare used by all sides in a conflict. This inevitably implies the existence of a distinction between combatants and civilians. Civilians may never be deliberately targeted by attacks. Parties to the conflict are required to take all practical precautions to minimise harm to civilians and civilian property and to refrain from attacks that fail to discriminate between combatants and civilians, or would cause disproportionate harm to the civilian population.

Common Article 3[54] stipulates a number of fundamental rights for civilians and people who are no longer actively taking part in hostilities, such as captured combatants and those who have surrendered or are unable to fight. It restricts the use of violence against them – particularly murder, cruel treatment, and torture – as well as affronts against their personal dignity in the form of degrading or humiliating treatment. Thus, no attack may target directly civilians or civilian objects. Indiscriminate attacks are also a violation of the laws of war. An indiscriminate attack targets both military objectives and civilians or civilian objects without any distinction. This means an indiscriminate attack either doesn't strike a specific military objective or involves weapons that cannot be directed at a specific military objective.[55]

Banned attacks include carpet bombing or bombardment of an area, which are attacks by artillery or air that target a whole area in order to destroy a single military objective found within the area, especially if the area is densely populated. Military commanders have a duty to choose weapons and tactics that can precisely strike military targets in order to minimise collateral damage. In case all the means available are so inaccurate that they cannot be deployed without a high risk of substantial collateral damage to civilians or civilian objects, they should not be used.[56]

It is easily noticeable that the conflict in the Eastern Ukraine violates many of these rules. But the most obvious is a result of hybrid lawfare, aimed at hiding responsibility of one side for the military and combat actions that lead to the non-observance of the laws, regulations and conduct against its own combatants. So regular Russian soldiers have been recruited, asked to withdraw or resign or taking holidays from the regular Russian Army in order to become overnight volunteers or combat soldiers in Eastern Ukraine, without a proper status. People died, were captured or were wounded, but the rules that should be applied to a regular soldier defending Russia, his country, could not be applied to the non-assumed combat soldiers in Eastern Ukraine, so their families also lost the benefits from the status they were conferred when entering the Army. That's also a piece of lawfare, or a self-inflicted lawfare if you will for Russia.

Artificial Islands: Lawfare in China's seas

According to the "United Nations Convention on the Law of the Sea" China, as a coastal state has the right to build artificial islands within its territorial waters.[57] The two original civil constructions are still in use. Apart from Chinese islands, The United Arab Emirates has successfully built artificial islands for tourism. Based on this Convention, Brazil and Japan built in the 1970s artificial islands benefiting the salt and coal industry, with both civil constructions still in use,[58] so China is not the first country to exercise this right.

In 1977 Nikos Papadakis, in his book "The International Legal Regime of Artificial Islands", distinguishes six types of artificial islands covering the whole range of state interests: city islands, islands for economic development, communication and transport hubs, islands providing facilities for scientific research and islands intended for tourism and entertainment. A sixth category is the artificial island structure for military purposes.[59]

But if in the case of Brazil, Japan and UAE the purpose of building these islands was obviously a civil one, China's case is different, and this is why its progress undertaken in building artificial islands is closely monitored. Also, the speed and scale of China's island-building spree have alarmed other countries with interests in the region. And this because China has constructed port facilities, military buildings and an airstrip on the islands, while some imagery taken in 2015 revealed the evidence of two more airstrips under construction.[60]

In 2014, sources say due to changes in the international situation and the need to resolve South China Sea issues, the Chinese military drew up a plan to conduct reclamation at Mischief and Fiery Cross Reefs. The construction of the two artificial islands there will be equivalent to that of building an aircraft carrier, but the strategic gains will be very big. But the financial burden of 5 billion US dollars needed to build the Fiery Cross and Mischief reef area was considered too high by the state leadership and was postponed. However, the solution came from the economic area – it was decided that Mischief reef would be a fishery centre at the South China Sea to provide fishing and fish farming income enough to recover the construction costs so that the construction of the artificial islands would not be a financial burden on the state. But despite this justification, the first purpose for the artificial islands was that of a military outpost, more precisely an unreplaceable military base with great strategic significance due to its location and size, while, for Beijing, such a base will amplify the value of the South China Sea for China and ensure China's status in South East Asia.[61]

At the end of 2014, international analysts published reports on major Chinese projects that would enable China to land military aircrafts on an artificial built reef, expanding its reach into the contested South China Sea. The report, along with several declarations and articles, came as a response to an international conference held in Beijing, which intended to promote President Xi Jinping's call for a new regional security architecture established on the concept of "Asia for Asians" (an idea that reduces the role of the United States in the Asia-Pacific region). Almost two years later, China appears to have installed weapons, including anti-aircraft and anti-missile systems, on all seven of the artificial islands it has built in the South China Sea, The Asia Maritime Transparency Initiative (AMTI) at the Centre for Strategic and International Studies reported, citing new satellite imagery.[62]

Published comparative images of the same geographical areas (Spratly Islands) were made public in mid-February 2015. The pictures show the size of the project put in to action by the Chinese state: it essentially consists of using existing geologic formations and reconfiguring them so that the end result will be thousands of times bigger. Despite the scale of the project which proved surprising: thorough preparation allowed its implementation very quickly and without the formalities of traditional foreign policy.

The actions drew protests both from regional actors who claimed they had territorial rights and from the United States. Protesters accused China of aiming to build airport facilities necessary to impose a Chinese Air Identification Area in the South China Sea. For now, however, economic motivation (initial) seems to be the most obvious. The area is rich in resources, and Chinese naval presence will prevent other interested parties from benefitting from the region.

Later, other protests from the US followed. In April 2016, China's apparent landing of a military jet on a man-made island in the disputed waters of the South China Sea drew a protest from the US military. But Beijing explained that the Chinese military aircraft landed on Yongshu Reef, also known as Fiery Cross Reef, to give emergency assistance to three severely ill civilian workers. Even so, for the US it was unclear why the Chinese used a military aircraft as opposed to a civilian one.[63]

The reef's central location in the broader South China Sea region positions it as a strategic location for an island-based airstrip. It would be capable of supporting a runway and apron, and have a harbor that would be large enough to dock warships. This is directly linked with previous Chinese actions – the footprint expansion in the Spratly archipelago, which involved moving sand onto reefs and shoals and creating at least three new islands (in Cuateron Reef – the southernmost of China's reclamation projects, Gaven Reef, and Johnson North Reef) that could serve as bases for Chinese surveillance and as resupply stations for navy vessels.

Furthermore, the dredging operations at Fiery Cross Reef (situated in an area where China claims the territory as part of Hainan province and exerts *de facto* control) are interpreted as methods to coerce other claimant states in the archipelago such as Vietnam and the Philippines to eventually relinquish their claim to the territory.

Bonnie S. Glaser, senior advisor for Asia at the Center for Strategic and International Studies in Washington, noted that the plans for an airstrip were intended to "land military aircrafts that could monitor an air defense identification zone, which China appears likely to desire".[64] Usually, states create these zones to monitor, identify and take military action against aircraft that enter the designated area without approval.

In November 2013, China unilaterally undertook similar procedures and established a zone over a region in the East China Sea, comprising the airspace over the contested islands with Japan.

The South China Sea (SCS) is subject to numerous rival territorial claims (disputed areas include potentially rich reserves of undersea natural resources) made by China, Malaysia, Brunei, the Philippines, Taiwan and Vietnam who dispute ownership of several island chains and nearby waters. It has been the centre of discussion of several international summits (ASEAN 25th Summit especially), regional gatherings, security dialogues, and numerous bilateral meetings.

The SCS is situated in an important geostrategic position, linking the most important trading countries in Asia, America and Europe. Nearly all the principal shipping and air traffic lanes through the SCS pass near or over the Spratly islands. The proximity of the islands to the coastal areas of the littoral states, where ports, cities and industrial zones are situated, underscores the strategic importance of the islands. In theory, occupation of the islands leads to direct or indirect control of most sea lanes from the Strait of Malacca to Japan (China is particularly concerned about the Strait of Malacca remaining open because approximately 80% of its oil and LNG imports pass from the Middle East through the Strait) from Singapore to Hong Kong and from Guangzhou to Manila.

The broader geopolitical environment of the region is one important factor leading to, and thereafter affecting, the process of the disputes. Geopolitical issues include power politics among major countries – China, the US (in some cases even Russia) – and the development of the Association of Southeast Asian Nations (ASEAN) as a regional organisation.

Disputes over the political jurisdiction of the Spratly Islands escalated, as China, Vietnam, Malaysia, the Philippines and Taiwan established continuous human presence on different small islands and some major reefs. These disputes were further complicated by the entitlement to a 200 nautical mile exclusive economic zone (EEZ) under the 1982 United Nations Convention on the Law of the Sea (UNCLOS).[65]

The construction of an airstrip capable island is not a new initiative for the Chinese Government. In March 2012 official documents attested to the presence of an island in the place of a formerly submerged reef created by dredging seabed material. China has set up on the new island additional satellite communication equipment, anti-aircraft and naval guns, additional radars, a helipad and a dock. Moreover, Malaysia, the Philippines and Taiwan have employed the same tactics and use airfields they have constructed on reefs and islands in the contested waters. Vietnam has constructed a harbor and other land formations in Southwest Cay (that belonged to the Philippines), Taiwan built an airstrip on Taiping Island, while the Philippines plans to build an airport and pier on Thitu Island.[66]

In sight of all the military initiatives and infrastructure building in the South China Sea, China is the sole regional power that possesses the resources and military capabilities to dramatically alter the status quo in the SCS.

There is a dearth of reliable data and sources that detail the capacity in which regional states have dredged or pursued island-building tactics.[67] Even without accurate data, it is evident that none of the regional states have the capabilities to match what China could achieve. China's construction capacity surpasses by far the means other states possess.

The size of China's internal market, its economic performance, the stability and strength of its currency, its competitiveness, its ability to use and develop new technology, the regional bilateral agreements, alongside political influence and military might position China well in a fierce competition for influence and resources. The ongoing military developments strengthen China's position as the paramount regional strategic challenger, based on its expanding economy (although its economic growth is slowing down, the resources made available for military spending are being increased) and particular infrastructure projects (linked with the increased budget spending in certain parts of the military sector[68]).

Protecting Chinese territorial waters and airspace have been primary missions for the Chinese military for decades. During the past 20 years, this mission has expanded further from mainland China to protect expansive Chinese claims to parts of the South China Sea. Future developments include the possibility that China might declare another air identification defense zone in disputed areas of the South China Sea as it did in November last year in the East China Sea. Even if, as analysts argue,[69] China is unlikely to do so in the immediate future, ongoing developments (expanding reefs into islands that can support large buildings and surveillance equipment) and the military projects to increase air and naval capabilities suggest that this is a future possibility. For China, the island on Fiery Cross Reef could fulfill the strategic role of an "unsinkable aircraft carrier".[70]

Military presence in the contested waters not only asserts *de facto* sovereignty, but also strengthens territorial claims. Civilian and military infrastructure leads to a permanent structure and framework, expanding China's power projection. "Island building" expands territory and enables China to have control of the security landscape, potentially building air and sea supremacy in the vast archipelago setting.[71]

Aside from the military scenario, China's approach manifests restraint. The long-term plans and perspectives on China's agenda do not comprise antagonising numerous states and the ASEAN community. Invasive and violent military developments in the South China Sea are at Beijing's disadvantage, and might risk triggering an increased US presence. China conducts intensive diplomacy with the states in the region, discussing energy policies, institutional arrangements, institutional loans, and energy cooperation. It engages in numerous forums and ongoing institutional frameworks, and promotes a particular type of soft power "Asia for the Asians". Nevertheless, as a key source of demand and investment, China can use its position as leverage to influence numerous situations in its favour.

Inspired by other states and understanding the provisions imposed by UNCLOS, as well the limitations to which it is subject (there is no real mechanism to enforce its provisions), China has created a situation which shows its ability to discern the shades of foreign policy: if forced integration of claimed territories directly and fairly quickly leads to international isolation, the construction of islands, especially developed from an existing territorial "seed" insignificant in size but significant in theory, can be sustained in the context generated by the official policy "Peaceful Development".[72]

Apart from these the financial aspects are not negligible: maintaining the occupation of a territory in dispute involves costs that are hard to recover. In this sense the direct action of building in an area rich in resources achieved two objectives: the costs are recoverable at least in part and it establishes a *de facto* exclusive economic zone by suggesting indirect military force.

UNCLOS states that artificial islands may not be accompanied by a "shelf" like coastal areas. Moreover, it limits the protection zone to 500 meters round them, not 12 miles as natural islands.

The issue is considered of lesser importance, China claiming that the structures are not artificial islands, but in fact the state only brought to surface what that were otherwise submerged reefs. The surfaces obtained also meet one of the requirements of Article no. 121 of UNCLOS on the relationship between human life and economic sustainability and the establishment of an exclusive economic zone and continental shelf.

The ambiguity of the situation in the Spratly archipelago (Philippines opened an arbitration process against China, which added to the complex situation) did not prevent Beijing asserting that "China's determination to defend the sovereignty and territorial integrity is unshakable".[73] "But on 12 June 2016, an international tribunal in The Hague delivered a sweeping rebuke of China's behaviour in the South China Sea, including its construction of artificial islands, and found that its expansive claim to sovereignty over the waters had no legal basis".[74] Meanwhile, the US is acting in accordance with its strategic interests in

Asia-Pacific, defying China's position and its legal lawfare in the region. In October 2016, the US Navy conducted freedom of navigation operation (FONOP) in the South China Sea. It was the first recent FONOP to openly and decisively reject a Chinese claim of maritime sovereignty. But it was a manoeuvre that did more than that and should open the legal door to a more aggressive US challenge to China's island-building in the South China Sea.[75]

Daesh IS and the Sharia as a basic Islamic law in a type of "religious lawfare"

Starting from its definition, when we refer to *lawfare* we should take into consideration a situation that we can describe as a form of asymmetric warfare. Thus, the word refers to a situation in which the domestic and/or international law are used in an inappropriate way, meaning that an international actor, usually a country, illegitimately uses them in order to obtain some advantages (political, economic, military etc.).

Domestic law, also called national law, refers to the "internal affairs" of a country, while international law represents a set of rules that are generally accepted and regarded in relations between countries, international organisations and other relevant international actors.

If, at least lately, we have examples of lawfare in which countries were involved, in the case of some international organisations it is less clear if we intend to establish whether their actions are part of such a lawfare category or warfare. And this because, if we speak about states, is much easier to identify their actions even if they cannot be classified as illegal, being obvious that their actions are used following the speculation of some legislative gaps, or that certain laws are interpreted in such a manner in order to ensure some advantages for a country while its competitors are disadvantaged.

Starting from the definition of lawfare, we might be tempted to consider states as potential users of such practices, an idea sustained by the reality on the ground. And this because they are directly involved in compliance with their own domestic law and international law, as subjects of international law. In reality, the non-state actors[76] can also be the initiators and supporters of such practices, in order to influence the evolutions of a situation in their favour, either by invoking regulations related to rules in international law, of laws that they recognise and promote, but in an interpretation favourable to them.

Extrapolating the discussion regarding the implication of an international actor in a war by using an asymmetric form like lawfare, the question of if the Islamic State group can be considered to be engaged in such actions becomes pertinent. The lack of a clear response to this question derives both from the fact that in this case, we talk about a terrorist organisation, being in this situation precluding any interest to respect the law (domestic or international), so we cannot talk about using a rule or a set of rules in a manner that legally covers its less than legal intentions.

On the other hand, it is about invoking some laws by the jihadist organisation[77] in order to justify maybe the most barbaric actions in the recent history of humanity, like the laws of Islam, a religion so different from the set of rules of the international law, but became the basis for the domestic law of the territories controlled by the jihadist group.

So, in the case of the emergence of the Islamic State group[78] we should pay attention to its goals and how it tries to implement them, to see if in the case of the evolutions in countries like Syria and Iraq, where jihadists intend to establish a caliphate, meaning a state ruled by a single political and religious leader according to Islamic law, also known as Sharia,[79] we can talk about a type of lawfare.

If regarding the actions that can be classified as being part of lawfare, we speak mainly about international actors like states, who deliberately use some rules of international law to gain advantages either by putting a rival state in a difficult situation or through actions targeting earnings that doesn't affect other countries, in the case of the jihadist group called the Islamic State, we are dealing with the interpretation of some internal, domestic norms, the ones applicable in the territory controlled by this terrorist organisation, namely Sharia, understood as the Islamic legal system, which is based on the commands found in the most important text of the Islam, the Quran and Hadith.

Even the term itself means in the Arabic language "a body of moral and religious laws", being a combination of sources: the Muslims' holy book, known as the Quran, the sayings and the conduct of the prophet Muhammad, gathered in what Muslims call Hadith (a collection of the reports of the teachings, deeds and sayings of the Great Prophet), but also *fatwas* which refer to the rulings of Islamic scholars.[80]

The Islamic law, known as Sharia, influences the legal code in most Muslim countries, guiding all aspects of Muslim life, from familial and religious obligations, to political ones and financial dealings.[81] More precisely, its rulings are meant to help Muslims understand how they should lead every aspect of their lives according to God's wishes.[82]

For many non-Muslims, Sharia represents a way of living associated with punishments that cannot be accepted today: amputations of limbs, lashes, death by stoning etc., all practices considered to belong to times long gone. Seen as ancient punishments, this kind of actions are considered to be, especially by the people in the West, archaic and unfair social ideas imposed upon people who live in Sharia-controlled countries. On the other side, on Muslims side, Sharia is seen as something that nurtures humanity,[83] a viewpoint that contrasts with the Western view regarding the Islamic law.

Sharia in the Islamic State interpretation

In countries where Islam is the official religion, Sharia is declared to be the source of the law. Even though some voices say that it has the potential to overcome tribal conflict and to quiet chaotic regions, Sharia is prone to abuses and manipulation in volatile regions where Islamic militants are active.[84]

If we take into consideration the evolutions in Iraq and Syria after the establishing of the Islamic State group, we can see that what should be a system of rules, Islamic rules, is used by jihadist militants through their own interpretation, making Sharia even more dangerous for some people in the region controlled by the IS group. Even if the Islamist group is not the first to apply the harsh rules of Sharia, the magnitude of its actions is bigger because of the huge number of people condemned to death for reasons such as their religion or their refusal to convert to Islam.

The Islamist organisation is using its own interpretation of the Sharia rules, bringing in the forefront some controversial issues like public executions and the execution of somebody for refusing to convert to its religion – Sunni. No matter what explanations the jihadist group invokes to justify its actions, including the rules of Sharia, they cannot be accepted. So, regarding public executions, in many cases we are talking about Christians, like the Egyptians killed in February 2015[85] and the Ethiopians killed in March 2015, in Libya.[86] Their execution cannot be explained by the rules invoked by the group known as the Islamic State because they are crimes against a population of a different religion (Christians, YAZIDIS), a situation equivalent to a serious violation of international norms.

The kidnappings of dozens of Assyrian Christians but also the beheadings of the Egyptians and Ethiopians Christians indicate that the jihadist group is not interested in accepting Christian people in the territories it controls, even if the holy book of Islam offers them a special status, more precisely, in return for a fee, the Quran mentions that their safety will be ensured by the Muslims. The payment of a fee is not something new, being the result of a consensus among the scholars of the Islamic world, which guarantee a special status for Christians and Jewish people in the Islamic territories, as adherents of monotheist religions.

But even if the holy book, the Quran, recognises that they have a special status, the jihadist group treats this rule in a different way than the Islamic law does, in its approach, a special status for Christians and Jewish being rather an exception than a rule. Thereby, invoking the refusal of the Christians to convert to Islam, the jihadist group decided to kill a large number of people of different nationalities only because "they were found guilty" of not abiding by the rules preached by the terrorist organisation. Briefly, the Islamic law is interpreted by the jihadist group in its own way, based on its rules and its own decisions and not on the rules of the Quran which offers a special status for the adherents of the monotheist religions. And this misinterpretation of Quran is deliberately made by the Islamic State group, not as a result of a misunderstanding of Sharia, but as part of the "Islamic lawfare" against Christianity and international law, which forbids the killing of a population on religious grounds.[87]

Another tragic episode of a deliberate misinterpretation of Islamic law is the execution of Moaz al-Kasasbeh, a Jordanian pilot, burned alive in a cage.[88] His execution, made public on 3 February 2015 by the Islamic State group, presents a short "story", a narrative video showing the implication of the Jordanian country in the international coalition against the terrorist organisation. The video shows a fighter aircraft launching a missile, being explained that the execution of the Jordanian pilot represents a "punishment" for what he did to the Muslims in Syria.

Killing Moaz al-Kasabeh in such a horrible manner (burning him alive) shocked the international community not only because such an execution has not been used until that moment by the jihadist group, but also because such actions are not normal in our times. In the history of Islam, executions like this are not known, so the clerics of the terrorist organisation issued immediately a *fatwa* to justify the Jordanian death, while other Muslim clerics claimed that the burning of a person is prohibited by Islam.

Not even the verse 16:126 in the Quran, which is the base of the so-called "quisas", the concept in the Islamic law that speaks about an equal punishment for crimes, based on the model of "eye for an eye", can be used as an explanation for the execution of the Jordanian pilot. And this because it is not clear who would have been "burned" by him or on behalf of the Jordanian country which he served, even if the jihadist group obsessively repeated the word "mumathala", which in their language means "reciprocity".

Notes

1 Carlson, J., Yeomans, N., *Whither Goeth the Law - Humanity or Barbarity*, September 2000, http://www.laceweb.org.au/whi.htm, Dec 2013 (accessed 19 September 2016).
2 According to the FBIS Editor's Note: The following selections are taken from "Unrestricted Warfare", a book published in China in February 1999 which proposes tactics for developing countries, in particular China, to compensate for their military inferiority vis-à-vis the United States during a high-tech war. The selections include the table of contents, preface, afterword, and biographical information about the authors printed on the cover. The book was written by two PLA senior colonels from the younger generation of Chinese military officers and was published by the PLA Literature and Arts Publishing House in Beijing, suggesting that its release was endorsed by at least some elements of the PLA leadership. This impression was reinforced by an interview with Qiao and laudatory review of the book carried out by the party youth league's official daily *Zhongguo Qingnian Bao* on 28 June. Published prior to the bombing of China's embassy in Belgrade, the book has recently drawn the attention of both the Chinese and Western press for its advocacy of a multitude of means, both military and particularly non-military, to strike at the United States during times of conflict. Hacking into websites, targeting financial institutions, terrorism, using the media, and conducting urban warfare are among the methods proposed. In the *Zhongguo Qingnian Bao* interview, Qiao was quoted as stating that "the first rule of unrestricted warfare is that there are no rules, with nothing forbidden." Elaborating on this idea, he asserted that strong countries would not use the same approach against weak countries because "strong countries make the rules while rising ones break them and exploit loopholes ... The United States breaks [UN rules] and makes new ones when these rules don't suit [its purposes], but it has to observe its own rules or the whole world will not trust it" (see FBIS translation of the interview, OW2807114599 https://web.archive.org/web/20061119123552/http://www.terrorism.com/documents/TRC-Analysis/unrestricted.pdf).
3 Goldsmith, J., *Thoughts on Lawfare*, https://www.lawfareblog.com/thoughts-lawfare, 8 September 2010 (accessed 15 February 2016).
4 *The Alliance's Strategic Concept*, Approved by the Heads of State and Government participating in the meeting of the North Atlantic Council in Washington D.C., Press Release NAC-S(99) 65, http://www.nato.int/cps/en/natolive/official_texts_27433.htm, 24 April 1999 (accessed 15 February 2016).

5   Goldsmith, J., *Thoughts on Lawfare*.
6   unlap, C. J., Jr., *Lawfare amid warfare, The Washington Times,* http://www.washingtontimes. com/news/2007/aug/3/lawfare-amid-warfare/, 3 August 2007 (accessed 21 February 2016).
7   Goldsmith, J., *Thoughts on Lawfare*.
8   Dunlap, C. J., Jr., *Lawfare amid warfare, The Washington Times*.
9   The Lawfare Project is a New York-based organisation devoted to exposing alleged abuses of the international legal system. *About Us*, THE – LAWFARE PROJECT, http://www.thelawfareproject.org/about (accessed 16 December 2010).
10 *What is Lawfare?*, THE LAWFARE PROJECT, http://www.thelawfareproject.org (accessed 16 December 2010).
11 The Lawfare Project, Mission http://thelawfareproject.org/mission-2/.
12 *About Us*, THE - LAWFARE PROJECT (last visited Dec. 16, 2010), http://www. thelawfareproject.org/about, idem
13 Martins, M., *Reflections on "Lawfare" and Related Terms*, The Lawfare Project, http:// www.lawfareblog.com/2010/11/reflections-on-%E2%80%9Clawfare %E2%80%9D- and-related-terms/, 18 November 2010 (accessed 16 December 2010).
14 Hill, H., *Lawfare and the International Criminal Court: Questions & Answers*, The American Non-Governmental Organizations Coalition for the International Criminal Court, 14 January 2008, http://www.amicc.org/docs/Lawfare.pdf (accessed 21 February 2016).
15 Ibid.
16 Ibid.
17 Dunlap, C. J., Jr., Lawfare amid warfare *The Washington Times*.
18 Ibid.
19 *Lawfare amid warfare,* The Washington Times, 3 August 2007, http://www. washingtontimes.com/news/2007/aug/3/lawfare-amid-warfare/
20 Ibid.
21 Ibid.
22 Hill, H., *Lawfare and the International Criminal Court: Questions & Answers,*
23 *One-Year Follow-up Response of the United States of America to Recommendations of the Committee Against Torture on its Combined Third to Fifth Periodic Reports on Implementation of the Convention Against Torture and Other Cruel, Inhuman, or Degrading Treatment or Punishment*, U.S. Department of State, 27 November 2015, https://www.state.gov/j/drl/rls/250342.htm.
24 Hill, H., *Lawfare and the International Criminal Court: Questions & Answers,*
25 *Special Warfare,* March-April 2008 | Volume 21 | Issue 2, https://static.dvidshub.net/ media/pubs/pdf_8252.pdf (accessed 7 March 2016).
26 Martins, M., *Reflections on "Lawfare" and Related Terms*, The Lawfare Project p.12.
27 The Mavi Marmara incident started with the killing by Israeli commandos of 10 Turkish activists on board a ship that was part of an aid flotilla attempting to breach the blockade of Gaza on 31 May 2010. The six ships in the flotilla were boarded in international waters, about 130km (80 miles) from the Israeli coast. Commandos landed on the largest ship, the Turkish-owned Mavi Marmara, by descending on ropes from helicopters. Clashes broke out immediately and the Israeli commandos opened fire. The activists say the commandos started shooting as soon as they hit the deck. Israeli officials say the commandos opened fire only after being attacked with clubs, knives and a gun which was taken from them. Video released by the Israeli military stops just before the shooting begins. A UN inquiry was apparently unable to determine at exactly which point the commandos used live fire. Source: *Mavi Marmara: Why did Israel stop the Gaza flotilla?*, BBC News, http://www.bbc.com/news/10203726, 27 June 2016 (accessed 21 March 2016).
28 *Belgium Drops War Crimes Cases,* Deutsche Welle, 25 September 2003, http://www. dw.com/en/belgium-drops-war-crimes-cases/a-978973.

29 Erlanger, S., *Rights Group Says NATO Bombings in Yugoslavia Violated Law*, The New York Times, http://www.nytimes.com/2000/06/08/world/rights-group-says-nato-bombing-in-yugoslavia-violated-law.html, 8 June 2000 (accessed 21 March 2016).

30 *Chronology of US actions related to the International Criminal Court, The American Non-Governmental Organisation for the International Criminal Court*, http://www.amicc.org/docs/US%20Chronology.pdf (accessed 12 April, 2016).

31 The Rome Statue was sign under the Clinton Administration (2000), the Bush Administration stated that the US would not join the ICC, while under the Obama Administration, a relation between the US and ICC was reestablished, the US having the status of observer. Source: *US Engagement With the ICC and the Outcome of the Recently Concluded Review Conference*, U.S. Department of State, https://web.archive.org/web/20120112210935/http://www.state.gov/j/gcj/us_releases/remarks/143178.htm, 15 June 2010 (accessed 17 April 2016).

32 Leverett, L. F., *Why Libya Gave Up on the Bomb*, The Brookings Institution, https://www.brookings.edu/opinions/why-libya-gave-up-on-the-bomb/, 23 January 2004 (accessed 24 April 2016).

33 Laufer, M., *A.Q. Khan Nuclear Chronology, Carnegie Endowment for International Peace*, http://carnegieendowment.org/2005/09/07/a.-q.-khan-nuclear-chronology, 7 September 2005 (accessed 24 April 2016).

34 On July 1, 2010, President Obama signed into law the Comprehensive Iran Sanctions, Accountability, and Divestment Act of 2010 (CISADA.) The Act amends the Iran Sanctions Act of 1996 (ISA) which requires sanctions be imposed or waived for companies that are determined to have made certain investments in Iran's energy sector. CISADA expands significantly the energy-related activities that are sanctionable and adds new types of sanctions that can be imposed. These new authorities address the potential connection between Iran's energy sector and its nuclear program that was highlighted in UNSCR 1929. They support an effort to increase pressure on Iran to return constructively to diplomatic negotiations to address the international community's concerns about Iran's non-compliance with its international obligations (including those under the relevant UNSCRs, the Nuclear Non-Proliferation Treaty, and the IAEA Safeguards Agreement.) The United States is resolved to make full use of ISA and the other authorities in CISADA as additional tools in our efforts to convince the Iranian Government to change its strategic calculus, comply with its full range of nuclear obligations, and engage in constructive negotiations on the future of its nuclear program. Source: *Fact Sheet: Comprehensive Iran Sanctions, Accountability, and Divestment Act (CISADA)*, U.S. Department of State, Bureau of Economic, Energy and Business Affairs, http://www.state.gov/e/eb/esc/iransanctions/docs/160710.htm, 23 May 2011 (accessed 15 May 2016).

35 *Iran charged over Argentina bomb*, BBC, http://news.bbc.co.uk/2/hi/americas/6085768.stm, 25 October 2006 (accessed 15 May 2016).

36 McCarthy, A., *Lawfare Strikes again*, National Review, http://www.nationalreview.com/article/221258/lawfare-strikes-again-andrew-c-mccarthy, 12 June 2007 (accessed 20 May 2016).

37 Goldsmith, J., *Thoughts on Lawfare*.

38 Dunlap, C. J., Jr., *Lawfare amid warfare The Washington Times*.

39 *Chapter VII: Action with respect to threats to the peace, breaches of the peace, and acts of aggression*, Chapter VII, http://www.un.org/en/sections/un-charter/chapter-vii/ (accessed 15 June 2016).

40 *Transcript: Putin says Russia will protect the rights of Russians abroad*, The Washington Post, https://www.washingtonpost.com/world/transcript-putin-says-russia-will-protect-the-rights-of-russians-abroad/2014/03/18/432a1e60-ae99-11e3-a49e-76adc9210f19_story.html?utm_term=.dd6b41874732, 18 March 2014 (accessed 15 June 2016).

41 United Nations High Commissioner for Human Rights (UNCHR), Report on the Human Rights Situation in Ukraine (15th April 2014), http://www.ohchr.org/Documents/Countries/UA/HRMMUReport15June2014.pdf (accessed 15 June 2016).

42 UNGA, Territorial Integrity of Ukraine (1st April 2014) A/RES/68/262, http://www.securitycouncilreport.org/atf/cf/%7B65BFCF9B-6D27-4E9C-8CD3-CF6E4FF96FF9%7D/a_res_68_262.pdf (accessed 15 June 2016).

43 UNGA, Res.3314 (XXIX), The Definition of Aggression (14th December 1974) UN Doc A/Res/3314, http://hrlibrary.umn.edu/instree/GAres3314.html (accessed 15 June 2016).

44 Ibid., Art 1.

45 Murray, Euan. "Russia's Annexation of Crimea and International Law Governing The Use Of Force", https://www.academia.edu/10068890/RUSSIA_S_ANNEXATION_OF_CRIMEA_AND_INTERNATIONAL_LAW_GOVERNING_THE_USE_OF_FORCE, pg. 6 (accessed 15 June 2016).

46 UN Charter (n30) Art. 2(4), Purposes and principles of the United Nations, http://www.un.org/en/sc/repertoire/principles.shtml#rel2 (accessed 17 June 2016).

47 Charted of the United Nations (October 24 1945) 892 UNTS 119, http://www.un.org/en/charter-united-nations/ (accessed 17 June 2016).

48 *Vienna Convention on the Law of Treaties* (Into force 27 January 1980) 1155 UNTS 331 Art.31, https://treaties.un.org/doc/Publication/UNTS/Volume%201155/volume-1155-I-18232-English.pdf (accessed 19 June 2016).

49 United Nations Conference on International Organization, Vol.6 (United Nations Information Organizations, 1945), https://archive.org/stream/documentsoftheun008818mbp#page/n351/mode/2up, p.344-345 (accessed 19 June 2016).

50 *Budapest Memorandums on Security Assurances, 1994,* Council on Foreign Relations, http://www.cfr.org/nonproliferation-arms-control-and-disarmament/budapest-memorandums-security-assurances-1994/p32484, 5 December 1994 (accessed 22 June 2016).

51 Bacynska, G., *Russia says no proof it sent troops, arms to east Ukraine,* Reuters, http://www.reuters.com/article/us-ukraine-crisis-lavrov-idUSKBN0KU12Y20150121, 21 January 2015 (accessed 22 June 2016).

52 Definition of Aggression (n28) Art 3, UNGA, Res.3314 (XXIX), The Definition of Aggression (14th December 1974) UN Doc A/Res/3314.

53 *The Geneva Conventions of 12 august 1949,* ICRC, https://www.icrc.org/eng/assets/files/publications/icrc-002-0173.pdf (accessed 29 June 2016).

54 *Common Article 3 of the four Geneva Conventions of 1949 and Additional Protocols I and II*, https://ihl-databases.icrc.org/ihl/WebART/375-590006 (accessed 29 June 2016).

55 *Practice Relating to Rule 13. Area Bombardment,* https://www.icrc.org/customary-ihl/eng/docs/v2_rul_rule13

56 *Eastern Ukraine: Questions and Answers about the Law of War,* Human Rights Watch, http://www.hrw.org/news/2014/09/11/eastern-ukraine-questions-and-answers-about-laws-war, 11 September 2014 (accessed 5 July 2016).

57 UNCLOS, Art. 60, http://www.un.org/depts/los/convention_agreements/texts/unclos/part5.htm (accessed 5 July 2016).

58 Alfred Soons, *Artificial Islands and Installations in International Law,* Law of the Sea Inst., Occasional Paper, 1974, https://repositories.tdl.org/tamug-ir/bitstream/handle/1969.3/27383/10857-Artificial%20Islands%20and%20Installations%20in%20International%20Law.pdf?sequence=1 (accessed 27 July 2016).

59 Nikos Papadakis, *The International Legal Regime of Artificial Islands*, Sijthoff Publications on Ocean Development, Vol. 2), A.W. Sijthoff, Leyden, 1977.

60 Watkins, D., *What China Has Been Building in the South China Sea,* The New York Times, http://www.nytimes.com/interactive/2015/07/30/world/asia/what-china-has-been-building-in-the-south-china-sea.html?_r=0, 27 October 2015 (accessed 15 December 2016).

61 *China to Build USD5 Billion South China Sea Military Base at Fiery Cross Reef,* Tiananmen's tremendous Achievements, https://tiananmenstremendousachievements. wordpress.com/, 15 December 2016 (accessed 15 December 2016).
62 Brrunnstrom, D., *China installs weapons systems on artificial islands: U.S. think tank,* Reuters, http://www.reuters.com/article/us-southchinasea-china-arms-exclusive-idUSKBN14310K, 15 December 2016 (accessed 15 December 2016).
63 Crawford, J., *U.S. protests after Chinese military jet lands on South China island,* CNN, http://edition.cnn.com/2016/04/18/politics/chinese-military-jet-lands-on-island/, 19 April 2016 (accessed 15 December 2016).
64 Jan Perlez, *China Said to Turn Reef Into Airship in Disputed Water,* The New York Times, 23 Nov 2014, https://www.nytimes.com/2014/11/24/world/asia/china-said-to-be-building-airstrip-capable-area-in-disputed-waters.html?_r=0.
65 United Nations Convention on the Law of the Sea, http://www.un.org/depts/los/ convention_agreements/texts/unclos/unclos_e.pdf (accessed 15 December 2016).
66 Ma, A., *Here's What You Need To Know About The South China Sea Disputes,* The World Post, Huff Post, http://www.huffingtonpost.com/entry/south-china-sea-disputes-explained_us_56ccd9ede4b041136f18ad3d, 26 February 2016 (accessed 15 December 2016).
67 Frey C., *China's opening moved in south China Sea,* Regional and International Developments in the Asia-Pacific Region, 6 December 2014, https://rieasiapacific. wordpress.com/2014/12/06/chinas-opening-moves-in-south-china-sea/.
68 Ibid.
69 Ibid.
70 Ibid.
71 Panda, A., *China's Spratlys Airstrip Will Raise South China Sea Stakes,* The Diplomat, http://thediplomat.com/2014/11/chinas-spratlys-airstrip-will-raise-south-china-sea-stakes/, 25 November 2014 (accessed 15 December 2016).
72 White Paper: China's Peaceful Development, September 2011, Beijing, http://english1. english.gov.cn/official/2011-09/06/content_1941354.htm (accessed 17 June 2016).
73 http://www.pca-cpa.org/showpage.asp?pag_id=1529 (accessed 17 June 2016).
74 Perlez, J., *Tribunal Rejects Beijing's Claims in South China Sea,* The New York Times, http://www.nytimes.com/2016/07/13/world/asia/south-china-sea-hague-ruling-philippines.html?_r=0, 12 July 2016 (access 19 July 2016).
75 Ku, J, *The Latest US Freedom of Navigation Operation Opens the Legal Door to More Aggressive US Challenges to China's Artificial Islands,* Lawfare, https://www. lawfareblog.com/latest-us-freedom-navigation-operation-opens-legal-door-more-aggressive-us-challenges-chinas, 24 October 2016 (accessed 9 November 2016).
76 Joey, A., *The Role of Non - state Actors in International Relations,* https://www. academia.edu/5124220/The_Role_of_Non-state_Actors_in_International_Relations (accessed 27 November 2016).
77 Gardner, F., *Jihadist groups around the world,* BBC, http://www.bbc.com/news/world-middle-east-27930414, 19 June 2014 (accessed 17 September 2016).
78 *Syria Iraq: The Islamic State militant group,* BBC, http://www.bbc.com/news/world-middle-east-24179084, 2 August 2014 (accessed 17 June 2016).
79 *What is Islamic State,* BBC, http://www.bbc.com/news/world-middle-east-29052144, 2 Decembre 2015 (accessed 17 June 2016).
80 *Sharia,* BBC, http://www.bbc.co.uk/religion/religions/islam/beliefs/sharia_1.shtml, 3 September 2009 (accessed 19 June 2016).
81 Toni Johnson, Mohammed AlySergie, *Islam: Governing Under Sharia,* Council on Foreign Relations, http://www.cfr.org/religion/islam-governing-under-sharia/p8034, 24 July 2014 (accessed 19 June 2016).
82 Dominic Cascian, *Q&A: Sharia law explained,* BBC, http://news.bbc.co.uk/2/hi/uk_ news/7234870.stm, 4 July 2008 (accessed 19 June 2016).

83 *Sharia*, BBC.
84 Toni Johnson, *Sharia and Militancy,* November 30, 2010, Council on Foreign Relations, http://www.cfr.org/religion/sharia-militancy/p19155 (accessed 25 June 2016).
85 *ISIS Releases Video Purporting To Show Beheading Of 21 Egyptian Christians in Libya,* The World Post, Huff Post, http://www.huffingtonpost.com/2015/02/15/isis-libya-video_n_6688376.html, 15 February 2015 (accessed 25 June 2016).
86 *ISIS releases video purportedly showing killing of Ethiopian Christians in Libya,* fox News World, http://www.foxnews.com/world/2015/04/19/isis-video-purports-to-show-killing-ethiopians-in-libya.html, 20 April 2015 (accessed 25 June 2016).
87 Muir, J., *Islamic State group: The full story*, BBC, http://www.bbc.com/news/world-middle-east-35695648, 20 June 2016 (accessed)
88 Jordan pilot hostage Moaz al-Kasasbeh "burned alive", BBC News, http://www.bbc.com/news/world-middle-east-31121160, 3 February 2015

Bibliography

Comaroff, J. L., 'Colonialism, Culture and the Law: A Forward', *Law and Social Inquiry* 26(2), 305-314

Dungan, C. Peter 'Fighting Lawfare at the Special Operations Task Force Level', *Special Warfare*, no. 2, March–Apr 2008

Dunlap, C. J., Jr., *Law and Military Interventions: Preserving Humanitarian Values in 21st Conflicts* Prepared for the Humanitarian Challenges in Military Intervention, Conference Carr Center for Human Rights Policy Kennedy School of Government, Harvard University Washington, D.C., 29 November 2001

Dunlap, C. J., Jr., 'Lawfare Today: A Perspective', Yale Journal of International Affairs, 3 YALE J. INT'L. AFF. 146, 146 (2008)

Gerstenfeld, M., *Ahmadinejad Calls for Israel's Elimination and Declares War on the West: A Case Study of Incitement to Genocide*, Jerusalem Center for Public Affairs, Israeli Security, Regional Diplomacy and International Law, Jerusalem Viewpoints, No. 536, 29 Tishrei 5766, 1 November 2005

Holzer, M. W., *Offensive Lawfare and the Current Conflict,* Harvard Law School, National Security Journal, http://harvardnsj.org/2012/04/offensive-lawfare-and-the-current-conflict/, 10 April 2012

Kittrie, O. F., *Lawfare and U.S. National Security,* Case Western Reserve Journal of International Law, School of Law, Case Western Reserve University, Volume 43, Issue 1, 2010

Liang, Q., & Xiangsui, W., *Unrestricted Warfare*, Beijing: PLA Literature and Arts Publishing House, February 1999

Newton, M. A., Illustrating Illegitimate Lawfare, Case Western Reserve Journal of International Law, Vol. 43, Vanderbilt Public Law Research Paper No. 10-41, 2011

Scharf, M. P., & Andersen, E., *Is Lawfare Worth Defining* – Report of the Cleveland Experts Meeting, Is Lawfare Worth Defining – Report of the Cleveland Experts Meeting, Volume 43 | Issue 1, 2010, School of Law Case Western Reserve University

Waters, M. A., *"Lawfare" in the War on Terrorism: A Reclamation Project*, School of Law, Case Western Reserve Journal of International Law; Volume 43 | Issue 1, 2010

6 The pattern of Russia's informational war[1]

Iulian Chifu

The informational war: Concept, instrumentation, functionality

The informational war: A concept and an instrument

A component of hybrid war, but also a self-contained instrument, is the informational war. The informational war represents the creation of alternative realities by perverting the objective truth – based on concrete data, facts and arguments – it is misconstruing by using a combination of elements, facts and pieces of truth that are selected, interpreted, combined with altered reasoning through the use of syllogisms, fallacies, propaganda, forced interpretation, everything stuffed with a multitude of lies (Chifu & Nantoi 2016: 15). Most times, it represents a "contactless" conflict that is fought in the realms of perception and the human mind. It continues through both official peace and wartime. (Lucas & Nimmo 2015: 8).

The battle of alternative narratives, of "alternative truths", became the most insidious way of constructing beliefs. But it relies on the groups and audiences targeted for each individual operation, on a vast contexture of preparation knowledge, inclinations and expectations of the target audience, its propensities, frustrations. Obviously the instruments do not concern only the information as such, but refer to other subtler components as well, related to basic emotions, context and the capitalisation of opportunities provided by the events in progress and the state of mind created in a target population, in order to inoculate a certain reference to the subject.

The alternative reality perverts the perception of the target population, in a combination of psychological operations (PsyOps), together with disinformation and propaganda, using fundamental beliefs, feelings and images with impact, aiming to lead the target audience towards a pre-defined perception. And, finally, as the public already built an opinion, its perception has taken the place of reality (Stern 1999) and no matter what argument or proof of the truth are presented, these would confront the blockage of the already formed perception.

In a world in which information travels quickly to a large number of people, in real time, via television, the Internet and social media, the perception of an event is easy to form, derail, alter and impose. The subsequent submission of the truth will lead to a minimal change of opinion on a large scale due to the lack of critical thinking of the majority of the population, a conservative approach in assuming the recognition of their own mistake at the level of the wider population, and the ease of using the already interiorised explanation by an ordinary person, especially one located within a community that has developed conformism and has its own description, perception and its own "truth".

The main overall objective of the informational war is to determine, to control or at least to alter the strategic decisions of foreign policy, security and defence, to pervert or hinder the instruments intended for the military component of a state, and to hinder the functioning, if not to block some elements related to the security of a state. The instrument and mechanism to achieve this goal are to ensure that the public, the citizens, the pressure groups that are prepared and conditioned, organised and directed, to put pressure on the authority in order to alienate it from the objective solution identified for the decision, at some point, due to the lack of support, or even due to public opposition.

Therefore, the characteristic elements, principles and values of an open and democratic society are being capitalised against the states and their institutions; an undermining from the inside through building groups of enemies from within. Moreover, the approach is unitary, integrated, and frequently a fact or a component of the informational war, taken separately, appears only as an oddity, a singularity, an accident, in no circumstances an act aggressively planned together with a suite of other elements. The insidious manner of action and this integrated approach creates the favourable elements for a credible denial of such action of informational aggression on a target population.

The informational war uses three distinct levels of action, with different relevance and degree of legal and moral significance. Together, through the integrated and sequential approach dependent on the targeted audience, increases the efficiency of the informational war.

The first component is visible, and concerns the engagement in altering the public space of a subjected target. It involves the media, which in our time is considered an instrument of war, because winning modern wars is as much dependent on carrying domestic and international public opinion as it is on defeating the enemy on the battlefield (Payne 2005: 81). As well, it involves the Internet and the social media area, but also it can be found at other more subtle levels, where we are talking about an injection of ideas and information that valorises the principles and fundamental values of democracy and human rights, including: the freedom of expression, freedom of speech, free circulation of ideas. These elements are not only legal and moral, but stand among the fundamental values that the democratic societies defend. At a lower level we deal with an open injection of propaganda, the propaganda being seen as a form of coercion without the appearance of coercion (O'Shaughnessy 2010: 29); manipulation and disinformation which is difficult to prove. Moreover, this type of action requires constant replication, analyses, investigations and public exposure of counterfeits and deliberate misinterpretations of facts, of alternative narratives that are behind these ideas and which are using the manner of interpretation of facts particularly to support the alternative package of truth proposed by the author of the propaganda. Also, selective news coverage can be a powerful tool of propaganda by tending to promote the kind of reporting that is favourable to an actor and its cause, and by restricting information that could be damaging (Zhukov & Baum 2016: 8).

Not infrequently the actions capitalise on the vulnerabilities of the system, habits in failing to comply with, or bypassing, or avoiding the sanctions based on the law, or vulnerabilities of the control institutions, legal limits, or the absence of professional institutions capable of morally sanctioning the use of such excesses in promoting an approach or another on an embraced subject or narrative, the absence of responses in the same news, the lack of expertise to qualify the released information, the speed and poor training of employees in the media area, the information dissemination and peddling. The false information, coming from obscure sources and penetrating the mainstream, the selected information, forcibly interpreting and piloting judgements to a default conclusion, the absence of alternative independent media, which would strictly keep to the rules of narrating some events, balanced news, providing in the same area alternative approaches, polemic, or at the same time the pros and cons arguments, all these help to build this informational war element.

In mature developed societies, with mass media that are developed, rich and with many alternatives, the component of takeover, guidance and control of the public space is much lower. Education matters as well, and so does the democratic culture of the target population. But there are societies where the public space is controlled by third party actors, such as the case of the Republic of Moldova An official report about news in Republic of Moldova (CCA-The Audiovisual Coordinating Council) says that 80% of the news, reports and ideas spread in the public space of the Republic of Moldova were made in Russia (both in Romanian and Russian).And when they are packaged in extremely well made and attractive entertainment programmes, these genuine news "injections" situated in the space of a preconceived narrative means that the impact of the projected alternative truths is major. Propaganda has its limits. Hence the use of a set of integrated instruments is required, developed and utilised at the same time, with target audience destinations and a distinct approach. On this point we reach the second element, lobbying, Public Relations if we are dealing with a company or a personality, or public diplomacy if we are talking about a state. This is a perfectly legal approach in the countries where laws on lobbying or equivalents exist.

The instrument works as follows: the decision makers must be influenced by ideas launched in the public space by legitimate and credible sources, with impact on its own population and the decision makers that lead a state at a certain time. Herein sums of money are used, paid so that the credible persons, analysts, experts, former and current politicians that have an impact on a target population, or even foreign carriers of messages, but again credible and legitimate to the target population to defend the theses proposed by the party that makes the payment.

The paid media or the expert, the analyst who is expressing an idea, are paid to create a certain image, to defend a certain actor, to carry a certain message, a vision, a narrative previously prepared. Therefore, a a credible or highly appreciated character, suddenly speaks out in the public space, spreading ideas that are not the result of his own analysis, of his thinking, but are the result delivered to be broadcast as such for an amount of money, paid by the silent partner. The public is not warned and does not know that the one standing in front of them does not speak his own mind, but that he expresses ideas about which he has been ordered to speak. Therefore, an assessment is made in the context of credibility and legitimacy of the person concerned (actually this is what the analyst is selling, the message carrier in the lobby). Moreover, after fulfilling the mission, the person in question returns to his analyses, legitimate, correct, a result of his own thinking, knowledge and ideas. The person becomes once again himself or preserves his credibility further on and may be used subsequently, on another project regarding the informational war or spreading another theme.

While in the USA there is lobby law, the public exposure of paid positions in this category, and a transparent formula of the amount of money received to convey certain themes, this instrument is missing in Europe, but not the lobby agencies. It is a legal instrument, sometimes immoral, but which is used in combination with propaganda and taking control or altering the media space in the informational war framework.

The third level of action is the most insidious. It is highly illegal, which targets subtler components of the informational war. It is linked to PsyOps – elaborate psychological operations, geared towards influencing the behaviour of the target. The target can be military or civilian depending on the situation.[2] This component of informational war has a much more profound level of access, where it reaches deep into the common beliefs, psychological state and deeper fears of the social organism. Here the disseminated information matters, and especially the effect created by information on the target audience, namely the shaping and creating or deepening of fears, creating collective emotions, preparing the public to react to future events in a directed way, previously prepared and pondered.

The objectives are achieved using false news, personalities and experts with known moral references within society, directed to certain positions, but the target is not the immediate information but creating the context for an emotional public reaction facing a subsequent event, that will appear. Dirigisme in relation to the subsequent reaction is created by accessing subtle levels of the subconscious and creating patterns of thought by repeating some sequences of this kind at predetermined intervals, teaching the brain and the subconscious to react in a certain manner to this type of information and emotional pre-set stimuli. And the goal is to determine a specific collective public response, when it is needed to pressure and alter the action of a decision maker in times of crisis.

The instruments used are a combination of narratives, alternative ideas, planting of doubt, promoting and validating lies as credible. They will enter the subconscious as perceptions of truth, exaggerated and directed interpretations, exaggerations, manipulation, misinformation, with all the components, the effects of trolls' actions (directed commentators in cyberspace). Here as well, the components for conditioning the target audience are built through actions at the subliminal and subconscious level, the inoculation of constructed perception, accessing the basic emotions and their orientation – fear, humiliation and hope.

The functioning of the informational war is done in an integrated manner, on all three dimensions, with deliberate dosages and a vast instrumentation built in time. Important resources are used for such actions and the component is most frequently moved towards the military space. It is an instrument whose relevance is just being discovered and its impact can be extremely powerful.

The informational war in Russian documents

It is important to know what the Russian Federation understands by "soft power", by informational war and its mode of action, which are its instruments and the way it intends to apply them. More than this, the practical application must be understood and how these policies have been addressed in clear terms must be analysed. In order to form an overall picture, there are three important documents of the Russian Federation: "The Concept of the Foreign Policy of the Russian Federation" (2013), "The Military Doctrine" (December 2014) and the statement of Vladimir Putin on 18 March 2014, the day the Crimea was annexed by the Russian Federation. These three documents are the benchmark in Russia's foreign affairs, defence and security.

We have identified the development and the presence of concepts such as soft power, hybrid action and informational warfare, concepts that are important parts of Russian soft power. Furthermore, the content description of these concepts, shows us how that these instruments are perceived and defined, and by means of such research we can see how they have been applied and used in reality.

From a certain point of view, the humanitarian dimension of Russia's foreign policy involves "soft power" only as an additional instrument. Thus, soft power becomes "a practical means of the humanitarian dimension in the foreign policy, which could be an answer to the dilemmas Russia is facing at the regional level".[3] More than this, the concept of "soft power" is not limited only to the ability to influence, or even the one to manipulate the public opinion in a target country, but *"includes a well formed partnership idea with benefits in the short and long term"* (Makarychev 2011: 2).

In Russia, Soft power is considered a part of "Humanitarian Affairs". It is link to the use of Russian language in the post-Soviet space (and special status of the Russian language), as well as to the special rights of the Russians, Russian speakers and "Compatriots" (persons living in the former Soviet Union or their decendents). Russia still holds some attractive sources to the post-Soviet countries, elements which are being exploited: language, common culture, energy resources (Ćwiek-Karpowicz 2012: 5).

In addition, an important period in which the policies of this kind have been experienced and when it was necessary to apply soft power was during the "colour revolutions", in Georgia (2003) and Ukraine (2004), in which Russian propaganda outlined the idea that the colour revolutions are an instrument designed by the Occident to change the regimes in the former Soviet space and to impose Western liberal democracy and not an "independent system".

The soft power concept is included in the *"Concept for the Foreign Policy of the Russian Federation"* and is correlated to the informational war, public diplomacy and cultivating the international image of Russia. More than this, there is a definition of a good and legitimate kind of soft power and an illegitimate and wrong soft power.

In Article 20, Chapter II of *"The Foreign Policy of the Russian Federation in the Modern World",* for example, soft power is defined as "a comprehensive instrumentation for achieving foreign policy goals, which build on the potential of the civil society, information, cultural methods and other technologies and alternatives to the traditional diplomacy".[4] The document stresses that the soft power "is an indispensable component of the modern international relations".[5] The same article also remarks that "at the same time, the increasing global competition and the existence of some crises generate a risk towards the destructive and illegal use of soft power and of the concepts regarding human rights. These negative interpretations make possible the political pressures on sovereign states, the intervention in their internal affairs, destabilising their political situation, manipulating the public opinion, inclusively under the pretext of financing projects regarding the cultural and human rights abroad".[6]

Here we outline the definition of a negative type of soft power, which actually describes the perception of the Russian Federation regarding the influence created by projects in the field of human rights, which in part have an "illegal and destructive" use, "presume the immixture in the internal affairs of a state", "exercise political pressure "and "destabilize the political situation by manipulating the public opinion". This approach emphasises, through a number of negative nuances and attributes, the fear of the colour revolutions and the monitoring of human rights, as well as the fear of hierarchy in the principles of stability versus democracy and human rights. Also, it is the point in which soft power is directly related to "manipulating the public opinion" – this way it has components of informational warfare.

In Chapter III, "International Humanitarian Cooperation and Human Rights", Article 39, the "foreign policy" objectives of Russia are stated, "as a country dedicated to the universal democratic values, including the human rights and liberties".[7] In addition, a "priority" is to establish "a positive image of Russia, worthy of the high status of its culture, education, science, sport and the achievements in the development of the civil society, as well as the participation in assistance programmes for the development countries ... modelling instruments to improve its perception in the entire world improving the application of soft power and identifying the best forms of activities in this field, which would take into account both the international experience, as well as the national peculiarities and would participate in building mechanisms of interaction with the civil society and experts ... the further development of the regulatory framework in the aforementioned domain".[8]

Once again, Russia sees soft power as having an important influence in building an international image and perception regarding its developments and policy and insists on promoting the international experience and national achievements. But do not forget about the "negative soft power", as described above, including "the development of a regulatory framework", in order to limit the negative effects, meaning the colour revolutions.

The same concern for accurate information and international perception (which aim at avoiding the effects of negative soft power and of the informational warfare) appeared in a special chapter entitled "Information Support for Foreign Policy Activities". Its main concern is "the real and accurate information" correlated with Russia's actions, which means promoting its own narratives and perspectives on the evolutions and events. Article 40 states that "an important element of the foreign policy activities of the Russian Federation is making available (for the world wide audience) the complete and precise information regarding its position on major international issues, the foreign policy initiatives and actions of the Russian Federation, the development of processes and plans on social and economic development policy, as well as the cultural and scientific achievements in Russia".[9]

Even clearer is the description from Article 41, in which the emphasis lies on an "objective perception"[10] of Russia, achieved through "effective means of influence on the public opinion and the information from abroad".[11] We have here a direct description of an informational war and the projection of an alternative reality for a specific audience, an endeavour called "public diplomacy", an activity standing at the limit of propaganda and informational war:

Russia, through public diplomacy, will try to ensure an objective perception, to develop its own effective means of influence on information, to strengthen the role of mass media in the international information environment, offering them the essential support. At the same time, it will actively participate in the international cooperation regarding the information domain and will take the necessary steps to counter the cyber threats to its sovereignty and security. The possibilities offered by the new information and communication technologies will be widely used in these activities. Russia will try to develop a set of legal and ethical rules for the safe use of these technologies".[12]

We find here a reference to "the informational threats" and to the need to take "the necessary measures" to "counteract" these threats. We do not have a precise description of what these "informational threats" might mean, but the text, and especially the context, provide insight of what it might assume as threats to the sovereignty and security of Russia: ideas and information that are different from those issued by the Kremlin and the affiliated mass media. The precise meaning is found in the rest of the document, having several directions. Firstly, it is based on cultivating prestige and forming an image of Russia by promoting its interests and defending the Russian citizens, the Russophones – Russian language speakers and compatriots, meaning residents of the former Soviet Union (together with citizens who left the Russian Federation). These categories do not exist in real life, but they are tools of the post-imperial syndrome. And assuming a protection of rights represents a powerful instrument of the informational war in the post-Soviet space. In a given case, the one regarding the Russian speakers, conceptually, it was taken over from Francophonie, the French institution created as an instrument to cure France of its own post-imperial syndrome. Similarly, the Compatriots Policy – people who remember and cherish life in the former Soviet Union – is an alternative to the British inhabitants of the British Commonwealth/ Commonwealth of Nations, an institution of the United Kingdom. The difference is that Russia adapts these institutions and assumes special rights in the countries where these categories exist and creates instruments to intervene in the internal affairs of these countries.

Thus, if we look at the country's objectives, Article 3 notes that "the rapid acceleration of the global processes, in the first period of the 21st century and the new tendencies in the global development, require new approaches to key issues and a new vision on Russia's foreign policy priorities, being taken into account Russia's increased responsibility to establish the international agenda and its ability to shape the international relations system".[13] In Article 4 we find out that "in line with the main objective of national security – ensuring the protection of the individual, the society and the state – the foreign policy should concentrate primarily on pursuing the following fundamental objectives: a) ensuring security, by protecting and strengthening sovereignty and territorial integrity and ensuring a central position within the international community, as an influential and competitive pole in the modern world... g) ensuring the legitimate rights and interests of the Russian citizens and compatriots, as well as promoting Russia's perspective, in various international formats, on issues related to human rights; h) promoting the Russian language and strengthening its position in the world, disseminating information regarding the achievements of the Russian population and strengthening the Russian diaspora".[14]

Russia's policy, which presupposes its own interpretation of democracy, human rights and the rule of law, the so-called sovereign democracy, has a facet in Chapter II "The Foreign Policy of the Russian Federation and the Modern World", Article 13 "for the first time in modern history, the global competition takes place at a civilization level, through values and development models, based on the various universal principles of democracy and market economy, that are starting to compete. The cultural and civilisation diversity of the world becomes increasingly obvious".[15]

In the same document we have references to hybrid warfare and the use of all instruments in order to achieve the goals and objectives of the Russian foreign policy, inclusively the informational war. In Chapter III, "Priorities of the Russian Federation in addressing the global issues", Article 27, it is mentioned that "the diverse and complex nature of international problems requires prioritisation in the foreign policy of the Russian Federation. The use of political instruments, diplomatic, legal, military, economic, financial, et cetera in solving the foreign policy problems must correspond with the interests of Russia's foreign policy; additionally, these instruments must be in coordination with all branches of power, as well as with the appropriate agencies". When discussing

"The emergence of a new world order", Article 28 points out: "Russia is pursuing a policy aimed at creating a stable and sustainable system, based on the international law and the principle of equality, mutual respect and non-interference in the internal affairs of states. The system proposes to offer security for every member of the international community in the political, military, economic, informational, humanitarian sector etcetera".[16]

The Intelligence domain is often used, as well as the combination of political, military, economic, informational sectors, with the humanitarian field. The first relates to the description of hybrid war as well as to the informational war. Through the humanitarian field, Russia understands defending its population and compatriots, but, also tries to assume a special responsibility towards "the Slavic nation", a precursor of the "Russian World" concept which Moscow promotes, as shown in the "Humanitarian International Cooperation and Human Rights" chapter.

In Article 39 it is written:

> "as a country dedicated to the universal democratic values, including human rights and liberties, Russia considers that its objectives are:
>
> c) the integrated development of the diplomatic and consular protection system of the Russian citizens abroad that are subject to international law and international treaties concluded by the Russian Federation to strengthen its effectiveness, including by expanding the network of consular offices abroad;
>
> d) protection of legitimate rights of the compatriots living abroad, based on international law and treaties signed by the Russian Federation as partner, inclusively through expanding and consolidating the area of Russian language and culture;
>
> e) supporting the compatriots' organisations to enable them to effectively back up their rights, in their countries of residence, while preserving the cultural and ethnic identity of the Russian diaspora and its links to the historic homeland; to provide conditions for the voluntary relocation in the Federation of the compatriots who wish to do so;
>
> f) facilitating the learning and the widespread use of the Russian language as an integral part of the world culture and an international and interethnic instrument of communication;
>
> g) promoting the interstate cultural and humanitarian relations among the slave peoples".[17]

Perhaps the most interesting element is the relationship Russia has with the symbolism linked to the Second World War and its role in this context. This symbolism is of primary importance, and the same Article 39 contains a reference to the canonical defending of its approach, its role and to the symbolic victory in the wartime: h) the strong counteracting of the extremist manifestations, neo-Nazi, or any forms of racial discrimination, the aggressive nationalism, anti-Semitism and xenophobia, as well as the attempts to rewrite history using confrontation and revanchist politics at the world level; help de-politicize the historical discussions in order to ensure their exclusive academic character".[18]

Equally important for soft power are the previsions found in "The Military Doctrine of the Russian Federation", issued in December 2014. Soft power, its negative form, has a special relevance in the military field. Firstly, Russia divides the security threats in two: "dangers" and "threats". "Danger" is a less significant threat, present, but included into a second method of reaction.

Therefore, Article 12 differentiates between "the main external military dangers":

> "k) the use of information and communication technologies for military – political purposes against actions contrary to the international law, which affects the political independence, the territorial integrity of states and that threatens the international peace, at the global level and the regional stability
> l) setting in the states neighbouring the Russian Federation, regimes imposed inclusively as a result of diverting the legitimate public authorities, whose policies threaten the interests of the Russian Federation".[19]

Therefore, the informational war is noted as such in the military doctrine, as well as a description of the meaning of such dangers in the international as well as the national arena. But more important is the fact that the danger represents "establishing in the neighbouring states imposed political regimes, whose policies threaten the interests of the Russian Federation".[20] The Russian Federation tries to supervise the type of regime (Liberal Democrat) in the neighbouring countries and considers them to be a threat to Moscow's interests. This is a form of limited sovereignty, a Soviet-era Brezhnev doctrine, in which the very sovereignty of its neighbours must be imposed by the Russian interests.

The document also illustrates the content and substance of the hybrid war concept in Article 15 "The nature and characteristics of modern conflict":

> "a) the integrated use of military, political, economic, informational force and other non-military measures, implemented with the widespread use of the protest potential of the population and of the special operation forces;
> c) the effect on the enemy from its territory, simultaneously in the global informational space, the industrial, aerospace, land and sea one;
> j) the use of political forces and financing some social movements.[21]

This definition, which includes the sphere of information, is of prime importance because its perception and definition show us the manner in which the Russian Federation wishes to use this type of war. And this could be found in the entire post-Soviet space, in eastern Ukraine, but also in Central and Eastern Europe and in the Western Balkans.

And this is already mentioned in Article 21 "The main duties of the Russian Federation to prevent the armed conflicts": "creating conditions to bring back the usage of information and communication technologies in the military and in formulating the political objectives of action, contrary to the international law, sovereignty, political independence, territorial integrity and which constitutes an international threat".[22]

Now to the analysis of the third document, Vladimir Putin's speech, dated 18 March, 2014, 3:50 pm. After Putin outlined a complete historical context and references to international law (referendum and the will of the people), other arguments entered the process. The possibility of Ukraine joining NATO, a fact connected to the military doctrine and linked to the free will and sovereign decision of a country, but limited to Russia's interests, appeared eight months later: "we expected Ukraine to remain our good neighbour, we hoped that the Russian citizens and the Russian speakers in Ukraine, especially in the Southeast and in the Crimea, will live in a friendly condition, democratic and civilized, one that would protect their rights in accordance with the international law". President Vladimir Putin said that this did not happen and that "Ukraine had a different agenda: they prepared another government; they wanted to seize power and stopped at nothing. They resorted to terror, murder and riots. The nationalists, neo-Nazis, Russophobes and anti-Semites executed the coup. They continue to set the tone in Ukraine". "It is also evident that there is no legitimate executive authority in Ukraine at this moment, no one with whom to discuss".[23]

Therefore, the revolution and the Maidan in Kiev were presented as "a military coup" supported by the United States and the West, and not as a natural protest of the Ukrainian people. The declaration states that "those who opposed the coup were immediately threatened. Of course, the first line here was the Crimea, the Russian-speaking part from the Crimea. Given this, the residents of the Crimea and Sevastopol have appealed to Russia for help".[24]

So the annexation addresses the protection of rights of the Russian population, Russian speakers and the compatriots, that created a special right for Russia to interfere through a hybrid war in the Crimea, by taking institutions and blocking the Ukrainian troops, holding a referendum and by the annexation of Ukrainian territory. The Russian President raised the following problem "secondly, and most importantly – what exactly are we infringing? True, the president of the Russian Federation received permission from the upper house of the Parliament to use the Armed Forces in Ukraine. However, strictly speaking, no one has acted on this permission yet. The Russian Armed Forces have never entered the Crimea; they were already there, in accordance to an international agreement. It is true that we have increased the presence of the forces. However – this is something I want everyone to hear and know – we have not exceeded the staff limit in the Crimea, which is established at 25.000, because it was not needed".[25]

Hence, there is no invasion, since the Russian forces were already on the field and new forces "were introduced" on the basis of an international agreement, even without Ukraine's consent. Russia did not need this consent, because "they do not have a recognized government" and in Kiev "the nationalists, neo-Nazis, Russophobes and the anti-Semites executed the coup".[26]

The most interesting part of the speech is the direct reference to the colour revolution: "Here were a whole series of "controlled colour revolutions".

Evidently, the people in the nations where these events took place, were over-whelmed by tyranny and poverty, by their lack of perspectives; but these feelings have been cynically taken advantage of. Standards that do not correspond to these nations and their way of life, their culture etcetera have been imposed. As a result, instead of democracy and freedom, it was chaos, outbreaks of violence and a series of transformations".[27] "A similar situation took place in Ukraine. In 2004, in order to push the necessary candidate to the presidential elections, they thought of some kind of the third round, which was not provided by the law. It was absurd and a mockery to the Constitution. And now, they invented an organised army and well-equipped with militants".[28] "We understand what is happening; we understand that these actions were directed against Ukraine and Russia and against the Eurasian integration".[29] Thus the Russian perception and moreover, the perception of President Vladimir Putin on soft power, is shaping the informational war and the colour revolutions. Everything is against Russia: these actions were against Ukraine and Russia, against the Eurasian integration – the new project to rebuild the Soviet Union in a different form. This is achieved through using Russia's soft power policies, the humanitarian policy, the policy of the Russian compatriots. Because President Putin tells us in other words "let me say one thing. Millions of Russians and Russian-speaking people live in Ukraine and will continue to do so. Russia will always defend their interests through political, diplomatic and legal means. But it should be above all in the interest of Ukraine".[30]

And, here again, we find indications regarding the informational war from Vladimir Putin's perspective. In the same speech, he remarked: "obviously, we will encounter opposition, but this is a decision that we must take for ourselves. Are we ready to constantly defend our national interests, or are we holding back? Some Western politicians are already threatening us with sanctions and problems on the domestic front. I would like to know what exactly goes through their minds: a disparate bouquet of "national traitors" or will they put us in a social and economic situation that is getting worse, so as to cause public discontent? We believe such statements are irresponsible and clearly aggressive and we will respond to them accordingly".[31]

The actions conducted by "a disparate bunch of national traitors", these are the elements of informational warfare, along with NGOs financed by the West, or the political forces which finance and lead the social movements. This explains the policy against the NGOs funded from external sources in Russia, considered as "foreign agents".

Militarising the information in the Russian Federation

The Russian Federation proposed, at the beginning of the 21st century, as a way to engage in conflict, the hybrid war. It employed it in Crimea, when the "little green men" – who were, in fact, the special troops of the Russian army, as explicitly acknowledged by President Putin – led the assault against the public institutions in the region, blocked the Ukrainian military units in the peninsula and overthrew the legitimate authorities, replacing them with a bunch of poorly trained adventurers, supported by a pseudo-referendum realised after the model of the Austrian Anschluss, with guns loaded and ready to fire.

They did it afterwards in Eastern Ukraine, combining in the same space all the instruments of this war, which also has a classical component, and insurgency war, and terrorist actions, and war through intermediaries, and organised crime and cyber warfare, and economic warfare, and asymmetric warfare and informational warfare and psychological warfare, and limited war, and war without limits, without rules. These instruments of war were used all together, in a combination appropriate for the time, place, the operation or the objective to be achieved.

The Kremlin's use of information as a weapon is not new, but its sophistication and intensity are increasing. (Lucas & Pomeranzev 2016). Russia's concept of hybrid warfare relies heavily on information warfare, being clear that Russia is actively using its information warfare techniques in support of a hybrid-warfare effort to achieve its current objectives (Snegovaya 2015: 9-10). Since 2012, Putin accelerated efforts to resurrect "active measures", while the full range of the Kremlin's active measures capabilities was on display during the early stages of Russia's intervention in Ukraine following the 2013 Maidan revolution (Polyakova et al. 2016: 3).

The Russian informational war carried out in Ukraine and worldwide, was led directly from the Kremlin. Former employees of the Russian public television stations recently showed that the TV stations have turned into a propaganda machine for the regime, just as in the ideological war period. The transcript of the meetings with former employees of VGTRK mass media holding (which includes the channels "Rossia-1", "Rossia-2", "Rossia-24" and many others) – was presented by the former deputy editor of the channel "Rossia-24" and "Rossia-2", Aleksandr Orlov. Orlov was dismissed in July 2014 because of the commentaries on social networks in support of the Russian opposition politician Aleksei Navalnîi.

It all started with the meeting in February 2014, when in Kiev, in Euromaidan, and the first protesters were dying. All employees were brought together and told that "the Cold War" had begun. "An epoch beside which the years 70–80 represented a trill of birds was brought into discussion and that those who do not wish to participate can find another field of activity outside the news channel" – affirms Orlov. The Russian authorities wanted blood on the screens and an increased media pressure on the public in order to counter the relative natural closeness between Russia and Ukraine and the sympathy of the Russians for the Ukrainians, who were having success in a new orange type of revolution and recalibrating the path towards West.

On Fridays, the chiefs of the television stations were summoned for the briefing meeting in the Kremlin, where the publishing plans for the next week were handed over to them. It was compulsory to have at least one story per day about the Crimea, Donetsk and Kiev. At first, the meetings were led by Alexey Gromov, the first deputy secretary of the Presidential Administration of Vladimir Putin, and later by the press secretary of Vladimir Putin, Dmitry Peskov.

The approaches taken regarding the events in Ukraine, the new leadership in Kiev, was exclusively the official one: at first, the *"coup d'etat"* in Ukraine dominated the screens as well as "the revolt in Eastern Ukraine", fearing "the fascists" had installed themselves in Kiev. These were considered a junta, a bunch of extremist nationalists going in to kill the Russian minority, which is why the Eastern regions, Novorossia in its entirety, had to leave, either by becoming independent under the Russian protectorate, or by incorporating with Russia. All new leaders in Kiev were called "bandirovtsi", meaning members of the nationalist–anarchist groups of Bandera's robbers, the legendary hero who fought against the Russians and Germans for Ukraine's independence.[32] As for the Crimea, "a legal referendum" decided to join Russia which was "ready to rescue them from the clutches of the Ukrainian fascists", from Kiev. Crimea may be considered a test-case for Russia in trying out this new form of warfare where hybrid, asymmetric warfare, combining an intensive information campaign, cyber warfare and the use of highly trained Special Operation Forces, play a key role (Bērziņš et al. 2015: 4).

There was not one word in the papers or in the public political arguments about the fact that the Parliament in Kiev, the Verkhovna Rada, with the same composition chosen during Yanukovich's administration, had voted the new leaders and the new government; about the legal elections and the little Russian green men, the regular troops that seized the government buildings and blocked the military units, taking over the Crimea with a referendum made within the range of automatic rifles belonging to the unmarked occupation troops. "Everything was under personal control. When the first negotiations took place in Minsk and there were rumours some kind of peace may be concluded, the ban on using words like "fascist", "Bandera", "junta" appeared. Then the situation was tense again and everything was resumed" – says the former assisting chief editor. As a result, the competition between TV channels disappeared – all the materials were shared among televisions, so the TV stations had about the same topics. Propaganda was made unitary with the same materials, the same images and the same message to deliver, as in wartime, without the opportunity to treat subjects freely. Even during Perestroika, the media in Russia had more freedom.

The VGTRK employees acknowledge that, in terms of editorial policy, they lacked freedom – everything was done in accordance with the instructions coming from the Kremlin. "The personal control regime encompassed even the weather news. By all means we had to invite a certain meteorologist – a famous fortune-teller in Russia, so that he may announce that in Ukraine it will be a terrible winter. There is a general tendency to exaggerate, "Ukraine depends on Russia, Moscow will no longer give gas, and the rebellious Ukrainians will freeze without the Russian gas", was the message that was repeated in the winter of 2014–2015, the first winter of the war in eastern Ukraine. As the Russian television stations employees claim, only a quarter of the journalists believed in the content of reports about Ukraine, made after scripts written by the Kremlin.[33]

Hence, the presence of the informational war represents a reality in Donbas. But not only there: in the rest of Ukraine as well, and in all the independent states in the post-Soviet space, and in Eastern Europe, and in the founding states of the European Union, and overseas. Everywhere. Where propaganda, political technologists and classic agitprop combine with psychological operations in an effort to create a parallel reality, consisting of bits of truths, interpretations, syllogisms, sophistries, inferences with logical fractures, juxtaposition of facts without direct causal link, massive propaganda and a great deal of lies. A figment with scent of veracity in regard to which the arguments, facts, reality and truth of evolution of actions no longer matter, because all are replaced with the altered perception and directed from the outside of the target audience.

The fact that Russia has applied this technique for a long time on worldwide subjects did not make the Russian Defence Minister try to avoid public exposure on this subject, on the contrary. Present at the "Media-As" award ceremony for Russian journalists, mainly from the official and officious media, the Russian Defence Minister, Sergei Shoigu, declared that the mass media represents one of the new types of modern weapons, which over the years brought both victories and defeats to Russia.

"Lately, the mass media encompasses a great deal of aspects and can bring serious damage. We realise now that a picture, a word, a camera, the Internet, the information, in general, have become a type of weapon, which can be well or poorly used. Currently, a piece of information held by a wrong person can become evidence, a prosecutor, a judge, an executioner. I would not like to use this weapon, the mass media, in a negative way", added Sergey Shoigu, according to the Russian media.[34]

Basically, the Russian Defence Minister reveals unusual things. It is known, but never acknowledged officially and formally, in no case at this level and by a Russian Minister of Defence. Thereby, the press has been considered for a long time as a weapon. The press is extensively used, and its new capabilities are exploited by Russia within the bosom of the West and the states concerned. Wins and losses are recognised of a war in which Moscow uses the media as a weapon.

Shoigu indirectly explains censorship as well as controlling the mass media in Russia, and avoiding democratic rules. The open society and fundamental human rights are considered by the Russian military structures for informational war as a weakness and a vulnerability of democratic Western societies and is viewed as a vulnerability by Russia. Against the societies where media is used in its real capacity, with its proper purpose, to offer a public service, to inform the population. The media is a weapon strategically used, with planned actions and specific military objectives. And the Internet, websites and the social media in any language, were flooded with a regiment of trolls paid 500–700 euros per month.[35]

The US administration was informed by the Foreign Affairs Committee of the House of Representatives about the need to counter the "militarization and the conversion of information into a weapon of war by Russia". The notification represented the result of some hearings within the commission and referred to the need of the US government "to invest in the global media war".[36]

Ed Royce, the chairman of the committee, argued that Russia's propaganda machine undermines democratic stability and promotes violence and cleavage in Eastern European societies. Among those interviewed included critics of Russia, from the former journalists of the Russia Today station in English, currently a member of the Sputnik platform for propaganda and informational war of the Russian Federation.[37]

Peter Pomerantsev, Helle Dale and Liz Wahl were those involved in these hearings and offered accounts of their own experiences from the time when they worked in the Russian media in English, this experience occurring even before the creation of the new instrument of Russia's informational war.

Peter Pomerantsev from the Legatum Institute in London, being questioned before the committee of the Chamber, said that a European and an US instrument were urgently needed in order to counter the propaganda, falsehoods and distortions widely promoted by Russia, actions that affect many spectators in the West and in the post-Soviet states. Operations setting up groups fighting against the national interests of the concerned countries, against the US, the NATO membership and for embracing the "equidistant" positions of Russia are being observed. "Russia launched an informational war against the West, and we are losing it today", says Pomerantsev.[38]

The debate is not new and was conducted at the European level as well. Although in a less virulent and more reserved manner in considering information as part of war, the EU decided to set up appropriate instruments at the European level to genuinely present what the European Union stands for and which are the benefits of the EU membership or implementing the Association Agreements reforms. Frank-Walter Steinmeier, the German Foreign Minister, promised the Baltic States aid regarding this war, consisting of preparing journalists in Germany with the right tools to counter Russia on this front.[39]

The most exposed countries to this propaganda are those where political parties or supporters of Russia, as well as those of a "balanced policy" – all of them financed by Russia - already exist. Their aim is to fight for imposing a narrative saying that Russia's interests should be observed, calling them the "legitimate concerns" of Russia, referring specifically to Russia's involvement in the agreements with the Eastern Partnership states. The post–Soviet states are the most exposed because here the Russian minorities already exist and they promote parallel agendas favourable to Moscow. But the instrumentation extends to other national minorities in these countries as well, as it recently happened in the Odessa region, by establishing the "Verkhovna Bessarabia", a separatist project conducted under Russian influence.

Moreover, in such states, the Russian media is still dominant. The Republic of Moldova is the most influenced by Russia and the Baltic states at the tail of the rankings, slightly behind Georgia. The capacity of Russian television to influence other states is based on Russian linguistic affinity, especially of the minorities in the former Soviet space, and this capacity to influence creates a formidable weapon that was countered only by banning the stations or blocking news dissemination and the electoral programmes on these stations. This is an interim solution, in states with fragile and emerging democracies, but this solution cannot last.

But propaganda and the subtler elements of the informational war can be found also in the countries resistant to Russian propaganda from historical experience.

Romania, too, has been the target of such an offensive by creating groups from the social networks, by building instruments of the civil society (NGOs) or by the inoculation in the mainstream media of topics that would serve the Russian plans. The freedom of speech and of assembly means that, in these EU countries, the combating of such propaganda is to be done through arguments, correct information, transparency and appropriate communication, at the official level, as well through discussions with various categories of the population for the demystifying or the public display of methods used by the instruments of the informational war.

And to take this step, first, it is necessary to acknowledge that Romania is in a full informational war and that it needs instruments to counter the aggression on this informational component of the fourth generation hybrid war (Chifu & Nantoi 2016: 40).

How the informational war works. The components of the informational war

The informational war[40] substantially exceeds trivial propaganda and even strategic communication exercises. Indeed, we are not talking about the legal free circulation of ideas, not about the lobby campaigns, PR, and public diplomacy in the case of a state. Propaganda is the first pillar, lobbying (which involves using important resources to promote inherent ideas, narratives or images) is the second pillar, whereas the informational war concerns the actions which alter decisions, influence the decisions in foreign policy, security and defence, mostly through mass media and the pressure that the citizens, having an inoculated certainty, can artificially exert over the authority. The Russian Federation, according to the previous categorization, has several categories of objectives.

Firstly, the direct explicit promotion of Russia through its leaders' messages, promotes its version of the truth and its official narratives. Here propaganda and lobbying are mainly used in a non-transparent form but largely legal.

The second component aims at planting doubt, amplifying artificial dilemmas, using conspiracy theories, but already using a whole scaffold of psychological warfare instruments and for creating forgeries and using instruments to confuse the target population. The matter is no longer about questioning any statement made by officials, nor about developing the critical spirit (which is part of an extremely healthy society and even the main instrument in fighting the informational war, together with education), but about inoculation through fakery, lies, subtle propaganda elements, playing on areas of personal sensitivity, capitalizing on the democratic inclinations of the Western populations, of pseudo-credible narratives, plausible, but artificially constructed on fake news. The purpose is not to promote Russia, but to create a mass of people who practice suspicion as a rule, profess criticism at any cost, and absorb and circulate conspiracy theories and abolish any element of decision or of internal or relational construction.

The third component is aimed at building the common enemy, the adversary, who is necessary to keep Russian society united, to impress the need for unity and support of the leadership on account of the existence of the common enemy. It is about the US, NATO, the EU as main enemies, and liberal democracy, the open society, human rights, "the colour revolutions", as instruments of a Western informational war. Also, on this level, the enemies are identified, and campaigns to derogate them from their credibility are promoted.

It is the classic case informational war where Turkey and President Erdoğan became targets after the downing of the Russian aircraft which entered the Turkish territory and the killing of the pilots by the Turkmen populations in Northern Syria. We observed in Romania a campaign to equate Turkey with Russia, and Putin with Erdoğan, which was designed to collapse political and general public support at the population level, for Turkey and for Turkey's entrance into the EU.

Fourthly, the objectives of the informational war campaigns aim not only at immediately achieving those objectives, through the content of information, but, as we saw above, building some states of mind and approaches based on fears and common reactions, as an effect of the created context, accessing the subtle levels of the subconscious, conditioning reactions and conducting certain future reflexes towards possible actions, facts and events that will unfold. At the appropriate time, as we saw above, conditioned groups react as they were scheduled to do and alter the objective option of the decision maker for a solution to the ongoing crisis.

The fifth objective that we identified is that of building the instrumentation for the informational war, based on the actions conducted using this precise instrument. Herein the losers and the discontented of the liberal democracy are identified and taken over, the mistakes of the administration are exploited as well, and the facts of the events are wrongly interpreted and willingly so, and then combined with blatant lies and misinformation. Within this component of Russia's informational war, the recruitment of supporters is conducted, creating supporting groups, the mass of manoeuvre, that will form the local instruments, "the enemy within the fortress" in the informational war, namely:

- groups of operative agents and neither of the local Russian network of spies or supporters is involved;
- the mass of manoeuvre consisting of useful idiots who embrace indiscriminatingly any topic they find appealing, without understanding it, due to the feeling of imitation, rebelliousness, silliness or adventure. Herein join those who follow a certain fashion of the moment, whether the inclination towards "being equidistant towards various options" or those who argue "listening to the Russians as well, they might also have their righteousness" (Chifu &

Nantoi 2016: 41) as approaches *per se*, and not respecting the real arguments of the discussed topics;

- the most complicated and valuable part of an action meant to build some instruments from the pressure and support groups is represented by the identification, selection, preparation and conditioning of those who became convinced by the alternative narratives, who are aware and consenting multipliers in the informational war, who have discernment and the intellectual capacity, sometimes they even come to recognize the falsehoods, their manipulation and use by third parties in the informational war, but are driven by the pride which prevents them to recognize, in time, that they have been used. It is the most dangerous area, which is being built today in all the targeted Western countries (Chifu & Nantoi 2016: 41).

Beside these, we can add other dimensions of informational war located in the visible spectrum:

- the construction of attacks towards third parties or directing some interpretations on matters of interest, in order to achieve or support Russian interests;
- actions to break transatlantic cohesion and European cohesion, building doubt and exaggeration of the national ideal of exceptionalism in order to block the common projects and the solidarity of the West;
- the war of trolls and controlling and directing discussions in social networks and the Internet and guiding them towards different directions of ideational development;
- controlling the ideas and the social constructs in the virtual field in the form of blocking the unwanted comments and debates and promoting advantageous actions;
- the artificial amplifying of the visibility of some ideas, people and groups and, of course, removing the visibility of others who are inappropriate to the objectives of the abuser (see the famous law of oblivion and the instrumentation used for the transformation into a ghost on the Internet,[41] not accessible to the public). (Chifu & Nantoi 2016: 44)

Most of the time the action unfolds in a concerted, planned and integrated way, on all three dimensions – media propaganda, lobbying and psychological operations. All the objectives are simultaneously pursued: those to achieve immediate, direct results and those to build a favourable context or preparation for the instruments of informational warfare developed in the future – conditioning or creating pressure and support groups, inclusively of the convinced groups.

Approaching and planning the informational war is conducted at three levels: global – the themes of interest to the Russian Federation, of context, where the narrative should be maintained; then regional – the former Soviet space (with the particularity of the "humanitarian" instrument, of defending the Russians, the Russian speakers and the compatriots), the Eastern Flank of EU-NATO, the heart of the West i.e. the EU and the US; and the third area of interest, and respectively local – at the national level.

The brains of the whole operation, most likely situated at the Russian military body level, have the force to adapt and exploit in real-time any opportunity that has arisen based on the events conducted globally, regionally and locally. Not infrequently, our analysis has demonstrated the ability to bring on to the field Russian actors with declarations of opportunity, but also other well-thought-of international actors with credibility in the third spaces or local actors stimulated and motivated to react in times of need.

Everything seems like a great devised machinery in which everyone is both an actor, and a pawn, and a player, and a leader, at the same time, the President Vladimir Putin, the Defence Minister, the Chief of the General Staff, and the Foreign Minister. On one side we have a thorough and strict planning, to access and capacity to determine these outputs of frontline leaders in the case of Russia. In defense, the reaction should be an ideological profound cohesion of all the targeted actors, in an informational war, a cohesion that must be so strong and reactions so precise, that they can consult react immediately, accurately and coherently to any such attack.. This variant is just as implausible as the ability to plan strictly and extensively, hence the possibility that we might deal with a combination between the two components – planning and internal impulse due to strong ideological cohesion – that makes such a mechanism of informational war function so precisely and have such an impact.

Ways of counteracting the informational war

The awareness of the informational war's existence and the creation of national, international and institutional counteracting mechanisms, subsequently of rules and norms of action in the instrumentation related to the informational warfare would be the first variants of reaction. We have international players that are more experienced or others that are weaker, more vulnerable to informational attacks. Aggression using the instrumentation of informational war is extremely broad as form of emergence.

We must remember that the informational war launched by the Russian Federation, according to their own public programmatic documents, cover the entire world, does not stop at the post-Soviet space, nor at the level of the former socialist states situated today in the Eastern Flank of the EU and NATO. Moscow felt aggressed by the extension of the values of a liberal democracy, universally declared, and invented the sovereign democracy, subsequently the administered democracy, controlled. It felt attacked by enlargement of the EU and NATO values area, inclusively through the instruments of the free trade space, culture, and of values and ideas. It considered the colour revolutions as a means of informational war, and sought to build its own instruments such as the so-called humanitarian policies and defending the rights of the Russians, of Russian speakers and of compatriots.[42]

Then the Russian Federation rejected the liberal democracy and proposed instead Dugin's conservatism and traditionalism, subsequently his Eurasianism (Clover 2014), and later on supported the nationalisms in order to counter the European communitarism. The fact is that the informational war proved to be implemented in the very heart of Europe – see the case of the famous Russian girl who had allegedly been raped by immigrants, a case that, amplified and sanctioned too late by the German institutions, strongly shook the Chancellor Mrs. Merkel.[43]

And operations like these can be found in France, in Europe as a whole and in the US. It concerns everybody, and the lack of attention or of reaction to the informational war can create monsters and late reactions, when control over the public space is already lost.

The Western states, the established democracies, are the best equipped to deal with the informational war. But they are also not immune. Thus, the existence of real media pluralism, of controlling instruments for the audio-visual media in terms of ethics, of the journalist profession, the education and the level of democratic culture, the critical spirit developed at the level of the society, at an early age, in school, seeking alternatives should provide a natural reaction and real antibodies against the elements of the informational war. But democracies are not perfect, the modern man has access to an enormous amount of information and is often sufficiently comfortable to believe that, if the information is easy to obtain, then he knows it without consulting it. The case of the UK referendum and the great game around the Brexit, was an opportunity for Russia to step in and use informational war instrument in support of the Brexit, which even its current followers have admitted,[44] demonstrated the limited action of antibodies against the informational war even in most highly developed societies.

Moreover, a vulnerability in the West, the penetration of informational war elements in the high quality and prestigious media, the insight and seizure of some prestigious politicians or opinion leaders in the informational war instrumentation carousel of the Russian Federation may at any time represent a major problem for the Eastern Flank states, former socialist states – through the legitimacy and credibility given to the informational war elements by passing through this Western filter – and it is a true earthquake and a catastrophe for states in the post-Soviet space and their populations, being subjected in the long term and constantly to a much stronger aggression, having reduced institutional antibodies and a more precarious responsiveness.

In the long term, the reaction formula, the most appropriate in the case of informational war, is education. Starting from middle school introducing into the curricula courses for developing civics and the critical spirit, in which the informational war is to be presented, but also elements for developing the critical spirit, separating critique from criticism at any cost, teaching the basic elements of advertising psychology and its working mechanism, the structure of lies, disinformation techniques, the limits and use of the conspiracy theories, communication strategies, elements and examples of propaganda and manipulation, all these drive towards building a balanced personality and a citizen who has the instrumentation, the discernment and the ability to fight the informational war and avoid its effects. But for such a step a period of about 20 years at least is needed, of a generation that is confronted with these elements, in order to have citizens immune to the informational war.

In the short and medium term, and even afterwards, the instrumentations qualified to manage the informational war elements are necessary. Awareness of this war's existence must be doubled by assuming, at the security documents level, of the specialised institutions responsibilities in the security domain and designating an integrative institution responsible for countering the informational war that would utilise all the resources of the other institutions involved.

Then, it is necessary for an official website to employ decryption elements to expose the instruments of informational war. The US State Department became accustomed to put materials on its website such as "the lies of the Russian Federation about …". It is an authorized official source where these elements can be found.[45,46] Then, in the nongovernmental sector, there are sites such as www. stopfake.org, a site as the one in Kyiv Mohyla University, Kiev (a private university named after Peter Mohyla, the first Metropolitan of Ukraine) is also very important. It exposes all the misinformation found by its volunteers in the media regarding the case of the war in Eastern Ukraine, but the experience could be extended to the level of some institutions in each country.[47]

Media coverage of the most flagrant cases of informational war is also useful. It is the case of the stratcom groups, for strategic communication, established at the NATO and the EU level. And other experiences and good practices or results could be shared, such as the studies of the NATO Centre of Excellence in Latvia for strategic communication in the Russian language space (Chifu & Nantoi 2016: 44).

The European Alliance to counter Russia's informational war

The supporting countries of the transatlantic relationship and that consider the US presence in Europe as indispensable for the strategic balance and for countering the Russian influence in the EU, have passed strong individual measures to counter the informational war waged by Russia in Europe and the world. The approach emerged after the EU considered that such a threat must be countered with plenty of public diplomacy, namely by promoting its own version of reality. Although it is faced with a sophisticated instrumentation of military origins and psychological operations – PsyOps, not merely with trivial propaganda generated from the cold war memory and the bipolar ideological battle.

The initiative belongs to the Netherlands and Poland, the first being the main subject regarding the impact of the bringing down of the Malaysian MH17 plane in July 2014, by a surface-to-air Russian missile, launched by a Buk device, brought from across the border into the separatist area, and afterwards moved back to Russia and destroyed.[48] One year after the tragedy in July 2014 that killed hundreds of Dutch citizens, the international community demanded the appointment of a special UN court to judge the guilty. This proposal was blocked by

Russia by veto in the Security Council.[49] Russia came back with a counter-proposal avoiding responsibility and would not allow the investigation on the humanitarian catastrophe generated under Moscow's responsibility, by a device belonging to the Russian Army, operated by soldiers of the Russian army, entered illegally on the occupied territory in eastern Ukraine and that have brought down the airliner.

Poland embraced the project, being the most financially potent and economically solid state in the first line of the Eastern front of the EU and NATO, which is the major target of Russia's propaganda and informational war. The two states have established and will launch a Russian-language news agency, an instrument to counter the informational war conducted by Russia through the Sputnik compound and other media channels.

Bert Koenders, the Dutch Foreign Minister, and Grzegorz Schetyna, the Polish Foreign Minister, declared that the instrument allows the Russian press and the social networks space to operate with balanced information in Russian, identifying and analysing all points of view, providing an important tool in the informational war. The purpose of this instrument to counter propaganda and media aggression, including media aggression psychologically targeting an audience in order to alter its perception of events and directed its mindset, with arguments, analysis and scrutiny, by the exposing of gross misinformation manoeuvres and public exposure of elements related to the sequential and evil-minded interpretation of facts combined with Russia's syllogisms and many malicious lies.[50]

The idea of launching a news agency of this kind, that will have television, radio, an online format and all the social media sites for, emerged after a study of the European Endowment for Democracy (EED), which targeted the counteracting formula of the Russian informational war in Europe.[51] The model is that of a European BBC, a factory of content, analysis and demystification of Russia's informational war elements.

The External Action Service of the EU decided also to act, since March 2015, to find ways to counter Russia's disinformation campaigns. Five experts called East StratCom Team were employed from the Czech Republic, Denmark, Estonia, Latvia and the UK to lead this cell for strategic communication and counteracting the informational war. The most important part of their work will be to decrypt and display the lying reports and stories of the Russian media and of the official propaganda carried out by Russian officials, information to be supplied to the Member States, the diplomatic representatives of the EU, the mass media and the partner states from post-Soviet space (Chifu & Nantoi 2016: 49).[52]

The project and the work methodology

This project (Chifu & Nantoi 2016) aimed to support the research in order to identify and present the model and content of the informational warfare in the region based on the actions using "soft power", interventions in the public space, strategic communication on behalf of a certain country that owns an important part of the media and public space in Republic of Moldova, informational warfare and psychological operations done below the radar in social media and cyber space in Romania.

In order to ascertain the Russian informational war, we proceeded from two complementary realities. First we considered the Republic of Moldova, where the penetration of the public space is complete and the access level reached the penetration of the political space, the control of a political force – the most important party – which promotes the interests of the Russian Federation. Here the study is aimed at the direct visible elements of the informational war, where the message carriers are the decision makers, the politicians and the opinion formers in the media space, the majority of content is produced directly in Moscow, and some content produced in Kishinev.[53]

For the second component, the one situated "under the radar", we used the case of Romania, where the deep reticence to accept everything coming from the Russian Federation, in terms of policies, information, motivations, is major. This fact is showed by a study made by the Centre for Conflict Prevention, in 2009, on the perception regarding Russia, the Russians and the Russian policies in Romania. Back then, Romanian perception of the Russians was substantially positive, with an acceptability level of the Russian citizens of 60%, regarding the acceptability of the Russian Federation, it was 45–45%, pro and con, meaning a half acceptability, however, there was a major rejection of Russian policies at 75%. In this context, the action of the Russian informational war in Romania must adopt the most insidious and less visible alternatives, not to generate negative virulent reactions. That is why, here, the components of the informational war in Romania: trolls' manifest, of the psychological operations, of the conditioning elements and most especially here and at this stage the recruitment actions unfold as well as the establishing of the influence groups, the supporting groups, the mass manoeuvre and especially the recruitment of the "convinced".

In both cases we studied the public space and the public events that are make up Russia's informational war in Romania. We didn't follow the traceability of the action. It is the responsibility of other institutions to start from these observations and to identify "the smoking gun", meaning the facts that proving the link between the Russian authorities – direct, at the level of the intelligence services, by means of some supposed NGOs or through the Embassy – and those who bear this action of informational war. In the Republic of Moldova there is the Centre for Investigative Journalism, a RISE Project collaborator, with whom we worked together, which partially handles this component as well. But the project aimed at identifying the working methods, the instruments and the goals of the informational war, and certainly not identifying the money circuit and the action orders.

In the Republic of Moldova, our partner, the Institute for Public Policies, along with numerous institutions and NGOs involved in the project, realised the monitoring and assessment of the complete visible spectrum of Russia's informational war, establishing the following access levels:

- control in the public space;
- control in the political space – parties and message carriers that defend Russia's interests;

- media instruments;
- non-governmental organisations and civil society formulas that are instrumentation projections for waging the informational war, at the civil society level and at the grassroots level, in the territory.

The level of control and influence, and even of determining decisions, is at the very core of the political life and covers, to a great extent, about half of the political spectrum in the Republic of Moldova, approximately 80% of the media space and an important part of the civil society and the ideas disputed. Also, although it was not possible for us to conduct the study in detail, at national level, at the grassroots level, Russia's informational war components seem to have exceeded half of access, at the level of the population, according to the estimates of those who worked on this component of the programme.

Regarding Romania, our methodology targeted an analysis of the public space, the news and the information targeting the strategic decisions and the reporting of the Foreign, Security and Defence Policy. We selected the most important TV channels, all the TV news stations, the most important radio stations, news agencies, newspapers, news websites as audience and evaluated their content for the period starting from the Vilnius Summit, the Eastern Partnership, November 2013, to March 2016. We have assessed the information and analyses content and the troll war, the aim being as follows:

- to identify the action patterns regarding Russia's informational war in Romania;
- to achieve the profile of the publication from the Russian informational war point of view;
- to see the extent to which the informational war is acknowledged;
- to identify the self-defence measures taken by the media institutions regarding this war, especially in the war of trolls;
- to determine the vulnerabilities and problems of the media institutions in the informational war;
- to track the themes of the informational war during this period and to decant the main themes promoted in the action directions of Russia;
- to supervise the virtual space, especially Facebook – highly appreciated in Romania – and the yahoo-groups, as forms of direct influence, in cyberspace, central to the informational war.

With certainty the study cannot cover the niche publications or the marginal media institutions, with low audience (under 5000 followers), meaning below the level of a Facebook user at its capacity limit without becoming a public figure. Starting from these two components, studied in distinct environments, where their manifestation is the most important, we managed to achieve this definition of the Russian informational war. We also managed to create a system of thresholds and levels of influence that we propose as a reference for assessing the impact of Russia's informational war in a third country.

We also believe that the most important role of the project is to disclose the informational war working systems and to bring awareness on the existence of this war and the institutional and individual formulas for protection against the informational war. Furthermore, the project publicly exposes, including for any internet user or genuine commentator on the news sites, the dangers they expose themselves to and the manner in which they could be used or recruited in this informational war (Chifu & Nantoi 2016: 52).

The Troll War

One of the most important weapons of Russia's informational war is represented by the armies of the so-called "trolls,"[54] groups of very well paid young people identifying highly visited sites and media tools and where they post comments to direct the readers' debates towards the conclusions imposed by the financier, the Russian state. The procedure has already been revealed by people on the inside, who worked in these factories of parallel truth, for building and supporting the stories inoculated by the Kremlin in a target population.

According to the statements, the trolls work in teams of three and simultaneously attack an article published electronically on the most famous websites of television and media, or NGOs and professional publications related to Russia, the war in Ukraine, Novorossiya – Putin's imperialist project to occupy the northern coast of the Black Sea to the mouths of the Danube – or other targets. One of trolls plays the role of the one who launches a comment on an extremely debated idea, another one gives him a reply, taking the opposite position, and the last draws the conclusions of the dispute in the direction in which the sponsors want. Clearly the comments come on previously prepared scenarios and were tested so that the postings have maximum impact on the target population, using samples of local cultural references, formulations and commonalities apropos of the targeted region.

The strongest strike was recently launched by "The Daily Beast", which revealed on 20 August 2015, where the Kremlin's "factories of trolls" on the Internet and used in the informational war, are placed.[55] And the way in which these factories were identified is interesting: they used an application that showed where the aberrations occurred regarding search terms such as Sector right, Novorossiya, the DNR – People's Republic of Donetsk, the separatist region in Ukraine. The geographical research showed that there are areas in Russia showing aberrations, where a larger number of computers seek certain terms excessively, several times more than the rest of the region and the national average.

This is how it was demonstrated that the most important trolls' factory used in the informational war in Eastern Ukraine and that projected worldwide is at Olgino, a suburb in Putin's hometown, Sankt Petersburg. The factory of trolls, entitled "Internet Research, Inc.", moved, at the beginning of this year, from Olgino to Savushkina street no. 55, in St. Petersburg.[56]

Thorough research revealed other locations as well: Perekatny, a suburb with 244 inhabitants and Yablonovsky, with a population of 30,518 in the autonomous republic Adygeia, in North Caucasus, near the city of Krasnodar. To these, we add Zelyony Gorod, a suburb in the Nizhny Novgorod city, the last specifically specialising in the war in Ukraine and preoccupied with the military terms and technique involved in this war. Just as the separatist republics were the responsibility of a troll factory in Taganrog, a town near the border with Ukraine, where convoys of Russian armament are passing towards the separatists, then this responsibility moved to Perekatny and Kursk and only afterwards, at the end, the Olgino trolls factory.[57]

The informational war is a war as real as it could be, which plays with perceptions, with the will and beliefs of the target populations. A fact as real as possible that may affect the support for the public policies of the concerned governments. It is not a coincidence that defence tactics have appeared worldwide and the news media institutions have decided to control the comments published on their websites in order to avoid being subject to this type of attack or to the forgery instrument of truth by the Russian troll factories.

Russia's informational war does not strike only the post-Soviet states or the ones on NATO's Eastern Flank, the former socialist states, more exposed to the Russian propaganda and sophisticated psychological operations, but it also attacks the heart of Europe. Germany has experienced it, when it faced a real offensive designed to oust Angela Merkel using its support for the refugees waves entering the country, when the Russian media invented a 13-year-old girl, from a family originally from Russia, who was allegedly raped in Cologne, and provoked public demonstrations inciting 2 million Russian Germans who held a public manifestation, whose magnitude was amplified by the Russian news network Sputnik. Germany reacted and sanctioned the informational operation accusing it of false, but the damage had already been done.[58]

Apparently, recently the US became the target of the same type of informational attacks on American soil. The Russian troll army, the pseudo-Institute for the Study of the Internet in Saint Petersburg, is behind the generalised attacks of trolls at the address of the most prized, most visited news sites, those with the largest audience. Thus, Fox News, Huffington Post, The Blaze, Politico, and WorldNet Daily are the most attacked sites by the Russian troll-agents as The Ghost of Marius the Giraffe, Gay Turtle, and Ass. These activities were exposed for the first time the trolls referred to the speculation of the public perception on the annexation of Crimea and on the Russian military aggression in Ukraine.[59]

The explosion of interest and the massive emergence of trolls on social media, also the comments in the electronic media, marked the Kremlin's interest in generating control over the Internet, specifically over the ideas conveyed on the Internet, an army of trolls being launched, financed with several millions of dollars to affect and divert the American public opinion and also to block freedom of expression on the Internet at home. According to the informational war strategy documents, the balance of forces is 20-80% to the detriment of the Russia brand advocates, according to one of the heads of Svetlana Boiko project, which is why they are trying to amplify the pro-Russian answers, targeted and coordinated in order to increase their efficiency, to give the feeling of an overwhelming number and power of those who support the views of Russia through activism, frightening the actors with opposing opinions and covering the independent and anti-system ideas from Russia itself.[60]

The instructions set the work level for the employees and the efficiency targets: every working day, the Russian trolls must post comments on the news articles at least 50 times, every blogger must maintain at least five Facebook accounts, with at least three posts a day for each, to discuss the news on the groups at least twice a day. After the first month they must have at least 500 subscribers and five media posts from each of them monthly. On Twitter, each must manage 10 accounts with a minimum of 2,000 members, and to drop messages at least 50 times a day. The postings reach two themes, "the American Dream", attacking the actions of the US, its history, the favourite themes of the American dream and creating the anti-system and anti-American current in the world, and respectively "I Love Russia", messages praising Russia's actions. The identities adopted, without having an explanation for the reason of their choice, are Handkerchief, Gay Turtle, The Ghost of Marius the Giraffe, Left Breast, Black Breast and Ass.

The Project Leader at the moment of the interpellation, Igor Osadchy, declared that he is not an employee of the Agency for Studying the Internet, denying also the documents about his hundreds employees situated in the suburbs of Sankt Petersburg. Moreover, Osadchy declined to comment for BuzzFeed also about the funding of the project that brings him 35,000 dollars a month salary, claiming that it was only a "missed challenge". He refused to comment upon the interceptions and the data obtained by the American hackers from the activity of the Agency that is being led by him, just as the Kremlin proceeded regarding the official and formal questions.[61]

Concerning Romania and the trolls' manner of action, our study determined the following conclusions:

- The war of trolls in Romania exists with certainty. The fact that the news with strategic impact and the ones targeting Russia are primarily commented on, singles out these issues.
- The alleged impact of the war of trolls is difficult to estimate. However, given the strict comments on a number of issues and the fact that a user reads an article and its 368 comments to write the 369th means that there is a public and a target for the trolls, the consumers of these materials.
- The trolls war is underlined also by the number of postings, by their daily repetition at the same 3, 5 or 7 news reports at most, the reports concerning geopolitics and Russia on the major news sites, as well as the confrontation between these trolls and the outside observers or trolls of another colour. It is obvious that those who are concerned with the posting have a permanent mission, a permanent job in order to do that.

- The overwhelming majority of trolls are Romanian citizens. This conclusion results from the writing, the formulations, et cetera. There is a small number of posts that seem to be translated with Google Translate, therefore not misused Romanian language or spoken in the Republic of Moldova, but transferred and translated formulas, however, they do not exceed 1% of the posts.
- The purpose of a battle of this kind is to direct the dispute conclusions under interpretation, in a constant way, towards the positions imposed by the Russian area. But the approaches are different from one media instrument to the next. Thus, to those that are permeable and where such a battle could be won, arguments are carried through to their conclusion. In those that are declaredly and explicitly pro-Western or pro-American, the interest is only the presence in the space of these disputes and the equal affirmation of the indicated themes, received through contract.
- Not infrequently, the postings have nothing to do with the commented topic. In 5-10% of the cases, there are posts with comments on some historical sequences which highlight that the Russians were of help in a certain historical moment or, on the contrary, that the Romanians were betrayed by the West. Furthermore, the same postings are to be found on more news and more sites at the same time, even if the user names are different and humorous.
- The user names that comment are either comments per se, or relevant acronyms, that draw attention, or proper names (probably false) but that give credibility to the message.
- Neither the swearing, nor the pressure on the authors of the commented materials are missing, especially if the approach is unsuitable to the programme of the trolls. Direct pressure, swearing, the attempt to have a more relevant ensemble to press pressure, highlighting the number of agreements obtained at a posting, altering the rating, all of these are used to generate a reaction.

Last but not least, the troll wars are used for recruiting, involving in the comments, exploitation in blind or convincing a number of objective users to multiply the trolling activity unknowingly. A user can genuinely believe that the Crimea belonged to the Russians. From a simple comment follows the involvement in bilateral talks and supporting the targeted one, then the invitation to comment on other news, subsequently even his direct hiring, in the real world. Based on this type of recruitment the pressure groups and "the convinced users" are achieved, therefore not the operative agents, not the mass manoeuvre and the slowcoach, but people with relevant intellectual base, who are convinced by the Russian approaches and are directed in groups, precise gatherings and other forms where to be used (Chifu & Nantoi 2016: 56–61).

Examples of the informational war waged by Russia and modus operandi

It is important to realise how the informational war works and how the parallel narrative first contours itself as an alternative viewpoint, then how the false is achieved and the amplification of marginal news stories, finally how the space and the psychological context for the informational war are built. From the period we monitored we selected news and public disclosures of the informational war so that we would have specific elements, tangible samples of news of this informational war. We split the material in two, news and external information from other areas (but broadcast worldwide), and the news and the information part of the informational war in Romania.

Russia conquers Ukraine in 3-5 days

We cannot start our discussion in other way than with Ukraine, one of the main targets of the Russian informational war. The objectives of the news are transparent in undermining the state power, attacking the prestige and inoculating the themes of the parallel narrative created by the Kremlin.

The President of the Russian Federation State Duma, Sergey Naryshkin, recently announced (material published Thursday 30 July 2015) that Russia does not want to occupy Ukraine but, if it would have wanted it, it would do it in 3 to 5 days, without a problem.[62] The declaration was meant to calm the spirits and to de-legitimate the cries for help of Kiev, that repeatedly demanded the delivery of weapons in order to defend the *de facto* border of the West on the Donbas demarcation line, proved to be the clearest evidence of Russia's bellicose inclinations, aggressive, revisionist and revanchist, against the states that did not fold under the neo-imperial ambitions of the Kremlin, which wants to transform the post-Soviet states into new colonies and to impose sovereignty limited to the supreme interests of Russia, by threatening with protecting the Russians, the Russian speakers and the compatriots.

If we take Naryshkin's statement as such, it is clear that we are dealing with bravado. Russia does not have the resources, the weapons, or the prepared manpower to lead a war in Ukraine, let alone to conquer it in 3–5 days. What Russia can really do is to occupy different parts of Ukraine, which can only be maintained with enormous effort and with the bankruptcy threat of its own state, in economic and financial terms.

A great deal has been discussed[63] about a corridor towards the Crimea, once the bridge across the Kerch Strait has proven not to be feasible, and the supply of the Crimea is made only by water, or it is dependent on the supply from the mainland to the peninsula, meaning from Ukraine, from which it was torn away. The link was organic as we can see today, while the annexation had no real planning for the day after the occupation. What could this mean?

The occupation of the thoroughfare towards the Crimea would not be a super-human effort for the regular Russian troops. Obviously, in this case also, as in the case of Ukraine's occupation, the story of the separatists fighting with the regular troops of Ukraine no longer has coverage and the Russian regular troops and technique must penetrate openly and in plain sight in order to fight. Admitting avoiding the cities (whose conquest would be more expensive and sustained) starting with Mariupol, a corridor to the Crimea could be achieved. But could it be defended? At what cost?

The corridor to the Crimea could be established in about two weeks, also providing the supply of the frontline troops. The operation could even be launched from two directions, namely Russia via Mariupol and the Crimea. But maintaining control would be extremely difficult and would require about 30,000 people for that distance. Moreover, as in the case of any transit corridor, it would be under pressure and simple incursions, groups of 10–15 people, who could attack and disrupt the corridor in multiple points and would constantly harass the Russian troops. Hence, it would be a never-ending effort.

In order to maintain the corridor's viability, entire regions would have to be occupied. Donetsk, until its end, Zaporoje and Kherson, at least to the isthmus that makes the connection to the Crimea. But for such an undertaking the support of the population is necessary – while, after the disaster in Donbas, Russia no longer has even the support of the Russian minority in Ukraine – and a much higher number of troops, in principle with military effort supported for 18–24 months and the involvement of 150–200 thousand soldiers. Without the support of the population, as an occupation army, the Russian Army would be able to maintain in exchanges the extended region for a medium-term of 3–5 years, a quasi-impossible fact at the level of the available resources and the endowment/ training degree of the Russian army nowadays.

Obviously the idea to occupy Novorossiya, eventually until the mouth of the Danube is also a utopia on the short and medium term. Destabilisation, strikes and terrorist actions could take place, but the occupation of the Odessa region alone requires an effort that today Russia is not capable of. It should be added that the Ukrainian Army is no longer the the same as it was in 2014, when it succumbed without a single shot fired in the Crimea, passing mostly to the enemy, or it has been pushed back in the Donetsk and Lugansk attack, due to the hybrid war form of aggression. But even maintaining the occupied territory claimed, at the end of last year, the almost open intervention of the regular Russian troops, as the regaining of a contiguous territory. But starting with this year, at the tentative resumption regarding the Mariinka operations, it has been clearly seen that the operations are not so easy to conduct once the Ukrainian army has been trained, armed with modern weapons, and has new soldiers and volunteers. It has dramatically improved its capacity to fight and defend the country. Russia needs 1–1.5 million soldiers, trained and armed, to occupy today's Ukraine. That number of soldiers is only to occupy Ukraine, not to maintain Russian presence. At this stage, it has only 300,000. And the national bankruptcy is behind the door (Chifu & Nantoi 2016: 62–65).

The USA introduced the Zika virus as biological weapon against Russia

The second development direction of the informational war is represented by absurd news, an obvious subject of blatant misinformation, but which proved in our study to have an audience as well. As some believe in aliens, others think that AIDS is a laboratory product launched by the USA in the world as a biologic weapon. On the same pattern, this time the star was the Zika virus:

The famous chief of the Russian Federation sanitary inspector, Ghenadi Onishchenko, one of the most blasphemed characters in the Republic of Moldova after he repeatedly provided "political evidence" to suspend the exports to Russia of wines, vegetables and other industrial products from the area, became the author of the latest attack in Russia's informational war with the entire world. Onishchenko declared that nothing more nor less that the much dreaded Zika virus - a virus that has wreaked havoc in South America, being carried by mosquitoes and being responsible for microcephaly in new-born babies from infected mothers - is actually a biological weapon created by the US to attack Russia.

The commentaries were made by Ghenadi Onishchenko at the BBC post in Russia,[64] claiming that unspecified Russian scientists identified the appearance of the disease in 2012 in mosquitoes in Abkhazia – a Georgian separatist region under the control of the Russian Federation, militarised and integrated in the Russian security system. "This thing worried us because, at 100 km of the place the mosquito lives, a microbiological laboratory of the US Army is located". Onishchenko, currently adviser to Prime Minister Medvedev, made reference to a facility in Georgia where The US Agency of Defence, despite threats built, in 2011, a laboratory for the epidemiological diseases control, which is currently located in Georgia's National Centre for the Control of the Infectious Diseases.

The reference to "an American chain of biological laboratories in the former Soviet states" must not be forgotten, that would be used to produce the biological weapon against Russia, appeared in Russia's last Security Strategy, a reference that was sent into oblivion and became an important part of in determining the loss of credibility for the document approved by the Security Council of Russia, which marks the US, NATO and the EU as enemies and threats to the security of the Russian Federation. The Zika virus spread exponentially in South America but formal cases did not register in the rest of the world, even less so from 2012 and in an area around the Black Sea.[65]

The only known case in the Russian Federation is that of an infected woman in the Dominican Republic, but who did not even infect the other passengers in in the plane that she travelled in, neither her relatives, nor other Russian citizens. As for Onishchenko's statements, they come to revive an older theory of Russian propaganda, which once said that even AIDS was a disease resulting from a virus, HIV, which is the product of biological warfare launched by the US against the USSR.[66] Returning to these practices, in 2016 emphasises the low level of the bilateral relations of Russia with the West and the total lack of mutual trust, a fact that leads to the reactivation of such message carriers for Russia's informational war.

In the meantime, the UK has identified a formula to combat the Zika virus by attacking the responsible genes directly in the carrier mosquito. London formed a veritable army made of millions of genetically modified mosquitoes, that freely mate with the females carrying the Zika virus and transmit a lethal gene, thereby resulting in mating mosquitoes that die before becoming adults and before transmitting the virus. "The good mosquito" was created by a British company and has so far been successfully tested in a locality in Brazil (Chifu & Nantoi 2016: 65–67).

"American soldier shooting the Koran"

Another eloquent example is that of the double action, by absorbing some false information, even some excogitations, concocted in the communication laboratories, slipping them through abstruse sources and absorbing them into the mainstream, possibly through an intermediary Western source to give credibility to the news story. The second objective of such news is to fundamentally undermine the image of the enemy, the US, in relation to the third parties, the Muslim world in this case, and to generate reactions from the third parties, creating new problems to the intended target

The trolls factory, commentators and "postphiles" (persons that post frequently comments to the articles published on the Internet) funded by Saint Petersburg to alter and influence the virtual space and international media, has produced a new infamy, disinformation through a huge lie, which they multiplied exponentially: the movie in which an American soldier allegedly shot a copy of the Koran. The Agency for Studying the Internet, which covers the trolls' factory, was revealed as author of the forgery by an investigation effected by the BBC in Russia.[67]

The film showed a man dressed in the uniform of a US soldier shooting three bullets in a blue book, apparently a copy of the Koran.[68] Launched in September 2015, the clip has generated inexplicable interest in Russia, being fiercely criticised by the Muslim community in the country, in terms of "the American soldier who shoots the Koran", even though the film does not explicitly reflect this reality, furthermore it is a fake.

The film involves a black man – to clearly reflect that he is an American – dressed in an American uniform and tests a semi-automatic Saiga 401K rifle of Russian provenance, firing 10 bullets towards a blue book with Arabic writing on it, which seems to be a Koran. Out of the 10 gunshots, only three hit the book, and the one who is filming, with a completely un-American English accent, proffers obscenities and claims that the gun is not good. The movie commented in English with many grammatical mistakes ends with the conclusion that the American weapons are the best.[69]

The film was posted on YouTube and was assumed by the alleged National Gun Forum, the forum of the national weapons that would host "the debates for the proud owners of weapons". The Derr86 user is the one posting the video claiming that he persuaded his friend not to buy a Russian Saiga 410K and shows how badly it works through the mounted video. The user has this as single posting and has vanished since then.

According to the BBC investigations, the man claiming to be a US soldier is dressed in a desert camouflage uniform that can be purchased by anyone in stores.[70] The soldier is wearing a cap belonging to Ops-Core FAST Base Jump and not a cap belonging to the US military, and has on the band visibly written the message "INFIDEL STRONG". All seem to be subliminal symbols, from the skin colour, the message on the cap, the discussion between the two, the bullets into the alleged Koran. The video on YouTube is registered on Mayaese Johnson, Google Plus claiming that the person is an employee of a high school in Moscow.

On Google Plus there are over 50 accounts on the name Mayaese, many of those registered on it claiming that they are working for high schools in Moscow. The video was broadcast on 11 September 2015, on two twitter accounts @ComradZampolit, with 33,000 followers, and @NovostiSPb, with more than 81,000 people who have seen it. In both of the tweets, the message claims that an American soldier shoots a copy of the Koran. The NovostiSPb Twitter account spreads news into the Nevskie Novosti website, belonging to the Russian businessman Evgeny Prigozhin, the one credited with financing the Agency for Studying the Internet, the trolls factory in Saint Petersburg, according to the BBC. Within a few hours, the film studded Facebook and Vkontakte (the Russian Facebook) accounts creating a true hysteria about how an American soldier shot the Koran. After three days the movie reigned also on the pro-Kremlin website Politonline.ru. So it entered the mainstream Russian press.

However, the first media institution, which is of reference, in noticing the posts on the websites and on YouTube was The Popular News, registered at 55 Savushkina Street in St. Petersburg –precisely at the address of the Agency for Studying the Internet, the Russian factory of trolls. Moreover, according to the BBC, the IP addresses used to promote the movie belong to the agency, one of them promoting the film as "the killer of the Koran" at a forum in Saratov. The BBC also found the person who impersonated the American soldier in the clip, a bartender from Sankt Petersburg, a friend of a woman employed at the trolls factory. Here is how a fake news story is achieved, and a lie that became an absolute truth is multiplied in Russia and the Islamic world: the American soldiers are shooting the Koran (Chifu & Nantoi 2016: 67–69).

Russia invents the Romanian separatism at Chernivtsi

Certainly the informational war needs some facts as well. Facts that are invented, directed, placed in abstruse spaces, as we saw above, but subsequently interpreted and amplified by the Russian official media in order to create major effects. As we approach Romania, here is a fake with credibility publicly attached to it, in order to create public disagreements between Romania and Ukraine at a time of maximum closeness and of support offered by Romania and the Romanians in Bucovina, on the field, for the war in Eastern Ukraine:

The alleged founding conference in Chernivtsi of the so-called Assembly of Romanians in Bucovina – an organisation that demanded a special autonomy status for the Romanians in Northern Bucovina – was actually a diversion intended to destabilise the situation in the region.[71] Russia invented from nowhere the Romanian separatism in Northern Bucovina, as part of the classic informational war that it orchestrates in Ukraine as in Romania. Thus, it achieved two objectives: to incite the weak-spirited Romanian audience and the marginal Romanian nationalist parties, keen to assert themselves, to loudly defend the compatriots from Chernivtsi; then to simultaneously artificially create and deepen divergences and rifts between the two neighbours, Romania and Ukraine, to demonstrate that it is not only about the Russian minority or about the Hungarians and the Ruthenians influenced by the two states with revisionist policies, which were accusing the government and the regime in Kiev of repressive policies against minorities, but it is about all of Ukraine's neighbours that might have such views.

The meeting in question proved to be a flash in the pan. A fake that, the falser and non-existent, the more it hoped to have a greater influence. The informational attack was meant to destabilise the situation in tolerant Bucovina, to provoke an ethnic conflict in the background of the Donbas crisis, where Russia carries out military aggression against Ukraine, in the Eastern regions, Donetsk and Lugansk.

In fact, it turned out that the meeting was never held. Then, as their leaders some non-existent leaders from the Romanian community were placed, the Assembly for the Romanians in Bucovina being led by "Dorin Chirtoaca and Cornelia Rusu" – an innovation to sound familiar, by the proximity with the name of the Chisinau mayor, Dorin Chirtoaca (who at that time was establishing the Local Council) and of Corina Fusu, Liberal deputy in the Republic of Moldova. Finally, the images from that meeting proved to be false, montages made from other occasions and in other circumstances, as resulted from studying the broadcast pictures, which accompanied the story originally aired in the Russian media, by ricochet via the Western media, from abstruse sources.[72]

According to the broadcast news, the Romanian minority organised as such was committed "to fight for a special autonomy status for the Romanian ethnics in Ukraine, and all those present voted unanimously in favour of this resolution".[73] If the information were initially denied at the individual level, several leaders of the Romanian cultural association in Chernivtsi denied the respective information. The Romanians in Bucovina had nothing to do with the reunion, neither with the media invention, the separatist claims require that the same status Donbas will obtain should be granted for the Romanians in Bucovina, just as gatherings of Ruthenians or Hungarians in Transcarpathia are prepare to claim, under the same Russian inspiration, for their region, a region where they don't have a majority, since Romanians also live there.. If Barna Csibi, the known symbolic hangman of Avram Iancu, wandered through the region inciting for separatism and the Ruthenians/Russians are coordinated by Moscow in their separatist claims, in the case of the Romanians in Bucovina, the situation is completely different.

Bucpress states: "In this context, the media, that fell victim – directly and indirectly – to the Russian propaganda, must disprove the respective information because it is nothing but a copy of the story invented in the context of a comprehensive informational war, which should not affect the interests of the Romanian community in Ukraine".[74] And about the interests of the Romanians in Chernivtsi, firstly the native Romanians have the right to speak about this, claims the news portal of the Romanian ethnics in Chernivtsi.[75]

Not that the Romanians in Bucovina would not have their own grievances and needs. That is a fact. But they do not evoke them in these terms and in any case not to give arguments for the Russian separatism in Donbas. Romanians proved to be a minority loyal to the state in which they live, fought alongside the majority Ukrainian countrymen in East, have defended their state of residence, and consider that they can solve their problems better if they can have representation in Parliament and in the regional and local leaderships. Unlike the self-proclaimed Moldavians in the area under Bessarabia, the Odessa region, here as well with many nuances, the Romanians in Ukraine proved to be the second largest minority that has behaved loyally to the Ukrainian state in which it lives. Maybe here as well some officials in Kiev reflect more on the Stalinist separation of the Romanian minority in Romanians and Moldavians (Chifu & Nantoi 2016: 69–72).

A Russian general, some armament, a pump and many fireworks

The articles in the media capitalise the media flaws and the vulnerabilities in the target country, namely in Romania, in this case: chasing the sensational, the uncritical takeover, without verification and without offering the other opinion of rumour circulated by the Russian media. Thus, a base for scaring the population was created by distributing fake news and amplifying it by linguistic artifices and the inventiveness of the titles of the media publishers. Thereby, no more and no less, the allegations of a "Russian general" became overnight "The Russian army that supports", "the Russian Ministry of Defence that threatens" and even it is presumed the position of Russia itself that "warns" (news from 18 June 2015).[76]

The ingredients are clear and impactful: "a Russian general" (necessarily), even though his belonging or rank and position are unknown, therefore the relevance of the character is built on his legitimacy. Then news about armament – in fact Russia's reaction to the future placement of the prepositioned military capabilities in Eastern Europe. It is about heavy weapons intended to serve in exercises with various NATO types of forces and to allow collective defence if an attack looms in the future. A decision taken at the NATO Summit in Newport, Wales, September 2014, transparent and known to everybody, to which the alleged general gives the destructive response just when the actual placement of weapons to defend the Eastern Flank is being negotiated. Finally, a pump to fill out the headlines in the tabloids, indifferent to the fact that the effect is the unnecessary frightening of the public. And a lot of linguistic artifices to boost the title: extraordinary, unseen, danger! et cetera.

In fact, a clear decryption of the conveyed news was necessary to avoid confusion: General Yuri Yakubov, used on other occasions as well for catastrophic messages like "it is necessary to think Russia's pre-emptive nuclear strike in case of threat,"[77] allegedly said that "Russia will offer an adequate response if the United States will deploy heavy artillery in Romania and other Eastern European countries". The speculation of what Russia might do as response follows. Next to him immediately appears also the declaration of a Romanian military official, this time of the Minister of Defence (previously at a similar construction, as Chief of the General Staff) to give his reply and potentiate the news. In reality the Army General Yuri Yakubov, the coordinator of the General Inspectors Directorate of the Russian Defence Ministry, does not have responsibilities in the matter and speaks from a personal point of view, even more since the Kremlin refused to speak on the subject. It was not Russia that spoke, neither the Ministry of Defence, not even the Russian Army, as the headlines in our newspapers presented it. His commentary runs:

"If the heavy military technique of the US, composed of tanks, artillery systems and other military equipment, will appear in a number of countries in Eastern Europe and the Baltic countries [so Romania is not explicitly mentioned], this will be the most aggressive step of the Pentagon and of NATO since the Cold War. In this case Russia can only increase its forces and means in the West strategic direction," after which he speculated "in the first place the military group will be strengthened over the whole western border of Russia, inclusively with new formation of tanks, artillery and air units. The missiles brigade in the Kaliningrad region will be quickly rearmed with new Iskander tactical missile systems, while the Belarusian Interarms group will undergo substantial changes".[78]

It should be well understood: I do not think that the general spoke from his beliefs, without having the consent from his superiors. Only that a speculation made on a direct addressed question, of an over-gauged and irrelevant character in the Russian planning system, is upgraded to being news and attributed to Russia. And Moscow knows very well about NATO's plans from last September, knows that placed force it brought from outside precisely because the states on the Eastern border of NATO did not make purchases and did not restructure the army and the level of troops and capabilities is downright irrelevant in front of the reduction of the level of troops and armaments in the region. Moreover, all are part of the all the agreements such as the Treaty on Conventional Forces in Europe, including the revised version.

NATO does not violate the arms control agreements and is arming itself, but Russia does. The amount of weapons and military equipment brought to the Crimea exceeds any level previously accepted, 25,000 soldiers and the tanks and planes limit, because Moscow considers it "Russian territory", by means of the annexation. And it has been announced that even nuclear weapons may be brought, in violation of the INF Treaty of the intermediate-range action nuclear forces. And in Donbas, the number of forces and conventional weapons go beyond what is supposed to be placed throughout the whole Eastern Flank of the Alliance, Russia preparing here its future frontier but also capabilities to take Ukraine by storm (Chifu & Nantoi 2016: 72–74).

On 5 June 2015, in the mainstream media, a classical fake appeared, a montage of cascading information, having a single source, nuanced views and presumed news, quoting unspecified sources, so as to build a successive sequence of statements and mutually interdependent allegations, and apparently reinforcing one another, in order to highlight the relative and apparent veracity of a lie, of a blatant lie/lies. Nothing actually happened however, on paper, the informational war masters started almost a war of truth: Romania against the separatist Transnistria.

The Russian media released the theme of a possible war in Transnistria, trying to accredit, by all possible means, the idea that the blame for such evolutions belonged to Ukraine, Romania and the constitutional authorities in the Republic of Moldova, but in any case not to Moscow.[79] In fact, the creation of this idea was not about facts but about *blame*, who is to blame and who is not. It does not matter for what. The entire string of information broadcast on this subject, from official statements, to speculations with reference to anonymous sources, that appear on lesser known sites, seemed coordinated from a single source, the Kremlin, is used to proceed in case of informational attacks.

On Wednesday, 3 June, the Moscow agency Interfax published a story about a possible extraordinary meeting of the Federation Council, the upper house of the Russian Parliament. It was the first brick in the building of the story. Shortly afterwards, on a virtually unknown website, Jurnalistkaia Pravda, another story appears which states that the Federation Council meeting could be dictated by the need to declare Transnistria as part of Russia!

Immediately after the battle training, the main attack emerged: the official post of the Russian Armed Forces, Zvesda TV, broadcast – as news on its website, of course, in the space for external comments – a statement (we cannot call it an analysis) of an alleged political analyst in Kishinev, Ernest Vardanean, who mentioned something about some "impression" that Romania would be the one currently analysing a military intervention in Transnistria. Thus, the character that was arrested, released, legitimised and validated through Transnistria, precisely as a great hero and objector, claims, with no factual or argumentative basis, that "the leadership in Romania (there you are!) is defined by two views on the actions in Moldova and against Transnistria. Prime Minister Victor Ponta is strongly looking to organise "a small victorious provocation", to build a reason to send armed forces in Moldova. President Klaus Iohannis is more moderate".[80]

The first brick of the construction is immediately taken, namely the story by Interfax, which reports that Valentina Matvienko, Chairman of the Federation Council in Moscow, is the one who asked her colleagues to be careful, because an extraordinary meeting is a possibility, and validating the statement "I do not exclude that, taking into consideration the agenda of the State Duma, it might be necessary to organise an additional meeting of the Federation Council, therefore, do not go too far and keep in touch. If such a decision will be taken, you will be informed in due time". There was nothing about Transnistria, only the smoke without fire version and construct, a figment of the informational war. An earlier statement of the Vice President of the State Duma, Sergei Jelezniak, was immediately juxtaposed, only as context, when declaring in a TV show that Russia is ready to enter the war, on the pretext of an alleged attack on the Russian peacekeepers in Transnistria, after the nomination of the former Georgian president, Mikhail Saakashvili, as Governor of the Odessa region. Finally, on this basis, the carrier of the main strike of the lies bomb, an absurdity and ineptitude to claim on his blog that "the German Chancellor Angela Merkel personally persuaded the leader in Bucharest not to take any action yet. However, in principle, Romania and the Western countries have not given up a military scenario". It all culminates when a news agency in Tiraspol claiming that the separatist administration in Transnistria could mobilise, within two weeks at maximum, 50 thousands of reservists in the region.

News, facts, syllogisms, forgeries, blatant lies and the construct of a parallel reality with claims of truth. This episode should be placed in Shakespeare's play, "much ado about nothing" if were is not, in fact, about something else, something very serious. In their chase after the sensational, views, visits and spectators, no less than three TV news stations and important sites in the country have taken over the stupidity, claiming to be news, which they have inflated, placing them proudly in sight in the newspapers to make the story visible. As if they were not living in Bucharest, they did not know what the agenda looked like and if someone discussed such a subject, they could ask, but a Moscow-Tiraspol-Kishinev fake was necessary to come and tell us what was discussed in the Bucharest chancellery and to validate the forgery. Here is the blame: exploiting the inclination towards cheap sensational news, Russia gave us a strike with our own hand. The best description of the story and of the news came from Minister Bogdan Aurescu: "deeply ridiculous". And, at this exam, the press from Dâmboviţa took a deeply ridiculous note, failing to pass the responsibility exam (Chifu & Nantoi 2016: 74–77).

Guantanamo-type prisons in Ukraine and Eastern Europe

Another case dates back to 25 April 2015, and highlights the involvement of the Russian Federation and the official propaganda in the informational war, aimed at the human rights violations in the CIA prisons in Guantanamo and Abu Ghraib in the programme for interrogating and torturing the terrorist suspects. Starting from a fact, combined with plenty of mythology already rooted in public perception, the official platform Sputnik built pseudo-news, which represents a complete fake, whose unique references are the unspecified sources between the separatists in Eastern Ukraine. By juxtaposition, conjugation and amplification, the creation of a reality is attempted, in which any ambiguous statement, leaving space for speculation and interpretation, is used in mounting the fake.

Behold the side effects of a rash statement, obviously inappropriate, by President Ion Iliescu about a building ceded to CIA for the operations in Bucharest. Immediately, Sputnik, the informational war platform of the Russian Federation has launched a new enormity, this time the target being Ukraine and, the second-ary elements, the European and NATO states in Eastern Europe, while the EU is also held responsible. Russia Today released the news according to which the "concentration camps such as the famous prison in Guantanamo, but funded by the European Union would exist in Ukraine, Romania, Bulgaria, Lithuania and Poland! Two such camps have been conquered by the Novorossia militias, which published a video material on the Internet", declared Russiatoday.ro.[81]

Russiatoday.ro cites those from the "Novorossia militias". A source that does not designate anyone, due to its ambiguity, but which introduces and circulates the Novorossia name, a region from the time of Catherine the Great that never existed as such, and that today is synonymous with the expansion of the neo-imperial Russia and the take-over of Ukraine's territories bordering the Black Sea.[82]

The news relates about the fact that, near Donetsk, there would not be just one, but two "military prisons", "actually an unfinished Ukrainian Nazi concentration camp, in a village in Zhdanovka, built for the people accused by the pro-American regime in Kiev of separatism and terrorism". Here are some other symbols with emotional impact on the target population: concentration camp, Guantanamo, the "Ukrainian Nazis" and "pro-American regime", terms used in juxtaposition. A school-construction of a non-news, without real basis, if it might have a collec-tion of symbolic subliminal messages to support Russia's position and condemn the US, Ukraine and their policies by their association with Nazism, concentra-tion camps, Guantanamo, prisons. This story was perfectly timed after the new launch of the theme of Ukrainian prisons build on the site of unfinished Ukrainian Nazi concentration camps in Romania.

It is obvious that, for credibility, "the news" – obviously exclusive and sensa-tional – must also contain details: in this story prison documents have been found according to which the construction was financed by the European Union. Formally, this camp was designed to be a detention centre for the illegal immi-grants. The buildings were located on the territory of some military units. So it emerged, in the story of the Russian propaganda laboratory citing a non-existent anonymous organisation, but with symbolic name, and the European Union. The organisation is guilty, the organisation was the sponsor, even if the EU wanted something else, this is where the European money goes!

But the delirium continues, because not all the propaganda targets have been achieved. The beneficiaries of the association with the prisons, Guantanamo, the Nazis, must also have a label or an anathema gave by Russia, that they disregard Russia's interests in Ukraine.. Thus, besides the "two such complexes in the Zhdanovka village, in the Donetsk region", as far as the anonymous source knows, "there are 20 such detention centres in Ukraine. These are not detention centres for the illegal immigrants in the civilized Europe. These are NATO pris-ons as the ones existing in Romania, Bulgaria, Lithuania or Poland. It is not too hard to include these facilities on the list of prisons for the war prisoners. These camps are Eastern Europe's Guantanamo".[83]

In this pseudo-news, Russia tries to hit Ukraine and, at the same time, Romania, Bulgaria, Lithuania and Poland – countries from NATO's reassured

Eastern front – as well as the Alliance itself. They do that by using "the absolute fact", that put together the image of abuse in "Guantanamo type camps", American rendition program and secret prisons, all associated with Nazism and extermination camps, that might exist in Eastern Europe states and NATO/EU border states. Using a number of images associated with abuses, human rights breaches, torture and Nazi camps, the image created harms all the states and organisations involved.

We are right in the middle of the informational war. Who does not realise it, risks being the subject of this mass manipulation, which already addresses the public of the Soviet space, but also the elites and opinion makers in Eastern Europe, those who do not have the time to verify the source of each idea "consecrated" by the Russian, pro-Russian and affiliated, at the global level. It is time to go back to the classical rules of fact journalism and accurate narrations, to the direct communication of institutions, and with no double meaning, to explain the phenomena and professionalise the mass media. Otherwise, anybody will induce any kind of ideas, and will induce any wanted perceptions in the population. Romania's security strategy should explicitly contain this threat and the SCND will have to appoint a national coordinator, responsible for the integrated inter-institutional formula in order to fight this type of threat, with all due respect to the freedom of expression and the free flow of ideas and opinions. (Chifu & Nantoi 2016: 77–79).

The informational war in the virtual space

We left until the end the elements of the informational war that appear in cyberspace. The informational war is a component of the hybrid war, but also a particular form of waging war which proposes replacing reality and facts by building an alternative reality and projecting it towards the target population to achieve objectives of military nature, respectively demobilising the population, creating doubt regarding the national interest objectives, but also direct actions, to block the possibility of engaging the population in the battle training or convincing the young people not to become volunteers for professional positions within the National Army.

A group suggestively called "We do not want to fight against the Russians"[84] was established and haunts the social networks with "alternative approaches". Beyond its strange name – I do not remember someone asking for the arming of the population and declaring war on Russia, if such a madman exists, he should be quickly calmed down by the appropriate bodies – the programme of the group is important as well. It is more than a Romanian-Russian friendship group and the project speaks about the fact that "the USA wants by any means to provoke war with Russia" and "if this happens, Romania will be a certain target of the Russian assault".

After showing us that the USA is the enemy and the word with a strong emotional impact "war", to induce fear and draw attention, the authors also tell us within the programme that "the US and the EU have gradually destroyed

Romania" and that "they want to take our lives as well". After establishing the enemies, the programme of the boys clearly says that "We do not want to fight for the interests of the Western invaders. We want them out and the liberation of Romania". And to conclude in high feather, the parents of the group – who are not yet 21 years old– tell us that "all young people between 20 and 35 years old will be enrolled and sent to fight against the Russian Federation. They will die for the profit of the Americans, who will win from the sale of weapons". Naturally aberration and nonsense is present in these claims, the group is fighting for Romania's liberation but says that "there is nothing done in the interest of the Romanian people, there's nothing left to defend (!)".

I will not go into the group's details and its authors. Neither the promotions made to the members to enter the "more friendly" Russian social network Vkontakte is not necessarily coincidental. We have just submitted a qualified sample of informational war waged against Romania. And this happens directly in our home, in Romania. What is there left to say about approaching the Russian non-governmental, nationwide online Regnum news agency, fundamentally Romanophobic when speaking about anything that Romania does in Moldova. Thus, everything that is Romanian is automatically qualified as anti-Russian, Russophobe or, alternatively, "unionist", characteristics that have become equivalent to the supreme crime of violating other Russian policy in the territory left of the Prut River.

Here is the description of the transparent projects of the Department for the Relations with the Romanians Everywhere in Regnum's vision, the Russian Intelligence and propaganda factory: "Most of the funds will be allocated to support the mass media in the Republic of Moldova, especially the one of Romanian-unionist and Russophobe orientation [...] Bucharest will provide around 22,700 euros to the nationalist and Russophobe publication Timpul (The Time) [...] The Publicația Uniunii Scriitorilor din Republica Moldova (The Publication of the Writers Union in the Republic of Moldova), Literaturășiartă (Literature and art), whose editor is the Russophobe writer Nicolae Dabija, will receive around 7,300 euros [...]. Bucharest will award another 6,500 euros to IDIS Viitorul (IDIS The Future), with the aim of studying the situation of Romanians in ATU Gagauzia, the self-proclaimed Dniester Moldavian Republic Transnistria, Taraclia and from the northern part of the Republic of Moldova, but also for promoting the Romanian values"[85] (Chifu & Nantoi 2016: 80–81).

Narratives of the informational war in Romania's public space

In assessing the topics approached by the Russian informational war in the public space we have managed to identify no less than 162 addressed themes, within the studied time frame, namely:

- 47 themes in televisions (ProTV and Antena 1, plus news televisions), of which only 41 on news channels (Realitatea TV, Romania TV, Antena 3, B1 TV);

- 34 themes in quality print newspapers (Romania Libera, Adevarul, Evenimentul Zilei, Gandul);
- 31 themes in the news agencies (Mediafax, Hotnews, DC News);
- 41 themes in news sites (ziare.com, ştiripesurse.ro);
- 9 themes in yahoo groups.

Following the streamlining of these topics, we observed that there are five fundamental themes recurring throughout the media and which constitute the strong themes of Russia's informational war:

1. Anti-Americanism and Romania as slave to the US
2. Propaganda and anti-NATO attacks
3. The missile shield – the base at Deveselu
4. The cleavage / breakup / disappearance of the EU
5. Undermining Turkey's position in Romania. Turkey equals Russia, Erdoğan equals Putin.

At bottom, these findings underscore very clearly the action direction of the Russian Federation in the region as well, and the categorisation of enemies– the US, NATO, the EU – and the supreme military concern – The missile shield – and the willingness to undermine the public support that Turkey enjoys in Romania at the level of the media, the public space and the public opinion, our country being one of the three – along with Poland and Sweden, according to Transatlantic Trends – which supports the EU and NATO integration of Turkey (Chifu & Nantoi 2016: 82–83).

Romania slave to the US and anti-Americanism

Since NATO's enlargement was identified as a main threat to the security of the Russian Federation (the national security concept from 2000[86] – however, it was mentioned in the previous documents as well), the Russian media close to the regime tried to discredit the US and NATO. Creating a negative image of the Alliance and its most powerful member among the population of the states that might become NATO members, could stop the Atlantic aspirations of that state. Thus, this strategy becomes a method of defence against NATO's expansion.

But the Russian propaganda instruments' objectives do not end here. The image of the alliance can be attacked among the populations of the member states as well to weaken it from within. Even though a state is already a NATO member, or has US bases on its territory, attacking the image of Washington or of the alliance is a method through which Russia is trying to weaken the cohesion from among the alliance and to press for the withdrawal of the bases (long term).

Moscow's attempts to weaken the EU by supporting the ultra-nationalist parties in the member countries is not necessarily a secret and such a strategy can be applied at all levels (political, public opinion) and in the case of NATO.

Romania is both a NATO member and a host for the US military bases so that it becomes a priority target for the Russian propaganda instruments.

The anti-Americanism is divided in two main themes. The first is represented by the simple attempt to generate hatred against the US and the Americans, against anything that can be identified as American, such as the culture and values. This is defined as anti-Americanism. The second is related to taking advantage of the dissatisfactions regarding the political class in Romania and turning them against the US. This theme presupposes portraying the political class as one servile to the interests of the US and implicitly the US as a colonial power, one that only seeks to exploit Romania. This second theme was called "Romania slave to the US" after the message it is trying to convey. The analysis does not include official sources of Moscow and includes only written materials from independent media sources or from social networks.

Conclusions

The informational war of the Russian Federation reaches all the levels of social and political life, targeting, in particular, the influencing formulas of decisions at the political, strategic, military and security level, directly at the level of the decision makers, by means of the public space and the mass media, by creating groups of "alternative" opinion and of public pressure. We identified influences, at the political level, up to political parties and personalities openly assuming the Russian agenda, political figures in pro-European parties (Republic of Moldova), who assume this agenda, the Russian mass media, opinion formers and journalists, representatives of the academic and cultural area, who embrace the agenda of Russia's informational war through direct grants or responsively, genuinely, and retrospectively remunerated in indirect formulas, organisations of "the civil society" resulted from designing in a certain space such centres of debate and assumed pro-Russian opinion, or through projects within genuine organisations of the civil society which assume the Russian projects and opinions to be promoted, going to the influences "below the radar", the trolls' warfare, the psychological operations, pressure or influence over the mass media, the public space or the decision makers on agendas indirectly favourable to Russia, fulfilling objectives of the Russian informational war.

The trolls' operations and the ones influencing the media space are directed from Moscow, however the most insidious take aim at the internal resources from the target area. Russia seems to have made an important map of resources and of the opinions of the decision makers and opinion formers, and approaches each objective in a nuanced and targeted manner. It uses equally groups of opinion favourable to Russia, peacekeepers in favour of avoiding a conflict, as well as nationalists, Orthodox, anti-immigrationists, Islamophobes, xenophobes of Europe, together with forces of the left or statists that oppose the passing of powers to the supranational institutions – the EU, NATO; it also uses the people who believe in conspiracy, all the anarchists, the anti-capitalist left structures, as well as the anti-system people-structures. Most importantly, it tries to engage in blind persons who, genuinely, take a position that leads to achieving a goal of its informational warfare, exploits the person in blind, involving him in such operations or proceeds with the direct recruitment, employing him in his own operations, without apparently constraining him in any way.

At the level of the trolls war, Russia seems to have employed the development of the capabilities on Internet during the presidential campaign in 2014, when they identified individuals, groups, bloggers, trolls, opinion formers useful for this war and, after the campaign ended, it provided financing for continuing the genuine business, for creating independent platforms for the people employed, at the local level, subsequently intervening with themes, obligations, intervention descriptions in groups of three to determine the arguments and direct the speech and debate in the right direction, in order to achieve their goal. It is aimed at spaces of intense debate, of audience, where they intervene methodically and in a planned fashion, sometimes outside the original topic and direct the discussion towards their area of interest.

The sudden activation of a large number of "conserves" was recorded, persons left in the space of interest to develop their own personalities and positions, and suddenly reactivated by using them on certain themes in the informational war. Opinion makers, decision makers, journalists, bloggers with their own personality, formed in time, suddenly embrace strange positions, previously difficult to identify, promoting one or another theme, one or another sequence of the psychological operation. It is hard to discern if it is about an objective exploited blindly, at call, or paid through a clear financial scheme, in order to develop the respective activity. It is the task of the specialised agencies to determine the traceability. Instead, what we can say is that, at the level of the activity conducted by the trolls and bloggers, many of those affected make a living from it, and use too much time in such activities to be mere genuine impulses or natural individual concerns, but rather appear to be a source or complementary source of their income. In the "conserves"[87] case, the family ties and kinship of some young people that appeared overnight and the old abandoned and reactivated "Soviet conserves" are to be identified.

Russia seems to develop types of themes for each country in particular, outside the general topics of interest and the specific objectives. They go from underlying Russia's strength and position in international scaffolding, the role and place that it deserves, the need for a "big bargain" with it in the East, a new Yalta, to painting the West in black colours, placing the blame for all the ills in the world on the US, NATO, the EU, the West, cleaving transatlantic relations and attracting Europe into a deal with Russia then, the cleavage of Europe, supporting the anti-EU nationalisms, going to specific topics in each country. The action is calibrated to each country and each interesting media instrument and used as vector, or to each employed group.

Russia uses intermediaries in order to always have the possibility of credible denial of its actions. That's why it uses numerous intermediaries for these operations. It also creates the appearance of respecting the law, and invokes for its actions the freedom of expression, free flow of ideas and other democratic values.

Notes

1 The chapter has been realised based on a report done after a study of the Conflict Prevention and Early Warning Center Bucharest and IPP Chişinău, on the informational war in the region. The full results could be found in Iulian Chifu, Oazu Nantoi, *The Pattern of the Informational War of the Russian Federation*, Romanian Institute for Political Sciences and International Relations of the Romanian Academy, Bucharest, 2016.
2 Naef, W. E., *Psychological Operations Interview with Larry Dietz*, London: Infocon Magazine Issue One, October 2003, http://www.iwar.org.uk/infocon/psyop-dietz.htm, 29 April 2003 (accessed 17 July 2015).
3 *The Humanitarian Dimension of Russian Foreign Policy Toward Georgia, Moldova, Ukraine, and the Baltic States*, 2nd, supplementary edition Riga, 2010, p. 38.
4 *Concept of the Foreign Policy of the Russian Federation*, approved by President of the Russian Federation V. Putin on February 12th, 2013, 303-18-02-2013, unofficial translation, The Ministry of Foreign Affairs of the Russian Federation official site, athttp://archive.mid.ru//brp_4.nsf/0/76389FEC168189ED44257B2E0039B16D (accessed 17 July 2015).
5 Ibid.
6 Ibid.
7 Ibid.
8 Ibid.
9 Ibid.
10 Ibid.
11 Ibid.
12 Ibid.
13 Ibid.
14 Ibid.
15 Ibid.
16 Ibid.
17 Ibid.
18 Ibid.
19 *Military Doctrine of the Russian Federation*, approved by the President of the Russian Federation, V. Putin, Russian Federation Embassy in Malaysia, at http://malaysia. mid.ru/web/embassy-of-the-russian-federation-in-malaysia/press-release/-/asset_ publisher/rAwX0ikSv3ua/content/29-06-2015-the-military-doctrine-of-the-russian-fe deration?redirect=http%3A%2F%2Fmalaysia.mid.ru%2Fweb%2Fembassy-of-the-russian-federation-in-malaysia%2Fpressrelease%3Fp_p_id%3D101_INSTANCE_ rAwX0ikSv3ua%26p_p_lifecycle%3D0%26p_p_state%3Dnormal%26p_ p_mode%3Dview%26p_p_col_id%3Dcolumn-1%26p_p_col_count%3D1 (accessed 17 April 2015).
20 Ibid.
21 Ibid.
22 Ibid.
23 *Address by President of the Russian Federation, March 18th, 2014,* The Kremlin, Moscow, President of Russia, athttp://en.kremlin.ru/events/president/news/20603(accessed 16 April 2015).
24 Ibid.
25 Ibid.
26 Ibid.
27 Ibid.
28 Ibid.
29 Ibid.
30 Ibid.
31 Ibid.

32 *Kremlinul vrea cât mai mult sânge la TV. A început războiul rece,* Dechide.md, http://deschide.md/ro/news/externe/17897/Media-rus%C4%83-R%C4%83zboiul-rece.htm, 7 August 2015, (accessed 15 August 2015).

33 Ibid.

34 *Shoigu: Information becomes another armed forces component,* Interfax, http://www.interfax.com/newsinf.asp?id=581851, 28 Mach 2015, (accessed 15 August 2015).

35 Shaun Walker, *Salutin' Putin: inside a Russian troll house,* The Guardian, https://www.theguardian.com/world/2015/apr/02/putin-kremlin-inside-russian-troll-house, 2 April 2015, (accessed 15 August 2015).

36 *Confronting Russia's weaponization of information,* Hearing before the Committee on Foreign Affairs House of Representatives, One Hundred Fourteenth Congress, April 15, 2015, Serial No. 114-37, http://docs.house.gov/meetings/FA/FA00/20150415/103320/HHRG-114-FA00-Transcript-20150415.pdf.

37 McGreal, C., *Vladimir Putin's 'misinformation' offensive prompts US to deploy its cold war propaganda tools,* the Guardian, https://www.theguardian.com/world/2015/apr/25/us-set-to-revive-propaganda-war-as-putin-pr-machine-undermines-baltic-states, 25 April 2015, (accessed 28 August 2015).

38 Pomeranzev, P., *Confronting Russia's Weaponization of Information,* House Committee on Foreign Affairs, http://docs.house.gov/meetings/FA/FA00/20150415/103320/HHRG-114-FA00-Wstate-PomerantsevP-20150415.pdf, 15 April 2014 (accessed 28 August 2015).

39 Troianovski, A., *Germany Seeks to Counter Russian 'Propaganda' in Baltics,* The Wall Street Journal, http://www.wsj.com/articles/germany-seeks-to-counter-russian-propaganda-in-baltics-1429294362, 17 April 2015 (accessed 28 August 2015).

40 Molander, R. C. & Riddile, A. S. & Wilson, A. P., *Strategic Information Warfare: A New Face of War,* RAND Corporation, http://www.rand.org/pubs/monograph_reports/MR661/index2.html, 1996, (accessed 25August 2015).

41 The law of oblivion: every unwanted subject, group or person in the internet can be locked in order that nobody from Russia cannot find or reach him. The page will not open in Russia. It doesn't mean that it could be erased from servers situated in the US or anywhere in the world. They are there and stay as ghosts on the internet since the persons originally involved and interested can no longer access them.Deutche Welle, "Russian parliament approves 'right to be forgotten online' law", 03.07.2015, http://www.dw.com/en/russian-parliament-approves-right-to-be-forgotten-online-law/a-18560565.

42 *Concept of the Foreign Policy of the Russian Federation,* approved by President of the Russian Federation V. Putin on 12 February 2013" (accessed 17 July 2015).

43 McGuinness, D., *Russia steps into Berlin 'rape' storm claiming German cover-up,* BBC News, http://www.bbc.com/news/blogs-eu-35413134, 27 January 2016 (accessed 28 February 2016).

44 Chatham House London, UK, *What Now for Britain and the EU?, debate,* 27 Jun 2016, at: https://www.chathamhouse.org/event/what-now-britain-and-eu?gclid=CjwKEAjwtb PGBRDhoLaqn6HknWsSJABR-o5sWSvy669YjOfBXcUYwIfbm65m8koamicmhkEn doA4nBoCRBjw_wcB#sthash.DlX7oRG1.dpuf. See also Patrick Sawer, *Russia accused of waging secret warfare against Britain using cyber attacks, espionage and fake news,* The Telegraph, 17 December 2016 http://www.telegraph.co.uk/news/2016/12/17/russia-accused-waging-secret-war-against-britain-using-cyber/, citing UK Government enquiry on Russia's involvement in Brexit

45 *President Putin's Fiction: 10 False Claims About Ukraine,* Fact Sheet, Office of the Spokesperson, U.S. Department of State, Washington DC, http://www.state.gov/r/pa/prs/ps/2014/03/222988.htm, 5 March 2014(accessed 21 July 2015). http://iipdigital.usembassy.gov/st/english/texttrans/2014/03/20140306295487.html?CP.rss=true

46 *Russian Fiction the Sequel: 10 More False Claims About Ukraine,* Fact Sheet, Office of the Spokesperson, U.S. Department of Stat, Washington DC, http://www.state.gov/r/

pa/prs/ps/2014/04/224759.htm, 13 April 2014(accessed 21 July 2015). http://xoxol. org/putin/ten-more-false-claims.html

47 http://www.stopfake.org/en/news/ (accessed 21 July 2015).

48 Rettman, A., *EU mulls response to Russia's information war,* EU Observer, https:// euobserver.com/foreign/127135, 8 January 2015 (accessed 21 July 2015).

49 *Security Council Fails to Adopt Resolution on Tribunal for Malaysia Airlines Crash in Ukraine, Amid Calls for Accountability, Justice for Victims*, Security Council, 7498th Meeting (PM), United Nations, http://www.un.org/press/en/2015/sc11990.doc.htm, 29 July 2015(accessed 30 July 2015).

50 Rettman, A., *Dutch-Polish 'content factory' to counter Russian propaganda,* EU Observer, https://euobserver.com/foreign/129724, 21 July 2015 (accessed 30 July 2015).

51 Dempsey, J., *The European Endowment for Democracy Goes Russian,* Carnegie Europe, http://carnegieeurope.eu/strategiceurope/59377, 16 March 2015 (accessed 30 July 2015).

52 *Questions and Answers about the East StratCom Task Force*, European Union External Action, http://collections.internetmemory.org/haeu/content/20160313172652/http:// eeas.europa.eu/top_stories/2015/261115_stratcom-east_qanda_en.htm, 26 November 2015(accessed 5 December 2015).

53 *Responding to Russia's weaponization of information. Recommendations for policy makers in the Baltic States, Ukraine, Georgia and Moldova*, BBSA, http://bbsa.lv/ wp-content/uploads/2015/10/Recommendations_BBSA_final.pdf, September 2014 (accessed 30 November 2015).

54 Chen, A., *The Agency,* The New York Times Magazine, http://www.nytimes. com/2015/06/07/magazine/the-agency.html?_r=0, 2 June 2015 (accessed 12 November 2015).

55 Fitzpatrick, C. A., *Russian Blogger Finds Pro-Kremlin 'Troll Factories',* The Daily Beast, http://www.thedailybeast.com/articles/2015/08/20/russian-blogger-finds-pro-kremlin-troll-factories.html, 20 August 2015 (accessed 30 August 2015).

56 *Everything you wanted to know about trolls but were afraid to ask,* Share America, https://share.america.gov/trolls-everything-you-wanted-to-know/, 4 November 2015 (accessed 7 November 2015).

57 Fitzpatrick, C. A., *Russian Blogger Finds Pro-Kremlin 'Troll Factories'.*

58 McGuinness, D., *Russia steps into Berlin 'rape' storm claiming German cover-up.*

59 Max Seddon, *Documents show How Russia's Troll Army Hit America,* BuzzFeedNews, 2 June 2014, https://www.buzzfeed.com/maxseddon/documents-show-how-russias-troll-army-hit-america?utm_term=.shWKyw78e#.ykXk7dzE0.

60 Ibid.

61 Seddon, M., *Documents show How Russia's Troll Army Hit America,* BuzzFeed News World, https://www.buzzfeed.com/maxseddon/documents-show-how-russias-troll-army-hit-america?utm_term=.br2EEljZP#.dp3NNwAbG 2 June 2014 (accessed 30 July 2015).

62 Sharkov, D., *Putin ally warns open war with Ukraine would last just four days,* Newsweek, http://europe.newsweek.com/russian-parliament-speaker-compares-baltics-trained-dogs-444683?rm=eu, 6 April 2016 (accessed 15 April 2016).

63 For example: *Bridge to Crimea: Putin strives to complete a 'historic mission',* Kathrin Hille, Max Seddon, 23 September 2016, https://www.ft.com/content/1c266a70-8160-11e6-8e50-8ec15fb462f4, for instance. A big number of military Ukrainian and Western personnel, pundits, journalists analysed this possibility. Please see also http:// euromaidanpress.com/2017/03/15/moscows-objective-gain-land-corridor-to-crimea-by-seizing-mariupol-ukrainian-analyst-says-euromaidan-press/, https://www.google. ro/search?q=A+corridor+from+Russia+to+Crimea&espv=2&tbm=isch&tbo=u&sour ce=univ&sa=X&ved=0ahUKEwieqtPsteDSAhVIVhQKHXSYDpYQsAQIFw&biw= 1366&bih=638&dpr=1, http://www.cbsnews.com/news/us-concerned-russia-may-carve-out-path-to-crimea/

64 Balmforth, T., *Former Russian Health Chief Suggests U.S. Plotting Zika Attack,* Radio Free Europe Radio Liberty, http://www.rferl.org/a/former-russian-health-chief-suggests-us-plotting-zika-attack/27555365.html, 16 February 2016 (accessed 15 April 2016).

65 Ibid.

66 Thomas Boghard, *Operation INFEKTION. Soviet Bloc Intelligence and Its AIDS Disinformation Campaign,* Studies in Intelligence Vol. 53, No. 4 (December 2009). Posted 26 Jan 2010, https://www.cia.gov/library/center-for-the-study-of-intelligence/csi-publications/csi-studies/studies/vol53no4/soviet-bloc-intelligence-and-its-aids.html.

67 http://www.bbc.com/russian/society/2016/03/160315_smj_trolls_make_haram_video

68 Logan, R., *Video of 'US soldier shooting Qur'an' is a fake made in Russia,* Mirror, http://www.mirror.co.uk/news/world-news/video-us-soldier-shooting-quran-7654058, 30 March 2016 (accessed 15 April 2016).

69 Steward, W., *'I'm going to shoot this mother ***er': Shock footage of a 'US soldier' blasting the Koran with a machine gun is FAKED by Vladimir Putin's anti-West 'troll factory',* MailOnline, http://www.dailymail.co.uk/news/article-3515146/I-m-going-shoot-mother-er-Shock-footage-soldier-blasting-Koran-machine-gun-FAKED-Vladimir-Putin-s-anti-America-troll-factory.html, 30 March 2016 (accessed 15 April 2016).

70 Logan, R., *Video of 'US soldier shooting Qur'an' is a fake made in Russia,* Mirror, http://www.mirror.co.uk/news/world-news/video-us-soldier-shooting-quran-7654058, 30 March 2016 (accessed 15 April 2016).

71 *"Romanii din Ucraina NU au cerut unirea cu patria-mama, cum a scris presa rusa. Cine sta in spatele acestei dezinformari(Romanians from Ukraine did not demand the reunification with the Mother Land, as the Russian Press wrote. Who stays behind this disinformation?),* PROTV, 31 July 2015, http://stirileprotv.ro/stiri/international/romanii-din-ucraina-nu-au-cerut-unirea-cu-patria-mama-cum-a-scris-presa-rusa-cine-sta-in-spatele-acestei-dezinformari.html

72 *Cernăuți: Adunarea Românilor din Bucovina s-a fondat și cere autonomie în cadrul Ucrainei,* RussiaToday.ro, http://news.russiatoday.ro/cernauti-adunarea-romanilor-din-bucovina-s-a-fondat-si-cere-autonomie-in-cadrul-ucrainei/, 28 July 2015 (accessed 15 April 2016).

73 *"Romanii din Ucraina NU au cerut unirea cu patria-mama, cum a scris presa rusa. Cine sta in spatele acestei dezinformari(Romanians from Ukraine did not demand the reunification with the Mother Land, as the Russian Press wrote. Who stays behind this disinformation?),* PROTV, 31 July 2015, http://stirileprotv.ro/stiri/international/romanii-din-ucraina-nu-au-cerut-unirea-cu-patria-mama-cum-a-scris-presa-rusa-cine-sta-in-spatele-acestei-dezinformari.html

74 Vadim Vasiliu, *Încă o făcătură a propagandei ruse-„Adunarea românilor din Ucraina"(Another fake made by the Russian propaganda – The Reunion of Romanians in Ukraine),* Adevarul, 30 July 2015, at http://adevarul.ro/moldova/actualitate/Inca-facatura-propagandei-ruse-adunarearomanilor-bucovina-1_55b9ef6bf5eaafab2c16ba6a/index.html

75 Bucpress(http://bucpress.eu/)

76 *Russian General Demands Preemptive Nuclear Strike Doctrine Against NATO,* Global Intel Hub, http://globalintelhub.com/russian-general-demands-preemptive-nuclear-strike-doctrine-nato/Ewen MacAskill, The Guardian, *NATO held a massive training exercise to warn Russia,* Jun. 18, 2015, 10:20 PM, at http://www.businessinsider.com/nato-held-a-massive-training-exercise-to-warn-russia-2015-6Moscow will respond to NATO approaching Russian borders 'accordingly' – Putin* in Russia Today, https://www.rt.com/news/267661-russia-nato-border-weapons/.Published time: 16 Jun, 2015 21:17, Edited time: 18 Jun, 2015 12:25

77 Ibid.

78 Baczynska, G. & Szary, W., *Russia says will retaliate if U.S. weapons stationed on its borders,* Reuters, http://www.reuters.com/article/us-russia-usa-europe-idUSKBN0OV17A20150615, 15 June 2015 (accessed 15 April 2016).

79 *Scenariu rusesc: România vrea să atace Transnistria. Reacția purtătorului de cuvânt al Guvernului*, digi24, http://www.digi24.ro/stiri/actualitate/evenimente/scenariu-rusesc-romania-vrea-sa-atace-transnistria-reactia-purtatorului-de-cuvant-al-guvernului-399789, 3 June 2015(accessed 21 June 2016).

80 *"România analizează posibilitatea unei intervenții MILITARE în Transnistria", susține un analistmoldovean*, Mediafax, http://www.mediafax.ro/externe/romania-analizeaza-posibilitatea-unei-interventii-militare-in-transnistria-sustine-un-analist-moldovean-14397280, 4 June 2015 (accessed 21June 2016).

81 *Milițiile din Novorossia afirmă că ar fi descoperit LAGĂRE tip Guantanamo lângă Donețsk*, Nașul TV, http://www.nasul.tv/incredibil-militiile-din-novorossia-afirma-ca-ar-fi-descoperit-lagare-tip-guantanamo-langa-donetsk/, 24 April 2015 (accessed 21 June 2016).

82 Ibid.

83 Ibid.

84 https://lookup-id.com/dir/654524471326324.html (accessed 21June 2016).

85 Chifu, I., *Pulsul planetei. Războiul informațional împotriva României*, evz.ro, http://www.evz.ro/pulsul-planetei-razboiul-informational-impotriva-romaniei.html, 17 April 2015 (accessed 21 June 2016).

86 NATIONAL SECURITY CONCEPT OF THE RUSSIAN FEDERATION, Approved by Presidential Decree No. 24 of 10 January 2000, 10 January 2000, http://www.mid.ru/en/foreign_policy/official_documents/-/asset_publisher/CptICkB6BZ29/content/id/589768

87 "Conserves" are people from the Soviet / Russian external security services that immigrated in the West with false Western identities, become local citizens, integrated completely, building themselves a history, without doing any activity. Then, when the time comes and there's a need to use them, they are re-activated. It happens with them and their children, as well. This is inherited from the Russian Soviet era. There are conserves in all Western countries as well as in the former socialist countries. See Christopher Andrews, Oleg Gordiewski, *KGB: The Inside Story of its Foreign Operations from Lenin to Gorbachev*, Harper Collins Publishers, 1990; Peter Hennessy, forward to *Understanding Intelligence in the Twenty-First Century*, LV Scott and Peter Jackson, eds. London: 2004; *"Melita Norwood: A secret life". 13 September 1999 – via bbc.co.uk*. at http://news.bbc.co.uk/2/hi/uk_news/444519.stm

Bibliography

Bērziņš, J. & Jaeski, A. & Laity, M. & Maliukevicius, N. & Navys, A. & Osborne, G. & Pszczel, R. & Tatham, S., Analysis of Russia's information campaign against Ukraine, Riga: NATO StratCom Centre of Excellence, 2015

Chifu, I. &Nantoi, O., *The Pattern of the Informational War of the Russian Federation*, Bucharest: Romanian Institute for Political Sciences and International Relations of the Romanian Academy, 2016

Clover, C., *In Moscow, A New Eurasianism*, Washington DC: The Journal of International Security Affairs, Fall/Winter 2014, No. 27

Ćwiek-Karpowicz, J., *Limits to Russian Soft Power in the Post-Soviet Area*, Berlin: DGAP analyse, 8 July 2012

Lucas, E. & Nimmo, B., *Information Warfare: What is it and how to win it?*, Washington DC: CEPA Infowar Paper No 1, November 2015

Lucas, E. & Pomeranzev, P., *Winning the Information War. Techniques and Counter-strategies to Russian Propaganda in Central and Eastern Europe*, Washington DC: CEPA's Information Warfare Project in Partnership with Legatum Institute, August 2016

Makarychev, A. *Hard Questions About Soft Power: A Normative Outlook at Russia's Foreign Policy*, Berlin: DGAP analyse kompakt, no 7, October 2011

O'Shaughnessy, N., *The death and life of propaganda,* Journal of Public Affairs, Volume 12, number 1, John Wiley & Sons, Ltd, 2012

Payne, K., *The Media as an Instrument of War,* Parameters, Spring 2005

Polyakova, A. & Laruelle, M. & Meister, S. & Barnett, N., *The Kremlin's Trojan Horses,* Washington DC: Atlantic Council, November 2016

Snegovaya, M., *Putin's informational warfare in Ukraine. Soviet origins of Russia's hybrid warfare,* Washington DC: Institute for the Study of War, 2015

Stern, E., *Crisis decision making. A cognitive institutional approach*, Dept. of Political Science, Stockholm: University of Stockholm, 1999

Zhukov, M. Y. & Baum, M. A., *Reporting Bias and Information Warfare,* International Studies Association Annual Convention Atlanta, GA, March 2016, https://www.hks.harvard.edu/fs/mbaum/documents/zb_isa_v5.pdf

7 Strategic Messages in the August 2008 Georgian–Russian War

Greg Simons

The informational aspect to waging war has steadily increased in importance. It is a virtual and intangible war that is fought in parallel with the physical hostilities. The reach of an informational war can be much wider, more insidious and invasive. It is directed at everyone, combatants and non-combatants alike. Public diplomacy and propaganda use a variety of tools that are intended to alter the perception of an event, and therefore following from this, patterns of thought and behaviour. This use of perception and deception is often assisted by the fact that many audiences are remote from the event and/or an effective gatekeeper system is in place, which narrows the choices available to the 'consumer' (the public) of the information in terms of informational pluralism.

One of the problems that are to be encountered in researching a topic such as this is the use of deception. Therefore it is important to not always accept things for what they appear to be. This has the effect of compounding the confusion caused by the *fog of war*. The word and concept propaganda, which has been so well used and abused in the past, has a controversial and even perhaps sinister connotation that comes with it. This necessitates the use of another word or term not associated with it and therefore does not attract the negative associations. In this regard, it proves quite difficult to separate propaganda from public diplomacy.

This chapter intends to look at the motivation and use of public diplomacy and propaganda in modern conflict, firstly from a theoretical point of view and then moving to a practical example to back up the theory. Material is sourced from books, media material and from journals and newsletters on the subject. The basic questions being explored in this work are: what are the reasons behind using this kind of attempted influence; what does it look like in a practical application; and does it work?

While the world's attention was seemingly focused on the Olympic Games being opened in Beijing, China in early August 2008, a five-day war broke out in Georgia. Many quickly blamed Russia's actions as reckless and aggressive (Asmus 2010), but others framed Russia's actions as emanating from a sense of insecurity and were in fact defensive in nature (Tsygankov 2016). The empirical focus of this chapter is on the August 2008 South Ossetian conflict, from the perspective of the failings of the Western mass media in giving an accurate or objective account of events. Certainly, when speaking of a term such as *objectivity* it is not possible to speak of it in absolute values. Instead one can speak of something being more or less objective. It makes for an interesting exercise when exploring the reasons behind the failing of the Western mass media, exposing a number of exploitable weaknesses in the structure of news production that can be used by unscrupulous actors.

A number of serious failings in the mass media coverage are revealed (for further information on this subject see Bennett et. al 2007; Norris et. al. 2003; Zelizer & Allan 2002). This can call into question the effectiveness of the perception of the mass media acting in the role of the Fourth Estate, acting in the capacity as a watchdog and protecting the public from the excesses of political power (or at least exposing it). Media acted within the framework of being active participants of an information war and they were in the capacity as public relations amplifiers, seeking to win the hearts and minds of their audiences in pursuit of a political agenda (Akhvlediani 2009). In effect many media acted as an amplifier of a political agenda and consequently the notion and role of a public guardian was lost.

The 2008 war has been framed by some along the lines of von Clausewitz, with this war representing politics by another means (Gordadze 2011). One of the fundamental problems, which need to be brought up, is that journalists may actually think they are serving the public interest. This can be found in the news frame of *defending Georgian democracy against unprovoked Russian aggression*. However, this in effect does not serve the public interest of the countries where this information is being disseminated (Western Europe and North America for example). If public opinion is manipulated to the point where it demands action from the nation's political leaders (whether or not the political establishment are receptive to the idea), on a false pretext, policy is conducted by deception and is most likely to inflame rather than dampen down the conflict.

News production and framing

During a conventional war (two standing armies meeting face to face on a defined battlefield) between two recognized states (by the UN as a means of measure), it is not unusual for the antagonistic actors to both possess a range of domestic mass media assets (print, broadcast and electronic media). This is also complemented often by the fact that mass media often rally behind the state during times of war (see Willcox 2006 for example). In the case of this chapter though it is not the domestic public (that of Georgia and Russia) that are of greatest interest, rather we are interested in the international public that are targeted by both sides in an attempt to win hearts and minds, in order to harness any potential political mobilization that can be achieved.

Bearing the above in mind, it is necessary to turn the attention of this chapter to look from a theoretical perspective at the process of producing news. In turn, this shall make sense of some of the empirical information that comes later. A news story can be said to consist of a number of different and interrelated parts. As such a news story consists of four main parts;

- Framing – establishing the topic.
- Focussing – the event's significance is explained.
- Realising – story confirmation and the process of authentication.
- Closing – alternative views are discounted. This process occurs throughout the story. Bignell (1997: 119–121)

The above describes the process of framing the news, after the information enters the system of news production. But what determines what information is allowed to enter the system in the first instance? News production is the result of a number of components and considerations added together. Therefore one can characterise news production as the sum of:

News = national priorities + national politics + media framing

The above formula describes in a very abstract and theoretical way the culmination of considerations that decides what makes news and what does not. In practice this is not a uniform process across the globe owing to different national priorities, different national politics and different media framing. Variation can enter the system when comparing the different national media systems with each other.

A final consideration in this section deals with the issue of gatekeeping and censorship. It should be understood that censorship is not necessarily something that is imposed by an outside agency on the mass media and journalists. When a frame becomes dominant in the mass media or a dominant frame theme is inserted into the mass media, then that frame shall be defended against information that runs contrary or is in any way dissonant with the central theme frame. A homogenous media workforce is easier to manage due to less pluralism of thought present in the workplace. In such circumstances, it is easier to gain consensus on issues of majority of opinion. Ultimately, a spiral of silence will develop ensuring effect discursive management by the dominant elite. The media's

> [...] gate keeping and agenda-setting roles have the capacity to set in motion a 'spiral of silence.' This means that social discourse is progressively closed because people fall silent if their views do not coincide with what the media portray as 'majority opinion'. (Louw 2001: 160)

Thus it is potentially a theoretical possibility, if a mass media savvy communicator knows the mechanisms and factors that determine news production, they may be able to 'hijack' the news frame. If this is done successfully, the mass media system shall do the policing for the sender (inserter) of the message by preventing competing or contradictory messages out of the system (i.e. it is a self-policing closed system). Such a scenario would give the actor a tremendous advantage in terms of persuasion and influence potential over their rival. An operational concept is needed to package the message in order for it to be noticed and transmitted by the mass media.

Defining public diplomacy and propaganda

In its most neutral and 'pure' form, propaganda is about the spreading of ideas. Philip Taylor states that it is "a process for the sowing, germination and cultivation of ideas and, as such, is – or should be – neutral as a concept" Taylor (2003: 2). However, the process is not left in isolation from the society in which it operates. There is a tendency by society to weigh the ethical and moral standards of such a practice, and under such conditions if it falls short of public expectation it is condemned. A fact that does not help is the cynical and deceptive use of propaganda by interest groups to push forward their political and economic agenda.

The term "propaganda" is a controversial one that has many negative connotations attached to it over the years as the result of an association with events in history, such as the Nazi and Soviet use of propaganda. It is also viewed as being a manipulation of the masses through deception. Hence many political figures in Europe and North America have made strenuous efforts to distance themselves from any hint of use or association with the practice. In effect there is the desire to state that *we do not do propaganda here*. According to the liberal view, there are a great number of negative aspects that affect society.

> Propaganda, it is felt, forces us to think and do things in ways we might not have otherwise done had we been left to our own devices. It obscures our windows on the world by providing layers of distorting condensation. When nations fight, it thickens the fog of war. Propaganda thus becomes the enemy of independent thought and an intrusive and unwanted manipulator of the free flow of information and ideas in humanity's quest for 'peace and truth'. (Taylor 2003: 1)

Thus resistance to the idea and practice of propaganda is based upon central human values within the individualistic spirit of freedom of thought, choice and actions. But what about public diplomacy, what is it and how does it work? A traditional role of public diplomacy is to try and persuade a given audience to hold a desired view on a subject, whether it is a favourable attitude toward a particular country or even a specific regime. In the current context of the Global War on Terrorism, this goal is sometimes moderated to encompass the desire to prevent the manifestation of certain unwanted behaviour. This can also be the case between countries during periods of peace, which is intended to influence the behaviour of citizens of the targeted country. For instance, an attempt to try and channel dislike or hatred in a given population away from acts of physical violence and extremism to something else. The nature and practice of public diplomacy differs from that of propaganda. Rather than having a purely 'passive' audience, as in a propaganda campaign, public diplomacy seeks to engage members of its audience in order to influence their thoughts and behaviour. How this functions in practice was expressed by the Under Secretary of State for Public Diplomacy and Public Affairs, James Glassman in a press briefing.

Our aim in public diplomacy is to engage foreign publics to make it easier to achieve U.S. foreign policy goals, both short term and long term. People frequently see my job as winning a beauty contest or an 'American Idol' vote. I disagree with that. My job is to help achieve the national interest, not necessarily by making America more popular, although certainly popularity, or more importantly a respect and trust, those are important things. But we focus on policy goals.

The key goals are to diminish the threat to Americans and the rest of the world posed by violent extremism and weapons of mass destruction, and to help people around the world to achieve freedom. Now, those two goals are linked. As the National Security Strategy puts it, championing freedom advances our interest because the survival of liberty at home increasingly depends on the success of liberty abroad. Governments that honour their citizens' dignity and desire for freedom tend to uphold responsible conduct towards other nations.[1]

Glassman's comments concerning the necessity for the sender to have credibility demonstrate that public diplomacy is still very much tied to the basic fundamentals of public relations and the formation and management of political relationships with foreign publics. An initial and crucial step is that the sender of a message must have credibility in order for their message to have any hope of its intended effect. In effect, public diplomacy serves as a form of informational plan that is designed to achieve the business plan (to enable successful prosecution of, in this instance, U S foreign policy).

One of the weak points of the public diplomacy theory, though, can be found in one of its basic assumptions. It seems to be the belief of many that cultural or educational exchanges are a good conduit for the host country to export its values to another country via those participants who engage in such exchanges. That is, by immersing a student in the lifestyle and values of the host country, these values and ways of thinking 'rub off' on them and they become an ambassador of these values and ways of thinking in their native country upon their return. However, I argue that this does not necessarily have to be the case, i.e. the participant internalising those values and adopts them as their own. There can be at least one more scenario, where the participant may not adopt those values. But, after living in the host country they come to understand how that society works and the finer points and meanings of the language. They therefore can appear to be 'like' people from the host country as they are able to communicate with the same technical language.[2] And therefore communication is much more effective as it sounds familiar and has a greater chance of achieving its intended effect.

Historical perspective

The use of propaganda stretches back across the vast expanse of time, from the use of visual art (frescos for example) and literature, to the modern equivalents seen and heard on film, TV and other mass media. One of the elements used in the informational aspects of war is military censorship, and more recently the use of front groups and pressure groups. The first aspect, military censorship, is designed to constrict the flow of information. Pressure groups and front groups are attempts at trying to 'steer' the course of the debate once it has started. The establishment of the Committee for Public Information in the United States by President Woodrow Wilson in 1917 can be argued to fall into this category. In the sense of this work, a pressure group is defined as being:

> On one view the activity of politics is facilitated by pressure groups, since they can obtain the ear of government; on another view it is hindered by them, since they drown out the individual voice. A pressure group that is consulted regularly, and which has enduring institutions and a body of legislation to protect its aims, has ceased to become a pressure group, and has become instead part of the establishment (Scruton 2007: 549–550).

There are a number of different strategy options open to pressure groups in order for them to try and attain their goals. The first group of strategies involve the use of action; such as bribes, boycotts and the use of violence. Another set of strategies involves two possible options; the use of propaganda and the use of censorship. These strategies are carried out in response to what a group perceives as being a threat. This raises the question, within the context of this chapter, what exactly is a threat? It can be described in the following manner: "The ideas that pressure groups perceive to be threatening fall into two general groups: those that relate to the public interest, or core values of the society, and those that relate to the welfare of the particular groups in question" Elkin (1960: 75). According to the Copenhagen School of thought, anything can be constructed and perceived as a threat as security is a socially constructed concept.

The use of front groups (also known as front organisations) is more noticeably used in the capacity of trying to put a positive spin on modern war. A front group can only be called such if it purports to represent one agenda when it in fact is working towards another agenda. An organisation may work with the use of deceptive means, but at the same time may make no secret of the interests it truly represents. It is also something that has been around for some time now. A definition of a front group in this context is as follows:

> Organisations which profess acceptable aims, in order to conceal the unacceptable aims which really motivate them. Usually the term describes organisations which are ostensibly liberal, democratic and constitutional, with respected and respectable members […] (Scruton 2007: 264).

It is a matter of trying to exert influence through stealth. A key point to be understood at this point is that what is seen on the surface is not what it appears to be. The audience, in an 'ideal' situation should not know the true agenda of the front or lobby group. An appearance or facade of legitimacy is gained by not being seen as being associated with an interest that could be unpopular. There are other ways and means of attempting influence too.

Public diplomacy was a tactic employed during the Cold War by both sides. Glassman stated that "after a slow start, the United States became good at public diplomacy, with such institutions as the Congress of Cultural Freedom, Radio Free Europe, and the USIA." However, after the perceived need for public diplomacy ended with the Cold War, then the mechanisms of persuasion were dismantled.[3] Propaganda can be seen as an attempt to influence opinion, a relatively short-term strategy. However, public diplomacy is designed to affect influence at a deeper level, impacting upon attitudes and values. This is done over the long term and is brought about by attempting to build a mutual 'relationship' with its target audience.

One of the 'victims' of the end of the Cold War, in the arsenal of propaganda and influence activity in general was ideology. With the end of the Cold War, and the demise of communism, it was assumed that there was no place and no need for ideology anymore. However, with the rise of the Global War on Terrorism and combating a politico-religious opponent that uses ideological concepts has forced the return of ideology. This was hastened by the fact that the Western forces were declared as losing the propaganda war to the terrorist/insurgent groups, such as al Qaeda and the Taliban. This also defeats the notion that countries like the United Kingdom and the United States do not engage in propaganda.[4]

Until this point where the use of ideological propaganda had regained currency, wars and conflicts were initiated and waged through the notion of justifiable concepts, often based upon highly laudable reasons (Willcox 2006). In 1986, American President Ronald Reagan justified the bombing of Libya as "the peaceful mission of America to counter the savagery of the brutal enemy wherever he threatens freedom" (Gonzalez & Tanno 1997: 15). In addition to *defending freedom*, other reasons based upon humanitarian concerns have been used – preventing genocide and famine for instance.

Logic and reasoning of influence

Influence is most effective when it becomes internalised within a target audience. That is, instead of consciously thinking and processing information and events in one's environment, the process becomes 'automated' due to a certain level of psychological conditioning. An individual's world view is formed by people and events around them, and this is then used as a means with which to process and interpret further information and events as they unfold. In this way, views and reactions to particular events, if they cannot be 'guided' it can be to some extent anticipated or predicted.

One of the key driving factors behind influence is that it is about being able to have a target audience think or react in a certain way that is beneficial to the promoted agenda. This must be done in such a way that the target audience perceive the process to have originated internally and not 'imposed' from an external source. Thus the process becomes policy making by perception. It is a process that is waged by emotional rather than logical means. It is also very much a process that is based upon emotion rather than information. One of the main reasons behind this is that information may inform an audience about the alternatives that are available to it and it gives a certain element of freedom of will and choice, which may not satisfy the agenda of the message sender. The use of emotion on the other hand, produces a sense of purpose and motivates the audience into action (see Johnson-Cartee & Copeland 2003).

This is tied to the nature of modern warfare and the way it is currently waged, which is guided by and determined by political factors much more intensely than in the past. The advances in modern mass media communications mean that an actor can reach and potentially influence a much larger audience than they could in the past. Therefore when a country is at war, an additional edge may be gained via politically mobilising the international audience to its cause and rallying their potential to sway the opinion of the national politics of their respective countries. In effect this is a means to carry out political lobbying via effective mass communications.

Influence on the battlefield and in the living rooms

Influence is perhaps best achieved when the target audience feels comfortable and at ease in their home environment. Their guard may be somewhat lowered by an increased perception and sense of security that comes with being in a familiar environment that is considered to be theirs. Therefore the living room, where the public sphere meets the private sphere becomes an important site in the struggle for influence.

Information and messages sent must contain the appropriate (in terms of values and understanding) use of symbols and meaning. Without this, the message can be misinterpreted, ignored or rejected. Glassman in his press briefing gave some hints as to the aims of public diplomacy, what the goals are and the means of the intended influence.

> While winning hearts and minds would be an admirable feat, the war of ideas adopts the more immediate and realistic goal of diverting impressionable segments of the population from the recruitment process. The war of ideas is really a battle of alternatives, alternative visions, and our goal is to divert recruits from the violent extremist vision. Our role is as a facilitator of choice. We help build networks and movements, put tools in the hands of young people to make their own choices, rather than dictating those choices.[5]

There are a number of points that can be gleaned from the text; the impression given by looking at what is said without any hidden meaning it seems to be a very noble quest. However, a basic point that is understood when discussing the issue of influence and persuasion is that a public that knows it is being manipulated are more likely to try and resist the message given. As Glassman stated on a number of occasions during his briefing, it is his job to ensure that the interests of American foreign policy are served. Therefore, following from this, it is in his interests that his intended public believe that it is them who are in charge of making their own choices and they are not being 'steered' into one choice or another.

A number of different means exist in the arsenal of public diplomacy which may seem to be 'innocent' or even benevolent. Such spheres as culture, entertainment, music, technology, literature, politics, sport, religion, education and business can all be used as part of a public diplomacy campaign. Traditionally, public diplomacy efforts have been spearheaded by the use of such tools as educational and cultural exchanges, sending 'experts' abroad (the US State Department sends some 800 experts abroad each year), the use of multilingual websites (such as www.america.gov and www.president.kremlin.ru) and the ownership or control of mass media assets.

The size of the American public diplomacy effort, in terms of the volume and size of mass media assets, is impressive. Glassman outlined some of the various media assets that are engaged in the public diplomacy programme around the world.

> The state of our broadcasting effort is helping. Every week, 175 million Americans – I'm sorry, 175 million adults around the world tune in to programming of US international broadcasting, in a total of 60 languages – that is more than any other international broadcaster – from the Voice of America, Radio Free Europe, Radio Liberty, Al Hurra, Radio Sawa, Radio and TV Marti, Radio Free Asia. That's a 75 percent increase in audience since 2002. And of the 75 new – 75 million new listeners, about half are Arabic speakers. But the BBG is also having an impact in places like Tibet, Burma, Kenya, North Korea, Cuba and Iran. In Iran, VOA Persian TV broadcasts 7 hours a day and reaches more than one-quarter of adult Iranians every week by satellite. Al Hurra has a bigger audience than Al Jazeera in Iraq, and a very large audience as well in Syria and other Arab countries. And it's viewed every week by more than – as I said, by more than half the adults in Syria.[6]

One potential flaw in this deluge of facts and figures that ignores a necessary condition,is that the information relayed on this array of media must be done in an understood and recognised format. Therefore it is not enough to communicate in a language that is understood by the target audience (English, Arabic, Russian … etc), but the message must also contain a recognised and accepted format (in terms of rhetoric, symbolism, technical language and general presentation). Therefore when communicating to a foreign public, foreign journalists maybe employed as they know the appropriate routines, codes and means of communication. In this regard, it is much easier to understand and record the Measure of Activity than the Measure of Effect.

Information and modern warfare: 2008 Georgian–Russian War

The focus of this section will be on the August 2008 conflict between Georgia and Russia over South Ossetia. This war was remarkable not only for its short duration, but the wildly contrasting projected realities, causes and consequences of the war (Pukhov 2010). One of the greatest failings shown in this conflict was by the mass media. They displayed a remarkably short historical memory in their reporting. As a rule, there seems to have been a general inclination to take events from August 2008 and not before, which greatly oversimplified events. This was combined with ingrained frames and prejudices (concerning both Russia and Georgia) that already existed in the mass media. Some observers noted that this war marked a turning point in East–West relations – "the rhetoric, used by both sides, bears all similarities with the Cold War period which officially ended in 1990, but it also became clear that the West is not in a position to provide real protection to its ally Georgia" (Bloed 2008: 322). A long period of spiralling poor relations existed between Georgia and Russia, especially in the wake of the Rose Revolution in 2003 that brought Mikhail Saakashvili to power. These antagonisms were based upon competing and clashing sets of norms and values that were framed in terms of interests and questions of honour. Russia, for its part, was said to have lost its desire to continue compromising with the West on geopolitical matters as they saw this as solely a one-way process (Tsygankov & Tarver-Wahlquist 2009; Karagiannis 2013).

In the period leading up to the war, all of the sides involved in the coming conflict increased tensions through deployments of forces and military exercises on their respective sides of the border (Toal 2008: 684). By the time of the Georgian attack, 12,000 soldiers, 4,000 interior ministry forces, 75 T-72 tanks, 70 Cobra armoured fighting vehicles and artillery had been massed on the border. At 23.30 hrs on 7 August 2008, the Georgian Army received their orders to open fire (Lavrov 2010: 47). It did take some time before it became more publicly accepted that Georgia was in fact the side that launched the initial military attack, possibly owing to the rational logic of a small and militarily weaker country attacking a much larger and militarily stronger one seems somewhat suicidal.

The evidence was already there, but some people choose to ignore the signs with such catchphrases as "the jury is still out" on who launched the initial attack. In order to make sense of the information and the way in which the information war was waged, and to put into context the serious shortcomings of many mass media, it is necessary to look at some of the pre-existing frames and prejudices that were cycled and recycled in the information sphere. There is a projection and the assumption that Georgia is a fully functioning democracy 'just like us', which is crucial to the functioning and viability of the constructed perception. This is due to the image that they can be seen to be more like a Western nation, seeking to rid itself of the Soviet colonial past (Toal 2008: 690–694; Wertsch & Karumidze 2009: 385). In this manner, it is made easier for the target audience to relate and sympathise with an entity that is perceived as being familiar.

The then president of Georgia, Mikhail Saakashvili, having been educated in the West and in a Western style of dress and talk is familiar in his presentation. However, the last elections were the source of a number of concerns (see for instance the OSCE report – http://www.osce.org/odihr/elections/georgia/30959) including a crackdown on political opposition and the closure of independent media (Antonenko 2008: 25). An important point being that this report came after the early media declarations that the elections were free, and therefore this report was relegated from public memory. The use of riot police against political opposition and the closure of opposition mass media during late 2007 and early 2008 are justified and dismissed as being an 'unfortunate' and are not condemned as such. Also an indicator of concern is the number of former political allies of Saakashvili that have been dismissed from government and are now opposing him. The former Chair of the Georgian Parliament, Nino Burjanadze (left voluntarily) provides one such case, some former allies have been pushed and others have left voluntarily. An effect of this situation is a shortage of long term political supporters in the Saakashvili regime.

A definite advantage that is held by Georgia over Russia is the fact that it is a fraction of Russia's size in terms of population and territory. In this regard, it is not difficult to frame Georgia as being the victim. Added with this are the taken-for-granted frames of the *Soviet past*, *Russian aggression* (and imperialism) and *Putin-era authoritarianism* versus *Georgian Western-style democracy* and their desire for independence. The picture was portrayed as a brave and independent Georgia defending itself against "the 21st century hordes" and a "good and evil, between David and Goliath" struggle.[7] References were made to the Soviet Union's crushing of the 1956 Hungarian Uprising and the 1968 Prague Spring. There was little basis to use these comparisons in an accurate and meaningful manner, not the least that the Soviet Union no longer exists and the whole of Georgia was not occupied and the political regime replaced. These particular frames already existed within the mass media sphere, so it was a matter of working within the existing frames that already favoured the Georgian position. Therefore there was no need to 'create' and then 'sell' a media frame to the mass media and journalists.

A divide existed between the real causes of the war and the public justifications for the event. On the one side, Georgia presented its launching of a military offensive to re-take South Ossetia as a response to what it termed as being large-scale provocations from the South Ossetian side. The fact that Georgia launched the initial attack leads to an attempt by Russia to label and characterise them as the aggressor in the conflict (along with the associated and implied guilt). Whereas Russia attempted to justify its actions as a means to protect innocent Russian citizens present on the territory. In addition, Georgia was deemed to fall within an area described as being a privileged sphere of interests, bearing some resemblance to the Brezhnev Doctrine that permitted operations beyond the national borders in countries to protect 'vital' national interests in areas where concentrations of its citizens reside (Bloed 2008: 322; Toal 2008: 694–698). This bears some similarities with the United States and its Monroe Doctrine, which is applied to Latin America.[8] Russia also used the international precedent that was set by the US-led intervention and independence of Kosovo as a means to legitimise their actions during and immediately after the August 2008 war (Toal 2008: 695–696). There was an information war that was run parallel to the physical fighting, which sought to win over hearts and minds in the quest for legitimacy and justification.

On both sides there were a number of media assets that were aimed at influencing an international audience, rather than the purpose of communicating to their domestic audiences. On the Russian side, *Russia Today* broadcast one version of events, and on the Georgian side *Civil Georgia* dutifully relayed all messages from Saakashvili. Not to mention the Georgian government hiring the Brussels-based PR agency, *Aspect Consulting* (http://www.aspectconsulting.eu/) and Patrick Worms[9] (as a former European Commission official knows the codes and practice of journalism in a Western media context). The Russian government in the meantime used the *GPlus Consulting Group* as its means of international audience 'outreach' in Brussels (http://www.gpluseurope.com/). *Ketchum* in Washington was used by the Russian authorities to try and deliver their message there (http://www.ketchum.com/). The agencies hired by the Russian government were done so to improve Russia's international image, and were oddly enough not engaged during the Georgian–Russian War of 2008. In the sum of things, the initial Georgian efforts in communicating to the international publics were much more successful than the Russian side because they were communicating more familiar norms and values, and projecting themselves as the beacon of democracy that was fighting for its existence against Russian 'aggression' (Heinrich & Tanaev 2009: 246).

It was a rush by both sides to try and prove that their side was suffering more and therefore the victim, which implies an absolution of guilt or culpability, together with the need to punish the aggressor. The yardstick that is intended to measure the suffering in this case, used by both sides, is the amount of civilian casualties. Given the existing frames and perceptions in circulation, this was not a strategy that Russia was going to win in this instance. Saakashvili with his experience of living and studying in the United States, together with the hired PR help, had a greater appreciation of what is likely to have a greater impact upon an international audience. Therefore he used messages and images that hit the target audience, such as 'threats' to European energy supplies (alleged Russian attack on Georgian oil pipelines),[10] accusations of ethnic cleansing by Russia,[11] and that Georgia was being occupied by Russia.[12] These various message narratives can be understood by a Western audience and are therefore more likely to resonate with them.

One of the biggest failings of the media is their buying into 'facts' and 'figures' quoted by American and Georgian sources that would be somewhat difficult to verify from other sources. Therefore, information that was at best vague and at worst outright fiction were not checked and verified. This is in spite of the fact that Georgia had been declared a political priority by the Bush administration for some time, and in April 2008 there had been an intense effort by the US to persuade NATO members to accept Georgia and Ukraine.[13] Thus Georgia was an obvious political priority for a number of years, even more obviously a mere four months before the conflict. This in turn exerts an influence on mass media framing and reporting. Other political relations should also be taken into account, such as the poor relations existing between the United Kingdom and Russia over the issue of a number of extraditions and the protection of wanted persons (Zakayev and Berezovsky wanted by Russia and residing in the UK, and Lugovoi wanted by UK living in Russia).

Partisanship and bias in reporting on the conflict was observable, which was split along the lines of the countries involved directly and indirectly in the conflict. Furthermore, "several journalists and editors confirm in private email conversations that censorship was particularly harsh during the brief war with Russia in August, with a demand for the media to portray Georgia as both victim and victor" (Akhvlediani 2009: 387). Additionally, the 'questions' asked by journalists contained a number of serious flaws, namely they had an ingrained bias and were not open questions (assumption of Russian guilt). This provided Georgian officials with the ability to continue the official line that was not only going unchallenged, but one could argue was being assisted by the international media. In a reflection upon the failings of the Western media, Peter Wilby of the *Guardian* summed up a number of reasons why they fell short. One of these was the timing of the war, not only during the summer holidays, but also on the opening day of the Olympic Games in Beijing. This meant many journalists were not available to cover the event, let alone cover it adequately. The dilemma being that the news must go on, as the saying goes. "They need to be told who are the goodies and baddies. News, remember, is part of the entertainment industry."[14] The 24/7 nature of the news industry pushed the story forward, which left journalists more vulnerable to 'information' being offered by the associated PR companies involved in the conflict.

The wording and framing of the news relating to the conflict demonstrates Wilby's comment about 'goodies' and 'baddies', with the internal mechanisms of the news industry being the ultimate decider of this 'reality'. Georgian actions were variously described in the press as follows: tanks were "moved", when shelling civilians it was "reprehensible", Saakashvili was "paying the price" for his pro-Western stance. Russian forces, on the other hand, were: "rampaging", and was also "offending every canon of international behaviour", meanwhile a "resurgent Russia" was "itching to flex its muscles and burning with post-imperial hubris."[15] These keywords and ways of phrasing the events set the way that news consumers set about interpreting and understanding the news, in a manner that was more to do with entertainment than imparting knowledge of an event that would enlighten the news consumers.

Both sides had planned for this conflict. There are no 'innocent' political parties, civilians on both sides bearing the brunt of the political course to war. But, by taking the Georgian assertion that they were the victim of aggression is to ignore many signs and facts. Among the first of these signs and indicators of Georgian intentions came in the spring of 2008 with the numerous reconnaissance flights by drones over Abkhazia and South Ossetia. The motivation of such actions is to know the territory that a military force may soon be crossing, and any potential military obstacles. Another possible use of the drones was to provoke the Russians into shooting down the drones and use this against them. This implies a certain level of premeditation in the use of military force by the Georgian side. Such news was omitted, for the most part, from Western media reporting.

Another assumption that was mostly taken for granted was that the attack was initiated by the Russians. One circulated version was that the Georgia move was in response to the alleged Russian offensive. However, little is done in explaining why so much Georgian military hardware (armour and artillery) was already concentrated in the area (which takes time and resources to move and assemble).

> After the Russian columns arrived through the Roki Tunnel, and the battle swung quickly into Russia's favour, Georgia said its attack had been necessary to stop a Russian attack that had been already underway.
>
> To date, however, there has been no independent evidence, beyond Georgia's insistence that its version is true, that Russian forces were attacking before the Georgian barrages.[16]

This *New York Times* article throws some doubt upon the generally assumed and held belief in the perception that Russia attacked first. Another perception that was challenged by this same article was that only military targets were subjected to artillery fire (as opposed to the belief that this was the standard Russian practice).

> In the field, there is evidence from an extensive set of witnesses that within 30 minutes of Mr. Saakashvili's order, Georgia's military began pounding civilian sections of the city of Tskhinvali, as well as a Russian peacekeeping base there, with heavy barrages of rocket and artillery fire.[17]

There is another issue raised in this brief quote, concerning the role of the Russian peacekeepers in the conflict. According to Georgian sources, the Russian peacekeepers were not neutral observers in what had been a frozen conflict, but had exceeded their mandate. The Russian and South Ossetian side deemed the presence of Russian peacekeepers as a necessary precondition to prevent a resurgence of the conflict and maintaining a measure of stability. Regardless of the level of involvement, whether it is as agitators or keeping the peace, it becomes somewhat of a superfluous argument when one nation attacks another's armed forces. The Russian peacekeepers were deliberately targeted, such a deliberate action is a clear act of war. A fact that has been omitted from many media reports.

A statement by Saakashvili in the *New York Times* that seemed to go pretty much unnoticed (or ignored) happened in early September 2008. In spite of the dominant frame used by Georgia that it was a victim of Russian aggression (and that this aggression could spill over in the future to include other neighbouring countries), it was announced that Georgia's "leaders hoped to rebuild and train its armed forces as if another war with Russia is almost inevitable."[18] In addition it was announced that Georgia had not given up on its ambition of re-uniting Georgia. The statements made by Saakashvili, although a matter of fact statement, are extremely inflammatory and unhelpful in the process of resolving the crisis by political means. One year after the 2008 War, the EU Report confirmed that it was Georgia that opened the conflict with a military offensive (IIFFM 2009). In addition, tensions were maintained through the provocative use of deceptive communications, including to domestic audiences. One such example was the news mockumentary that featured on Georgian TV in March 2010, which caused widespread panic, fear and disorder as Georgians believed the conflict had become hot once more.[19]

Conclusion

This conflict was a mix of disinformation practices. 'Classical' uses were applied, such as minimising one's own military casualties and maximising the enemy's, demonising the leadership of the opponent, hyping the number of civilian casualties (own). The Russian side attempted to make detailed explanations in order to refute Georgian claims. This however, proved to be ineffective against the somewhat vague or at least imprecise Georgian assertions (that generally went unchallenged). The media messages contained a number of elements, including demonization, stereotypes and prejudices, ideology and censorship (self imposed as well as externally enforced). The August 2008 Georgia–Russia War was an armed confrontation that witnessed a parallel information war being fought, which was based upon the use of competing projections of values and norms as well as credibility. There are a number of reasons why the Georgian propaganda efforts were initially very successful. Although Georgia initially enjoyed some brief success in its communications to the international publics, Russia's message did not resonate and it suffered various diplomatic and communication failures. The end sum is that this was a war without any clear winners in the end (Antonenko 2008).

Many of the reasons for this initial success relate to the ability to exploit the news production process of the mass media. An almost complete lack of background to the conflict, in terms of its origins and history, ensures that those relying on mass media for their information have a significant gap in understanding it. Although, given the various biases in terms of framing and agenda, covering the background could have worked against these, and perhaps is the reason for its omission from the media's reporting. The effect of this omission is to leave the conflict out of context and to be 'floating' on the political landscape with no apparent logic, apart from the offered logic of Russian aggression.

The value of perception was very much in Georgia's favour, with the odds being stacked against Russia in terms of values and assumed qualities due to the asymmetry involved in the conflict between the two primary actors. Russia is a country that is vastly bigger than Georgia in terms of population and area.

Although South Ossetia is much smaller than Georgia in terms of population and area, Georgia was able to frame the conflict as being between Russia and Georgia. Thus to an extent, South Ossetia as an actor became a neglected and even a somewhat irrelevant side issue, thereby rendering it as an object rather than a subject within the frame of a larger event and process. This simplification of the conflict's actors played into Georgia's hands as it was able to project itself as a victim of 'unprovoked' aggression. Various negative historical prejudices and stereotypes were attached to Russia (especially those with Soviet connotations and overtones), whereas Georgia was promoted as being Western in terms of values and outlook. As such, Georgia was intended to be something the target audience could 'understand' and relate to, therefore empathise with. Saakashvili as the face of Georgia was a good choice from their perspective as he had an understanding of how Western society and mass media functioned, and looked and talked like someone from the West. This meant that the international audience could relate to him and his message.

Information that does not exist or agree with the predominant discourse is either rejected or ignored and at times information is concocted to fit. There were instances where interviews (with Putin by a German media company ARD[20]) were doctored to bring out the media's political agenda, where eyewitnesses' testimony was ignored because it contradicted the primary media frame (Georgia as the victim) such as when Fox News interviewed a teenage girl coming from Tskhinvali.[21] In this regard, mass media tended to be the most effective censors by creating a spiral of silence around any competing or contradictory information and views.

If anything can be demonstrated from media coverage, by all mass media (US, UK, Georgia, Russia, Sweden … etc), the so-called *fog of war* was actually increased rather than decreased as the result of reporting. Definite political biases and agenda dominated the information space, with little or no room left for alternative opinions on the matter. To sum up in a short and concise manner the effect of the mass media reporting; it promoted rather than dampened tensions thereby potentially prolonging the political and military conflict. By dividing the actors of the conflict into 'good' and 'bad' countries, the picture is overly simplistic and laden with value judgements, which makes the prospect of reconciliation between the parties ever more remote.

Notes

1 Glassman, J. K., *US Public Diplomacy and the War of Ideas*, Foreign Press Centre Briefing, Washington D.C., http://fpc.state.gov/107034.htm, 15 July 2008
2 When speaking of technical language I refer to the intricacies that are to be found in every different language – the mechanism and symbolic meaning, and not whether it is German, French, English … etc.
3 Glassman, J. K., *US Public Diplomacy and the War of Ideas*, Foreign Press Centre Briefing, Washington D.C., http://fpc.state.gov/107034.htm, 15 July 2008
4 For example see the article in the Guardian, www.guardian.co.uk/world/2008/aug/26/alqaida.uksecurity?gusrc=rss&feed=uknews.
5 Glassman, J. K., *US Public Diplomacy and the War of Ideas*, Foreign Press Centre Briefing, Washington D.C., http://fpc.state.gov/107034.htm, 15 July 2008

6 Glassman, J. K., *US Public Diplomacy and the War of Ideas*, Foreign Press Centre Briefing, Washington D.C., http://fpc.state.gov/107034.htm, 15 July 2008

7 *'Georgia will bury Russian Imperialism' Saakashvili*, Civil Georgia, 1 September 2008. Johnson's Russia List, 2008-#163, 2 September 2008

8 To read further on the impact of the Monroe Doctrine please see http://www.history.com/topics/monroe-doctrine.

9 Martirosyan, S., *Information Support to the South Ossetian War*, Noravank Foundation, www.noravank.am, 13 September 2008

10 See following link as an example of the news in this frame: http://www.dailymail.co.uk/news/worldnews/article-1043185/The-Pipeline-War-Russian-bear-goes-Wests-jugular.html

11 See the following link as an example of a news item in this frame: http://www.reuters.com/article/asiaCrisis/idUSL9329769

12 See the following link as an example of a news item in this frame: http://www.abc.net.au/news/stories/2008/08/23/2344394.htm

13 Erlanger, S. & Myers, S. L., *NATO Allies Oppose Bush on Georgia and Ukraine*, The New York Times, http://www.nytimes.com/2008/04/03/world/europe/03nato.html?_r=1&scp=14&sq=Georgia%20Priority%20US%20interest&st=cse, 3 April 2008

14 Wilby, P., *Georgia has Won the PR War*, The Guardian, http://www.guardian.co.uk/media/2008/aug/18/pressandpublishing.georgia, 18 August 2008

15 Ibid.

16 Chivers, C. J. & Shanker, T., *Georgians Eager to Rebuild Army*, The New York Times, 3 September 2008

17 Ibid.

18 Ibid.

19 Kramer, A. E., *Panic in Georgia After a Mock News Broadcast*, The New York Times, http://www.nytimes.com/2010/03/15/world/europe/15georgia.html, 14 March 2010 (accessed 1 December 2016)

20 Please see the assessment of the doctoring of the interviews here - http://thesaker.is/full-videos-of-the-cnn-and-ard-interviews-with-putin-in-russia-and-with-english-subtitles-updated/

21 To see the Fox News video clip, please see the following link. http://www.foxnews.com/video2/video08.html?maven_referralObject=3023509&maven_referralPlaylistId=&sRevUrl=http://search2.foxnews.com/search?access=p&getfields=*&sort=date%3AD%3AS%3Ad1&output=xml_no_dtd&ie=UTF-8&client=my_frontend&filter=0&site=video&proxystylesheet=my_frontend&q=Shepard%20Georgia#|

Bibliography

Akhvlediani, M., The Fatal Flaw: The Media and the Russian Invasion of Georgia, *Small Wars and Insurgencies*, 20(2), 2009, pp. 363–390

Antonenko, O., A War with No Winners, *Survival*, 50(5), 2008, pp. 23–36

Armistead, L. (Editor), *Information Operations: Warfare and the Hard Reality of Soft Power*, Washington D. C.: Brassey's Inc, 2004

Asmus, R., *A Little War that Shook the World: Georgia, Russia, and the Future of the West*, New York: Palgrave Macmillan, 2010

Balabanova, E., *Media, Wars and Politics: Comparing the Incomparable in Western and Eastern Europe*, Aldershot: Ashgate Publishing, 2007

Bennett, W. L., Lawrence, R. G. & Livingston, S., *When the Press Fails: Political Power and the News Media From Iraq to Katrina*, Chicago: The University of Chicago Press, 2007

Bernays, E. (Introduction by Mark Crispin Miller), *Propaganda*, New York: I G Publishing, 2005 (originally published 1928)

Bignell, J., *Media Semiotics: An Introduction*, Manchester: Manchester University Press, 1997

Bloed, A., Georgian–Russian War, the Turning Point in East–West Relations?, *Security and Human Rights*, No. 4, 2008, pp. 322–325

Borg, J., *Persuasion: The Art of Influencing People*, 2nd Edition, London: Pearson/ Prentice Hall, 2007

Chomsky, N., *Media Control: The Spectacular Achievements of Propaganda*, 2nd Edition, New York: Seven Stories Press, 2002

Edwards, L., *Media Politik: How the Mass Media Have Transformed World Politics*, Washington D. C.: The Catholic University of America Press, 2001

Elkin, F., *Censorship and Pressure Groups*, Phylon, Clark Atlanta University, Vol. 21, No. 1 (1st Qtr.), 1960, pp. 71–80

Ewen, S., *PR! A Social History of Spin*, New York: Basic Books, 1996

Gonzalez, A. & Tanno, D. A., (Editors), *Politics, Communication and Culture*, Thousand Oaks: Sage Publications, 1997

Gordadze, T., 'Georgia-Russia Conflict in August 2008: War as a Continuation of Politics' in Jafalian, A. (Ed.), *Reassessing Security in the South Caucasus: Regional Conflicts and Transformation*, Farnham: Ashgate, 2011, pp. 11–31

Heinrich, H-G. & Tanaev, K., Georgia & Russia: Contradictory Coverage of the August War, *Caucasian Review of International Affairs*, 3(3), Summer 2009, pp. 244–259

Herman, E. S. & Chomsky, N., *Manufacturing Consent: The Political Economy of Mass Media*, New York: Pantheon Books, 2002

Independent International Fact-Finding Mission on the Conflict in Georgia (IIFFM), *Report* (Volumes I-III), September 2009

Johnson-Cartee, K. S. & Copeland, G. A., *Strategic Political Communication: Rethinking Social Influence, Persuasion, and Propaganda*, Lanham (MD): Roman & Littlefield, 2003

Karagiannis, E., The 2008 Russian-Georgian War Via the Lens of Offensive Realism, *European Security*, 22(1), 2013, pp. 74–93

Lavrov, A., 'Timeline of Russian-Georgian Hostilities in August 2008' in Pukhov, R. (Ed.), *The Tanks of August*, Moscow: Centre for Analysis of Strategies and Technologies, 2010, pp. 37–76

Lippmann, W., *A Preface to Politics*, New York: Prometheus Books, 2005 (originally published 1913)

Louw, P. E., *The Media and Cultural Production*, Thousand Oaks: Sage, 2001

Norris, P., Kern, M. & Just, M., (Editors), *Framing Terrorism: The News Media, the Government, and the Public*, London: Routledge, 2003

Pratkanis, A. & Aronson, E., *Age of Propaganda: The Everyday Use and Abuse of Persuasion*, Revised Edition, New York: W. H. Freeman & Company, 2001

Pukhov, R. (Ed.), *The Tanks of August*, Moscow: Centre for Analysis of Strategies and Technologies, 2010

Scruton, R., *The Palgrave-Macmillan Dictionary of Political Thought*, 3rd Edition, Basingstoke: Palgrave Macmillan, 2007

Taylor, P. M., *Munitions of the Mind: A History of Propaganda from the Ancient World to the Present Day*, 3rd Edition, Manchester: Manchester University Press, 2003

Toal, G., Russia's Kosovo: A Critical Geopolitics of the August 2008 War over South Ossetia, *Eurasian Geography and Economics*, 49(6), 2008, pp. 670–705

Tsygankov, A., *Russia's Foreign Policy: Change and Continuity in National Identity*, 4th Edition, Lanham: Rowman and Littlefield, 2016

Tsygankov, A. & Tarver-Wahlquist, M., Duelling Honours: Power, Identity and the Russia-Georgia Divide, *Foreign Policy Analysis*, 5, 2009, pp. 307–326

Wertsch, J. V. & Karumidze, Z., Spinning the Past: Russian and Georgian Accounts of the War of August 2008, *Memory Studies*, 2(3), 2009, pp. 377–391

Willcox, D. R., *Propaganda, the Press and Conflict: The Gulf War and Kosovo*, New York: Routledge, 2006

Zelizer, B. & Allan, S. (Editors), *Journalism after September 11*, London: Routledge, 2002

8 Communication management and the humanitarian war blueprint

The Libya War

Greg Simons

Communication management has become a common tool in the arsenal of the West in the context of trying to build the pretext for war, and then controlling the information flows after the fighting has begun. It is an attempt to justify the seemingly unjustifiable, where reason and logic are distorted, and the use of emotion is actively promoted. In the 21st century, its use has come to be commonplace in the enactment of controversial policy and the advancement of a narrow set of interests in international relations (Pashenstev & Simons 2009). Certainly, one may now even speak of a blueprint for going to war as being established. This has been gradually shaped and refined by events such as the 1991 Gulf War, 1999 Kosovo War and the 2003 invasion and occupation of Iraq. Libya gave the opportunity to operationalize the blueprint, which in political terms proved to be successful in terms of managing the information environment in order to promote a dubious political agenda (enact regime change against Gaddafi). The current situation in Syria points to the urgent need to be able to understand and to counter these subversive tactics.

The war has, officially at least, come to an end in Libya and the country declared as being 'liberated' (from the rule of Gaddafi) and 'democratic'. Corporate mass media have once again shown their complete inability to serve any kind of actual or real public interest in their coverage (DiMaggio 2009), and the corporate owners of those mass media are with national politics, and look forward to the prospects of further spoils from another war of choice.

Yet, at its very end, the war in Libya has raised more questions than it has answered. It is probably one of the most poorly managed information wars in recent times. There were a number of evident dilemmas and contradictions present in the mass media reporting on the war, and the 'neutral' role of NATO in this regime change that was enacted under the guise of protecting civilians. However, these vital questions are not being raised in the mass media, which tends to remain silent on a number of obvious key issues. The huge gaps, between what was being said and practiced by NATO, are in plain sight for many to see.

One of the motivations for this article therefore, is to briefly raise those issues, which I believe need to be articulated. These include the various false and misleading statements made by NATO concerning why and how they were involved militarily in Libya, the very worrying nature (and largely ignored) nature of the National Transitional Council, some of the results of the conflict, and the emerging conflicts that seem to be forming and shall follow.

Liberal wars

One of the issues that were recently debated was that of the notion of *liberal wars*. One needs to carefully ask the question, what exactly is a liberal war? This term has become some kind of brand, where it is uttered and the audience automatically understand (or at least assume to understand) what is meant. The fundamental flaw, as I see it, is that an action that is by its very nature inhumane can be considered as being 'liberal'. There is no use of logical or ethical argumentation to persuade your opponent, but the use of blunt force to beat them in to submission.

The nature of so-called liberal wars has been gradually evolving in the 20th and 21st centuries. There has been a move away from what can be termed as being negative motivations for going to war – to stop famine, to halt genocide and ethnic cleansing. Now the narratives revolve around 'humanitarian' reasons such as spreading democracy and 'liberating' oppressed peoples. Military interventions are increasingly being marketed and sold to the public by their governments (Western 2005). Thus the façade of a much more positive rhetoric and the appearance of a positive rather than negative international engagement appear before the public.

Another trend that seems to be emerging is the asymmetric nature of these wars that are heralded to bring about 'peace'. An alliance of numerous democratic Western countries aligned against some fanatical dictator, the disparity of military power obvious for those who choose to look – such as Iraq, Afghanistan and Libya. This takes some of the guesswork and unpredictability away from waging war, but not all of it. Therefore, the chance of military success makes them easier to sell a quick and just 'victory' to the domestic audience. However, eight months of war in Libya has shown that in spite of the overwhelming military superiority, things do not necessarily go smoothly and according to the media-narrated script. There is an academic theory which states that democratic countries do not go to war with each other (democratic peace), but this discounts the fact that 'democracies' are more likely to attack those labelled as being 'non-democratic' states than the other way around (Risse-Kappen 1995). The notion of liberal wars is that they are waged as a last resort and in a 'good' cause.

A uniform system of communication is in place, which theoretically is better placed to inform citizens about processes and events. However, there is a possible dark side to communication too. "Strategic communication has a dark side. And that dark side involves intentional ambiguity, which sometimes results in deception and lying" (Dulek & Sydow Campbell 2015: 135). These wars are generally pre-emptive, rather than preventative in nature, based upon, in many instances false and misleading information. You do not have to remember too far back, when the case was made against Iraq, the WMDs and links to terrorism that were so 'sincerely' sold to the world (Simons 2008; Simons 2010). But these are after all good wars that are fought against bad people who are out there to harm us, because they hate our freedom and way of life. So we are told … . Every 'good' war needs atrocities, real or imagined, in order to capture the public's attention and sympathy. The human dimension here revolved around the well-used excuses of massacres of civilians and mass rapes (Taylor 2003). "Washington is concerned by reports that forces loyal to Libyan leader Moammar Gaddafi are using rape as a weapon of war, the US secretary of state said. […] Susan Rice, the U.S. envoy to the United Nations, told the UN Security Council that Gaddafi was handing out Viagra tablets to his forces to encourage them to rape women."[1] These claims, like the WMDs in Iraq and many other tales used by the US as an excuse to go to war and fulfil their self-appointed global 'humanitarian' mission were based on very spurious allegations that were presented as facts to the world.

Libya has a number of other similarities with previous wars in this regard in addition to the production of atrocity stories. We were told that there were people aspiring for democracy and freedom from the tyranny of Gaddafi. The brave underdog and the much stronger, evil and brutal dictator provide the black and white dimensions of good and evil for the coming spectacle. Thus there is a ready-made script for the consumption and entertainment of domestic audiences.

All through the mass media, around the world, the headlines triumphantly proclaim a successful beginning in the latest war the West has initiated. With many echoes and similarities to previous wars fought, there is the necessity to protect the defenceless civil population that want to free themselves from a violent tyrant. And a favourite of a number of previous conflicts from Kosovo to Iraq, engaging in a limited war, where the superiority of 'Our' airpower shall win the day; taking few (if any) losses ourselves, causing limited civilian casualties and wreaking complete destruction upon the enemy.

Jus ad Bellum has been established in the mass media, announced proudly by politicians in Europe and the United States. This war, as have many in the Post-Cold War era, is being fought in the name of humanity. The logic that is meant to flow from this is that it is a just war, one fought selflessly and for the good of the Libyan people. However, when one gets away from this noble rhetoric, can war be classified as being something that is noble and just? The logic used is often in an emotional, rather than a rational basis, and the logos form does not need to be factually true, so long as it is accepted and/or believed by the target public (i.e. to resonate with the audience). The idea of Just War was revived in the 21st century with a plethora of small-scale armed conflicts being fought in the wake of the end of the Cold War and the result of the United States being the sole global hegemon with no competitor that could check and balance it in the international system.

There is a problem with notions, such as Just War and Responsibility to Protect (R2P), which is the broad and vague invocation and application of these concepts as a means to pursue interests under the guise and pretence of a 'defensive' military operation. This has been noted with the application of Just War as being an expedient means to legitimise war and otherwise difficult to justify policy (Booth 2000). Other newer conceptual tools for legitimising military intervention are being created, when older means lose their usefulness or effectiveness. R2P is one such example, which was created as "a reaction to the failure to generate consensus in the 1990s, after the contested humanitarian interventions, rather than a statement of political agreement" (McCormack 2010: 80). Superficially, the concept sounds appealing – to protect the population of another country whose government does not or cannot protect them. However, many questions remain unanswered – to protect whom, from what, and by which means? If invoked, it can becomes an open possibility for enacting wide ranging policy and operations to successfully bring about a hidden agenda by a militarily powerful actor. The current cycle of politics and conflict is seemingly based upon short term political goals, with a complete disregard for the long term impact and consequences. This makes the ultimate 'end-game' a very unpredictable and probably an unpleasant neverending cycle of violence and instability.

In less than one hour the UN Security Council voted on a course that has led to open war, and involvement in a civil war. Ten voted for war and there were five abstentions. "All necessary measures to protect civilians" was passed in an evening session that was marked by some concerns expressed, but no outright opposition (by using a no vote to block the resolution).[2] Effectively, carte blanche had been given to the use of force on Libya.

Revolutions past and present

Recently, waves of political and social unrest have shaken the decade's old established authoritarian regimes throughout the Middle East and North Africa. The Neo-Cons have been hailing this as a successful confirmation of President George W. Bush's claim that the US-led invasion of Iraq would lead to an eventual wave of democracy in the region.[3] This in itself seems to be rather overly optimistic as the dust has not even settled from the revolutions in Tunisia, Egypt, Libya and other countries.

The way that these revolutions were waged showed some similarities with the *Colour Revolutions* that swept through the countries of the Former Soviet Union in the 2003–2005 period (Georgia in 2003, Ukraine in 2004 and Kyrgyzstan in 2005). These revolutions were fuelled by youth organizations and New Communications Technology (the internet and mobile phones), which were able to circumvent the cumbersome mechanisms of control that were wielded by the authoritarian regimes of the time (Landolt & Kubicek 2014). The object of the revolutions was to remove the presidents of the countries, yet leave the political body essentially untouched, thereby gaining the support of the political elite. Looking at the leadership of the revolutions, the 'revolutionaries' were all at one stage serving in the ranks of the governments that were overthrown.

They were also supported materially, logistically and financially by the United States and their allies in the respective regions. The messages and means of rallying mass support and participation were based upon the goal of inducing an emotional response from the publics they were messaging, which included branding, reputation management and news management. These revolutions were hailed as being grassroots democratic movements, although the aftermath proved this to be far from the case. All of these countries have been racked by economic, social and political instability (even seeing the villain of the Orange Revolution in Ukraine eventually being elected President). Some have noted the seemingly inconsistent approach of the US to the various Arab Spring revolutions in the MENA area, some being supported and others opposed, being based upon geopolitical and not value/norm-based concerns (Salt 2012). There are three observable assumptions that make up the Western narrative on the Arab Spring: 1) the regimes under attack are overwhelmingly unpopular; 2) the 'opposition' represent the overwhelming will of the people; and 3) once the revolution began, its force would be unstoppable. In addition, Libya was "the focus of a significant Western intervention" (Friedman 2011: 2).

There has been the element of slogans and messages that are designed and intended to attract the attention and support of an international public – these messages being composed in English and using messages designed for a foreign audience. At the political marketing conference held in Uppsala, Sweden in August 2015, Noah Bakir noted the symbolism of the brand name Arab Spring. She said that this is understandable and offers a positive promise in a wider context, but from an Egyptian perspective, the word Spring has different connotations that involves a brief and intense time of year when sand is blown and gets everywhere. Not the colourful symbolism and promise of growth. In Libya one could even see a sign in English pointing the way to a Rebel international media centre, which draws attention to the significance paid to international opinion. There is also the evident use of mass slogans and symbols to rally the protestors on the street.

Competing versions of the future

There seem to be two primary competing versions predicting the future that awaits Libya after the fighting finally subsides. One of those predictions appears to be overly optimistic and the other predicts extremely negative trends taking hold. There have been many talks in the international community about shaping the future of this company, including the creation of the Contact Group on Libya.

So far there have been a number of meetings of the Contact Group on Libya, its fourth meeting in Istanbul in late August 2011 had delegations from over 40 countries attended. The latest meeting was in Paris, where "leaders of Libya's uprising were in Paris Thursday with delegates from 60 countries and world bodies to discuss a roadmap for Libya's humanitarian, political and economic future."[4] Creating such a group, and holding various meetings about dictating the future of this country (albeit with some representation from Libya), has similarities to events in the past, such as Tehran in 1943 and Yalta in 1945. As eloquently, and as beautiful as the spoken words and promises may be at this current time, it still does not bode well for the average Libyan citizen.

However, this has not halted attempts to try and paint a rosy picture of Libya's future. One such example of this came with a plethora of new acronyms. Harlan Ullman is a commentator for United Press International, and is also chairman of the Killowen Group (advises leaders of government and business) and senior adviser at the Atlantic Council. He began by deriding the term BRIC countries (Brazil, Russia, India and China) as being a 'virtual cliché' of the globe's *emerging* economic dynamos. This is ignoring the basic fact that China already owns more than US$1 trillion of US national debt and is starting to demand some conditions on their 'investment.' During the height of the recent debt crisis in the US, President Obama threatened not to pay American servicemen, but made guarantees to the Chinese[5], which provides a clear case of the changing system of international politics owing to changes in the possession of economic power.

Coming back to the issue of a new set of acronyms created by Ullman in the name of *political fairness*, there were two: AII (Afghanistan, Iraq and Iran); LES (Libya, Egypt and Syria). Proudly announcing Libya, Egypt and Syria as the *charter members* of this new 'club' that have been "drawn together by public rebellion against decades of autocratic rule." He gives a warning further on that "what happens in each represents the Arab Spring and the budding of democracy or turns into winters of discontent and chaos remains to be seen." But he remains mostly optimistic, and is careful to draw a distinct line between AII and LES countries. Ullman pointed to a number of historical warnings, and called for a need to be involved in deciding the future of countries or be prepared to accept the consequences.

In Iraq, the euphoria in April 2003 over Saddam's fall turned into looting and violence exacerbated by the inexcusable failure to plan for the peace. Aside from the benefit of ridding the planet of a particularly unsavoury character, the majority of Iraqis aren"t better off today; Iran has been the substantial benefactor whose influence has spread; and violence among Sunni, Shiite and Kurd is far from contained.

In Iran, the people celebrated the end of the Shah in 1979. Ayatollah Khomeini, orchestrating the rebellion from safety and luxury in France, was the returning hero. And from an autocracy, Iran became a mullahocracy in the grips of a ruling council of theocrats not democrats. One could also cite the false expectations after Fidel Castro routed Cuban President Fulgencio Batista over Christmas 1959 and what happened since as a further warning.[6]

What Ullman seems to ignore is that in these cases, US involvement and interference in domestic affairs leads to an intolerable situation for many citizens. When citizens ultimately have nothing to lose we see the rise and success of regimes, such as the current one in Iran. What we are offered are shallow warning stories and further nonsensical words that are intended to serve as some kind of rhetorical bogeyman, whether this is *Islamic Fascist* or *mullahocracy*. They simply make no sense and demonstrate the ignorance of those who wield them. Ultimately he does acknowledge, after a decade of war and with no end in sight, citizens in the West are weary of war and this is likely to affect their appetite to be involved in another long occupation.[7]

The West's façade: Public debates in the mass media

The 2011 Libyan War was initially portrayed as an ideal example of a popular uprising overthrowing a corrupt dictatorship with the aim of establishing democracy and human rights (Siebens & Case 2012). A revolution began in Libya on 15 February 2011 and initially the forces opposing Gaddafi were militarily successful. However, they were soon found to be on the defensive and outgunned. The UN Security Council Resolution 1973 gave carte blanche for the use of military force on Libya in the evening of 17 March 2011 (meeting closed at 1920), the military operation named Odyssey Dawn commenced by 0400 on 19 March 2011.[8] Although there were strenuous claims that the airstrikes were not in any way in support of the rebels the nature of the zones being attacked and the targets indicates otherwise. The role of NATO in Libya was so subjective that it began to attract the label as being "al Qaeda's air force" by various opponents of the war.[9]

This is not the first time that airpower has been directed against Gaddafi. In 1986 the US attacked Libya, President Ronald Reagan justified the bombing as "the peaceful mission of America to counter the savagery of the brutal enemy wherever he threatens freedom" (Gonzalez & Tanno 1997: 15). Once again, we see the double-speak about the use of war for 'peaceful' ends. The action was in response to Libya's involvement in the bombing of the Pan Am flight that crashed on the Scottish village of Lockerby in 1988.

There is an absence of even any pretence at presenting balanced coverage of this latest mass media spectacle. Once more the pro-war voice is amplified and the anti-war voice muted (Baum & Zhukov 2015). A number of subtle, yet detectable techniques can be readily observed. Everything that is said by Libyan authorities is stated and it is always said now that the information "has not been independently verified." Yet when Western military or political officials are quoted there is no such proviso. Of course, it is naturally understood how honest they have been with the public on information concerning the Global War On Terrorism (GWOT) (Bennett et al. 2007; Simons 2008; Zelizer & Allan 2002). Maybe it could in some regards be considered a good sign that at least the mass media have developed at least a selective understanding of their professional duty in publishing material from sources. However, this standard should be applied without prejudice, especially in time of war and not only against what is promoted as being the 'bad' side of an event.

Thus the GWOT has been expanded even further, becoming a Global War On Despots and Tyrants (albeit a very selective one) as well as the well established brands of the Taliban and Al Qaeda or simply AQ. Once more the focus is on the tactical questions and not the strategic ones. Strategic questions are absent from the media – should we fight this war? The mantra of a just war is the message to the public that is repeated again and again. Instead, the focus has been on the tactical questions. How do we best fight this war? It is a given in the mass media narrative that the war is a righteous one.

As with the Kosovo War in 1999, this Libyan war has been billed as one that is being reluctantly undertaken, somewhat of a burden for the Western alliance in the name of a good and righteous cause. Also similar to Kosovo is the frame of waging a limited war, where our fighting men will be in little to no danger or risk. This is to be a war that is to be fought from afar. It is a war that is fought with Tomahawk cruise missiles and airpower to enforce a no-fly zone over Libya. On Monday 21 March 2011 the *New York Times* announced that: An American-led military campaign to destroy Col. Muammar el-Qaddafi's air defences and establish a no-fly zone over Libya has nearly accomplished its initial objectives, and the United States is moving swiftly to hand command to allies in Europe, American officials said Monday.[10] In an effort to enforce political consensus on a foreign, US-led military intervention against Gaddafi, the process needed to be framed within R2P. There are two issues at stake, the first is having the right to intervene and the second point is to have the political will to intervene (Chesterman 2011: 279). Both of these questions are ultimately determined by political consensus, which requires a notion of legitimacy and urgency in order to be achieved.

This was in response to a rift that occurred in the unfolding media narrative, when events did not pan out as anticipated by politics and media alike. The early successes of the coalition against Gaddafi were cheered in the information sphere as the triumph of the oppressed masses yearning for democracy and freedom, and anticipating the 'inevitable' end to the regime very soon. However, when the 'inevitable' did not occur, and in fact Gaddafi rallied his forces and began to crush the rebellion, the narrative shifted to one that urged the protection of the rebels from the wrath of the dictator, who had pledged to show no mercy.

In 2011 there were also attempts by Sweden to get militarily involved. Many of these polls were being conducted, which gave the impression of public support for 'intervention.' A façade 'debate' occurred on TV 4 after the 0700 news at a time when the issue was heating up in Sweden owing to the government's desire to send military assets to assist the NATO mission. For the anti-war side was an unassuming and quietly spoken woman, her opponent was a tall man in a suit and loudly spoken, completely crowding her out. This so-called display of pluralism and debate on this issue was over even before it had begun. The much more adept public speaker, representing the pro-war side, was able to give a much more convincing presentation, not owing to the power and logic of his argument, but due to his ability to disproportionately project his voice and hence argument over the top of his opponent that enhanced the sense of ethos. Swedish TV managed viewer perception further by the techniques used to reinforce the pro-war position, with the use of interviews with Swedish military officials before and after the debate. There was a noticeable lack of impartiality in the media reportage and their calls for a military contribution by Sweden, from a supposedly neutral country.

There were a number of polls, which in a way echoed the lack of serious public debate on the issue of military intervention in Libya. According to polls conducted in Sweden, by *Demoskop* on behalf of the yellow newspaper *Expressen*, 9 out of 10 Swedes supported the UN's decision to intervene, and 65 per cent of respondents stated that Sweden should participate in the intervention.[11] Polls are a means to convey a certain perception on an issue, rather than being a solid fact. At very best they can be considered as being indicative of public sentiment (depending on the size of the poll and the questions asked). However, in this instance it seems to give the impression of public consensus. Sweden, it seems, were willing enough to throw away 200 years of neutrality and accumulated reputation that accompanied this position on a venture that was hastily assembled and poorly defined.

The dictator that everyone can hate

For every 'good' and 'just' war there needs to be a media presentable object or subject that everyone can hate. In many regards, Colonel Muammar Gaddafi was perfect for the task. His past associations with terrorism, his 'flamboyant' lifestyle when on foreign trips, the way he dressed and his behaviour, which seemed bizarre at times, made him the perfect candidate and object for misunderstanding and dislike. The clincher for his image as being a brutal dictator and a 'mad man' was the fact that he was not exactly photogenic, and appeared to be mad.[12] This mad image was easier to generate as there was no attempt to background or explain any potential cultural differences with a 'Western' audience.

A logic following from establishing someone as being mad is that they are incapable of reason and therefore cannot be negotiated or reasoned with in order to see 'common' sense. Gaddafi had been dictator of Libya since 1969, when a coup brought him to power. Until the events of February 2011 there was no sign of a domestic opposition capable of toppling him. To survive in this region for as long as he did required more than luck, and certainly skill and cunning. Not exactly the hallmarks of a mad man. So he was brutal, yes absolutely, as for being a madman there are strong doubts about that.

As for the future of Libya's dictator, there seems to be a lack of consensus on this issue too. On the one hand there were calls from Obama and Clinton that Gaddafi had to go. Therefore this military operation could be seen in the context as a means with which to remove him (and certainly by targeting his residences). However, British Prime Minister Cameron, when speaking before the House of Commons ahead of a vote on the issue of military action ruled this out. "It explicitly does not provide the legal authority for action to bring about Gaddafi's removal of power by military means."[13] Unfortunately the extreme vagueness of UN Resolution 1973 did not explicitly exclude it either!

Talk was intense on the issue of bringing Gaddafi before an international court on the charges of war crimes.[14] This not only contradicts one of the narratives that the war was not intended to overthrow Gaddafi, it was also sheer hypocrisy. Gaddafi was being held responsible for the actions of his armed forces, certainly as Commander in Chief the responsibility did ultimately rest with him. However, this should have then be evenly applied, rather than on a highly selective basis. On an equal footing and using these very criteria were being called for, President Obama should have been investigated. As Commander in Chief of the US armed forces he was ultimately responsible for their conduct. The conduct of US soldiers with murdering unarmed Afghan civilians[15] and the continued drone attacks in Pakistan that have killed numerous civilians over the years (the use of drone attacks were increased by Obama).[16] Or does the use of such attacks on civilians not matter when the label "Taliban Suspects" is used, which justifies the summary execution of civilians with no due legal process or right to recourse? There has also been remarkably little said, after a brief condemnation, of the brutal suppression of the unrest in Bahrain.[17] Certainly there are no hints or threats of investigation by the international criminal court.

Second thoughts and rifts

However, everything has not progressed as smoothly as anticipated, and there were already signs of discontent and suspicion surfacing in some spaces. The Arab League seemed to have had a revelation. In spite of calling on the West for this attack, realities of modern warfare started to dawn upon them. There are second thoughts just days after it began. Apparently there are civilian casualties and they don't like civilians being attacked. The whole 'show' takes on a rather farcical dimension. The Arab League's Secretary General Amr Mussa went as far as to say "what has happened in Libya differs from the goal of imposing a no-fly zone and what we want is the protection of civilians and not bombing of other civilians."[18]

These second thoughts are based upon, what in effect is a form of *Pavlovian Response* that has been cultivated by the media coverage of the new 'humanised' warfare. That is, the narrative that the West have superior soldiers and weapon technology, and fight in such a way that minimises civilian casualties. The use of 'smart' bombs and the like has the public believing and the expectation that few (if any) civilians should be killed in a war. This narrative is certainly promoted by the military officials of this concept of *War with a Human Face*. However, it also means that when civilian casualties do occur, the backlash is immediate and in some cases hard, owing to the dissonance with public expectation.

There were also cracks appearing in the Western alliance where there is fighting over who should take over responsibility after the US leaves. British Prime Minister David Cameron stated NATO should in a public statement, which was contradicted by the French Foreign Minister Alain Juppe, who stated that Arab League interests and wishes should be taken into account. Turkey who opposed the attacks stated that it does not want to see this war end with the occupation of Libya. Within the US ranks there was strife too. Law makers are complaining that the act of war was committed by President Obama without the consent and approval of Congress, thereby exceeding his constitutional authority.[19]

Obama's apparent vision in seeing NATO as being the organisation to take the lead role from the US seems to be in trouble too. The Italian Foreign Minister Franco Frattini warned that if NATO did not take over quickly, Italy shall take back control of NATO bases on its territory. This situation has been made even murkier by Juppe who has talked of NATO taking a supporting role (and not the lead).[20] Such statements not only demonstrate a very public rift in NATO and the

US on how to proceed, but also there has been remarkably little thought put into how to manage the war from the opening phases.

Russia and China, although stating their objection to the conflict, interestingly never used their votes to veto the resolution in the UN Security Council, have been upping their critical rhetoric. On 22 March 2011 Prime Minister Putin stated that although Gaddafi's regime was not democratic this was not reason enough to embark upon a military intervention. He also characterised the UN resolution as: "The resolution is defective and flawed. It allows everything [...] It resembles medieval calls for crusades."[21] The rhetoric is quite hard, but is in the end only symbolic. The real power, to veto the resolution, was not used.

There have been attempts and calls by the UN Secretary General Ban Ki-Moon to bring about a sense of unity in the international community.

> Out of the terrible massacres of the previous decades in which the international community had been accused of doing nothing – those massacres included the genocide in Srebenica, Rwanda and Cambodia – after those terrible incidents, the world said never again. [...] It is imperative that on this measure the international community speak with one voice.[22]

His emotional rhetoric though is very easily invalidated by the use of logic and facts. Certainly the world does not want to see a repeat of the genocides that he has mentioned. But he implies that only intervention by the international community would have seen these dark episodes averted. But there are a number of problems with his emotional call, international presence was already established in both Bosnia and Rwanda at the times these massacres took place, but those peacekeepers stood aside and let it happen. The third case of Cambodia was brought to an end not by the 'selfless' intervention of democratic countries but by the invasion of Communist Vietnam. This makes a mockery of these attempts to justify the crushing of an open and pluralistic debate on an issue of such importance.

NATO's involvement: Fiction and fact

The mandate given by the UN Security Council, which was essentially the mechanism that was used to permit and justify an illegal action that results in regime change, was to protect civilians from attack by armed formations in Libya. Among the claims by NATO were that its mission was to protect civilians, it was only targeting military objects, it was not targeting Gaddafi, there was no regime change agenda, there was no arming of the rebel factions and no troops were on the ground. The UK government through its communications tried to sell the war via a tangled and somewhat contradictory set of explanations that were supposedly founded upon the supposition that it was morally right to do so. Various reasons given included: reduce the threat of terrorism; protect Libyan civilians; safeguard the economy; minimise immigration; protect against organised crime; remove a tyrant; uphold international law; demonstrate global leadership; support its allies; and to spread freedom and democracy (Colley 2015: 67).

Therefore, the war was simultaneously a humanitarian intervention and in the national interest, but without any explanation of those supposed links. So, let's take a look at each of these claims by NATO and leading Western powers, the rhetoric expressed and the reality of their actions.

NATO's mission was to protect civilians only.[23] This gives the war of choice against Libya the thin veneer of a 'humanitarian' mission. The intended impression here is to have something that is otherwise repugnant, organised killing and violence, all done in the name of a seemingly good and just cause. The double standard of many journalists in how they treated sources of information differently is most evident here. Information from NATO and the National Transitional Council (NTC), i.e. the good guys in this war, was accepted at face value and without double checking, presented as facts. That is in spite of a long history of deception, by NATO especially, in earlier military conflicts. Gaddafi and his followers, in other words the bad guys of this plot, had their statements questioned and ridiculed.

Brigadier General Claudio Gabellini, from NATO's planning staff from Naples, stated that "all NATO targets are military targets." He also claimed that NATO had no interest in targeting Gaddafi, not even knowing his whereabouts. However, a statement by Colonel Ahmed Bani, the rebel military spokesman, casts doubt on NATO's alleged 'neutrality' in the conflict. With reference to NATO airstrikes, he said that "they are doing their jobs very, very well [...] We will need these airstrikes when we are planning to advance on the ground."[24] This statement shows that NATO was in effect engaged in a ground support operation for the forces opposing Gaddafi rather than for protecting civilians.

Yet there were plenty of journalists able and willing to produce propagandistic articles on NATO's prowess and care for Libyan civilians. One particularly blatant article had a headline that proclaimed *With 'God's Eye view' on Libya, NATO Strikes*. "Two F-16 fighter jets prowling the skies over Tripoli pinpoint a missile launch site near a building in the capital. They ask for clearance to drop a pair of 500-pound bombs. [...] This bombing past midnight Sunday highlights the complex choreography behind more than 2,500 air strikes conducted by the alliance over nearly four months in pursuit of Moammar Gaddafi's forces."[25] This propaganda was meant to soothe any concerns of civilians in the Western states about killing Libyan civilians. However, to work, this relies on an almost absolute ignorance of the power of modern weaponry. Dropping 500-pound bombs is almost certainly going to lead to civilian casualties, especially if this is done within urban areas! No matter how precise these weapons are guided. Additionally, it is interesting to note that the journalists referred to NATO pursuing Gaddafi's military forces, rather than protecting civilians. The thin coating of lies and spin does not take much to uncover.

Credibility of the precision bombing narrative was further eroded by a number of articles about the level of bombings by NATO. A *New York Times* article headline speaks for itself, *NATO bombs Tripoli in heaviest strikes yet*. In one day, 15 targets in the central city were bombed.[26] Other stories also suggested a less than precise use of the so-called smart bombs. A bombing raid on the Libyan intelligence chief's private residence saw approximately 10 bombs dropped on a residential neighbourhood.[27] This was neither a military target nor something that was directly threatening civilians. Although, the rationale that is used to try and justify this act is that the work nature of the person being targeted is a threat to civilians. Such logic though is working on a lot of assumptions and presumptions. It also ignores the fact that civilians and their dwellings will become, to use the military's politically correct term, *collateral damage*. Such rhetoric and logic ignores any sort of ethical or moral responsibility of war. For the greater part, journalists have allowed NATO's flawed public statements go unchallenged and therefore they remain unaccountable.

As in the Kosovo War in 1999, Afghanistan in 2001 and Iraq in 2003, state mass media assets were deliberately attacked. This presents an interesting dilemma from countries that lecture the rest of the world about media freedom and protecting journalists. But it also highlights the issue of the importance of trying to achieve information dominance in time of war and to deny your enemy this opportunity. Although, this is usually caged in much 'nicer' terms, such as their media is only used for propaganda argument. "NATO said Saturday that it had disabled three Libyan state television transmission dishes in Tripoli with airstrikes overnight, as the alliance took steps to remove the main instrument of Col. Moammar el-Gaddafi's propaganda from the airwaves."[28] Irina Bokovo, the Director-General of UNESCO, rightly condemned this action. "The NATO strike is also contrary to the principles of the Geneva Conventions that establish the civilian status of journalists in times of war even when they engage in propaganda [...] Silencing the media is never a solution. Fostering independent and pluralistic media is the only way to enable people to form their own opinion."[29]

NATO has an almost reflexive response when it comes to accusations that they have hit civilians in air raids. Such an instance occurred in June 2011 when NATO allegedly carried out strikes on a 'high-level command and control node', although it initially denied the strike. A Libyan government spokesman alleged that a number of children were killed in this raid. An allegation that was strongly denied by Canadian Lieutenant General Charles Bouchard, Commander of NATO operations in Libya. "This strike will greatly degrade Gaddafi regime forces' ability to carry on their barbaric assault against the Libyan people."[30] Within a period of two days, NATO admitted to striking the wrong target. Bouchard was then forced to say that a missile was intended for a "military missile site", but had missed and "may have caused a number of civilian casualties." He blamed "weapons system failure" and added that "NATO regrets the loss of innocent civilian lives."[31] Another headline read *NATO Admits Libya Airstrike, Not Civilian Deaths*. Thus the reluctance to admit what is common sense. "A NATO official said the alliance was aware of regime allegations that 15 people, including three children, were killed but had no way of verifying them."[32] This kind of makes one ponder and wonder then, how do NATO get such 'accurate' kill figures from the drone strikes that are done in the remote tribal areas of Pakistan, if they cannot do so on Europe's doorstep?

One of the articles that perhaps reveal what is likely to be one the real intentions behind the air strikes, which have hit civilian objects was found in *Deutsche Welle*. "NATO forces are continuing to expand their airstrikes over Libya and its capital, Tripoli, as the pressure builds on the country's leader, Moammar Gaddafi, to quit in the wake of more high-level defections."[33] This is in effect using military force as a means of psy-ops (psychological operations), in order to force people to leave Gaddafi, which implies that he was hardly the isolated dictator that he was painted to be.

One of the issues that came out clearly was the level of cooperation between NATO and NTC forces in the fighting. The level of cynicism and lack of tact in how this was carried out became gradually more observable as the war progressed. "Libya's new rulers urged the visiting leaders of Britain and France on Thursday to continue NATO airstrikes in the North African nation as rebels entered one of deposed dictator Moammar Gaddafi's last remaining strongholds."[34] This implies that NATO is far from acting as a neutral arbitrator, protecting the lives of civilians in this conflict, but rather providing air support operations for the rebel ground forces. An added implication is that if the rebels could not take the last remaining positions unassisted by NATO airpower, then it is unlikely that they would have ever been capable of winning this war without the foreign help.

At times, media openly discussed the help given by NATO to the rebels, in spite of no UN mandate to become involved with any one side in the civil war. "The officials also said that coordination between NATO and the rebels, and among the loosely organized rebel groups themselves, had become more sophisticated and lethal in recent weeks, even though NATO's mandate has been merely to protect civilians, not to take sides in the conflict."[35] Although the *New York Times* article raises the issue of violating the UN mandate, there is absolutely no criticism of this fact. In June 2011, a British official was quoted as saying "we will protect civilians by all means necessary while the UN mandate is in force, and that applies to everybody. If the NTC attacks civilians, the mandate would give the international community the grounds to intervene." In response to this issue being raised, one rebel commander was on record as saying "We object to being threatened by our allies. They are taking part in military action only at our invitation."[36] This is hardly a very convincing argument for NATO's so-called 'neutral' role in this war!

As the civil war came to its current bloody end in Sirte, it became apparent, that in spite of the fine statements and promises made above concerning the protection of all civilians, this was more about rhetoric than fact. The heavy shelling by the NTC ground forces and the continuous aerial bombing by NATO of the city was a direct military threat to civilians that were still trapped within the city.[37] Thus this situation completely contravening NATO's UN mandate for being there. Yet NATO took absolutely no action to attack NTC artillery positions outside of Sirte that were firing into the town.

One of the denials that were often made was that there were no NATO forces on the ground, and that it was only air and naval forces being used. "With no troops on the ground in Libya, NATO relies heavily on images taken by surveillance planes and drones to identify targets."[38] This statement is completely clear and has no ambiguity concerning its meaning: there are no troops on the ground. This appears to be another lie as other statements clearly contradict this assertion. "At the same time, Britain, France and other nations deployed special forces on the ground inside Libya to help train and arm the rebels, the diplomat and another official said."[39] The second statement is also very clear, NATO ground forces have been deployed in Libya. After this 'revelation', there were attempts to try and disguise this violation of UN Security Council Resolution 1973 by hiding the details with misleading definitions. "In an interview with the EU Observer website, an unnamed NATO official admitted Britain and France may have deployed troops in Libya, but said that it would be 'unfair to call them NATO forces.'"[40] Once more, there is an attempt to try and conceal the truth through the use of defining and redefining of words and meanings.

Timetables and inevitability

This war was billed as being one with an inevitable outcome, sooner or later Gaddafi would be ousted from power owing to the power of the forces aligned against him. We were told that he was isolated and unpopular, his remaining supporters would soon abandon him. Yet this war lasted some eight months, and Gaddafi had supporters to the very end. During the course of the war two mechanisms were employed by NATO on a regular basis. One was the expectation by the public, and NATO employed expectation management in this regard to control this aspect, which is when a war begins there is an expectation for a foreseeable end to it. Iraq and Afghanistan have violated this principle of war, and it seems like wars without an end (in spite of various vague promises of withdrawal). Deadlines and anniversaries are highly symbolic and crucial in the highly politicised nature of modern warfare. The other concerns the use of the rhetoric of inevitability. That is, an outcome is presented as a being a fait accompli.

To give just one example of the use of fait accompli, Defence Secretary Robert Gate's, stated in June 2011 that "It's just a question when everybody around Gaddafi decides it's time to throw in the towel and throw him under the bus."[41] The amount of time is not specified in this quote from Gates, and is avoided for good reason, as the war was expected to end much sooner than it did. He does give the impression of the course of events to be inevitable, and beyond question.

British Foreign Secretary William Hague tried to create a space for political manoeuvring using emotional rhetoric to avoid the issue of strict deadlines. "We're not going to set a deadline. You're asking about Christmas and who knows, it could be days or weeks or months, (but) it is worth doing."[42] As stated above, the war lasted much longer and NATO encountered more resistance from Gaddafi's forces than anticipated, therefore this is an attempt at expectation management. This is done by trying to emphasise the 'worthiness' of this war, but strictly avoiding any kind of timetable.

The earlier statements were made during a time when there was no immediate foreseeable end to the war. However, when events seemed to finally turn in NATO's favour, then some forecasts began to be made. "Asked for an assessment a day after NATO allies extended the mission by another 90 days, Lieutenant General Charles Bouchard told a press briefing: 'I'm highly confident we can complete this mission well within this timeframe.'"[43] The end-game scenario is painted by NATO, which then tries to capitalise on the perception of legitimacy as they are going to complete their mission within the extended 90-day UN mandate. The sense of inevitability of the finale is married with the deadline.

Bearing in mind that the UN mandate referred to protecting civilians only, there was a natural denial that there were any efforts to track or target Gaddafi. However, like a lot of the NATO narrative, there are many inconsistencies in terms of words and deeds. A *Washington Times* article quoted Marine Colonel David Lapan on this issue. "I've confirmed with folks at NATO and through the command structure that they are not involved in targeting any particular individual, that they are not involved in a manhunt." Yet, as was pointed out in the same article, British Defence Minister, Liam Fox, stated that NATO intelligence and reconnaissance assets are being used to try and hunt Gaddafi down.[44] Other contradictory messages from military and political actors also appeared in the media. The Commander of US Africa Command, General Carter Ham, stated that Gaddafi had very few men left fighting for him and that "it seems to me that his ability to influence day to day activities has largely been eliminated, probably not completely eliminated, but pretty significantly." This differs greatly from what the NATO Secretary General, Anders Fogh Rasmussen, was saying. Sticking to the mantra, he stated that "remnants of Gaddafi's regime still constitute a threat to the civilian population." Therefore NATO had a duty to continue to protect them while the threat remained.[45] The difference between the military and political assessments seems to be related to the subjective political objectives, rather than an objective military analysis of the situation.

One final clue as to the unreliable information given by NATO regarding Gaddafi not being a target was a triumphant announcement that vehicles that were likely to be carrying Gaddafi who was fleeing from Sirte were attacked. "A US defence official said Thursday a US Predator drone along with a French fighter jet had attacked a convoy of vehicles in Libya that Paris believed was carrying Moammar Gaddafi."[46] How does this action fit with the UN mandate of protecting civilians from attack? It is certainly the final nail in the coffin of the lie that NATO was acting as some kind of neutral actor for the protection and good of the Libyan people.

Breaking the law and constitution in a 'good' cause

One of the primary narratives of the war in Libya revolves around the issue of the adherence to rule of law, in addition to 'human decency'. That is, Libya and Gaddafi in particular, should follow the established legal guidelines pertaining to the use of military force. Yet another aspect of inconsistency, something that was relatively downplayed by the mass media and certainly by politicians, were the constitutional requirements that were violated during the United States' war against Gaddafi's Libya.

In spite of being kept uninformed, let alone part of the process for some time neither the US House of Representatives nor the Senate pressed for the imposition of the 1973 War Powers Resolution. This act was designed to limit a president's authority over placing armed forces in a state of hostilities without a declaration of war by Congress, but still leaves the president with room to respond to attacks on US armed forces. At the very most, the president is able to engage in a war for absolutely no more than 90 days without the imposition of the War Powers Resolution.[47] Operation Odyssey Dawn, the Pentagon's name given to military operations against Gaddafi, began on March 19 and ended on 31 October 2011. This far exceeds the constitutionally permitted time and that requires the enactment of the War Powers Resolution.

Was this a mere oversight or accident? Perhaps the thought of the greater good by violating the US constitution prevailed at the time? Such theoretical considerations seem to be naïve owing to some limited debate and comments from some sections of US politics. Representative Brad Sherman, Democrat from California clarified the situation and issue at hand. "It's time for Congress to step forward. […] It's time to stop shredding the U.S. Constitution in a presumed effort to bring democracy and constitutional rule of law to Libya."[48] The comments by Sherman seem to reveal not only a sense of indignity about the illegal aspects of the war in terms of the constitutional aspects, but also lack of belief in the stated objectives of the war.

This lack of belief in the stated 'moral' dimensions of the war is back up by some of the legislative actions that subsequently occurred. In May 2011 the US House of Representatives passed a $690 billion Pentagon budget bill. However, there were conditions that came with it. The conditions included limiting the Obama administration's handling of detainees at Guantanamo Bay and forbidding the use of US ground forces in Libya.[49] This shows a distinct lack of faith and trust between the executive and legislative branches of government.

Obama merely cemented the cynicism surrounding his receipt of the Nobel Peace Prize, through various attempts to try and hide violations of the US constitution, not to mention rules of war and the UN mandate through trying to hide in 'grey' legal and descriptive definitions of roles and events. A 38-page report was sent to lawmakers, describing and defending the Libyan operations. The situation was characterised as "US operations do not involve sustained fighting or active exchanges of fire with hostile forces, nor do they involve US ground troops."[50] However, these morally, ethically and legally dubious self-fulfilling definitions seemed to cause some disquiet among legal advisers at the Pentagon and Justice Department. Two lawyers stated their opinion was that continued involvement in the war amounted to 'hostilities', which was ignored in favour of legal council that did not characterise the war in this manner. The disagreement was downplayed as being a good example for democracy in action by the White House.[51] However, what is clear is that only opinions that favoured an illegal course of action were listened to, which was merely used as a means to give the appearance or façade of legitimacy to an illegal act.

The immediate aftermath of the regime change

There have been a number of different warning signs about the likely sinister nature of the new regime that has taken control of Libya. One of the first points of contention is the 'democratic' label that has been quickly assigned by self-appointed leading members of the international community. The basic question needs to be asked, what is so democratic about taking political power by armed force? There have been no elections, no mandate from the Libyan people. Starting from this premise, I shall lay out a number of different points.

In spite of the overriding narrative from Western politicians that the rebel movement that has succeeded Gaddafi is a democratic movement, there are a significant number of concerns that there are certainly non-democratic elements that stand to ultimately take political power. A short introduction to an article in *The Australian* sums up the situation that is unfolding. "'Who wants to join the mujahidin? The gates of jihad are open in Libya!' declares a message posted on a pro al-Qaida internet forum monitored by Western analysts."[52] This article is very detailed in the various extremist Islamic-based groups that were seeking influence in Libya with the removal of Gaddafi. In some regards there are a number of parallels here with Iraq, the removal of a dictator paving the way for extremist elements to move in.

By September 2011, there was growing concern about a possible takeover by the extremist elements. A number of concerns were even coming from inside the rebel ranks. Qatar had been noted as being very helpful to certain elements that have an established track record of extremist activity. This included shiploads of weapons that were destined for extremist factions.[53] This seems to be a contradictory act, to support the rebels in Libya, when they are fighting wars in Afghanistan and Iraq, with some people and organisations that have the same links.

Actions should correspond with the rhetoric and slogans that are assigned to them. In other words, deeds must match the talk. One of the points in which the nature of the new Libyan regime showed its true colours, yet again, was the handling of Moammar Gaddafi after his capture in Sirte on 20 October 2011 when he was beaten and summarily executed by his captors. A number of media outlets tried to minimise the damage that this crime would do by framing the event as being uncertain, such as allegedly, in very carefully chosen words and constructed sentences. Others, such as the *Financial Times*, highlighted the brutal nature of the Gaddafi regime. Stories focussed on the 'joy' and celebration of Libyans and world leaders at his death. Little attention was paid to the complete absence of due process. This should have been paramount owing the vast amount of propaganda that was used to paint the picture of a democratic movement seeking freedom versus a brutal dictator.

The NTC tried to offer a weak and feeble excuse to counter the allegations that Gaddafi was murdered. At first they tried to claim that he was killed in crossfire.

However, the various images and videos that were taken of the event already demonstrated quickly enough that this was yet another NTC lie. Gaddafi was shown being manhandled and beaten in a frenzied crowd, and ultimately bullet holes in his head that suggested it was an execution that killed him.[54] There were some brief, weak and basically symbolic calls by the United States and the UN for the NTC to provide more details on the death.[55] This was not the first or last time that prisoners have been executed by NTC and the allied militias. Another high profile case occurred on 28 July 2011 when the former rebel military commander, General Abdel Fattah Younes was murdered in custody. Not to mention the dozens of bodies strewn around Sirte after the fall, some with their hands tied behind their back, murdered as well.[56]

However, the reactions by the NTC to investigate Gaddafi's murder and the numerous other cases are likely to remain uninvestigated, in spite of some vague and illusive promises. Attempts to try and lay the blame for the murder of Gaddafi by his own supporters tend to support this less-than-optimistic forecast.[57] Such a lack of accountability and sense of justice is likely to result in a lack of trust and suspicion in society towards the new regime, which is beginning to consolidate its power base in the country through creating a sense of fear.

Human rights groups have expressed concern over how the rebel forces have been conducting themselves in terms of crimes against civilians and lynching captured soldiers. In a series of articles, United Press International outlined a number of concerns that were expressed by Amnesty International. "Amnesty International said civilians suffered most from crimes allegedly committed by forces loyal to the NTC. Several fighters loyal to fugitive leader Moammar Gaddafi were lynched after they were captured by rebel forces."[58] Human Rights Watch made similar observations concerning war crimes committed by the rebel forces. Sarah Leah Whitson, Middle East and North African Director for Human Rights Watch stated "Revenge against the people from Tawergha, whatever the accusations against them, undermines the goal of the Libyan revolution. In the new Libya, Tawerghans accused of wrongdoing should be prosecuted based on the law, not subject to vigilante justice."[59] Although UPI cover the story, there seems to be a sense of belittling the subject through the use of the word 'fret' in the title, which has a trivialising effect. The *New York Times* also carried a story about the Libyan town of Tawerga, whose citizens in effect endured a form of collective punishment from the NTC forces after they took the town.[60] There seems to be no effort to systematically investigate these grave allegations by the international mass media or politicians.

There have also been a number of documented cases of crimes against African peoples, by those forces that were opposed to Gaddafi. Some discussion circulated in the ranks that urged rebels not to take out acts of revenge against 'brother Libyans', however, no such consideration was given Africans present in the country. Large numbers of migrant workers from sub-Saharan Africa were present in the country and they were imprisoned and arbitrarily murdered. The evidence against these people seemed to be the colour of their skin. The event that seems to have initiated this prejudice originated from when African mercenaries were apparently used to quell the revolt in Tripoli in the early days of the civil war. However, since this time "western journalists began arriving in the city a few days later [...] they found no evidence of such foreign mercenaries." Those not lynched were imprisoned in appalling conditions, and their numbers far exceeded that of Libyan prisoners.[61] Africans seemed to provide a readily available and easily identifiable group to persecute at a time when the NTC needed to show some kind of responsibility to protect vulnerable groups in Libya.

It is certainly no secret that a number of the NTC have links to extremist Islamic organisations. Abdel Hakim Belhaj, by then put in charge of a military committee that was responsible for keeping order in Tripoli, was in 2004 subjected to rendition on the request of the US. And now he was re-branded as an ally of the US, the same ones that sent him to six years of hell in a Libyan prison.[62] Therefore this sudden change of mind, or at least rhetoric, appears to be very opportunistic and linked to short-term strategy.

The NTC and its Libyan allies have not shown restraint in terms of their desire and ability at disinformation and deception of international audiences through their public statements and orchestrated public spectacles. This was made a much easier task owing to a very obliging Western press that mostly publicised the words without analysis or question. A good example of this occurred early on in the war, when a Libyan woman just happened to go to a hotel that was occupied by foreign journalists. She declared publicly that she had been raped by forces loyal to Gaddafi.[63] The fact that of all of the places she could go was a hotel know to be full of foreign journalists, combined with the fact that she could be subjected to an honour killing by her own family (she can be killed by her own family for bringing shame to them) makes this story extremely suspicious. One does not have to remember too far back to the claims of Iraqi soldiers tossing infants from incubators in Kuwait. Every 'good' and 'just' war needs a good old fashioned atrocity story to ensure public support for an adventure that is fraught with ethical and moral shortcomings.

There was another example of the use of disinformation and deception later on in the war, which also highlights the attention that is paid to the political dimensions of modern warfare. The following is from an Information Operations and Influence Activity Symposium held at the UK Defence Academy in Shrivenham. This incident occurred when the NTC announced that they had captured one of Gaddafi's sons, Seif al-Islam, who showed up soon after for his own press conference in a very non-captured state. This deception did serve its short-term purpose though as 11 foreign governments recognised the NTC as the legitimate authority in Libya, at a time when there was a reluctance in the international community to take a stance on the war. The impression was conveyed that the war was about to end, by the implication of the NTC statement, which meant that there was a perceived need to take a stance at the last minute and support the winning side.

Libya's slide into anarchy does not seem to have finished. In spite of being completely 'liberated' the country is inundated with weapons throughout the population. The self-appointed liberators, in their numerous factions, terrify the local residents on a daily basis.[64] This seems to be a prelude to a power struggle between the various factions that were in a loose coalition against Gaddafi. The various militias are not disarming.[65] In spite of the NTC saying that these groups needed to be kept armed, the reality appeared to be that they were powerless to do anything about the situation.

The results of the war of choice

One of the likely benefactors of the war against Gaddafi's Libya is big business, and especially oil interests. They could hardly contain their glee during the war. Already on 23 August 2011, Libyan rebels stated that oil companies are "very interested" in what was going on in Libya. The pre-war level of production in Libya was 1.6 million barrels of oil per day. Keith Roberts, the Finance Director at British Oil Services Group Petrofac stated that "obviously we're going to be very interested in what they intend to develop. [...] We haven't found the right opportunity in the past and it's been a difficult country to do business in."[66] From this statement it is obvious that oil companies have a stake in seeing the Gaddafi regime deposed to enable the possibility of a more 'cooperative' regime to enable them to increase corporate profits.

In addition to the oil companies, other businesses were seeking to quickly jump on board and earn profits from the misery that has been imposed upon the Libyan people. The *New York Times* ran an article about the new 'prospects' for Western businesses in Libya. The complete absence of any form of ethics was amply demonstrated in the article.

> The guns in Libya have barely quieted, and NATO's military assistance to the rebellion that toppled Col. Muammar el-Gaddafi will not end officially until Monday. But a new invasion force is already plotting its own landing on the shores of Tripoli.
>
> Western security, construction and infrastructure companies that see profit-making opportunities receding in Iraq and Afghanistan have turned their sights on Libya, now free of four decades of dictatorship. Entrepreneurs are abuzz about the business potential of a country with huge needs and the oil to pay for them, plus the competitive advantage of Libyan gratitude toward the United States and its NATO partners.
>
> A week before Colonel Qaddafi's death on Oct. 20, a delegation from 80 French companies arrived in Tripoli to meet officials of the Transitional National Council, the interim government. Last week, the new British defence minister, Philip Hammond, urged British companies to "pack their suitcases" and head to Tripoli.
>
> "There is a gold rush of sorts taking place right now," said David Hamod, president and chief executive officer of the National U.S.-Arab Chamber of Commerce. "And the Europeans and Asians are way ahead of us. I'm getting calls daily from members of the business community in Libya. They say, 'Come back, we don't want the Americans to lose out.'[67]

This paints a grim picture for the future of the Libyan people, especially when taking into account the behaviour and the results of oil, reconstruction and security firms in Afghanistan and Iraq. Additionally, presumably in a manner similar to Iraq, they are likely to be robbed of their national wealth and assets.

If one was to take for granted what is being said by politicians and mass media, it would seem that the war was a complete success and that the Libyan people are now 'liberated' and able to enjoy the fruits of freedom. Various political 'pillars' of the international community could not rush quickly enough to Tripoli to be seen with the new regime, and to try and take credit for a war that had not only been started, but finished as well (unlike the early predictions in the campaigns in Afghanistan and Iraq).

In terms of the streams of information being carried by the international media in the information sphere, it was quickly apparent that the level of deception and disinformation was very high. I have enumerated a number of different examples, although not an inexhaustible list, by any means! However, how have journalists evaluated the situation and their performance in this recent war? In one rather surprisingly frank article in the *New York Times*, a number of the issues affecting the 'truth' were discussed.

> Truth was first a casualty in Libya well before this war began, and the war has not improved matters at all, on any side. [...] Information, or rather truthful information, is often difficult to come by in any war zone. Disinformation is a powerful tool that can be used to mislead the enemy, hide tactics, instigate fear or win public support. There is also the fog of war, the confusion in communications and the chaos of the battlefield that can obscure any objective understanding.[68]

Parallels were made with the lies and deception that was used in the Iraq War in 2003. This demonstrates the value that is placed in the role of information in influencing the political factors, which affect the outcome of wars (rather than individual battles of a war).

Another article probed even deeper into the role of information and Western media in promoting the cause of the insurgency. Questions were asked and the situation detailed, how had so-called sophisticated Western journalists been so easily fooled. This time the blame was being laid at the feet of the journalists and not the rebels.

> There is no better proof for the gullibility (or worse) of Western media than how easily they have been manipulated by rebel spokesmen for the Libyan insurgency. From Sunday through Monday evening for more than 24 hours, broadcast and cable media outlets reported the rebels had captured Saif Gaddafi and his brother Mohammad. Why did they believe and publicize these unconfirmed reports? Because the rebels told them so. No photos, no audio, no proof. We even heard that Saif's capture was confirmed by International Criminal Court prosecutors who apparently believed what they were told too.

But seriously, what has happened to journalism? NATO quickly morphed from being a force to protect civilians under its UN and Arab League Mandate into – 15,000 sorties later – being the air arm of the rebel ground forces, casualties be damned. In the same spirit, it looks now like the Western media have become the propaganda arm of the insurgency. Or maybe it's just terminal laziness. [...]

Every armed conflict is accompanied by a propaganda war, and I don't blame the rebels for reporting gossip or lies or wishful thinking if it serves their aims. That's war. But I expect our supposedly free and informed and sophisticated journalists to be cynics and to ask the hard, unsentimental questions, so that we can all get some sense of what the actual facts are before making our judgments and can help the rebels deal with all he hard problems they will face after Gaddafi is gone.[69]

This tract from the article reveals a significant betrayal of professional aspects of journalistic work and integrity: not checking the sources of information (verification), not offering alternative points of view, getting too close to their subject. The question is whether this was 'just' a case of very poor workmanship or some other even bigger problem that has become ingrained in modern Western journalism. As it seems to be becoming increasingly common occurrence for journalists to undertake similar self-critical evaluations after many of the contemporary conflicts that have taken place, implying the establishment of a certain pattern or at the very least a complete lack of an ability to learn from past errors.

Broader arguments of the war and its justification involve elements of bettering human security for the people of Libya. As has been demonstrated above, the result is quite the contrary. The security situation for people in the wider area, including Europe, has been further compromised by more short-term and short-sighted interference by NATO and the West. One of the results of the anarchy is that the significant arsenals of Gaddafi were plundered. Of particular interest is the fact that at least 5,000 (and perhaps as many as 10,000) of the 20,000 man portable surface-to-air missiles are missing. This includes Russian made SA-7s.[70] The European Union's Count-terrorism Coordinator, Gillies de Kerchove, stated in September 2011 that Al-Qaeda in the Islamic Maghreb have "gained access to weapons, either small arms or machine guns, or certain surface to air missiles which are extremely dangerous because they pose a risk to flights over the territory."[71]

This situation then, has some further potential implications and scenarios, which include a foreign presence in the country as a result of the very real risks brought about by the presence of uncontrolled weapon stocks, which has been facilitated by NATO interference in the country. This seems to be already happening in a limited manner. The US has sent a team of experts to help search for missing weapons, with an emphasis on the surface to air missiles.[72] This seems to be the start, the question being, where shall this eventually end? The prognosis is not very promising with emerging events and trends in Libya and the West's history of interference in other countries. A final point to dwell upon at this stage, which sets the 'humanitarian' tone of the Western enforced regime change came from a 'joke' by Hillary Clinton when being interviewed. While laughing and referring to Gaddafi, she said "we came, we saw, he died."[73] This is a fitting condemnation for those wonderful promises and explanations of humanitarian intent.

Libya as another Iraq

A narrative that is eagerly suppressed by politicians is comparing and contrasting Libya with Iraq. There are a number of reasons for doing this, which are tied to the perception that this tends to generate. Firstly, Iraq (in spite of the upbeat rhetoric) is a failure for the US. Eight years of occupation, no gratitude from the Iraqi people for their US installed 'democracy' and 'freedoms', thousands of soldiers dead, tens of thousands wounded. Another element is that Iraq is seen by many as an occupation, which they do not want to see Libya perceived as also. For now, there are no large numbers of foreign troops on the ground.

Datuk Mustapha Yaakub, Bureau Chairman of Perkasa International, was critical of NATO's attack on Libya. He was also critical of the lack of any form of protest from Islamic organizations in the region (Arab League, Organisation of Islamic Conference and Gulf Cooperation Council). "A civil war will occur in Libya if Gaddafi's successor possesses no charisma to bring together the various tribes, just like the inability of the late Iraqi president Saddam Hussein's replacement in providing the kind of leadership that could unite the Sunni and Syiah Muslims in that country."[74] A valid point is made insofar as in the view of war that is intended to bring about regime change, should consider the end result and answer the following question as a minimum. Is the situation of ordinary people going to be better or worse as a result of the war? If it is worse, then moral constraints should prevent any attempt to bring about change, even if they are against a 'dictator' or have some other non-democratic label.

There were also words or warning from key figures from Western countries too. The former head of the British Army, General Lord Richard Dannatt, warned that NATO's campaign in Libya was reminiscent of the 2003 campaign in Iraq. He openly stated that it was a "very naïve hope that a lightening campaign would bring about change in power and that all would be well."[75] The background and experience of Dannatt should make him a very capable judge of the situation, yet his voice as with other dissenting voices was largely shut out from public discourse in the pages and screens of corporate media. His comments seem to reinforce the idea of short-term thinking and planning of such military operations.

Iraqis have also offered their opinion on the issue. The *New York Times* interviewed a number of Iraqis about their experience of being 'liberated' and 'democratised', and what this situation means for ordinary Iraqis (and could mean for ordinary Libyans). This quick and easy process that is given by Western politicians of the process does not match the reality of average people that are forced to live through the process.

The men said they had learned the hard way what they never understood living under decades of repression: that democracy is not just the absence of oppression, but that it also involves challenging concepts of tolerance, compromise and civic responsibility yet to take root in Iraq, or in Libya.

> What emerged in Iraq after the fall of Mr. Hussein's government was a society of everyone for themselves, individually and in small groups, grabbing for what they could get – literally, through looting, and eventually through the political process. This has made many Iraqis weary of the chaos of Iraqi-style democracy. Increasingly, they want a strong hand – elected by the people — to wield power.[76]

This new reality of living in a 'democratic' country does not match the superficial rhetoric and deceit that is fed to the Western publics about the tremendous 'successes' of the various military ventures in the Middle East and Central Asia. Extremely interesting are the additional comments made by those interviewed. "Do not trust expatriates who rush back to stake a claim in the new government. Avoid a parliamentary system. And do not ostracize members of the former regime, as happened in Iraq under the so-called de-Baathification policy."[77] There has been and continues to be a power struggle to this day and very likely for some time to come. With experience, hindsight and a steady stream of revelations, the Iraq War of 2003 has proven to be serving as a benchmark for deception and the creation of an unnecessary war of choice. Libya certainly seems to be a confirmation of these tactics, where regret and 'errors' are admitted in hindsight and only after another disaster in terms of foreign policy and security interests has been confirmed. In September 2016 the House of Commons Foreign Affairs Committee released their report on the results of an investigation in to the impact of the Libyan War. The summary gives a good overview of the tone and conclusions of the report.

> In March 2011, the United Kingdom and France, with the support of the United States, led the international community to support an intervention in Libya to protect civilians from attacks by forces loyal to Muammar Gaddafi. This policy was not informed by accurate intelligence. In particular, the Government failed to identify the threat to civilians was overstated and the rebels included a significant Islamist element. By the summer of 2011, the limited intervention to protect civilians had drifted into an opportunist policy of regime change. [...] The result was political and economic collapse, inter-militia and inter-tribal warfare, humanitarian and migrant crises, widespread human rights violations, the spread of Gaddafi regime weapons across the region and the growth of ISIL in North Africa. (House of Commons 2016: 3)

Evident from this extract are a number of very worrying and repetitive points in the post-Cold War world of 'humanitarian' wars. A starting point is the misuse of the UN Security Council resolution as a means of political legitimacy to initiate regime change. The resolution was not limited and applied to Gaddafi's forces only. The failure of intelligence, the role played by misinformation (the threat to civilians exaggerated and the threat of Jihadist elements downplayed) in priming and mobilising a target audience to accept war. Not least, the usual catastrophic result of the war that has destroyed a country and threatened the security of a very wide region (Siebens & Case 2012: 35-36). The result has also been to further compromise the credibility and legitimacy of leading Western governments' and their ability to engage in further regime changes via military operations, thereby serving to reinforce the effect set by the Iraq War benchmark.

Democracy and freedom for some, but not for all

One of the matters that became most apparent in the rhetorical assault on Libya, and now Syria, is the issue of democracy and freedom. This has been waged in a very open manner, which reveals the deep rooted lack of consistency in the message. Demands are made for Libyans and Syrians to enjoy 'democracy' and 'freedom', but there is no such talk for equal treatment of the people in Yemen or Bahrain for instance. Interestingly, the question has not been asked by the non-functional Fourth Estate as to why such an obvious differentiation of treatment of the same issue between different countries in the same region exists.

During the largely neglected abortive attempt at an Arab Spring revolt in Bahrain, which was ruthlessly crushed with overwhelming armed force, there has been little coverage, let alone protest at the continuing social and legal injustice there. For instance, doctors and nurses that treated wounded protestors were given terms of 5–15 years for doing their job, by treating those who sought medical help. Doctors Without Borders had its offices raided by security forces in August 2011 and subsequently stopped working in the country. At the height of the protest security forces seized Salmaniya hospital![78] Yet there was no outcry from the self-appointed pillars of the 'civilised world' – Sarkozy, Cameron and Obama. Are the people of Bahrain less worthy of a free and democratic life than Syrians and Libyans?

Yemen is another country, where the element of hypocrisy has become very open and obvious. There have been numerous stories of the Yemeni Government using overwhelming force against protestors, including airpower. Dozens of protestors were being killed in the streets.[79] Just a couple of almost inaudible whispers from Washington when the excesses of the slaughter became a little too much to remain completely silent, but there was no threat of imposing no fly zones, economic or political sanctions. Human Rights Watch, one of the voices condemning events, called the UN response to events there as 'apathetic'.[80] This did not result in any form of reprimands by the international community in any form, and the President of Yemen received medical treatment in the US!

Where are we going from here?

One disturbing headline in the *New York Times* gives a hint of what may be in store for the future – *U.S. Tactics in Libya may be a Model for Other Efforts*.[81]

Although there was a lot of downplaying the situation in Libya being transferred to Syria, the fact is that the US tried to begin in very much the same way with a resolution that was very similar to the one used to open the way for the military attack against Libya. On this occasion, China and Russia used their veto powers to avoid a re-run. The US façade continued when, in response to their veto, US Secretary of State Hillary Clinton demanded that China and Russia explain their veto to the Syrian people. "We believe the Security Council abrogated its responsibility yesterday [...] The countries that chose to veto the resolution will have to offer their own explanations to the Syrian people, and to all others who are fighting for freedom and human rights around the world."[82] If this was equally applied around the globe, the US would be in for doing a lot of explaining to different countries around the world, where it has interfered and cost lives of countless innocent civilians. There are also some observable traces of the Libya model being used against Syria. Some alternative media reports have noted the similarities in the format and the tactics used against Libya are now being applied against Syria. Notably, are the use of exile communities in the UK and US that are used to speak on behalf of the people of the target country, the threat of the 'regime' against its own citizens, the funding of NGOs to shape the information space and create a 'favourable' public opinion, the Jihadist elements that are present among the 'moderate' opposition forces, the lack of alternative policy options presented, and the subjective application of sanctions and embargos by the West.[83]

Coming back to the issue of Libya, there was a lot of back patting and self-congratulatory celebration for a 'good' job done. The US flip-flopping continued here too, making it somewhat difficult to understand which version of the story was in fact true, if any. On 8 September 2011, the US thanked Britain and France for their "extraordinary" role in the Libya campaign.[84] Yet, by early October, the US was already criticising NATO allies that it cannot make up NATO shortfalls. This was in response to defence cuts, demanding that various countries 'coordinate' with the US when making the decisions on reducing defence expenditure.[85] However, if anything the US needs other countries more than other countries need the US currently, the various wars of choice around the globe mean that the defence capacity and capability is stretched to breaking point. Hence the attempt to make the Libyan campaign seem like a European-led operation.

Conclusion

In summing up the results of the Libyan War, the question needs to be asked, why was the execution of the communication management strategy so poor this time? Then answer to this question can be found in different aspects. First, relates to the practical and operational issue of mass communication, and the number of different actors that were in the messenger side. The basic dilemma applies, the more different actors or people that you have in any one particular political body the greater the diversity of opinion. In other words, there were many different political actors that constituted the coalition that attacked Libya, each with their own set of world views and values, which did not necessarily fit with the NATO message. Hence the result was a sense of a very split and divided organisation, owing to the absence of a commonly agreed upon message. The reasons given for regime change under the guise of R2P were often split, poorly explained, contradictory, lacking common sense, too vague/abstract and often with too much emphasis of the moral element at a time when this high moral ground had been lost with the deceptions applied to starting the 2003 Iraq War.

The second point touches upon the issue of politics. War has a tendency to heighten political sensitivity and reactions. By its nature it is something that is brutal and rather unpalatable for the general public. Therefore, political rhetoric needs to bill a war of choice in a very moral and ethical narrative in order to enable the chance of acceptance. A result of this is to create a readily apparent gap in terms of the public expectations that have been cultivated by the political sphere, and the bloody reality that is modern warfare. Thus a compliant mass media is required in order to try and perpetuate the myth for as long as possible. The political risks of going to war are different for different countries, owing to historical backgrounds and the shared values and beliefs of different societies. It results in some countries' political leadership being much more cautious about going to war and how wars should be ideally fought. The loss of military personnel is a more sensitive political topic in some countries than in others too. However, the ability to hide these potentially harmful and counter-images and messages are more difficult to control in the age of the internet and social media. Abu Ghraib, Haditha, the Kill Team and many other US atrocities committed in the name of the War Against Terror testify to this new facet. The tactic then shifts to trying to crowd out those opposing and damaging information streams, to establish information dominance.

An established means or blueprint for creating a favourable information environment promotes and gives the perception of a popular native demand for regime change. It is normally directed against a regime that is not compliant with political or economic demands that are forced upon it by Western countries and corporations. A concerted information war is initiated in the so-called free press of the West, which paints the picture of an oppressed majority rising up against a repressive and non-democratic political regime, only wanting basic freedoms, human rights and democracy. The underdog narrative is important for establishing sympathy for them. These rebels are depicted as being democratic and non-violent in character. It is then 'logically' extrapolated according to an emotional logic that it is the 'civic duty' of the West to interfere and intervene in other countries, which is where the use of concepts, such as, R2P become readily apparent.

The negative aspects and characteristics of the targeted regime are highlighted to demonstrate the 'need' for change. In the mean time, other countries with similar regimes have those negative characteristics downplayed or ignored. What has been unfolding in Yemen, the similar use of force against rebels and protesters for example, yet there are no sanctions let alone military action initiated against this regime. The numbers of those opposing the favoured regime are minimised, and overestimated in the cases where regime changed is desired.

Material and technical support is provided by the West to support the opposition. This ranges from know-how on organising unrest, the recent arrest in Egypt of an Otpor activist from Serbia tends to add credence to this aspect.[86] Informational support, in terms of harnessing the power of corporate and state media in the West to support the efforts of the rebels, is another means to support, spread and sustain the unrest or at least give the impression of this to Western audiences. One can clearly see the use of continuity in the branding of revolutionary waves, the Colour Revolutions and now the Arab Spring. They give the impression of something that is spontaneous and a positive wave of 'progress', all of which they are far removed from.

There is an attempt to legitimise Western interference in the domestic conflict, which is provoked and supported by the West, through such international instruments as the UN Security Council. This gives the façade of world consensus on the issue, which is then manoeuvred into directions that were not mandated as has been amply demonstrated in the Libyan operation. In the lead up to the planned war, there is an attempt to try and paint the image of a reluctant West that must become involved on the grounds of humanitarian concerns and not self-interest. A reluctant hero to the rescue of an oppressed people that merely seek liberation from their oppressor and to enjoy what the rest of the free world does already.

Once the fighting begins there is an attempt to 'clean' the war as much as possible. Only the brutal dictator kills civilians, NATO does not, for instance. The deaths of civilians at the hands of the dictator are deliberate, whereas NATO inflicted casualties cannot be confirmed or are collateral damage. Iconic images and moments are sought to promote the idea of an inevitable result of the righteous war, such as the capture of key figures or the defection of key members of the regime under attack. The destruction and splintering of an otherwise cohesive regime is encouraged through targeting, economically and militarily the assets (residential house and economic assets) of key people. This is a form of psychological warfare, which was also practised in 1999 in order to break the resolve of the Milosevic regime and Serbian military in order to hasten the end to a war that had dragged out longer than anticipated.

Notes

1 Libyan Rape Claims Concern Clinton, UPI, http://www.upi.com/Top_News/ Special/2011/06/17/Libyan-rape-claims-concern-Clinton/UPI-35201308326250/, 17 June 2011 (accessed 15 August 2011)
2 *Security Council Approves 'No-Fly Zone' over Libya, Authorizing 'All Necessary Measures' to Protect Civilians, by Vote of 10 in Favour with 5 Abstentions*, Security Council SC 10200, http://www.un.org/News/Press/docs/2011/sc10200.doc.htm, 17 March 2011 (accessed 23 March 2011)
3 Karl Vick, *Israel Has Faith Mubarak Will Prevail*, Time, http://www.time.com/time/ world/article/0,8599,2044929,00.html, 28 January 2011 (accessed 22 March 2011)
4 Hennessy, S., *Paris Conference Contemplates Libya's Future*, Voice of America, http:// www.voanews.com/english/news/africa/Paris-Conference-Contemplates-Libyas- Future-128893123.html, 1 September 2011 (accessed 4 September 2011)

5 http://www.dailymail.co.uk/news/article-2020651/US-debt-ceiling-crisis-American-troops-Afghanistan-paid.html

6 Ullman, H., *Outside View: The 'LES' Countries*, UPI, http://www.upi.com/Top_News/Analysis/Outside-View/2011/08/24/Outside-View-The-LES-countries/UPI-88941314181140/, 24 August 2011 (accessed 25 August 2011)

7 Ibid.

8 Associated Press, *Gaddafi vow Long War After Allies Strike Libya*, Herald Tribune, http://www.heraldtribune.com/article/20110319/WIRE/110319411/2416/NEWS?Title=Gadhafi-vow-long-war-after-allies-strike-Libya, 19 March 2011 (accessed 23 March 2011)

9 For one example, go to https://twitter.com/thelastrefuge2/status/769713179287060481

10 Elisabeth Bumiller and Kareem Fahim, *US-Led Assault Nears Goal in Libya*, The New York Times, http://www.nytimes.com/2011/03/22/world/africa/22libya.html?_r=1&scp=1&sq=US%20-%20led%20assualt%20nears%20goal&st=cse, 21 March 2011.

11 Sofia Strandberg, *Swedes positive to UN intervention in Libya, survey suggests*, Göteborg Daily, http://webnews.textalk.com/goteborg-daily/news/swedes-positive-to-un-intervention-in-libya-survey-suggests, 22 March 2011 (accessed 23 March 2011)

12 Karimi, F., *Gadhafi's Legacy in Africa: 'Madman or god?'*, CNN, http://edition.cnn.com/2011/10/05/world/africa/africa-gadhafi-legacy/, 5 October 2011 (accessed 4 December 2016)

13 *British PM Says No Authority to Topple Gaddafi*, Space War, http://www.spacewar.com/reports/British_PM_says_no_authority_to_topple_Kadhafi_999.html, 21 March 2011

14 Bruno Waterfield, The Telegraph, http://www.telegraph.co.uk/news/worldnews/africaandindianocean/libya/8359861/Libya-Col-Gaddafi-to-face-ICC-war-crimes-probe.html, 3 March 2011 (accessed 23 March 2011)

15 Marc Hujer, *Did US Soldiers Target Afghan Civilians? War Crime Allegations Threaten to Harm America's Image*, Der Spiegel, http://www.spiegel.de/international/world/0,1518,717127,00.html, 13 September 2010 (accessed 23 March 2011)

16 *US drone strike 'kills 40' in Pakistani tribal region*, BBC News, http://www.bbc.co.uk/news/world-south-asia-12769209, 17 March 2011 (accessed 23 March 2011)

17 Brull, M., *What Western Double Standard? Syria and Bahrain*, Overland, https://overland.org.au/2012/06/what-western-double-standard-syria-and-bahrain/, 8 June 2012 (accessed 4 December 2016)

18 *UN Security Council Opens new Libya Session*, Space War, http://www.spacewar.com/reports/UN_Security_Council_opens_new_Libya_session_999.html, 21 March 2011

19 Elisabeth Bumiller and Kareem Fahim, *US-Led Assault Nears Goal in Libya*, The New York Times, http://www.nytimes.com/2011/03/22/world/africa/22libya.html?_r=1&scp=1&sq=US%20-%20led%20assualt%20nears%20goal&st=cse, 21 March 2011.

20 AFP, *NATO Struggles to Overcome Decisions on Libya Action*, Space War, http://www.spacewar.com/reports/NATO_struggles_to_overcome_divisions_on_Libya_action_999.html, 21 March 2011

21 *Putin Rips 'Medieval Crusade' in Libya*, Reuters in The Moscow Times, http://www.themoscowtimes.com/news/article/putin-rips-medieval-crusade-in-libya/433447.html, 22 March 2011.

22 UN chief defends Libya air strikes against doubters, Space War, http://www.spacewar.com/reports/UN_chief_defends_Libya_air_strikes_against_doubters_999.html, 22 March 2011 (accessed 23 March 2011)

23 To see the text of the resolution please see http://www.guardian.co.uk/world/2011/mar/17/un-security-council-resolution

24 Associated Press, Fox News, NATO Forces Pound Tripoli as Rebels Claim Gains in East, http://www.foxnews.com/world/2011/05/10/nato-forces-pound-tripoli-rebels-claim-gains-east/#ixzz1eca7E8y8, 10 May 2011 (accessed 11 May 2011)

25 Staff Writers, AFP, *With 'God's Eye view' on Libya, NATO Strikes*, Space Wars, http://www.spacewar.com/reports/With_Gods_eyeview_on_Libya_NATO_strikes_999.html, 12 July 2011 (accessed 1 August 2011)

26 Burns, J. F., *NATO Bombs Tripoli in Heaviest Strikes Yet, The New York Times*, http://www.nytimes.com/2011/05/24/world/africa/24libya.html, 23 May 2011 (accessed 24 May 2011)

27 Staff Writers, AFP, Libya's Spy Master Home Destroyed in NATO Air Strike, Space War, http://www.spacewar.com/reports/Libyas_spy_master_home_destroyed_in_NATO_air_strike_999.html, 19 August 2011 (accessed 22 August 2011)

28 Kirkpatrick, D. D., *NATO Strikes at Libyan State TV, The New York Times*, http://www.nytimes.com/2011/07/31/world/africa/31tripoli.html, 30 July 2011 (accessed 10 August 2011)

29 Director-General deplores NATO strike on Libyan state television facilities, Media Services, UNESCO, http://www.unesco.org/new/en/media-services/single-view/news/director_general_deplores_nato_strike_on_libyan_state_television_facilities/, 8 August 2011 (accessed 24 November 2011)

30 Staff Writers, AFP, NATO Says Bombed Libya Military Target, Not Civilians, Modern Ghana, http://www.modernghana.com/news/335669/1/nato-says-bombed-libya-military-target-not-civilia.html, 21 June 2011 (accessed 1 August 2011)

31 Kirkpatrick, D. D., NATO Admits Missile Hit a Civilian Home in Tripoli, http://www.nytimes.com/2011/06/20/world/middleeast/20libya.html, 19 June 2011 (accessed 31 July 2011)

32 Staff Writers, AFP, *NATO Admits Libya Airstrike, Not Civilian Deaths*, Straits Times, http://www.straitstimes.com/BreakingNews/World/Story/STIStory_682117.html, 20 June 2011 (accessed 1 August 2011)

33 Benzow, G. & Mara, D., NATO Extends Libyan Airstrikes as More Top Officials Defect, Arab World, Deutsche Welle, http://www.dw-world.de/dw/article/0,,15125157,00.html, 2 June 2011 (accessed 3 June 2011)

34 Kumar-Sen, A., *Libyan Rebels Urge More NATO Airstrikes*, The Washington Times, http://www.washingtontimes.com/news/2011/sep/15/cameron-sarkozy-visit-post-gadhafi-libya/?page=all, 15 September 2011 (accessed 16 September 2011)

35 Schmitt, E. & Myers, S. L., *Surveillance and Coordination With NATO Aided Rebels*, The New York Times, http://www.nytimes.com/2011/08/22/world/africa/22nato.html, 21 August 2011 (accessed 22 August 2011)

36 Sengupta, K., *We'll Turn Our Guns on Libyan Rebels if they Attack Civilians, NATO Threatens*, The Independent, http://www.independent.co.uk/news/world/africa/well-turn-our-guns-on-libyan-rebels-if-they-attack-civilians-nato-threatens-2294933.html, 9 June 2011 (accessed 9 June 2011)

37 Staff Writers, AFP, *NATO, NTC Deadlier Than Kadhafi Diehards: Sirte Escapees*, Space War, http://www.spacewar.com/reports/NATO_NTC_deadlier_than_Kadhafi_diehards_Sirte_escapees_999.html, 6 October 2011 (accessed 7 October 2011)

38 Staff Writers, AFP, *With 'God's Eye view' on Libya, NATO Strikes*, Space Wars, http://www.spacewar.com/reports/With_Gods_eyeview_on_Libya_NATO_strikes_999.html, 12 July 2011 (accessed 1 August 2011)

39 Schmitt, E. & Myers, S. L., *Surveillance and Coordination With NATO Aided Rebels*, The New York Times, http://www.nytimes.com/2011/08/22/world/africa/22nato.html, 21 August 2011 (accessed 22 August 2011)

40 *NATO Admits UK and France may Have Troops in Libya*, RIA Novosti, http://en.rian.ru/world/20110829/166274046.html, 29 August 2011 (accessed 29 August 2011)

41 Staff Writers, AFP, *NATO Hits Tripoli as Gates Says Kaddafi's Time is Up, Space War*, http://www.spacewar.com/reports/NATO_hits_Tripoli_as_Gates_says_Kadhafis_time_is_up_999.html, 5 June 2011 (accessed 6 June 2011)

42 Staff Writers, AFP, *NATO Hits Tripoli as Gates Says Kaddafi's Time is Up, Space War*, http://www.spacewar.com/reports/NATO_hits_Tripoli_as_Gates_says_Kadhafis_time_is_up_999.html, 5 June 2011 (accessed 6 June 2011)

43 Staff Writers, AFP, *NATO Confident Libya Air War to End Within Three Months, Space War*, http://www.spacewar.com/reports/NATO_confident_Libya_air_war_to_end_within_three_months_999.html, 22 September 2011 (accessed 23 September 2011)

44 Associated Press, *Pentagon: U.S., NATO not in Manhunt for Gaddafi*, The Washington Times, http://www.washingtontimes.com/news/2011/aug/25/pentagon-us-nato-not-manhunt-gadhafi/, 25 August 2011 (accessed 26 August 2011)

45 Staff Writers, AFP, *Kadhafi Controls Few Forces, not a US Target: General*, Space War, http://www.spacewar.com/reports/Kadhafi_controls_few_forces_not_a_US_target_general_999.html, 14 September 2011 (accessed 15 September 2011)

46 Staff Writers, AFP, *US Drone hit Same Convoy Targeted by French Jet: US*, Space War, http://www.spacewar.com/reports/US_drone_hit_same_convoy_targeted_by_French_jet_US_999.html, 20 October 2011 (accessed 21 October 2011)

47 Tomkins, R., UPI, *U.S. Congress Remains in Dark Over Libya*, Space War, http://www.spacewar.com/reports/US_Congress_remains_in_dark_over_Libya_999.html, 23 May 2011 (accessed 24 May 2011)

48 Savage, C., *Libya Effort is Called Violation of War Act*, The New York Times, http://www.nytimes.com/2011/05/26/world/middleeast/26powers.html, 25 May 2011 (accessed 26 May 2011)

49 Staff Writers, AFP, *US Lawmakers, Pass $690 Billion Pentagon Bill*, Space War, http://www.spacewar.com/reports/US_lawmakers_pass_690_billion_Pentagon_bill_999.html, 26 May 2011 (accessed 27 May 2011)

50 Savage, C. & Landler, M., *White House Defends Continuing U.S. Role in Libya Operation*, The New York Times, http://www.nytimes.com/2011/06/16/us/politics/16powers.html?pagewanted=all, 15 June 2011 (accessed 31 July 2011)

51 Savage, C., *2 Top Lawyers Lost to Obama in Libya War Policy Debate*, The New York Times, http://www.nytimes.com/2011/06/18/world/africa/18powers.html?pagewanted=all, 17 June 2011 (accessed 31 July 2011)

52 Neighbour, S., Libya Ripe for Jihad's Rallying Cries, The Australian, http://www.theaustralian.com.au/news/features/libya-ripe-for-jihads-rallying-cries/story-e6frg6z6-1226044640098, 26 April 2011 (accessed 6 September 2011)

53 (1) Nordland, R. & Kirkpatrick, D. D., *Islamists' Growing Sway Raises Questions for Libya*, The New York Times, http://www.nytimes.com/2011/09/15/world/africa/in-libya-islamists-growing-sway-raises-questions.html?pagewanted=all, 14 September 2011 (accessed 15 September 2011)
(2) Sen, A. K., *Rebels Fearful of Islamist Takeover in Libya*, The Washington Times, http://www.washingtontimes.com/news/2011/sep/29/rebels-fearful-of-islamist-takeover/?page=all, 29 September 2011 (accessed 3 October 2011)

54 Fahim, K., Shadid, A. & Gladstone, R., *Violent End to an Era as Gaddafi Dies in Libya*, The New York Times, http://www.nytimes.com/2011/10/21/world/africa/qaddafi-is-killed-as-libyan-forces-take-surt.html?pagewanted=all, 20 October 2011 (accessed 21 October 2011)

55 Fahim, K. & Gladstone, R., *U.S. and U.N. Demand Details From Libyan Leaders on How Qaddafi Died*, The New York Times, http://www.nytimes.com/2011/10/22/world/africa/libyan-leaders-appear-to-wrangle-over-qaddafi-burial.html?pagewanted=all, 21 October 2011 (accessed 23 October 2011)

56 Daragahi, B. & Blitz, J., *Libya's NTC Under Fire For Killings*, The Financial Times, http://www.ft.com/intl/cms/s/0/f0ea02be-fe5a-11e0-bac4-00144feabdc0.html#axzz1epP0T1Le, 25 October 2011 (accessed 25 October 2011)

57 Fahim, K. & Nossiter, A., *In Libya, Massacre Site is Cleaned up, Not Investigated*, The New York Times, http://www.nytimes.com/2011/10/25/world/middleeast/libyas-interim-leaders-to-investigate-qaddafi-killing.html?pagewanted=all, 24 October 2011 (accessed 25 October 2011)

58 Libyan Rebels Accused of War Crimes, UPI, http://www.upi.com/Top_News/Special/2011/09/13/Libyan-rebels-accused-of-war-crimes/UPI-83181315922807/, 13 September 2011 (15 September 2011)

59 Rights Group Frets Over Post-Gadhafi Libya, UPI, http://www.upi.com/Top_News/Specia...ost-Gadhafi-Libya/UPI-83201320079633/, 31 October 2011 (accessed 7 November 2011)

60 Fahim, K., *Accused of Fighting for Qaddafi, a Libyan Town's Residents Face Reprisals*, The New York Times, http://www.nytimes.com/2011/09/24/world/africa/accused-of-fighting-for-qaddafi-tawerga-residents-face-reprisals.html?pagewanted=all, 23 September 2011 (accessed 25 September 2011)

61 Kirkpatrick, D. D., *Libyans Turn Wrath on Dark-Skinned Migrants*, The New York Times, http://www.nytimes.com/2011/09/05/world/africa/05migrants.html?pagewanted=all, 4 September 2011 (accessed 5 September 2011)

62 Nordland, R., *In Libya, Former Enemy is Recast in Role of Ally*, The New York Times, http://www.nytimes.com/2011/09/02/world/africa/02islamist.html?pagewanted=all, 1 September 2011 (accessed 2 September 2011)

63 *Libyan Woman Details Alleged Gang Rape*, CBS News, http://www.cbsnews.com/news/libyan-woman-details-alleged-gang-rape/, 12 April 2011 (accessed 4 December 2016)

64 Daragahi, B., *Gunfire and Fear Fill Tripoli's Security Vacuum*, The Financial Times, http://www.ft.com/cms/s/0/45de427a-0415-11e1-864e-00144feabdc0.html#axzz1fRMjSYEU, 31 October 2011 (accessed 11 November 2011)

65 Kirkpatrick, D. D., *In Libya, Fighting May Outlast the Revolution*, The New York Times, http://www.nytimes.com/2011/11/02/world/africa/in-libya-the-fighting-may-outlast-the-revolution.html?pagewanted=all, 1 November 2011 (accessed 7 November 2011)

66 UPI, Oil Majors Waiting for Libyan War to End, Dalje.com, http://dalje.com/en-world/oil-majors-waiting-for-libyan-war-to-end/378091, 23 August 2011 (accessed 25 August 2011)

67 Shane, S., *Western Companies See Prospects for Business in Libya*, The New York Times, http://www.nytimes.com/2011/10/29/world/africa/western-companies-see-libya-as-ripe-at-last-for-business.html?pagewanted=all, 28 October 2011 (accessed 7 November 2011)

68 Kirkpatrick, D. D. & Nordland, R., *Waves of Disinformation and Confusion Swamp the Truth in Libya*, The New York Times, http://www.nytimes.com/2011/08/24/world/africa/24fog.html?pagewanted=all, 23 August 2011 (accessed 24 August 2011)

69 Barber, B. R., *Western Media in Libya: Journalists or the Propaganda Arm of the Insurgency?*, The Huffington Post, http://www.huffingtonpost.com/benjamin-r-barber/western-media-in-libya-jo_b_933901.html, 23 August 2011 (accessed 24 August 2011)

70 1) Staff Writers, UPI, *Alarm Rises Over Missing Libyan Missiles*, Space War, http://www.spacewar.com/reports/Alarm_rises_over_missing_Libyan_missiles_999.html, 4 October 2011 (accessed 5 October 2011)
2) Nordland, R. & Chivers, C. J., *Heat-Seeking Missiles are Missing From Libyan Arms Stockpile*, The New York Times, http://www.nytimes.com/2011/09/08/world/africa/08missile.html?pagewanted=all, 7 September 2011 (accessed 7 September 2011)

71 Staff Writers, AFP, *Qaeda Offshoot Acquires Libyan Air Missiles: EU*, Space War, http://www.spacewar.com/reports/Qaeda_offshoot_acquires_Libyan_air_missiles_EU_999.html, 5 September 2011 (accessed 6 September 2011)

72 Staff Writers, AFP, *US Team Seeking Missing Missiles in Libya*, Space War, http://www.spacewar.com/reports/US_team_seeking_missing_missiles_in_Libya_999.html, 14 October 2011 (accessed 17 October 2011)

73 Please see the video clip here https://www.youtube.com/watch?v=Fgcd1ghag5Y

74 *Libya Could be Like Iraq or Worse: Perkasa*, MYsinchew.com, http://www.mysinchew.com/node/62683, 24 August 2011 (accessed 24 August 2011)

75 *Lord Dannatt: Libya 'Echoes' Iraq Campaign*, BBC News, http://news.bbc.co.uk/2/hi/programmes/hardtalk/9495064.stm, 24 May 2011 (accessed 24 May 2011)

76 Schmidt, M. S., *From a Few Iraqis, a Word to Libyans on Liberation*, The New York Times, http://www.nytimes.com/2011/08/30/world/middleeast/30baghdad.html, 29 August 2011 (accessed 30 August 2011)

77 Ibid.

78 Goodman, J. D., *Bahrain Court Hands Down Harsh Sentences to Doctors and Protestors*, The New York Times, http://www.nytimes.com/2011/09/30/world/middleeast/bahrain-court-hands-down-harsh-sentences-to-doctors-and-protesters.html, 29 September 2011 (accessed 30 September 2011)

79 Staff Writers, AFP, *Rival Forces Clash in Yemen Capital*, Space War, http://www.spacewar.com/reports/Rival_forces_clash_in_Yemen_capital_999.html, 29 September 2011 (accessed 30 September 2011)

80 *UN Falling Short on Yemen, HRW Says*, UPI, http://www.upi.com/Top_News/Special/2011/10/03/UN-falling-short-on-Yemen-HRW-says/UPI-60931317665393/, 3 October 2011 (accessed 5 October 2011)

81 Cooper, H. & Myers, S. L., *U.S. Tactics in Libya may be a Model for Other Efforts U.S. Tactics in Libya may be a Model for Other Efforts*, The New York Times, http://www.nytimes.com/2011/08/29/world/africa/29diplo.html?pagewanted=all, 28 August 2011 (accessed 29 August 2011)

82 *Russia, China Should Explain Their Veto to Syrians – Clinton*, RIA Novosti, http://en.rian.ru/world/20111006/167427841.html, 6 October 2011 (accessed 6 October 2011)

83 Carden, J. W., *How Libyan 'Regime Change' Lies Echo in Syria*, Consortium News, https://consortiumnews.com/2016/09/25/how-libyan-regime-change-lies-echo-in-syria/, 25 September 2016 (accessed 27 September 2016)

84 Staff Writers, AFP, *US Hails 'Extraordinary' French, British Roles in Libya*, Space War, http://www.spacewar.com/reports/US_hails_extraordinary_French_British_roles_in_Libya_999.html, 8 September 2011 (accessed 12 September 2011)

85 Staff Writers, AFP, *After Libya, US Cannot Bail Out NATO Shortfalls: Panetta*, Space War, http://www.spacewar.com/reports/After_Libya_US_cannot_bail_out_NATO_shortfalls_Panetta_999.html, 5 October 2011 (accessed 6 October 2011)

86 For further information on the interaction among different youth movements, such as Otpor in Egypt, see http://citeseerx.ist.psu.edu/viewdoc/download?doi=10.1.1.470.1197&rep=rep1&type=pdf

Bibliography

Baum, M. A. & Zhukov, Y. M., Filtering Revolution: Reporting Bias in International Newspaper Coverage of the Libyan Civil War, *Journal of Peace Research*, 52(3), 2015, pp. 384–400

Bennett, W. L., Lawrence, R. G. & Livingston, S., *When the Press Fails: Political Power and the News Media From Iraq to Katrina*, Chicago: The University of Chicago Press, 2007

Booth, K., Ten Flaws of Just Wars, *The International Journal of Human Rights*, 4(3–4), 2000, pp. 314–324

Chesterman, S., "Leading from Behind": The Responsibility to Protect, the Obama Doctrine, and Humanitarian Intervention After Libya, *Ethics & International Affairs*, 25(3), 2011, pp. 279–285

Colley, T., What's in it for Us, *The RUSI Journal*, 160(4), 2015, pp. 60-69

DiMaggio, A. R., *Mass Media, Mass Propaganda: Examining the American News in the "War on Terror"*, Lanham (MD): Lexington Books, 2009

Dulek, R. E. & Sydow Campbell, K., On the Dark Side of Strategic Communication, *International Journal of Business Communication*, 52(1), 2015, pp. 122-142

Friedman, G., *Re-Examining the Arab Spring*, Stratfor, 15 August 2011

Gonzalez, A. & Tanno, D. (Eds), *Politics, Communication and Culture*, Thousand Oaks: Sage Publications, 1997

Landolt, L. K. & Kubicek, P., Opportunities and Constraints: Comparing Tunisia and Egypt to the Coloured Revolutions, *Democratisation*, 21(6), 2014, pp. 984-1006

McCormack, T., The Responsibility to Protect and the End of the Western Century, *Journal of Intervention and Statebuilding*, 4(1), 2010, pp. 69-82

Pashentsev, E. & Simons, G. (Editors), *The Rising Role of Communication Management in World Politics and Business*, Moscow: Slovo Publishing, 2009

Risse-Kappen, T., Democratic Peace – Warlike Democracies? A Social Constructivist Interpretation of the Liberal Argument, *European Journal of International Relations*, 1(4), 1995, pp. 491-517

Salt, J., Containing the "Arab Spring", *Interface: A Journal for and About Social Movements*, 4(1), May 2012, pp. 54-66

Siebens, J. & Case, B., *The Libyan Civil War: Context and Consequences*, Special Report, THINK International and Human Security, Summer 2012

Simons G., Selling conflict in the 21st century: PR or advertising the way of public consent? in Topical Issues of Advertising: Theory and Practice: collection of Papers. Vol. II. / Editor-in-Chief A.V. Prokhorov. Tambov: The Publishing House of TSU named after G.R. Derzhavin, 2010, pp. 45-53

Simons, G., Mass Media and the Battle for Public Opinion in the Global War on Terror: Violence and legitimacy in Iraq, *Perceptions Journal*, Volume 13, Spring-Summer 2008, pp. 79-92

Taylor, P. M., *Munitions of the Mind: A History of Propaganda from the Ancient World to the Present Day*, 3rd Edition, Manchester: Manchester University Press, 2003

Western, J., *Selling Intervention and War: The Presidency, the Media, and the American Public*, Baltimore: John Hopkins University Press, 2005

Zelizer, B. & Allan, S. (Editors), *Journalism After September 11*, London: Routledge, 2002

9 Propaganda and the information war against Syria

The latest war for peace[1]

Greg Simons

War is Peace
Freedom is Slavery
Ignorance is Strength
Slogans on the wall of the Ministry of Truth from George Orwell's *1984*

The global publics have been bombarded with messages, which are not remote from the Orwellian doublethink that has been illustrated above (DiMaggio 2009). There is a notion that wars are being fought for good causes, and ultimately peace, which when subjected to a thorough and objective scrutiny simply does not make any sense. Yet a string of recent wars have been fought in the name of 'humanitarian' concerns, such as in Libya, and the push to create the pretext for an open war against the Assad government in Syria.

Propaganda seeks to exploit perception and emotion in order to create more favourable conditions for starting wars in order to fulfil foreign policy, especially with regard to 'sponsored' regime change. Public opinion is cultivated through the widespread use of presenting opinion as news. This makes the necessity to understand how this is done a critical issue in order to lessen the effectiveness of these campaigns. There have already been a number of works that have addressed the issue in a limited way, regarding the Global war on Terror (Bennettet al. 2007; DiMaggio 2009; Thussu & Freedman 2003; Zelizer & Allan 2002). However, there was less material at the time of those critical current events breaking out of the so-called Arab Spring (Korotaev et al. 2011; Primakov 2012).

A number of narratives exist that attempt to explain the Syrian war. There are those that describe it as a civil war,[2] however, others view this as a geopolitical war of opposing proxy forces (DIA 2012). Others have framed in as a geopolitical struggle in various frames, such as a geopolitical conflict within the Middle East by various regional interests (Dalacoura 2012; Salloukh 2013), and/or global geopolitics (Bagdonas 2012). In line with how the Libyan War was narrated, the Syrian War has been described as being a grassroots movement by the people against a repressive political regime, for human rights and democracy (Ismail 2011; Leenders 2013; Blanchard et al. 2014). In other words that this is a war, as was Libya, initiated for the people and by the people, which is a popular theme in the Western rhetoric that surrounds foreign-backed regime change.

Mass media and social media have played an important part in priming and mobilising audiences, especially by those seeking regime change. Studies have shown the role and importance of images that have been acquired from non-professional journalist sources with little or no means of verification, which has a tendency to elicit pathos in favour of the anti-Assad forces (Pantti 2013). There has also been evidence of the staging of media events in order to give the political advantage to one of the sides of the conflict (Simons 2016). This chapter intends to trace the different methods of propaganda that are used through mainstream news media reporting on the Syrian War in order to visualise the role of information and a means of support in contemporary armed conflicts.

As a point of departure it is necessary to create an understanding of propaganda and information war as a concept and as a practice. This will set the scene for screening and analysing media content on the Syrian conflict. News reporting from mass media outlets and information circulating on social media websites, such as LinkedIn, shall be categorised according to the type of propaganda that is being used in order to rally public sentiment and opinion to support a war against Syria. This chapter intends to take the first two years of the war in Syria as its point of focus, because it is in these opening phases of such conflicts that there is an attempt to set the public narrative of the event, which has the effect of restricting the permissible boundaries and manner of description.

Propaganda and information war

Propaganda is a highly charged term that has a long history of development and application. Yet, it is also a word where there is a great deal of disagreement about its exact meaning, in spite of most people having heard of and has their personal understanding. Renowned researcher of propaganda Philip Taylor defined propaganda in the following manner:

> The deliberate attempt to persuade people to think and behave in a desired way. Although I recognise that much of propaganda is accidental or unconscious, here I am discussing the conscious, methodical and planned decisions to employ techniques of persuasion designed to achieve the specific goals that are intended to benefit those organising the process (Taylor 2003: 6).

From Taylor's perspective, propaganda is a deliberate act by a group to advance its interests. According to Shabo (2008: 5), propaganda can be detected through identifying four simultaneous elements in messages – the persuasive function, attempting to reach a sizeable target audience, the representation of a specific group's agenda, and the use of faulty reasoning and/or emotional appeals.

But what motivates the use of propaganda? Referred to as the *Father of Modern Public Relations*, Edward Bernays, developed a tool for what he saw as bridging a divide in modern society. Bernays quotes Buckle, a historian, "when the interval between the intellectual classes and the practical classes is too great [...] the former will possess no influence, the latter will reap no benefits" (Bernays 2005: 126). Bernays identified PR as being that needed tool to bridge the divide. Walter Lippmann (1997) in his book *Public Opinion*, detailed the need to unite deeply divided public opinion as a means to create a united will. Jacques Ellul (1973: 232) tends to agree with Lippmann that democracy needs propaganda in order for a country to function in a competitive system. This connects with Bernay's characterisation of PR as a means to bridge divides in society. The ability and means to manipulate and form public opinion are becoming increasingly more far reaching with the advent of more powerful and instant information technologies and the accumulation of mass media assets in to fewer and fewer hands.

Herman and Chomsky identify a number of different filters in the mass media, which act as gatekeepers of all information passing through them. These filters are: size, ownership, and profit orientation of the mass media; the advertising license to do business; sourcing mass media news; flak (negative responses to specific media content, designed to pressure a media outlet) and the enforcers; anti-communism as a control mechanism (in this case anti-authoritarian/pro-humanitarianism); dichotomisation and propaganda campaigns (2002: 3–35). These filters represent a mixture of external and internal mechanisms. Not all censorship is externally imposed, for instance Rupert Murdoch's open and public support for going to war in Iraq serves to illustrate that the Fourth Estate in its corporate form is far from acting as a check and balance against the abuse of power by the political elite (Snow, 2003: 36–49). And in some instances it actually participates in those abuses along with the political authorities.

George Creel, the head of the Committee for Public Information, stated the need for a country contemplating going to war to convince international audiences of the 'self-less' reasons for doing so. This is done in order to try and sway foreign audiences in to accepting the reasons for going to war are 'good' or at least not to actively resist (Creel 1920). One of the subtle propaganda mechanisms that is employed in news production is a delineation between what are essentially deemed as being worthy versus unworthy victims. "A propaganda system will consistently portray people abused in enemy states as *worthy* victims, whereas those treated with equal or greater severity by its own government or clients will be *unworthy*. The evidence of worth may be read from the extent and character of attention and indignation" (Herman & Chomsky 2002: 37). This tactic is very evident in the string of so-called humanitarian wars that have been taking place in the post-Cold War, and especially in the post-9/11 period, where the recent examples of Libya and Syria offer numerous cases of defining the worthy and unworthy sides in a manufactured conflict.

This is fitting with one of the rules of propaganda that relates to lying: it is better to lie by omission rather than by commission. This means, rather than lying directly, it is better to selectively leave out unfavourable information (to the messenger's agenda) that may interfere with the intended message effect (DiMaggio 2009; Taylor 2003). In this case, if the ruse is discovered, it is easier to defend one's position if something has been 'accidentally' omitted rather than a deliberate and calculated lie.

These aspects are important tools for building a narrative that can sell the idea of war to a public that may be reluctant to engage in yet another war, and after a decade (and counting) of irregular warfare. It is in cases such as this where the notion of humanitarian warfare has risen (DiMaggio 2009: 179–215). In the GWOT, the narrative was about the necessity to go to war in a distant land, before war comes to the shores of the United States. The narratives in Libya and currently in Syria have changed and been replaced with heroes and villains. An oppressed, yet brave, defiant and democratic Libyan and now Syrian people who aspire to have the same rights and privileges enjoyed by the West are the heroes of the narrative. The villains cast in this scene are self-centred bloody and ruthless dictators that seek to continue to oppress their people and benefit financially and retain absolute political power. The storyline therefore is intended to produce a sense of empathy for the heroes and a sense of revulsion at the identified villains.

Events in Syria

An unnamed US officer spoke of defining the future of warfare in an article in 1997 in the US Army *War College Quarterly*. "….we are already masters of information warfare. Hollywood is 'preparing the battlefield.' (We) will be writing the scripts, producing them, and collecting the royalties. Our creativity is devastating."[3] Below are a number of different propaganda techniques that are employed in order to base decisions on emotion and perception, rather than on sound and reasoned logical thinking. They are designed to exploit a number of different human psychological conditions and needs. The exploitation of fears and desires for example: the desire for popularity or the fear of being left out; the desire for wealth or the fear of poverty; the desire for health or the fear of disease (Shabo 2008: 77); the desire for love or the fear of rejection (Shabo, 2008: 78–81). These personalised mechanisms can be very powerful motivators in a world that is increasingly perceived as being impersonal.

Other fears and desires are also taken advantage of, such as the desire for immortality/longevity and the fear of death (Shabo 2008: 88–92). Further mechanisms aim to generate empathy and sympathy, which can inspire generosity and giving (Shabo 2008: 95–103). This is often personalised, and motivation to help is inspired by the perception that through the requested help a positive difference can be achieved. Such pleas can also contain a sense of urgency, along the lines of help now before it is too late. Thereby, this has the effect of reducing the ability to weigh the pros and cons of the suggested course of action.

In some cases appeals are made that promote the idea or notion of civic responsibility. An attempt is made to try and capitalise on any possible benevolent feelings, and the course of action is promoted as being done for the welfare of a particular community or group. The call for civic responsibility is meant to bring about collective civic action, taking advantage of the sense of community or belonging. The 'payment' for engagement is a gratifying sense of personal

In terms of sources of information, the Western media have been often quoting the British-based Syrian Observatory for Human Rights. The main website is found at http://www.syriahr.com/, which is in Arabic. When the English language option is used, the reader is redirected to http://www.facebook.com/pages/Syrian-Observatory-for-Human-Rights/121855461256134. According to website, the Syrian Observatory for Human Rights was founded on 20 May 2012 and describes itself as being a NGO. The group has undergone an ownership dispute. One of those associated with the site declared himself an official spokesman and called for foreign intervention. The 'news' site also does not cover atrocities or acts of violence against pro-Assad forces and civilians as this is "not in their interest".[7] Other worrying issues, such as using social media, non-declaration of sources of finance to support the so-called NGO all have the hallmarks of a front group (a group purporting a certain public agenda, but which has a hidden agenda). Yet Western media quote this as a primary source of information.

Allegations of massacres by government forces are eagerly snapped up by the Western media, often without question or verification. The sources are treated as being trustworthy, in spite of glaring conflicts of interest at times. However, when allegations are made by the Syrian Government of massacres by anti-government forces the situation changes markedly. If the story makes the news, it is treated with a great deal of suspicion and with various noticeable caveats that are not applied to rebel sources, such as "massacre" appearing (rather than without quotation marks) or that the information has not been independently verified. At times a great deal of effort goes into denying or belittling the alleged massacre, such as gaining commentaries from rebel sources or applying rumour or suggestion that they were not civilians or that this is not what it seems.[8] There is no pretence at equal treatment of subjects and sources by the media, which is in some manner 'justified' by journalists taking upon themselves to identify the 'good' anti-government forces that deserve our understanding and sympathy and the pro-government forces that do not deserve such.

Glittering Generalities

Glittering generalities is a technique that involves the use of vague words, which go undefined, that are used to represent the position of the messenger. Lacking context or a specific definition, these words are intended to evoke an emotional response from the target audience. Should the words be accepted and the emotional response evoked, it is intended to produce an environment of unquestioning approval for whatever is said. Popular words used include: freedom/liberty; strength; security; prosperity; choice; equality; change (Shabo 2008: 30–33). One word missing from this group, especially given the rhetoric of regime change, is democracy.

There is a very specific rhetoric used by Western media when they are describing the government and anti-government forces in Syria. It is essential to recognise the significance of this vocabulary as it goes towards supporting the narratives concerning the identified 'good' and 'bad' sides of the conflict. Words are loaded by their very nature as they contain subtle cues that trigger perception and emotions. For instance, the *Washington Times* refers to the civil war in Syria as an *uprising*. This implies a sense of legitimacy against an authority, a rebellion against an imposed injustice.

When the people that constitute the anti-government forces are given a description, terms such as *activist* (*Financial Times*) on an individual level or *opposition* in the collective sense (*The New York Times*) are applied. At times the two words are put together – opposition activist.[9] In addition, the cause of the anti-government forces is hedged with references to freedom and democratic principles. When engaged in combat, the anti-government forces are referred to as being rebels, not as insurgents or terrorists (even though the tactics of insurgency and terrorism have been used). These words generate a more benevolent perception of who the anti-government forces are and what they represent. In doing so, the international public is more likely to empathise and sympathise with them and hold a negative perception of the government forces. This may render the public more receptive to later suggestions of generosity that seek to take advantage of any positive and empathetic/sympathetic feelings.

False dilemma

False dilemma is another commonly used tool of propaganda that reduces the complexity of a complex debate to a narrow number of alternatives, and where there is only one 'viable' option. The effect is to deny the existence of any neutral ground. Therefore the target audience is forced to choose the option that is labelled as being 'good', regardless of whether there is a good argument for doing so or not (Shabo 2008: 36–38). A clear example of this is President George Bush's statement after the 9/11 attacks in the United States, when he declared either you are with us or against us.

The conflict in Syria illustrates the false dilemma very clearly: either you are supporting the 'bad' brutal and bloody dictator Assad or the 'good' work and intentions of the international community. The US media, especially outlets such as the *Washington Times*, characterise Russia's non-compliance with the international community as being driven by self-interest (as opposed to the 'human' values of the international community). "Russia would lose a source of revenue and a Middle East power base if Syrian President Bashar Assad falls — two reasons why Moscow has armed the regime and blocked votes to let the United Nations punish Damascus."[10] No mention is made of any possible US interests in the conflict, and only American officials are used for expert commentaries. There is no platform or ability for the Russian side to respond to various unsubstantiated allegations that are presented in this so-called analysis.

Russia has been accused on numerous occasions of supporting Assad with military equipment. The chorus of condemnation by the self-appointed international community grew very loud with the revelation of attack helicopters being shipped to Syria. Clinton stated that it would "escalate the conflict quite dramatically." Another 'senior defence official' stated that Russia had "legions" of technicians in Syria working on military equipment for the Syrian Government. This is in spite of the fact that it was the fulfilment of a refurbishment contract from some four to five years earlier.[11] Thus accusations are made without the necessary understanding of the background, which appears in the mass media, conveying the perception that Russia is aiding the alleged massacres committed by the Syrian army.

The lesser of the two evils

Many dilemma techniques offer one 'good' and one 'bad' alternative, this one offers the target audience two 'bad' alternatives to choose from. This is used in an instance where an audience may be hesitant to adopt or accept a particular course of action, which makes the desired 'bad' alternative more appealing by introducing another choice that is even less appealing. Other alternatives are deliberately excluded and innovative thinking is discouraged (Shabo 2008: 41–43).

As with Libya, there is a chance of extremists taking political control from an authoritarian regime at the barrel of a gun. Likewise, the 'neutrality' of many journalists is questionable. Robert King, a photojournalist, when discussing the possibility of a religious government being installed stated that the rebels did not seem to be interested in doing so, but that could change with extremist sponsors becoming involved. "They are going to take help from wherever they can get it, and they are not wrong in doing so, because the Assad regime is killing their babies, blowing up their churches and mosques, they are humiliating them."[12] Therefore, King seems to suggest that any regime other than the Assad regime is the lesser of the evils, which violates the fundamental rule of a journalist becoming too emotionally attached to their subject and becoming a propagandist rather than an informer of events.

There has been a chorus of calls for becoming involved in arming the Free Syrian Army and other groups fighting the Assad regime. A series of 'articles' by Matthew van Dyke (who has variously describes himself as being a "veteran of Libya" and a "Middle Eastern and North African Expert" on his LinkedIn profile) have condemned China and Russia and called for arming the rebels. He stated six reasons for why the West should arm the rebel factions: rebels shall get weapons from other sources anyway; the longer the war continues the greater the level of radicalisation; lacking conventional weapons rebels shall resort to terrorism; Islamist militants will die early as they seek martyrdom; by supplying weapons the system is more transparent and accountable; not supplying weapons gives Islamic militants a chance to supply weapons and gain influence.[13] These weak arguments do not stand up to thorough scrutiny. There is little to no accountability for weapons supplied to the Libyan rebels for example. They are going to get weapons anyway, so why supply the weapons if they can get them from elsewhere? If we don't supply weapons they shall resort to acts of terrorism (which has already begin), so we should aid and abet terrorism in the name of a 'good' cause?

This is merely a defunct debate however, owing to the fact that external assistance in terms of supply of weapons, safe havens and so forth already exist.[14] It was also the case in Libya, when the arming of Libyan rebels took place, it was some time before it was admitted publicly, with a number of the above mentioned reasons offered as a form of justification. Both Turkey and Lebanon have been used as points for smuggling and harbouring rebels from the Syrian army.[15] The shooting down of a Turkish military aircraft in Syrian airspace, together with a scheduled meeting on how NATO shall respond to the incident[16] provides a possible window for NATO to 'justify' a military strike based on the grounds of Syrian 'aggression'. This is in spite of the aircraft violating Syrian airspace, and Turkey's active and open help in supplying weapons and safe areas for anti-government forces.

Another public spectacle has been the pretence at the options being considered to solve the conflict. British Foreign Secretary William Hague laid the blame at the feet of Assad, and stated that Damascus was making matters worse by calling opponents terrorists, which had the effect of encouraging Syrians to take up arms to defend themselves. "We do not want to see the Annan plan fail, but if despite our best efforts it does not succeed, we would have to consider other options for resolving the crisis, and in our view all options should then be on the table."[17] Given the use of this newspeak on the eve of other 'humanitarian interventions' this does not bode well for Syria. Other advocates have been more open in their call for further external interference in Syria, citing the massacre in Houla as an iconic moment that proves the need for military action.

> It is true that Syria does not lend itself to an easy military solution, and such a move would hold enormous risks. But there are ways of securing both international and regional legitimacy for the creation of a Nato-protected zone in the Idlib province near the Turkish border and possibly also in Dera'a, near Jordan. There, a more disciplined rebel force could be assembled and higher-level defectors would find shelter. Only then can the serious cracks within the regime that western governments have been hoping for become possible, and only then will Mr Assad understand that he must sign up to a transition plan that ends his presidency.[18]

This is purely opinion, which is being paraded as news. It is not about informing the public about events in Syria, but about agitation and propaganda that favours a specific course of action, and offers no effective counter-argument or alterative avenues. What is advocated here is little to do with resolving the conflict, but allowing the rebels an upper hand with safe havens and assistance. Russia has been understandably against foreign intervention and further inflammation of the situation, especially in the wake of events in Libya. Russian Foreign Minister Sergey Lavrov stated that "external forces are pushing the armed opposition toward taking an irreconcilable stance and continuing combat actions, which inspires these opposition groups with the hope of replaying the

Libyan scenario."[19] The Moscow Patriarchate opposes regime change in Syria, following the disastrous situation faced by Christians after the 2003 American-led invasion of Iraq and post-Arab Spring Egypt, where Christians were targeted and persecuted. Almost 2/3 of Iraq's Christian community have gone with the demise of Saddam Hussein.[20]

Name calling

Whereas glittering generalities uses positive words to evoke an emotional response, this technique uses negative and derogatory words to produce the desired effect. It has the effect of disparaging an enemy or opposing points of view. The target object can be attacked either directly (he is a crazy socialist) or indirectly (we have a great deal of respect for him. However, his views on the market economy require further scrutiny given his communist background) (Shabo 2008: 46–49). Even though this can be a crude form of propaganda, it is effective against unpopular targets.

An example of this type of reporting was found in the *New York Times*, on the attempts by the Assads to try and cultivate a more positive international image. The article is characterised by extremes in the depictions of Asma Assad (first lady) and President Bashar al-Assad. President Assad is blamed for the brutal crackdown that began in March 2011, without any reference to why this occurred in the first instance. He is described as being brutal and repressive. The various flattering and *fawning* articles from fashion magazines concerning Asma Assad are detailed with a certain sense of absurdity, irony and sarcasm.[21] Political marketing is the lifeblood of most politicians and political parties, including in the West. And like with the situation with the Assads, political marketing in the West is about working at creating image and perception, rather than something of substance. The Assads have been painted as the very representative face of all that is evil and the wrongdoing that is being done in Syria. Yet President Obama, as Commander in Chief of the Armed Forces, is not being held personally accountable for the string of war crimes being committed by American troops in Afghanistan.

Pinpointing the enemy

The issue of oversimplification of complex problems or issues comes to the fore when one single cause or enemy is identified as being at the root of it. This technique appeals to people's propensity to prefer clear-cut and uncomplicated explanations. If the enemy is thought of as being an 'other' this is made an even more effective form of propaganda (Shabo 2008: 52–55).

The BBC has been one of the most active news outlets in demonising the Syria conflict and painting a very black and white picture of what is a very complex reality. At times their reporting has crossed the border of journalism in favour of advocacy/propaganda. One clear example of this was exposed in May 2012 when the *Telegraph* detailed how the BBC had used a photograph from Iraq (March 2003) that showed a child jumping over bags of skeletons under the rubric "Syria massacre in Houla condemned as outrage grows" (May 2012).[22] This particular example demonstrates, in the best case scenario, that the BBC is incompetent and does not check it sources and engage in basic good journalistic practices. In a worst case scenario this is an illustration of outright deception that is aimed at provoking an emotional response from those viewing the article. This is intended as being another nail in Assad's coffin in the arena of public opinion.

During or even preceding a war, a 'good' reason is needed to meld public opinion as a means of unifying public opinion and solidifying the public for a course of action, to achieve these ends an *iconic moment* is needed. An iconic moment is a particular event or incident that occurs, which can be so terrible that it has the effect of creating conditions that make the public much more willing to engage in actions or policy that they would not otherwise do. In recent US history the 7 December 1941 Pearl Harbour attack and the 9 September 2001 terror attacks provides two instances of defining iconic moments. These can later be used as a shortcut and rallying point for later action as an emotional cry – avenge December 7, for example.

Atrocities are a convenient and very emotionally based source for creating an iconic moment. Various unconfirmed stories have been carried in the Western media, including the government use of child soldiers, sexual violence and massacres of civilians.[23] Fighting in the town of Dara'a for instance killed 17 people (some of them women and children), for whom the Syrian Government was accused of killing. Calls for war crimes were made. However, no such calls were made when an American Staff Sergeant in Afghanistan went from house to house killing 16 civilians in their sleep (including women and children). In fact, this soldier is not even charged with war crimes, but rather steroid abuse![24] The Syrian Government has been assigned the blame for its lack of cooperation and willingness to accede to the international communities' dictates,[25] even though the conditions imposed upon Assad leave him with nowhere to go and nothing to left to lose.

Very graphic and grisly accounts (both in text and images) of various massacres are given. The finger is often pointed at the government, which is based upon a mixture of rumour, guesswork and the testimony of anti-government representatives.[26] Some brief space is given to official rebuttals of involvement in the various massacres. But this is couched with descriptions that ridicule or destroy the credibility of those denials, such as Assad's reference to a surgeon getting blood on his hands, but saving the patient in the wake of the Houla massacre.[27] The insurgency began in March 2011, in the wake of the finalisation of the conflict in Libya. The Houla massacre took place on 25–26 May 2012, over 100 people were killed. Anti-government forces blamed pro-government fighters, which were denied by the Assad regime.[28] The US tried to frame this as a defining and iconic moment in the conflict, and as a means to pressure Russia into accepting the US position and policy.

There are however, a significant number of unanswered questions and assumptions hastily made. The Russian Foreign Minister made the point "that *certain countries* were attempting to use the deaths in Houla as a *pretext* for a military operation against Assad's forces, which have been, in part, armed by Russia. Lavrov also accused the head of the foreign-based opposition, Syrian National Council, of attempting to *incite a civil war* in the Middle Eastern country."[29] Russian reporter, Marat Musin's first-hand account casts significant doubt as to the supposed responsibility for the massacre. According to Musin this was a staged exercise by rebels in the area as a means to produce an iconic event that was significant enough to force China and Russia to allow direct foreign intervention. Materials were prepared beforehand by the rebels in Chinese and Russian languages to support the fabricated video material. The attempt at deception needed to be revised owing to gaps of consistency between what was being said and what the video showed.[30] An article that appeared in the *Frankfurter Allgemeine Zeitung* merely served to increase suspicions as to the reliability of information coming out of Syria. "Over 90% of Houla's population are Sunnis. Several dozen members of a family were slaughtered, which had converted from Sunni to Shia Islam. Members of the Shomaliya, an Alawi family, were also killed, as was the family of a Sunni member of the Syrian parliament who is regarded as a collaborator."[31] These media reports tend to allude to a deception employed at Houla as an attempt to affect the policy of other countries (in much the same way as Libyan rebels used this ploy when they announced Saif Gaddafi's capture during the Libyan war).

Conclusion

Syria is certainly not Libya, for a number of reasons. However, there are a number of rather disturbing similarities between how the 'spontaneous democratic' insurgencies against authoritarian regimes has miraculously appeared and how it is managed. Indeed, the word blueprint has already been applied to the Libya scenario for future 'humanitarian interventions' by Western military forces.[32] The Libyan military under Gaddafi, although seemingly strong on paper was in effect a paper tiger, Syria's arsenal is much more formidable, hence the delay in launching a military strike.[33] The Western public is in no mood to suffer heavy losses in a dubious military intervention, especially with no end in sight to the decade long Global War Against Terrorism.

The results of foreign interference in Libya are still fresh, with increasingly disturbing reports surfacing regularly. Large stocks of weapons, from small arms to surface to air missiles (SAMS) disappeared from the arsenals of the Libyan army. Some of these weapons have already found their way to other trouble spots on the African continent, such as Mali.[34] Other weapons, such as the SAMS are available on the black market and are available to the highest bidder,[35] right on Europe's doorstep.

There is the facade that all options are on the table, meaning that war is one of the possible options. However, when reviewing the nature of the propaganda in this latest information war being fought in the name of humanitarian concerns, it is obvious that war is not an option, it is the option. A similar scenario played out before the Libyan war, a move to head off a possible war in Syria has been initiated.[36] There is no attempt at any form of logical, reasoned and open public debate on the issue. The power of the argument is in the emotion of the discussion, rather than any solid and defendable basis. When using logos to try and justify and build their narratives, a common means is to employ an emotional rather than a reasoned logic. The logic can also prove to be a false logic that relies on the media consuming publics believing the message at face value. But when challenged, some of the false logics are relatively easy to debunk. As one example, the promise to supply the jihadist forces with lethal weapons (which was in fact already being done) if the fighting got worse as a means to help bring relief. Flooding a war zone with even more weapons and to those forces that are far from moderate is unlikely to bring about any reduction in violence; in fact the opposite is most likely to be true.

Earlier in this chapter I argued that propaganda can be detected through identifying four simultaneous elements in messages, which were the persuasive function, attempting to reach a sizeable target audience, the representation of a specific group's agenda, and the use of faulty reasoning and/or emotional appeals. The current situation regarding the facade of debate in the public sphere on the issue of what should be done to remedy the conflict in Syria easily meets all four of these criteria. Referring back to the quote from 1984, two of the three slogans stand out – war is peace and ignorance is strength.

Notes

1 This chapter is a revised version of a paper published in 2012. Simons, G., *Propaganda and the Information war Against Syria: The Latest War for Peace*, Государственное управление. Электронный вестник, Выпуск № 33. Август 2012

2 Nebehay, S., *Exclusive: Red Cross Ruling Raises Questions of Syrian War Crimes*, Reuters, http://uk.reuters.com/article/uk-syria-crisis-icrc-idUKBRE86D09B20120714, 15 July 2012 (accessed 5 December 2016)

3 Lendman, S., *Terrorists Portrayed as 'Opposition': BBC Wages Propaganda War on Syria*, Global Research, http://www.globalresearch.ca/index.php?context=va&aid=31126, 30 May 2012 (accessed 9 June 2012)

4 Meyssan, T., *Syria: What the Security Council Said*, Voltaire Network, http://www.voltairenet.org/Syria-What-the-Security-Council, 6 June 2012 (accessed 9 June 2012)

5 Clinton, Annan Discuss Syrian Political Transition Strategy, RIA Novosti, http://en.rian.ru/world/20120609/173930121.html, 9 June 2012 (accessed 9 June 2012)

6 Bohm, M., Putin has a Responsibility to Protect Syrians, The Moscow Times, http://www.themoscowtimes.com/opinion/article/putin-has-a-responsibility-to-protect-syrians/460075.html, 6 June 2012 (accessed 9 June 2012)

7 Bennet, I., *Deaths in Syria: Counting Them (Politically) Correctly*, RT, http://www.rt.com/news/syria-death-count-political-875/, 9 February 2012 (accessed 24 June 2012)

8 Mroue, B., *Syrian TV Says Gunmen Kidnapped and Killed 25*, The Washington Times, http://www.washingtontimes.com/news/2012/jun/22/syrian-tv-says-gunmen-kidnapped-and-killed-25/, 22 June 2012 (accessed 25 June 2012)

9 Peel, M., *Syrian Rebels Kill 80 Regime Soldiers*, Financial Times, http://www.ft.com/intl/cms/s/0/fd088892-ae5c-11e1-b842-00144feabdc0.html, 4 June 2012 (accessed 9 June 2012)

10 Analysis, Russia Clings to a Crucial Power Base in Syria Uprising, The Washington Times, http://www.washingtontimes.com/news/2012/jun/17/russia-clings-to-a-crucial-power-base-in-syria-upr/, 17 June 2012 (accessed 18 June 2012)

11 Schmitt, E., Landler, M. & Kramer, A. E., Copters in Syria May not be New, US Officials Say, The New York Times, http://www.nytimes.com/2012/06/14/world/middleeast/copters-in-syria-may-not-be-new-us-officials-say.html?pagewanted=all, 13 June 2012 (accessed 14 June 2012)

12 Barnard, A., *A Rare View of Conflict in Syria*, The New York Times, http://lens.blogs.nytimes.com/2012/06/13/a-rare-view-of-conflict-in-syria/, 13 June 2012 (accessed 13 June 2012)

13 Van Dyke, M., *Have the US and Europe Helped Arm and Empower Islamist Militants in Syria?*, The Freedom Fighter Blog, http://www.matthewvandyke.com/blog/arm-islamist-militants-syria/, 13 June 2012 (accessed 18 June 2012)

14 Khalaf, R., *Arming of Syria Rebels Gains Momentum*, Gulf News, http://gulfnews.com/news/region/syria/arming-of-syria-rebels-gains-momentum-1.1033593, 9 June 2012 (accessed 9 June 2012)

15 1) *Syria Thwarts Turkish, Lebanese Attacks*, UPI, http://www.upi.com/Top_News/Special/2012/06/07/Syria-thwarts-Turkish-Lebanese-attacks/UPI-80841339079001/, 7 June 2012 (9 June 2012)
    2) *Lebanon Rivals Agree on Syria*, Space War, http://www.spacewar.com/reports/Lebanon_rivals_agree_on_Syria_999.html, 11 June 2012 (accessed 12 June 2012)
    3) Landler, M. & MacFarquhar, N., *Heavier Weapons Push Syrian Crisis Towards Civil War*, The New York Times, http://www.nytimes.com/2012/06/13/world/middleeast/violence-in-syria-continues-as-protesters-killed.html?pagewanted=all, 12 June 2012 (accessed 14 June 2012)
    4) *Syria Rebels Gain Ground With Foreign Help*, Space War, http://www.spacewar.com/reports/Syria_rebels_gain_ground_with_foreign_help_999.html, 21 June 2012 (accessed 22 June 2012)
    5) Schmitt, E., *CIA Said to Aid in Steering Arms to Syrian Opposition*, The New York Times, http://www.nytimes.com/2012/06/21/world/middleeast/cia-said-to-aid-in-steering-arms-to-syrian-rebels.html?nl=todaysheadlines&emc=edit_th_20120621, 21 June 2012 (accessed 25 June 2012)

16 Hacaoglu, S., *NATO to Meet over Downing of Plane by Syria*, The Washington Times, http://www.washingtontimes.com/news/2012/jun/24/turkey-calls-nato-meeting-over-syria/, 24 June 2012 (accessed 25 June 2012)

17 *London: 'All Options' Open to Handle Syria*, UPI, http://www.upi.com/Top_News/Special/2012/06/12/London-All-options-open-to-handle-Syria/UPI-29411339520761/, 12 June 2012 (accessed 16 June 2012)

18 Khalaf, R., *Time to Consider Military Options in Syria*, Financial Times, http://www.ft.com/cms/s/0/d52fe084-ac15-11e1-a8a0-00144feabdc0.html, 5 June 2012 (9 June 2012)

19 *External Players Inspire Syrian Opposition with Hope for Libyan Scenario Replay – Lavrov (Part 2)*, Interfax, http://www.interfax.com/newsinf.asp?pg=2&id=338885, 9 June 2012 (accessed 11 June 2012)

20 Barry, E., *Russian Church is a Strong Voice Opposing Intervention in Syria*, The New York Times, http://www.nytimes.com/2012/06/01/world/europe/russian-church-opposes-syrian-intervention.html?pagewanted=all, 31 May 2012 (7 June 2012)

21 Carter, B. & Chozick, A., *Syria's Assads Turned to West for Glossy PR*, The New York Times, http://www.nytimes.com/2012/06/11/world/middleeast/syrian-conflict-cracks-carefully-polished-image-of-assad.html?pagewanted=all, 10 June 2012 (accessed 11 June 2012)

22 Furness, H., *BBC News Uses Iraq Photo to Illustrate Syrian Massacre*, Telegraph, http://www.telegraph.co.uk/culture/tvandradio/bbc/9293620/BBC-News-uses-Iraq-photo-to-illustrate-Syrian-massacre.html#, 27 May 2012 (accessed 25 June 2012)

23 Mroue, B. & Hadid, D., *Syria Observer Chief Says Violence Derails Mission*, The Washington Times, http://www.washingtontimes.com/news/2012/jun/15/syria-observer-chief-says-violence-hinders-mission/, 15 June 2012 (accessed 16 June 2012)

24 Lerman, D., *Bales Charged With Steroid Abuse Before Afghan Killings*, Bloomberg, http://www.bloomberg.com/news/2012-06-01/alleged-afghan-shooter-bales-charged-with-steroid-use-1-.html, 2 June 2012 (accessed 25 June 2012)

25 Kirkpatrick, D. D. & Sanger, D. E., *UN Suspends Syria Mission, Citing Increase in Violence*, The New York Times, http://www.nytimes.com/2012/06/17/world/middleeast/un-suspends-its-mission-in-syria-citing-violence.html?pagewanted=all, 16 June 2012 (accessed 17 June 2012)

26 Gladstone, R., *UN Monitors in Syria Find Grisly Traces of Massacre*, The New York Times, http://www.nytimes.com/2012/06/09/world/middleeast/syrians-bar-un-monitors-from-a-massacre-inquiry.html?pagewanted=all, 8 June 2012 (accessed 9 June 2012)

27 Peel, M., *Assad Denies Regime Role in Massacre*, Financial Times, http://www.ft.com/intl/cms/s/0/1a22391c-ad83-11e1-bb8e-00144feabdc0.html, 3 June 2012 (accessed 9 June 2012)

28 US Hopes Houla Tragedy Changes Russia's Stance on Syria, RIA Novosti, http://en.rian.ru/russia/20120529/173741996.html, 29 May 2012 (accessed 9 June 2012)

29 *Moscow Warns West Against 'Hasty Conclusions' on Houla*, RIA Novosti, http://en.rian.ru/russia/20120531/173770461.html, 31 May 2012 (accessed 9 June 2012)

30 Lendman, S., *Heading for War on Syria*, Freedom's Phoenix, http://www.freedomsphoenix.com/Article/112769-2012-06-03-russian-journalist-exposes-propaganda-lies-about-houla-massacre.htm?EdNo=001&From=,5 June 2012 (accessed 9 June 2012)

31 Von Rainer, H., Abermals Massaker in Syrien, Frankfurter Allgemeine, http://www.faz.net/aktuell/politik/neue-erkenntnisse-zu-getoeteten-von-hula-abermals-massaker-in-syrien-11776496.html, 7 June 2012 (accessed 25 June 2012)

32 Dejevsky, M., *Libya's Liberation Must not Justify a new Colonial Adventurism*, Independent, http://www.independent.co.uk/opinion/commentators/mary-dejevsky/mary-dejevsky-libyas-liberation-must-not-justify-a-new-colonial-adventurism-2373606.html, 21 October 2011 (accessed 25 June 2012)

33 *Russian Arms Make Move On Syria Costly*, Space War, http://www.spacewar.com/reports/Russian_arms_make_move_on_Syria_costly_999.html, 18 June 2012 (accessed 25 June 2012)

34 Wong, K., Pentagon: Libyan Weapons Entering African Trouble Spots, The Washington Times, http://www.washingtontimes.com/news/2012/jun/18/pentagon-libyan-weapons-entering-african-trouble-s/, 18 June 2012 (accessed 25 June 2012)

35 Johnson, R., *Missing Libyan Weapons are Reportedly on their way Hamas*, Business Insider, http://articles.businessinsider.com/2011-09-26/news/30203197_1_marketeers-sams-weapons, 26 September 2011 (accessed 25 June 2012)

36 Kasperowicz, P., Ron Paul Seeks to Block Military Intervention in Syria, Times 24/7, http://times247.com/articles/ron-paul-looks-to-block-military-intervention-in-syria, 19 June 2012 (accessed 25 June 2012)

Bibliography

Bagdonas, A., Russia's Interests in the Syrian Conflict: Power, Prestige, and Profit, *European Journal of Economic and Political Studies*, 5(2), 2012, pp. 55–77

Bennett, W. L., Lawrence, R. G. & Livingstone, S., *When the Press Fails: Political Power and the News Media From Iraq to Katrina*, Chicago: The University of Chicago Press, 2007

Bernays, E., *Propaganda*, New York: IG Publishing, 2005 (original 1928)

Blanchard, C. M., Humud, C. E. & Nikitin, M. B. D., *Armed Conflict in Syria: Overview and U.S. Response*, Congressional Research Service, RL33487, 17 September 2014

Creel, G., *How We Advertised America: The First Telling of the Amazing Story of the Committee on Public Information That Carried the Gospel of Americanism to Every Corner of the Globe*, Lexington (KY): Forgotten Books, 2010 (original in 1920)

Defence Intelligence Agency (DIA), *Information report* (14-L-0552/DIA/287), August 2012

Dalacoura, K., The 2011 Uprisings in the Arab Middle East: Political Change and Geopolitical Implications, *International Affairs*, 88(1), 2012, pp. 63–79

DiMaggio, A. R., *Mass Media, Mass Propaganda: Examining America's News in the "War on Terror"*, Lanham (MD): Lexington Books, 2009

Ellul, J., *Propaganda: The Formation of Men's Attitudes*, New York: Vintage Books, 1973

Herman, E. S. & Chomsky, N., *Manufacturing Consent: The Political Economy of the Mass Media*, New York: Pantheon Books, 2002

Ismail, S., The Syrian Uprising: Imagining and Performing the Nation, *Studies in Ethnicity and Nationalism*, 11(3), 2011, pp. 538–549

Leenders, R., Social Movement Theory and the Onset of the Popular Uprising in Syria, *Arab Studies Quarterly*, 35(3), Summer 2013, pp. 273–289

Lippmann, W., *Public Opinion*, New York: Free Press Paperbacks, 1997 (original 1922)

Korotaev, A. V., Zinkina, U. V. & Khodunov, A. S. (editors), *Systemni Monitoring Globalnikh I Regonalnikh Riskov: Arabskaya Vesna 2011 Goda* (Systematic Monitoring of Global and Regional Risk: Arab Spring 2011), Moscow: LKI, 2011

Pantti, M., Seeing and Not Seeing the Syrian Crisis: New Visibility and the Visual Framing of the Syrian Conflict in Seven Newspapers and Their Online Editions, *JOMEC Journal: Journalism, Media and Cultural Studies*, November 2013

Primakov, E., *Blizhni Vostok: na Stsene I za Kulikami* (Near East: On the Stage and Beyond the Link), Moscow: Rossiskaya Gazeta, 2012

Salloukh, B. F., The Arab Uprisings and the Geopolitics of the Middle East, *The International Spectator: Italian Journal of International Affairs*, 48(2), 2013, pp. 32–46

Shabo, M. E., *Techniques of Propaganda and Persuasion*, Clayton (DE): Prestwick House, 2008

Simons, G., News and Syria: Creating Key Media Moments in the Conflict, *Cogent Social Sciences*, 2: 1170583, 2016

Snow, N., *Information War: American Propaganda, Free Speech and Opinion Control Since 9–11*, New York: Seven Stories Press, 2003

Taylor, P. M., *Munitions of the Mind: A History of Propaganda from the Ancient World to the Present Day*, Manchester: Manchester University Press, 2003

Thussu, D. & Freedman, D. (editors), *War and the Media: Reporting Conflict 24/7*, London: Sage, 2003

Zelizer, B. & Allan, S. (editors), *Journalism After September 11*, Routledge: New York, 2002

10 Power through subversion

Shaping perception and opinion on Ukraine's Euromaidan through manufacturing knowledge

Greg Simons

Revolutions can have a profound impact upon international relations, with a number of different possible effects and outcomes. An initial effect is to increase the profile and importance of the country that is experiencing the revolution. Another point is that a revolution can upset existing alliance patterns. A final point to consider is that other countries often fear that revolutionary regimes may attempt to export their revolution (Katz 2001: 1). Therefore, the way and manner in which knowledge is manufactured on an event is one of the key elements that can assist in realising a successful overthrow of a country's government. It also can have an impact and constrain how domestic and international actors may respond to the action as it unfolds.

Events in Kiev rapidly degenerated into an orgy of violence on the streets as anti-Yanukovich forces and riot police fought pitched battles. A brand was established for this particular revolution – Euromaidan. As with previous revolutionary brands such as the Orange Revolution and the Arab Spring, Euromaidan was supposed to project positive (liberal or Western) norms and values by those attempting the seizure of political power. The event pushed Ukraine into the front pages of mass media around the world, and gave an apparent sense of urgency to the situation and how it should be dealt with. This chapter seeks to explore the manner in which knowledge was manufactured by the international media on Euromaidan in order to provide support for the insurgency that saw the successful overthrow of the democratically elected, but highly corrupt, President Viktor Yanukovich.

News reports from most Western countries were leading the way in shaping public perception of the emerging geopolitical battle, and in suggesting how the 'international community' should think and react to the crisis situation. The narratives used by the mass media demonstrated that the news media was far from neutral in this matter, choosing to depict the events in an entertainment format that was designed to influence and agitate the publics. Work in the information sphere was critical in helping to influence the political environment and make conditions more suitable for a successful overthrow of Ukraine's political regime through influencing the intangible elements at the domestic and international level. It is the intention of this chapter to investigate how an actor rhetorically explains, justifies and attempts to legitimise regime change when this very action may contravene their own expressed values and norms by doing so. How has information and knowledge management been used to support regime change in Ukraine?

This chapter covers the initial period of regime change that occurred in Ukraine from the opening of the Euromaidan protests until the opening of the so-called Anti-Terrorist Operation (ATO) that marked the beginning of open warfare in the east of the country. Those critical and/or suspicious of Euromaidan held a number of core beliefs and assumptions. Mass media coverage of the coup in Kiev was seen as being distinctly partisan, echoing and supporting the policy of regime change that was coming from political circles in leading Western countries, and ignoring the unsavoury far-right elements in the new regime (often referred to as being fascists or the 'coup regime') (Lendman 2014; Boyd-Barrett 2016). It was extremely critical of everything that was done by Yanukovich and the security forces, and reporting seemed to be serving the lobbying of specific political agenda rather than any notion of an effective Fourth Estate. One can for instance see these lines of argumentation with criticism and the frame that people should be allowed to express their opinion (even when throwing Molotov Cocktails), yet see the double standards with regards to how the Occupy movement was handled by US police and law enforcement.[1]

Pro-Euromaidan movement commentators used another set of values and norms, which were intended to highlight the process and event in a positive frame. In particular, they emphasised the spontaneous and grassroots nature of the protests, clash of civilisations element (Western versus Russian civilisational choice), a fight for independence of politics and identity from Russia, sometimes referred to as a 'revolution of dignity' (human rights, rule of law, democracy and other 'Western' values) (Diuk 2014; Gerasimov 2014; Ryabchuk 2014; Vinogradov & Sviatnenko 2014). Infringements committed by the insurgents were either ignored or buried, such as the recording of Catherine Ashton and the Estonian Foreign Minister on the matter of the snipers in Maidan.[2] Knowledge management was supporting a favoured policy line that was difficult to follow through under ordinary circumstances, hence the need for a crisis and the demand for intervention based upon norm and value based arguments.

Role of news in perception

News carries with it automatic connotations of something that is neutral, objective and balanced in nature, which is designed to inform its audience and arm them with the necessary knowledge that enables them to form accurate opinions that are needed to make decisions on various issues, topics and tasks (McQuail 2010; Allan 1999). However, the practice of news is somewhat remote from this utopian ideal. News is seen as a potential tool with which to shape audiences, to shape their perceptions and opinions in order to support a certain policy or agenda.

> Primarily, however, the engineer of consent must create news. News is not an inanimate thing. It is the overt act that makes news, and news in turn

shapes the attitudes and actions of people. A good criterion as to whether something is or is not news is whether the event juts out of the pattern of routine. The developing of events and circumstances that are not routine is one of the basic functions of the engineer of consent. [...] Newsworthy events, involving people, usually do not happen by accident. They are planned deliberately to accomplish a purpose, to influence our ideas and actions. (Bernays 1947: 119)

Here Bernays makes it clear that there is nothing random or neutral in the production of news, it serves a purpose, which is to support certain political objectives and policy through carefully 'massaging' public opinion. Entman notes that "public opinion cannot be divorced from the political discourse and media frames that surround it. The apparent impact of the public on government policy often arises from a circular process in which government officials respond to the polling opinions, anticipated or perceived majorities, and priorities that many of them helped to create" (Entman 2004: 142). Public opinion is highly coveted for the reason that it can be used in an instrumental sense to achieve the priorities and goals of the communicator. It may seem like a straightforward proposition, but in order to influence public opinion, an approach is needed in order to create an adequate political information environment in which to incubate it. Public opinion is the vehicle to realise tangible and concrete steps from intangible communicational interactions.

Public opinion is a construction: of governments, of the media, and of everyday conversation influenced by government and the media. It is accepted and treated as though it were an objective reality to be discovered by polling or otherwise taking account of expressed beliefs and assumed beliefs about public policy. But it reflects and echoes the claims of officials and of reports in the media respecting developments or alleged developments in the news. Dramatic news reports and interpretations of events and non-events are routinely deployed to evoke concern, anger, relief, and beliefs in general, and these are then labelled *public opinion* (Edelman 2001: 53).

As is seen above, shaping public opinion is an art that requires a specific and accurate approach to news telling. Words and images are used in a deliberate manner in order to try and induce the desired emotional state that is likely to stimulate the desired response to the event being depicted. To be able to bring about this situation, the aspects of magnitude (in terms of prominence and repetition) and cultural resonance must be considered. Words and images need to be "highly salient in the culture, which is to say noticeable, understandable, memorable and emotionally charged" (Entman 2004: 6). New information communication technologies play an increasingly significant role in the type and nature of news, and in the means to influence audiences. This enables the projection of strongly emotional material and themes, especially with regards to mobilising and/or rallying "global consciousness" and "moral actors" on the world stage.

"The admonition to "think globally" has undeniable ethical overtones: that we are part of one world whose condition should concern us all" (Bob 2007: 7). At its most basic point, this exercise is one of enacting influence on a target audience.

The term influence has become a 'dirty' word in some political circles as there are connotations with propaganda and manipulation. Thus, on a superficial level, there may be rhetoric about informing the public about events and not influencing them. However, this goes against the purpose of different forms of political communication, such as public affairs or public diplomacy, which is all about influencing publics. "The selection of facts cited to communicate information is inherently a subjective act, and the imperatives of governing require making the case that supports certain actions and policies" (Farwell 2012: 228). Every aspect of the news production and dissemination process is one that requires careful consideration, including the rhetoric, the topic/issue chosen, the timing and the information that is contained or excluded. This makes the narrative a vital aspect of managing communications and in conveying a uniform message to the target publics – not only in terms of information, but the tone and emotion as well.

The binds of the narrative

Narratives as noted by Brophy (2009: 50), "they enable us to share, discuss and debate all the multifaceted aspects of complex human relationships, systems and organisations. [...] They enable us to reveal ourselves to others in a way which represents not just our explicit, observable acts but includes our motivations, feelings, thoughts and beliefs." Therefore the narrative can function as a means to convey the tangible and intangible elements of an event, and the role of personalities within the framework of the narrated moment.

> In terms of ontologies, there is on the one hand belief in knowable, objective reality, a world which exists and can be described and known quite apart from any human observer. On the other hand, there is the belief that all depictions of reality are socially constructed. (Brophy 2009: 17)

As seen above, narratives are not only related to knowledge, but also to beliefs. Narratives are as much about reasoning and projecting as they are about describing an actual event objectively. They project and convey assumptions and embedded values and norms, and hence how an audience 'should' think and react to the narrated event.

> Narrative is a way of organising spatial and temporal data into a cause and effect chain of events with a beginning, middle and end that embodies a judgement about the nature of events as well as demonstrates how it is possible to know, and hence to narrate, the events. (Branigan 1992: 3)

This implies that the creator of the narrative must decide what to include and what must be excluded, what is relevant and what is not. Superficially, the narrative is for the telling of events. However, the situation is more complex than this suggests. Because the narrative is the key to creating the meaning making of an event, therefore the elements of judgement and other subjective factors play a key role in shaping how an audience that is exposed to the narrative makes sense of, forms opinions about and how they react to an event.

Narratives have in common a number of features/aspects – a setting (real or imagined place), causality (express cause and effect), a plot (inferred rather than explicit), style (way in which the narrative is presented), a point of view (a focus or angle), character(s) (for interplay between human elements), narrative presence (creates the audiences' relationship to the story), and the use of hermeneutic/proairetic codes (create suspense and tension – hermeneutic code raises unanswered questions, proairetic code actions that occur will have consequences causing anticipation) (Brophy 2009: 44–47). Through the use of narratives and frames the mass media attempt to engage in activating a number of different functions when covering political events, issues and actors – "defining effects or conditions as problematic, identifying causes, conveying a moral judgement, and endorsing remedies or improvements" (Entman 2004: 5). There is an attempt to promote norm implementation. This is done "by pressuring target actors to adopt new policies, and by monitoring compliance with international standards" (Keck & Sikkink 1998: 3). This seems to be 'innocent' enough, however, it ignores the basic fact that 'international standards' tend to be set by a powerful actor with good access to mass communicational assets. And those actors may have hidden interests in fields of monitoring and enforcing compliance to certain given sets of norms and values, which are masked by rhetoric and symbolism.

Symbolism and its interpretation is an integral part of the process of persuasion. "Activists frame issues by identifying and providing convincing explanations of powerful symbolic events, which in turn become catalysts for the growth of the networks" (Keck & Sikkink 1998: 22). Events, both past and present can be co-opted or created, which are meant to represent and convey values and norms. These moments are meant to be extraordinary moments, iconic events, which carry an emotional and symbolic significance within their reception and interpretation. "Iconic events are used to sell products, spin ideology, and legitimate war" (Leavy 2007: 2) or in this case to try and legitimise regime change. Furthermore, "from the moment that they occur, certain events seem to occupy a disproportionate space in the culture" (Leavy 2007: 3). Media focus on the event in order to try and demonstrate to the publics the event's importance and significance. Therefore, mass media tend to bombard the publics with constant saturation coverage in order to get the point across. According to Leavy, these events have a number of points in common: 1) event has undergone hyper-representation; 2) been appropriated for an ongoing political agenda; 3) transformed into commodities; and 4) been adapted into popular entertainment (2007: 5). Some recent examples include events that have occurred can be found within the frame of the Arab Spring brand.

An important point to make when communicating about topics concerning different forms of political violence is to make a distinction between a *crisis* and an *attack*. A crisis invites attention from the media and society, and is a 'naturally' occurring phenomenon. It presents an opportunity for defensive organisations or individuals to respond. Whereas an attack is "launched deliberately by groups or individuals, can be used either as an attempt to inflame a crisis, enhance an issue, influence outcomes or perceptions, or deflect attention away from one element of the crisis to another. Attacks can be very well funded, timed, and sponsored" (Eder 2011: 12). It is somewhat less problematic to communicate about and become embroiled in a crisis, rather than a war, especially with a war-weary Western public that has been at a state of war since September 2001 and therefore with little appetite for engaging in another new war.

Subversion and power: Use of force in politics[3]

What is power? Seemingly it is a simple question, but it is in fact, very difficult to answer. Many people talk about power, but there are variable definitions. It is one of those things that is much easier to experience than to define or be able to accurately measure. Nye defines power as "the ability to influence the behaviour of others to get the outcomes one wants" (2004: 2). There are two different paths to achieving power, through the use of attraction or the use of coercion. Owing to the nature of the topic of this chapter, the path using coercion is more appropriate. Coercive or command power relies on the use of demands "to change [my] preferences and do what you want by threatening [me] with force or economic sanctions" (Nye 2004: 6). Power involves the use of persuasion as a means to achieve a desired goal or objective. Anthony Lake, former National Security Advisor to President Clinton, stated that the US diplomatic responses to conflicts can be classified into two categories: as honest broker and powerful broker (Lake 2000: 116). An honest broker is defined as relying on reason, patience and non-coercion. Meanwhile a powerful broker relies on the use of force, and by the implied logic is consequently less patient and sincere.

Persuasion is a commonly heard and key element in the process, however it still requires further elaboration. It involves five different components: 1) It is a symbolic process, 2) in which people persuade themselves, 3) which involves an attempt to influence 4) the transmission of a message, and 5) which requires free choice (Perloff 2010: 12–5). In terms of impact, persuasion can be used for three broad effects. One effect is to *shape* attitudes and opinions on something. A second use is to *reinforce* attitudes and opinions in an audience. The third effect is to *change* attitudes and opinions (Perloff 2010: 24–25; Jowett & O'Donnell 2012: 33–34). This is achieved through the control of a two-way flow of information. "The most successful movements simultaneously seek information about their targets while managing facts about themselves" (Bob 2007: 52). There may in fact be different publics that need to be segmented as there may be incompatible goals between the different publics, for example an international public and a foreign government. The goal may be to garner support for regime change (although formulated in a more palatable and diplomatic form) among the international public, and to try and limit the perceived options available to a foreign government. There has been a refinement of tactics used in regime change that try to reduce the overall perception of deep rooted national interests in the process of regime change, which uses a variety of different state and non-state actors as well as international and domestic actors (in the target country). Keck and Sikkink make an interesting observation in the opening of their book on transnational advocacy networks.

> World politics at the end of the 20th century involves, alongside states, many non-state actors that interact with each other, with states, and with international organisations. These interactions are structured in terms of networks, and transnational networks are increasingly visible in international politics. (Keck & Sikkink 1998: 1)

The authors have an upbeat assessment of this new form of advocacy, which they associate with positive changes in international politics within such areas as human rights and the environment. They note that "advocacy networks are helping to transform the practice of national sovereignty" (Keck & Sikkink 1998: 2). However, these networks can and are used for other purposes as well. By eroding the concept and strength of national sovereignty, it potentially exposes a targeted country to informational attack for the purposes of regime change.

A broad coalition of actors is involved in the process of advocacy, but are controlled and directed from a central point and by common practices. In their study on the role and activity of transnational advocacy networks, Keck and Sikkink, identify a number of similarities among diverse networks and causes. "Despite their differences, these networks are similar in several important respects: the centrality of values or principled ideas, the belief that individuals can make a difference, the creative use of information, and the employment by non-governmental actors of sophisticated political strategies in targeting their campaigns" (Keck & Sikkink 1998: 2). These groups often work in issues areas where there is high value content and informational uncertainty. Information exchange is a central aspect in their relationships, which is used to mobilise informational strategically in order to persuade, pressure and influence their target group (Keck & Sikkink 1998: 2). These groups seek to influence the political environment by trying to use the implementation of certain norms and values as leverage.

In some regards, a political ideological tone can be detected in the various revolutionary waves that have witnessed regime change (Colour Revolutions and Arab Spring for example). There seems to be inherent in the overarching narrative a clash between grand ideologies, "each of which presented a totalistic view of the world offering perspectives on how society should be organised" (Schwarzmantel 2008: 111). This is clear in the frame where the political ideology of democracy/liberalism is projected as being superior to the stated or suggested oppositional political ideology of authoritarianism (this does not mean to say that the opposing side are authoritarian, but rather framed as being so).

Even if one regime is toppled and is replaced by another regime type that is rhetorically standing for democracy and against authoritarianism, there is no certainty of participatory democracy taking placing owing to external actors spoiling the scenario. "The process of democracy is often co-opted into programmes of polyarchy and neoliberalism by the United States and international financial organisations so as to prevent popular democracy from taking root" (Schock 2005: xxvi). However, this relates to unarmed revolutions that are used against a political regime. What happened in Kiev in early 2014 was something else, more akin to the notion of revolutionary warfare.

> Revolutionary warfare employs ancient military tactics in conjunction with political and psychological techniques in order to acquire political power as a prelude to transforming the social structure. [...] Revolutionary warfare strategists combine unconventional military tactics with political and psychological operations in order to establish a competing political and ideological structure. (Shultz 1989: 113)

There are tangible elements present in this type of political violence, however perhaps of greater importance are the intangible elements. Brute force is but one aspect, the psychological aspect is of greater significance and importance to the outcome of the struggle. Shultz named five principles in revolutionary warfare – primacy of propaganda and political action; mass mobilisation; establishment of a political and military infrastructure; military and paramilitary tactics; and acquisition of outside assistance (1989: 114–117). Subversion is the art of being able to turn the intangible into the tangible. Lawrence Beilenson, a friend of Ronald Reagan, once described Vladimir Lenin as being a *Prophet of Power*. "He grasped the opportunity by translating words into deeds to become the foremost theorist-practitioner of subversion. His employment of the tool was shaped by his character, ideology, and theory of power" (Beilenson 1972: 3). This is only half the picture though, the other half is found in the capacity and actions of the target government.

Beilenson also noted that "the capability of the subversive tool – like that of any weapon – depends partly on the capacity of its target to resist. A one-time subverter can concentrate on the particular strengths and weaknesses of the target government he wants to topple" (1972: 13). In addition to the characteristics of a political regime's institutional and ideological vulnerabilities, there is another aspect that needs to be considered as well – that of timing. There are different moments when a regime is either more or less vulnerable to subversion and overthrow. "The unpredictability of place and time of overthrow is a collar of the general rule that particular foresight is generally fallible. Experience illustrates the application of the rule to economics, war, and international politics" (Beilenson 1972: 28). The planners of a coup or revolution can take advantage of the state's reaction (especially concerning police and security forces), which in some senses has been compared to a 'machine' insofar as it behaves in a fairly predictable and automatic manner (Luttwak 1979: 21). Insurrections and rebellions are unpredictable events that can go in a number of different directions on account of different variables.

There are, however, a number of common factors that can be used to create the 'right' conditions and environment to initiate insurrection against a government. Luttwak proposed at least three conditions that needed to be simultaneously present. 1) "Severe and prolonged economic crisis, with large-scale unemployment or run-away inflation; 2) a long and unsuccessful war or a major defeat, military or diplomatic; 3) chronic instability under a multi-party system" (1979: 31). Lenin identified four elements that are needed – 1) foreign assistance to government or dissidents; 2) shifting immediate local grievances, in which underlying causes of discontent become particularised; 3) the failure or success of temporarily uniting diffuse dissident factions during an uprising; 4) the level of loyalty or disaffection in the security forces (Beilenson 1972: 44). Luttwak also notes, when a political regime (regardless of whether it is democratic or not) keeps open a channel for active dialogue, the chances of creating an environment of being overthrown are reduced (1979: 29). These are the necessary domestic conditions that are required in order to begin the process.

According to Stephen Walt there are a number of common elements and outcomes to revolutions. "First, revolutions become possible when the administrative and coercive capacities of the state have been weakened by a combination of internal and external challenges." Second, there is a rapid outburst of political activity. In mass revolutions, this is often carried out by individuals or groups that are marginalised. Third, the language of political discourse is altered and new symbols and social customs are nurtured. Fourth, the means and principles with which leaders are chosen are changed, they are drawn from the groups that were formerly excluded and now exclude members of the old regime. Fifth, violence is normally the method of revolution, and struggles between competing groups continue after the ouster of the regime (Walt 2001: 35). There are also external factors at play in subversion, which need to be taken into account.

When the subversion is directed from external sources, there are three distinct strategic characteristics. 1) "It was mainly auxiliary to war being waged or expected to come. 2) Decisive external subversion was always geographically spotty (i.e. not global). 3) In the particular country to be subverted, decisive external subversion was normally conducted in an opportunist manner" (Beilenson 1972: 90). There is coordination needed between the external sponsors and the domestic executors of the political power seizure. This is particularly important in shaping the external image and portrayal of those subverting a government, and in attempting to shape international public perception in order to try and mobilise support for the act and to condemn the target government and its actions.

Upon the successful seizure of power, there are two primary principles that are pursued by those who have taken political control. The first point is the need for a rapid transformation of and in society to take place, but simultaneously cloaked in anonymity so as to not alienate or mobilise any potential opposition. Secondly, is that all opposition in the form of armed formations needs to be crushed quickly

(Luttwak 1979: 58). Otherwise weaknesses may emerge that can be exploited by competing groups.

Euromaidan and geopolitics in Ukraine

The particular spark that is associated with the protests, which quickly developed into a revolution, occurred on 21 November 2013 when President Viktor Yanukovich suspended preparation for signing an Association Agreement and Free Trade Agreement with the European Union.[4] The primary narratives that come from Western governments and mass media depict events around Euromaidan and the seizure of political power in Kiev as being a spontaneous local grassroots action, by democratically-minded forces opposing the corrupt and authoritarian, pro-Russian regime of President Yanukovich.[5] A norm and value based catch phrase was used by those protesting – "Ukraine is Europe."[6]

The events in Ukraine have been characterised as a crisis, and not a revolution or war, which is important in trying to distance public perception of something that occurs 'naturally' rather than being contrived. By focusing attention on events as they unfolded in Kiev, and especially in Maidan (Independence Square) the information content was well suited to an entertainment-like news format for the international public and Kiev's Independence Square was developed into an iconic event (together with the symbolism, values and norms expressed by this act). Subversion of the Yanukovich regime has proved to be successful in this case for a variety of different reasons. 1) Ukraine has been suffering from a protracted period of economic crisis. 2) The perceived diplomatic defeat, symbolised by Yanukovich's refusal to sign the Association Agreement and Free Trade Agreement. This was used symbolically as a means to justify and try to crystallise public discontent. 3) The chronic instability of the political system in Ukraine (together with elections that were scheduled for May 2015). 4) Lack of active dialogue between the government and society. 4) Foreign assistance to those domestic actors seeking regime change, which weakened the Ukrainian Government's ability to meet the internal and external challenges it faced.

Some observers have characterised the events that lead to the violent phase of Euromaidan and the ATO are the result of geopolitical factors of competition and conflict between the US-led West and Russia (Jalilov & Kelly 2014; Götz 2015; Simons 2016; Boyd-Barrett 2017). Tsygankov (2015) argues more specifically that Russia's escalation in Ukraine was the result of a more assertive foreign policy to secure its interests in the wake of the West's lack of recognition of Russia's existing values and interests in Eurasia. However, other observers although emphasizing the geopolitical factor, highlight the struggle as one to get out of the Russian orbit of influence (Gerasimov 2014; Kuzio 2015). Foreign intervention and assistance came in a number of different forms – tangible and intangible. The tangible forms included financial support (Under-Secretary of State for Europe and Eurasia, Victoria Nuland's claim of US$5 billion spent[7]) as well as other support activities, such as the Soros Foundation support for creating the Ukrainian Crisis Media Centre to 'inform' the international community.[8]

Intangible forms included attempts at bolstering the coup government political legitimacy through symbolic speech acts and access to high level meetings with Western leaders. A statement by protestors on 29 November 2013 provided the tone for the ultimate aim of the Euromaidan movement. There were three primary demands from a letter that was signed by the organisers and leaders. First, was to form a co-ordinating committee to communicate with the European community. Second, the statement that the president, parliament and the Cabinet of Ministers aren't capable of carrying out a geopolitically strategic course of development for the state and calls on Yanukovich's resignation. Third, was the demand for the cessation of political repressions against Euromaidan activists, students, civic activists and opposition leaders.[9] This call is an attempt to impose a counter-political discourse to the Yanukovich regime as well as an attempt to begin the process of attacking his intangible elements of power and to open the door to external political pressure from the West. It also begins to establish the narrative of the coming crisis as a conflict between 'positive' Western and 'negative' Russian influence in the context of a geopolitical struggle. One of the conditions identified by both Lenin and Luttwak is the need for foreign assistance for the insurrection. This can be found in political rhetoric as well as coercive threats against the target government, and in support of those seeking to overthrow it.

The reaction of Western governments and organisations was to criticise the Ukrainian Government on a number of fronts and praised the 'activists' for their bravery. Secretary-General of NATO, Anders Fogh Rasmussen, stated that "first of all, I strongly condemn the excessive use of police forces we have witnessed in Kyiv. I would expect all NATO partners, including Ukraine, to live up to fundamental democratic principles including freedom of assembly and freedom of expression."[10] Remembering back to the use police force in the West to remove Occupy activists, his condemnation seems to be somewhat of a sense of dissonance in the attitude towards different street protests. The police response to the protests was predictable and probably calculated into the timeline of the growing revolution. Recalling Luttwak's statement that a state bureaucracy is at times like a machine, it acts according to a recognisable set of parameters and is therefore predictable. By the protestors being there, the organisers could count on an eventual response from police, which then could be used to 'justify' increasingly violent protests, which then developed into revolution when the conditions became 'right'. Russia was also accused of the usual assumed crimes, such as invasion, violation of international law and violations of human rights. To which, one of the responses of the Russian Foreign Ministry was to publish their 'White Book' on Ukraine with respect to various allegations of the violations of human rights and international law by the coup government and its supporters (MID 2014). Many generalities and taken for granted unsupported statements are made by Western leaders to try and increase the intangible balance in favour of the insurgents and against Yanukovich.

The United States was leading the rhetorical condemnation of Yanukovich and his government, making various assumptions about listening to and respecting the 'voice of the people' in echoes not dissimilar to Arab Spring events. President

Obama stated that he hoped that negotiations would create "some sort of demo-cratic process that creates a government with greater legitimacy and unity."[11] The text of Secretary of State John Kerry's statement on the situation was published (without any comment or interpretation) in the *New York Times*.

> For weeks, we have called on President Yanukovych and his government to listen to the voices of his people who want peace, justice and a European future. Instead, Ukraine's leaders appear tonight to have made a very differ-ent choice. We call for utmost restraint. Human life must be protected. Ukrainian authorities bear full responsibility for the security of the Ukrainian people. As church bells ring tonight amidst the smoke in the streets of Kyiv, the United States stands with the people of Ukraine. They deserve better.[12]

Both of the statements by the US President and Secretary of State, contain refer-ences and hints of desired regime change. Blame for the crisis situation is clearly and solely laid at the feet of Yanukovich and his government, the increasingly violent protestors are absolved of any wrong doing. This was not the worst and most damaging complicity of the United States in supporting regime change in Ukraine. The most obvious example was the recorded phone conversation between Nuland and the US Ambassador to Ukraine, Geoffrey Pyatt.[13] In the recording, which was broadcast on YouTube, Nuland and Pyatt discuss who should be included in the new government to be and who should be excluded. For example, Arseniy Yatsenyuk was approved and Vitali Klitschko (leader of the party UDAR) was not. A number of articles have appeared in non-mainstream and non-corporate media that refer to the events and result of Euromaidan as an exercise in nothing less than regime change. The primary argument being, what-ever his personal flaw, Yanukovich was the duly elected leader of Ukraine and he was overthrown by non-democratic means that was supported by the United States and the West at large.[14] This is in keeping with Lake's characterisation of the United States as a *powerful broker*. The specific form of power that is utilised is the coercive typology.

This begs the question, what does the US government want in Ukraine? On the one hand they are standing for the right to self-determination and right of assem-bly for the Euromaidan groups, criticising any attempts to stifle these rights and freedoms. But, on the other hand, they are claiming that the groups opposing the Kiev insurgents who seized power as being provocateurs and no sign of criticism of the 'anti-terrorist operation' that has killed numerous citizens in the East of the country.[15] The German newspaper *Bild am Sontag* published a report that cited unnamed sources in German Intelligence that CIA and FBI agents were advising Kiev on how to suppress the rebellion in the east and to help set up a functioning security structure. It also noted that the so-called anti-terrorist operation began not long after the Director of the CIA, John Brennan visited Kiev.[16] An article in *The National Interest* noted that "though the intensity of Western discourse about Ukraine might lead one to conclude that serious strategic interests are threatened by Russia's annexation of Crimea and meddling in Eastern Ukraine, and our past and present policies are at odds with the interests we have."[17] One of the problems here is the clouding of the issue between interests that are 'vital', and those that are 'interesting'. They may seem vital given the saturation media coverage, which hints to the audience how important a particular issue is through the amount of time and effort to cover it.

The US and EU-led efforts in regime change form only part of the picture though; there needs to be the element of revolutionary 'heroes' as part of the domestic scene, to battle with Yanukovich, the villain of the story. News frames and narratives, and political rhetoric were carefully chosen, to highlight positive values and attributes, and to mask or hide those attributes that were negative. The contrast in depiction between Maidan activists and those in Eastern and Southern Ukraine is striking. Euromaidan activists are the heroes of this story, they were presented as being revolutionaries, democrats, from the pages of the 1989-style heroes, standing for decency, liberty and freedom. Those other protestors in the East and South of the country are depicted and denounced as 'mobs', 'vandals and occupiers of government property', 'balaclava wearing men', driven by 'secessionist hysteria' and Putin's personal puppets. Those who oppose the imposed narrative of Euromaidan are quickly attacked as being 'rabble-rousers', 'hysterical', 'fanatics', 'vandals' and agents of Russian interests.[18] For example, in the *Guardian*, one journalist wrote "I have little doubt that Russian security services were in some way involved in the recent escalation of violence in several towns in Eastern Ukraine."[19] Perhaps he has some suspicion, but beyond rumour or conjecture there is no solid evidence provided. A very subjective use of norms and values are assigned to the political representatives of the Euromaidan coalition.

Those who seized political power from Yanukovich have been characterised as standing for liberty, democracy and other cherished Western liberal norms and values. A great deal of effort went into trying to minimise the perception of any participation or involvement by radical groups in the new government that was formed. What is known is the composition of the Western-backed government. It included five members of Svobodo, seven members from Tymoshenko's party, one member of the Stepan Bandera Tryzub, four from Lviv with unclear affiliations, two from among the Euromaidan activists and one former minister of the Tymosheno government (from 2010).[20] One article noted that "who's in charge? Certainly not the bought-and-paid-for-moderates that Washington and the EU hoped to install as the new government of Ukraine." It also noted a number of comments from one of Right Sector's leaders, Aleksandr Muzychko,[21] such as he will fight "Jews and Russians until I die", law and order will prevail or "Right Sector squads will shoot the bastards on the spot" and "the next President in Ukraine will be from Right Sector."[22] Right Sector responded to the death of Muzychko by threatening retaliation and refusing to give up their weapons, which was demanded by the Interior Minister Arsen Avakov.[23] This demonstrates a rapid rift developing between those who took political power and former allies of the Euromaidan. Right Sector gained prominence during Euromaidan as 'protectors' of the protestors, and been highly organised, motivated and ideologically driven.[24]

Although Euromaidan started off as a fairly peaceful event, it soon degenerated into wholesale violence. The Western media narrative places the blame on Yanukovich. One observer blamed the Yanukovich regime for the violence based on a number of institutional reasons – "the absence of clear institutional channels for a swift resolution, the increased politicisation of the judiciary, and the use of selective justice against protestors, which strengthened the far right segment" (Popova 2014: 64). Russian media narrative assigns the blame for the violence to those protestors on the street and especially the far right wing elements. The role of the neo-Nazi and far-right groups' participation and influence on the Euromaidan movement was emphasized by the Russian authorities and those opposed to the overthrow of an elected national leader. In reference to the seizure of power, and with the active support of the US and EU, the White Book was blunt about the supposed results.

> These dramatic events were accompanied by widespread and gross violations of human rights and freedoms on the part of the self-proclaimed government and its supporters. As a result, manifestations of extremist, ultranationalist, and neo-Nazistic sentiments, religious intolerance, xenophobia, blatant blackmail, threats, pressure placed by the Maidan leaders on their opponents, purges and arrests amongst them, repression, physical violence, and sometimes plain criminal lawlessness have become commonplace in Ukraine (MID 2014: 63).

This extract reveals many of the official Russian narratives in terms of the negative values and norms that are presumed and projected as being the result of the revolution. The projected reality is portrayed in terms of absolutes and not nuances. There was some evidence that does point to the presence of some of those elements in the new authorities, which is something downplayed by the West and Ukraine. Svobodo has also come under a lot of scrutiny by those seeking to uncover the hidden aspects to the regime change. The EU Parliament in 2012 passed a resolution that condemned the party as being "racist, xenophobic and anti-Semitic." Yet in 2014 the Prosecutor-General of Ukraine and the Minister of Defence were Svobodo members (Deputy Secretary of National Security in Ukraine was from Right Sector).[25] One of the Svobodo members of parliament established a think tank in 2005 called the Joseph Goebbels Political Research Centre and praised the Holocaust as a "bright period" in human history.[26] These are two neo-Nazi factions, but what role in general did the far right wing play in the regime change?

The Western media and political narrative, which was carried in mainstream news was Euromaidan was a democratic movement, which may have had some very marginal extremist elements in it. Russia narrated the regime change as a fascist coup. The US State Department spent some time and effort trying to defend the Western narrative and simultaneously attack the Russian counter-narrative.[27] Expert on Russian nationalism, Stephen Shenfield, claimed that there were two aspects to the Euromaidan protests – *civic* (against a corrupt, unresponsive, incompetent and repressive government) that was shared by citizens in the west and east of the country alike, and the *ethno-national* (that thought the revolution was not 'Ukrainian' enough, which was perceived as being a threat to citizens in the east).[28] The ethno-national element is expressed in neo-Nazi sentiment and ideology. In the summer of 2013, for example, a prominent party leader of youth in Svobodo was distributing texts from Goebbels that had been translated into Ukrainian.[29] Shenfield concludes that "there is considerable truth in the claim that the change of regime in Ukraine was a 'fascist coup.'"[30] There are also a number of issues that demand closer scrutiny with regard to apparent double standards or by attempting to conceal damaging information that could harm the narrative of the new regime.

Based on the Western media narrative, some victims are apparently more worthy than others in Ukraine. Western leaders and media were very quick to denounce use of police force against Euromaidan activists, but give a free hand in the 'anti-terrorist operation' in the south and east of the country. An illustration that serves this point very well are the events that took place in the Trade Union building in Odessa in which more than 30 anti-Kiev protestors died. Outnumbered by Right Sector and football 'fans', they took refuge in the building, which was set on fire. Any of those inside trying to escape were attacked by the neo-Nazi groups waiting outside, who were chanting anti-Russian slogans while people were being burned alive. According to the Western narrative, those killed were guilty of 'provoking' the situation.[31] Military forces under Kiev's control had also begun to use artillery on Slovyansk, hitting civilian structures.[32] There was no word of criticism or calls for restraint from Western leaders, who used such excuses to unleash military action to remove Gaddafi from power in Libya (R2P – Libyan civilians from use of military force).

One of the 'early' controversies that emerged, and only did so thanks to an intercepted phone call between the EU foreign affairs chief, Catherine Ashton and the Estonian foreign minister Urmas Paet, concerned the story behind the Kiev snipers. This was assumed and blamed on Yanukovich. However, the leaked phone call[33] told another story, and indicated that it may in fact be snipers employed by someone within the Euromaidan movement that employed them.[34] The story was carried in some mainstream Western media, such as the Guardian, simply because this was too big a story and potentially damaging to just ignore. It was interesting to note the criticism of breaching a private call, especially with regards to the revelations concerning the NSA and PRISM. There was also an attempt to introduce a red herring into the political information space with the attempted deception of the hoax posters demanding Jews to register in Donetsk.[35] The news was carried without critique by Western media, Western politicians stood on their pedestals and criticised the separatists. The interim regime also took the time to make symbolic, value laden political speech acts to condemn the action.[36] There was little to no critical reflection concerning who stood to gain the most, in terms of political legitimacy, from this action, let alone delving into Right Sector's and Svobodo's anti-Semitic stance. There were also problems with 'loyalty' in the state apparatus inherited by the new regime too.

One of the problems faced by the new regime is that not all existing state machinery is loyal to it. This has been shown on a number of occasions, such as when Alfa units refused to deploy to the east of the country on the so-called anti-terrorist operation.[37] The story was absent from mainstream Western media sources. Another story that received scant attention occurred on 22 May 2014 when a unit of 57 Ukrainian army reservists refused an order to attack a nearby settlement because there were no terrorists there, only civilians (a non-aggression agreement had been signed between the unit and local residents too). Soon afterwards a convoy of vehicles belonging to Privat Bank (owned by the Oligarch Ihor Kolomoiski, who has in the past financially supported Svobodo and has been appointed governor of Dnipropetrovsk by the regime government) brought heavily armed men from the Donbass and Azov militias and attacked the unit, leaving all but seven soldiers dead. The attackers planted Saint George Ribbons on some of the dead before they left in an attempt to make it look the work of anti-Kiev forces. Independent videos and investigations by a BBC journalist confirmed the course of events.[38] The actions demonstrate a great deal of effort that has been put into creating the deception, but also sending a 'message' to Ukraine's security forces.

Conclusion

As noted by William Dunkerly, the US position on the regime change that took place in Ukraine, maintained a strict narrative that stayed 'on track', but ignored facts on the ground. The narrative stated that "the Ukraine crisis grew from its people's quest for Western democracy over Russian oppression, and its new leaders have formed a constitutionally legitimate government." However, it excluded 'uncomfortable' facts like the use of violence and lawlessness in Maidan, unconstitutional assumption of power by the new regime, discarding the legitimate constitution and the inclusion of extremist elements in the new government.[39] This was confirmed by other observers, "the Standard Western Media Narrative on Ukraine is a construction that plays up some facts, ignores others and avoids certain questions. In short, something manufactured by interests that are not necessarily concerned with improving the miserable situation in Ukraine but are playing some geopolitical game."[40] The narrative plays a critical role in trying to project and/or maintain legitimacy or detract from an opponent's image. When a narrative becomes established, it restricts the way a particular subject, object or event can be described. This instrumental use of the narrative is most obvious in the context of the event(s) that make up Euromaidan.

Rather than calling and naming the different factions involved in the violence of post-Yanukovich Ukraine, they are labelled according to the script of the narrative in which Russia is presented as being the villain against 'freedom' and 'democracy.' Therefore, anti-Maidan factions (which could detract from the imposed frame of popular legitimacy of those who took political power in Kiev) become pro-Russian separatists, and former President Yanukovich is a pro-Russian dictator instead of being self-serving. Because, in this story Russia is meant to be the catalyst for creating the image of threat and a wider crisis for the 'civilised' world, which is meant to drive the publics to a certain conclusion and course of action.

An attempt has been made to project the Euromaidan leadership as being legitimate political actors based upon a subjective evaluation of their techniques used, the success of the seizure of political power and their alleged representativeness among the Ukrainian people. The so-called interim government have inherited the old state bureaucratic machinery, which is potentially a source of resistance that needs to be neutralised, both before and after the coup. This accounts for the blanket 'international' condemnation of Yanukovich's use of security forces in Maidan against what became extremely violent and organised insurgents. After the seizure of power this accounts for the selective public show trials of members of the security forces from the time of the Maidan insurrection. In order to try and project the façade of legitimacy, any radical social change that is to be forced through, needed to take place after the elections in May 2014, in order for the coup government to successfully manage the election.

There is no doubt that many ordinary Ukrainians had a legitimate cause for concern and irritation by the manner in which Yanukovich ruled. This is perhaps one of the main underlying reasons why the concept of Euromaidan was soon transformed from words into deeds. However, mainstream Western media and politics were engaged in knowledge production and knowledge management. The knowledge that was produced and managed has been used to support and legitimise regime change, using arguments that were not based upon concrete arguments of law, but rather through using unclear and subjective systems of values and norms. Domestic and international actors joined forces, which increased the chances of a success regime change through force by mobilising domestic and international public support for the insurgents and by limiting the options available to the Yanukovich regime to defend their position and retain power. Those who criticised or tried to counter the narrative have found themselves under personal attack and subjected to norm and value based demonization.

A number of similarities exist in the use of information, perception and public opinion in the case of regime change in Ukraine, which are also seen to some extent in the Western backed cases of regime change and attempted regime change in Libya and Syria. There are a competing set of projected realities that are value and norm based in their nature. A notable use of pathos and logos (including false logics) are normally carried in an emotional and not a rational form. In this manner, the target publics are more likely to be primed and mobilised. Those projected realities are diametrically opposed sets or norms and values, one of which is intended resonate and to attract the sympathy and support of the audience (i.e. the 'hero' character of the particular event) that is intended to draw the audience towards that side and reality – the pull of attraction. The identified 'villain' is assigned repulsive and non-appealing sets of values, norms and practices. They are pictured as standing for the opposite of what are asserted to be acceptable international norms and standards – creating the push of avoidance. Therefore, the logic goes, the villain should be removed and replaced by the hero of the story. It is also assumed that the hero maybe assisted in defeating the villain by a 'benevolent' and 'responsible' foreign actor. If a particular narrative becomes hegemonic, the immediate effect felt is that it considerably narrows the permissible and allowable public discourse on a particular topic or issue, it enforces a spiral of silence in effect. For those that transgress the established boundaries of 'decency' run the risk of having their reputation tarnished and to become the victim of character assassination. Following from this, some dubious foreign policy practices then may remain unchallenged as a result, and the catastrophic results (immediately for the target country, and eventually the wider region) of the policies/practices of regime change and military adventurism are not subjected to transparency or accountability.

Notes

1 For example the activist from the Occupy Movement was sentenced to 90 days in jail in addition to the two years of incarceration already served (could have got seven years) for elbowing a policeman, for more see http://www.huffingtonpost.com/2014/05/19/cecily-mcmillan-occupy-wall-street-assault-officer_n_5351322.html. More recently, the conduct of heavily militarised police unites deployed against unarmed protestors against the North Dakota Pipeline highlight the apparent double standards seen in who is and is not able to openly express themselves without facing the threat of disproportionate force. See for example - http://www.aljazeera.com/indepth/inpictures/2016/10/north-dakota-native-americans-protest-pipeline-161028150518748.html.

2 MacAskil, E., *Ukraine Crisis: Bugged Call Reveals Conspiracy Theory About Kiev Snipers*, The Guardian, http://www.theguardian.com/world/2014/mar/05/ukraine-bugged-call-catherine-ashton-urmas-paet, 5 March 2014 (accessed 26 May 2014)

3 The terms *coup*, *insurrection* and *revolution* are at times used to describe the action of an illegal seizure of political power by forces that use means other than a democratic vote. Their origin of use is related to the respective author of the theoretical material being consulted and quoted.

4 *Ukraine Protests After Yanukovich EU Deal Rejection*, BBC News Europe, http://www.bbc.com/news/world-europe-25162563, 30 November 2013 (accessed 26 May 2014)

5 Woodruff, J., *Why Did Ukraine's Yanukovich Give in to Russian Pressure on EU Deal?*, PBS News Hour, http://www.pbs.org/newshour/bb/world-july-dec13-ukraine2_12-02/, 2 December 2013 (accessed 26 May 2014)

6 *Ukraine Protests After Yanukovich EU Deal Rejection*, BBC News Europe, http://www.bbc.com/news/world-europe-25162563, 30 November 2013 (accessed 26 May 2014)

7 American Conquest by Subversion: Victoria Nuland's Admits Washington Has Spent $5 Billion to "Subvert Ukraine", Global Research, http://www.globalresearch.ca/american-conquest-by-subversion-victoria-nulands-admits-washington-has-spent-5-billion-to-subvert-ukraine/5367782, 7 February 2014 (accessed 26 May 2014)

8 Weissman, S., *Meet the Americans Who Put Together the Coup in Kiev*, Reader Supported News, http://readersupportednews.org/opinion2/277-75/22758-meet-the-americans-who-put-together-the-coup-in-kiev, 25 March 2014 (accessed 26 May 2014)

9 Euromaidan Rallies in Ukraine – Dec. 9, Kyiv Post, http://www.kyivpost.com/content/ukraine/euromaidan-rallies-in-ukraine-live-updates-332341.html, 10 December 2013 (accessed 26 May 2014)

10 *Rasmussen Hopes Ukraine Lives up to Democratic Principles*, Interfax-Ukraine, http://
en.interfax.com.ua/news/general/178955.html, 3 December 2013 (accessed 26 May
2014)
11 *Obama Hopes for new Ukrainian Government 'with Greater Legitimacy and
Unity'*, Kyiv Post, http://www.kyivpost.com/content/ukraine/obama-hopes-for-new-
ukrainian-government-with-greater-legitimacy-and-unity-336068.html, 1 February
2014 (accessed 26 May 2014)
12 Kerry, J., *Kerry's Statement on Ukraine*, http://www.nytimes.com/2013/12/11/world/
europe/kerrys-statement-on-ukraine.html?_r=0, The New York Times, 10 December
2013 (accessed 26 May 2014)
13 A) *Nuland: Fuck the EU*, YouTube, https://www.youtube.com/watch?v=r5n8UbJ8jsk,
6 February 2014 (accessed 26 May 2014); B) Marcus, J., *Ukraine Crisis: Transcript
of Leaked Nuland-Pyatt Call*, BBC News Europe, http://www.bbc.com/news/world-
europe-26079957, 7 February 2014 (accessed 28 April 2014)
14 1) Giambrone, J., *Obama Off the Ukrainian Deep End*, Foreign Policy Journal, http://
www.foreignpolicyjournal.com/2014/03/17/obama-off-the-ukrainian-deep-end/,
17 March 2014 (accessed 26 May 2014); 2) McGovern, R., *Ukraine: One 'Regime
Change' too Many?*, Consortium News, http://consortiumnews.com/2014/03/01/
ukraine-one-regime-change-too-many/, 1 March 2014 (accessed 26 May 2014);
3) O'Neil, B., *Ukraine: This isn't a Revolution - its Regime Change*, Spiked, http://
www.spiked-online.com/spikedplus/article/ukraine-this-isnt-a-revolution-its-regime-
change#.U4NRK_mSyPU, 25 February 2014 (accessed 26 May 2014); 4) Weissman,
S., *Meet the Americans Who Put Together the Coup in Kiev*, Reader Supported News,
http://readersupportednews.org/opinion2/277-75/22758-meet-the-americans-who-put-
together-the-coup-in-kiev, 25 March 2014 (accessed 26 May 2014).
15 Paul, R., *What Does the US Government Want in Ukraine?*, Anti-War.Com, http://
original.antiwar.com/paul/2014/05/11/what-does-the-us-government-want-in-
ukraine/, 11 May 2014 (accessed 26 May 2014)
16 *CIA, FBI Agents 'Advising Ukraine Government': Report*, AFP via Yahoo News, http://
news.yahoo.com/cia-fbi-agents-advising-ukraine-government-report-101508429.
html, 4 May 2014 (accessed 26 May 2014)
17 Posen, B. R., *Ukraine: Part of America's "Vital Interest"?*, The National Interest,
http://nationalinterest.org/feature/ukraine-part-americas-vital-interests-10443, 12 May
2014 (accessed 26 May 2014)
18 O'Neil, B., *Ukraine: Western Double Standards hit a New Low*, Spiked, http://www.
spiked-online.com/newsite/article/ukraine-western-double-standards-hit-a-new-
low/14989#.U4Q1nvmSyPU, 7 May 2014 (accessed 15 May 2014)
19 Ishchenko, V., *Maidan or anti-Maidan? The Ukraine Situation Requires More Nuance*,
The Guardian, http://www.theguardian.com/commentisfree/2014/apr/15/maidan-anti-
maidan-ukraine-situation-nuance, 15 April 2014 (accessed 16 April 2014)
20 A) Penaud, A., *The Ukraine Crisis and Recent Russphobia*, 23 May 2014 in Johnson's
Russia List, 2014-#116, 25 May 2014. B) Zawadzki, S., Hosenball, M. & Grey, S., *In
Ukraine, Nationalists Gain Influence – and Scrutiny*, Reuters, http://in.reuters.com/
article/2014/03/07/ukraine-crisis-far-right-idINDEEA260DT20140307, 7 March 2014
(accessed 10 March 2014)
21 He was assassinated in a 'police raid' in March 2014, for more information please refer
to http://www.bbc.com/news/world-europe-26729273
22 Roberts, C., *Democracy Murdered by Protest: Ukraine Falls to Intrigue and Violence*,
Foreign Policy Journal, http://www.foreignpolicyjournal.com/2014/02/25/democracy-
murdered-by-protest-ukraine-falls-to-intrigue-and-violence/#.U4RMQPmSyPU,   25
February 2014 (accessed 27 February 2014)
23 A) McLaughlin, D., *Ukraine's Crisis Opens Rifts Among its Revolutionaries*, Irish
Times,   http://www.irishtimes.com/news/world/europe/ukraine-s-crisis-opens-rifts-
among-its-revolutionaries-1.1737912, 26 March 2014 (accessed 27 March 2014);

B) Roth, A., *Ukraine Faces Struggle to Gain Control of Militias, Including Those on its Side*, The New York Times, http://www.nytimes.com/2014/05/24/world/europe/ukraine-faces-struggle-to-gain-control-of-militias-including-those-on-its-side.html?_r=0, 23 May 2014 (accessed 26 May 2014)

24 Bidder, B., Neef, C., Pylyov, V. & Schepp, M., *Prepared to Die: The Right Wing's Role in Ukrainian Protests*, Spiegel Online, http://www.spiegel.de/international/europe/ukraine-sliding-towards-civil-war-in-wake-of-tough-new-laws-a-945742.html, 27 January 2014 (accessed 20 May 2014)

25 Dunkerly, W., *US Ukraine Position Falls Apart*, Omnicom Press, http://www.omnicompress.com/ukrcrisis/, 14 March 2014 (accessed 18 March 2014)

26 Foxall, A. & Kessler, O., *Yes, There are Bad Guys in the Ukrainian Government*, Foreign Policy, http://www.foreignpolicy.com/articles/2014/03/18/yes_there_are_bad_guys_in_the_ukrainian_government, 18 March 2014 (accessed 26 May 2014)

27 *President Putin's Fiction: 10 False Claims About Ukraine*, US State Department, http://www.state.gov/r/pa/prs/ps/2014/03/222988.htm, 5 March 2014 (accessed 27 May 2014)

28 Shenfield, S., *Ukraine: Popular Uprising or Fascist Coup?*, stephenshenfield.net, http://stephenshenfield.net/themes/international-relations/164-ukraine-popular-uprising-or-fascist-coup, 5 April 2014 (accessed 7 April 2014)

29 Bidder, B., Neef, C., Pylyov, V. & Schepp, M., *Prepared to Die: The Right Wing's Role in Ukrainian Protests*, Spiegel Online, http://www.spiegel.de/international/europe/ukraine-sliding-towards-civil-war-in-wake-of-tough-new-laws-a-945742.html, 27 January 2014 (accessed 20 May 2014)

30 Shenfield, S., *Ukraine: Popular Uprising or Fascist Coup?*, stephenshenfield.net, http://stephenshenfield.net/themes/international-relations/164-ukraine-popular-uprising-or-fascist-coup, 5 April 2014 (accessed 7 April 2014)

31 A) O'Neil, B., *Ukraine: Western Double Standards hit a New Low*, Spiked, http://www.spiked-online.com/newsite/article/ukraine-western-double-standards-hit-a-new-low/14989#.U4Q1nvmSyPU, 7 May 2014 (accessed 15 May 2014); B) Parry, R., *How the Media Sees no Nazis in Ukraine Even as they Burn Dozens to Death*, Stop the War Coalition, http://stopwar.org.uk/article/how-the-media-sees-no-nazis-in-ukraine-even-as-they-burn-dozens-to-death#.U4RX7PmSyPU, 7 May 2014 (accessed 7 May 2014); C) Golstein, V., *Why Everything You Read About Ukraine is Wrong*, Forbes, http://www.forbes.com/sites/forbesleadershipforum/2014/05/19/why-everything-youve-read-about-ukraine-is-wrong/, 19 May 2014 (accessed 21 May 2014)

32 Hoyle, B., *Civilians Prepare to Flee as Kiev Shells Rebel-Held City*, The Times, 23 May 2014. Johnson's Russia List, 2014-#114, 23 May 2014

33 https://www.youtube.com/watch?v=ZEgJ0oo3OA8, 5 March 2014 (accessed 27 May 2014)

34 Durden, T., *"Behind the Kiev Snipers it was Somebody from the New Coalition" – A Stunning New Leak Released*, Zero Hedge, http://www.zerohedge.com/news/2014-03-05/behind-kiev-snipers-it-was-somebody-new-coaltion-stunning-new-leak-reveals-truth, 5 March 2014 (accessed 28 April 2014)

35 Kramer, A. E., *Demands That Jews Register in Eastern Ukraine are Denounced, and Denied*, The New York Times, http://www.nytimes.com/2014/04/18/world/europe/efforts-to-register-jews-in-ukraine-are-denounced-and-denied.html, 17 April 2014 (accessed 28 April 2014)

36 Chasmar, J., *Ukraine PM Vows to Find 'Bastards' Behind Anti-Semitic Fliers*, The Washington Times, http://www.washingtontimes.com/news/2014/apr/20/ukraine-pm-vows-find-bastards-behind-anti-semitic-/, 20 April 2014 (accessed 28 April 2014)

37 Ukrainian Ant-Riot Police Unit Alfa Refuse to Obey the Orders of Interim Authorities and Storm Buildings, UNIAN, http://acenewsservices.com/2014/04/11/ukrainian-ant-riot-police-unit-alfa-refuse-to-obey-the-orders-of-interim-authorities-and-storm-buildings/, 11 April 2014 (accessed 27 May 2014)

38 *Ukraine SITREP May 22nd, 19:32 UTC/Zulu: Ukie Death Squad Murder Suspects*, The Vineyard of the Saker, http://vineyardsaker.blogspot.se/2014/05/ukraine-sitrep-may-22th-1932-utczulu.html, 22 May 2014 (accessed 26 May 2014). Go to http://www.bbc.com/news/world-europe-27515514 to see the BBC report
39 Dunkerly, W., *US Ukraine Position Falls Apart*, Omnicom Press, http://www.omnicompress.com/ukrcrisis/, 14 March 2014 (accessed 18 March 2014)
40 Armstrong, P., *Propaganda and the Narrative*, Da Russophile, http://darussophile.com/2014/02/propaganda-and-the-narrative/, 25 February 2014 (accessed 27 February 2014)

Bibliography

Allan, S., *News Culture*, Buckingham: Open University Press, 1999

Beilenson, L. W., *Power Through Subversion*, Washington DC: Public Affairs Press, 1972

Bernays, E., The Engineering of Consent, *The Annals of the American Academy of Political and Social Science* 250(1), 1947, pp. 113–120.

Bob, C., *The Marketing of Rebellion: Insurgents, Media, and International Activism*, New York: Cambridge University Press, 2007

Boyd-Barrett, O., *Western Mainstream Media and the Ukraine Crisis: A Study in Conflict Propaganda,* New York: Routledge, 2017

Branigan, E., *Narrative Comprehension and Film*, London: Routledge, 1992

Brophy, P., *Narrative-Based Practice*, Farnham: Ashgate, 2009

Diuk, N., Euromaidan: Ukraine's Self-Organising Revolution, *World Affairs*, 176(6), March-April 2014, pp. 9–16

Edelman, M., *The Politics of Misinformation*, New York: Cambridge University Press, 2001

Eder, M. K., *Leading the Narrative: The Case for Strategic Communication*, Annapolis: Naval Institute Press, 2011

Entman, R. M., *Projections of Power: Framing News, Public Opinion, and US Foreign Policy*, Chicago: The University of Chicago Press, 2004

Farwell, J. P., *Persuasion and Power: The Art of Strategic Communication*, Washington DC: Georgetown University Press, 2012

Gerasimov, I., Ukraine 2014: The First Post-Colonial Revolution. Introduction to the Forum, *Ab Imperio*, 3, 2014, pp. 22–44

Götz, E., It's Geopolitics, Stupid: Explaining Russia's Ukraine Policy, *Global Affairs*, 1(1), 2015, pp. 3–10

Jalilov, M. & Kelly, P., The Ukrainian Shatterbelt: A New Cold War?, *I Report dell'IsAG*, 30, October 2014

Jowett, G. S. & O'Donnell, V., *Propaganda and Persuasion*, 5th Edition, Washington DC: Sage, 2012

Katz, M. N. (ed.), *Revolution: International Dimensions*, Washington DC: CQ Press, 2001

Keck, M. E. & Sikkink, K., *Activists Beyond Borders: Advocacy Networks in International Politics*, Ithaca: Cornell University Press, 1998

Kuzio, T., Competing Nationalisms, Euromaidan, and the Russian-Ukrainian Conflict, *Studies in Ethnicity and Nationalism*, 15(1), 2015, pp. 157–169

Lake, A., *Six Nightmares – Real Threats in a Dangerous World and How America Can Meet Them*, New York: Little, Brown and Company, 2000

Leavy, P., *Iconic Events: Media, Politics, and Power in Retelling History*, Lanham (MD): Lexington Books, 2007

Lendman, S. (Ed.), *Flashpoint in Ukraine: How the US Drive for Hegemony Risks World War III*, Atlanta (GA): Clarity Press Inc., 2014

Luttwak, E., *Coup d'Etat: A Practical Handbook*, Cambridge (MA): Harvard University Press, 1979

McQuail, D., *McQuail's Mass Communication Theory*, 6th Edition, London: Sage, 2010

Ministry of Foreign Affairs of the Russian Federation (MID), *White Book on Violations of Human Rights and the Rule of Law in Ukraine (November 2013-March 2014)*, Moscow, April 2014

Nye, J. S. (Jr.), *Soft Power: The Means to Success in World Politics*, New York: Public Affairs, 2004

Perloff, R. M., *The Dynamics of Persuasion: Communication and Attitudes in the 21st Century*, 4th Edition, New York: Routledge, 2010

Popova, M., Why the Orange Revolution was Short and Peaceful and Euromaidan Long and Violent, *Problems of Post-Communism*, 61(6), November/December 2014, pp. 64–70

Ryabchuk, A., Right Revolution? Hopes and Perils of the Euromaidan Protests in Ukraine, *Journal of Contemporary Central and Eastern Europe*, 22(1), 2014, pp. 127–134

Schock, K., *Unarmed Insurrections: People Power Movements in Non-democracies*, Minneapolis: University of Minnesota Press, 2005

Schwarzmantel, J., *Ideology and Politics*, London: Sage, 2008

Shultz, R. H. Jr., "Political Strategies for Revolutionary War" in Lord, C. & Barnett, F. R., *Political Warfare and Psychological Operations: Rethinking the US Approach*, Washington DC: National Defence University Press, 1989, pp. 111–138

Simons, G., 'Euromaidan and the Geopolitical Struggle for Influence on Ukraine via New Media' in Suslov, M. & Bassin, M. (Eds.), *Eurasia 2.0: Russian Geopolitics in the Age of New Media*, Lanham (MD): Lexington Books, 2016, pp. 275–294

Tsygankov, A., Vladimir Putin's Last Stand: The Sources of Russia's Ukraine Policy, *Post-Soviet Affairs*, 31(4), 2015, pp. 279–303

Vinogradov, A. & Sviatnenko, S., Euromaidan Values From a Comparative Perspective, *Social, Health, and Communication Studies Journal*, 1(1), 2014, pp. 41–61

Walt, S. W., "A Theory of Revolution and War" in Kats, M. N. (ed.), *Revolution: International Dimensions*, Washington DC: CQ Press, 2001, pp. 32–62

11   Observations and conclusions

Greg Simons and Iulian Chifu

> *The management of foreign relations appears to be the most susceptible to abuse all of the trusts committed to a Government, because they can be concealed or disclosed, or disclosed in such parts and at such times as will best suit particular views.*
>
> James Madison in 1798

What lessons can be learned?

Foreign wars have been an activity of government that has for a long time been open to and subject to abuse. This has been in a part a product of some level of trust that did exist between the public and its government. The selective use of information and disinformation to steer public perception and opinion is another important factor. Changes have often been presumed on the basis of advances in technology and trends, such as the presumption of globalisation or other 'inevitable' cultural and political trends. This creates certain connectivity within the realms of politics and international relations. Betz claims that connectivity certainly has important implications for war, but that it does not substantially alter the nature of it as much is as presumed. For example, the element of chance has not been removed from war; the importance of passion (the will to follow and fight) has not diminished; and some sort of 'silver bullet' has not materialised to ensure and swift and safe form of war (2015: 179). Thus the effects of passion, chance and reason – Clausewitz's Trinity of War – remain today.

Madison noted the use of deception and misrepresentation by politics in the pursuit of foreign policy. This is not something that is especially new, and even before his time, the successful use of deception in times of war was considered an integral part of the road to victory. Sun Tzu noted that "all warfare is based upon deception" and adding that "the expert approaches his objective indirectly" (Tzu 1971: 41). Given the increasing tendency to resort to the use of armed force in order to achieve foreign policy goals (Western 2005), the link between foreign policy and war becomes clearer.

Madison's quote is amply illustrated by the recent revelations from the Podesta emails made public by Wikileaks. Within the context of the anti-ISIS coalition, on the face of it the political nature of it seems to be united. But underneath there is found to be a multitude of interests in the unpublicised part of where politics meets armed conflict. One of these emails, from 19 August 2014 clearly shows that Hillary Clinton knew and was aware of key members of the supposed anti-ISIS coalition was providing aid to the terror group.[1] This is illustrative of the hidden parts of politics and war, which can be regarded as being a part of the 'fog of war'. But it also illustrates a certain level of deception or secrecy that is intended to suit maintaining a particular political point of view. This particular case also reveals new non-state actors that are challenging the established set of state actors.

New means of Information Communication Technologies (ICT) are creating new mass communication potential. Willcox noted that "the nature of war is likely to remain virtual with technology allowing for the legitimisation of the conflict" (2005: 188). However, new ICTs are creating an increasingly complex environment in politics and the information sphere. What remains to be seen is whether they will fundamentally alter the way that armed conflicts are fought or merely the nature of the relationships between the actors involved in war.

Marketing and persuading for war

Western concludes "that decisions on military intervention and war are the result of active and aggressive campaigns for or against a particular war." Further, he identified that "four factors contribute to the success or failure of the information control and issue-framing advantages necessary for selling war: the role of the presidency and the cohesiveness of the executive branch, the resources of the opposition, the role of the news media, and the duration of the crisis" (2005: 224). Marketing is a form of mediated persuasion that builds an emotionally based political relationship between the messenger and the target public (Simons 2013), which is intended to create the requisite political conditions that would permit the waging of war.

> Given that media representations of war can have a defining impact on the maintenance or weakening of civilian morale and public support for war, the relationship between how a war is conducted and how it is portrayed is of crucial importance. The shift from the explicit censorship of the Falklands War of 1982 to the apparent transparency of the 2003 Iraq War is indicative of how militaries are increasingly concerned with developing highly sophisticated mechanisms to sell and justify war operations to the public. (Maltby 2007: 4)

The manner in which a military intervention is packaged and communicated to an audience is crucial, which requires a resonance with the target audience if there is to be any sense of legitimacy for the action and therefore the sought after public consent. This can certainly be seen in a CIA Red Cell report on US media strategies that were intended to shore up European support for the continued war in Afghanistan in 2010 based upon key issue topics (drugs and women's rights) that seemingly required further ISAF involvement if they were to be resolved (CIA 2010).[2] However, it is not only governments that rely on building emotionally based political relationships with target audiences. This is also actively performed by non-state actors too.

Iulian Chifu in Chapters 3 and 4 provides a good illustration of the use of marketing in communication by non-state actors, such as the terrorist groups as al Qaeda and ISIS that are currently operating in the MENA area. The issues of foreign fighter recruitment and the Jihadi brides demonstrate a fairly high level of communication savvy that is able to lure recruits from the relative safety of the Western lifestyles on to the dangers of the battlefields in places such as Iraq, Libya and Syria. In Chapter 6, Chifu also demonstrates the element of marketing in Russia's approach to informational war, and especially in regard to projecting alternative realities to those of mainstream Western politics and mass media. As Chifu rightly points out, the declaration of a Caliphate by ISIS was in itself a rather remarkable example of marketing by a non-state actor that tried to transform itself by such politically symbolic communications as being transformed in to a state actor. The examples in these chapters demonstrate the importance of perception over reality in the context of contemporary armed conflicts. It is what people perceive to be the reality that they react to and not necessarily the actual reality. Although this does not assume that the actual and perceived realities are always different, they may be the same.

Greg Simons in Chapters 2, 7, 8 and 9 also displays the hallmarks of attempts to sell armed conflicts through marketing means. There is a distinct clash of norms and values on offer by the different sides of the conflicts in Georgia, Libya and Syria. In addition, the Libyan and Syrian conflicts (Libya being the 'successful' example) show how Western governments attempt to manipulate the public consciousness through these alternative realities and key moments in order to push their foreign policy of regime change via legitimising military action to be undertaken in the name of humanity. The accusation of mass rapes in Libya by pro-Gadaffi forces, which were widely publicised by Hillary Clinton at the time, were not substantiated. Yet the plight of civilians in urgent need, which was even admitted as being overblown in the British Government report (House of Commons 2016), provided the emotionally charged logical basis for a NATO-led attack on the country.

Chapter 7 also showed how a great degree of marketing was used within the context of an armed conflict, even going as far as to have both Georgia and Russia employing professional PR agencies to engage in communication with audiences on their behalf in 2008. There was a high degree of news and perception management through the use of developed sets of narratives, at least initially Georgia proved the actor more capable of communicating with international audiences than Russia. In fact, Russian communications seemed to be more oriented toward a domestic than an international audience. In Chapter 10, the name given to the process of subversion that saw the toppling of the corrupt, but democratically elected President Yanukovich, saw the use of branding. Euromaidan not only captures the place context of this period, but also there is the element of values and expectations that are captured in the Euro part of the brand. Chapter 2 also provides concrete examples in Afghanistan of the use of marketing techniques to try and pacify public concerns of a seemingly endless war, which happened to create other problems for ISAF. Firstly, it trained public expectation to believe that a withdrawal was inevitable, which tended to make the Western publics even more adverse to casualties among their soldiers as it seemed to now be a 'pointless' loss. Secondly, this also sent a signal to those non-state actors, such as the Taliban, that ISAF was leaving and now this war became a waiting game where one actor put themselves on a timetable and the other did not.

Politics, information and communication

Information and communications in their own right are not neutral states of being, the levels of subjectivity increase markedly with the blending of politics and armed conflict in to this mix. According to Thussu and Freedman (2003: 4–5) there are three key narratives that cover how mass media communicate on contemporary armed conflicts – "the critical observer; publicist and, most recently, as battleground, the surface upon which war is imagined and executed." This very much undermines the assumption of mass media and journalism as serving as a Fourth Estate, a check and balance against the abuses of power by the political branches of power and the judiciary. Information in both its offensive and defensive understanding is a key element in engaging in the political pursuit of armed conflict. This requires a certain carefully considered information strategy.

Information strategy is a relatively new phenomenon and in the process of forming owing to the changes in technology and the human environment (politics, communication, economics and so forth). This requires a good understanding of not only the enemy, but oneself too.

> The good information strategist must be a master of a whole host of skills: understanding the kind of knowledge that needs to be created; managing and properly distributing one's own information flows while disrupting the enemy's; crafting persuasive messages that shore up the will of one's own people and allies while demoralising one's opponents; and, of course, deceiving the enemy at the right time, in the right way (Arquilla 2007: 1).

Traditionally it has been the state-level actor that has had a monopoly on information strategy, given the level of technological development and other factors that have acted as constraints on other actors being able to challenge the state monopoly on mass communication. However, there have been changes in technology and processes that have enabled other non-state actors to challenge the position of that monopoly.

> What has become clear, though, is the extent to which informationalisation has contributed to the decline of external state-on-state mode of war, dominated by a relatively small number of organised forces, and the rise of a more

internally focused warfare featuring a plethora of moderately organised and loosely affiliated non-state groups (Betz 2015: 169).

Technology has increasingly enabled non-state actors to challenge state-based actors in the information sphere. This has been witnessed in Libya and Syria, there has been a high degree of mediatisation of the conflict by the anti-government forces, such as the establishing of 'media communication centres'. This seems to be a mirror of how government actors establish 'information centres' in times of war, although this could be a reflection of the various assistance offered by Western governments to the different anti-government forces (including Jihadist elements) in the MENA region.[3] It is the goal of an actor to protect their own information flows, while attacking the enemy's at the same time. "Pursuing information superiority by affecting adversary information and information systems while protecting our own is the core theme of the first section of the doctrine [of information operations] and pervades the discussion throughout the entire document" (Paul 2008: 26). The informationalisation and mediatisation processes can exert a significant influence on the information space that surrounds an armed conflict in several ways.

Three dynamics have been noted within the context of mediatised conflicts. 1) Media act in the capacity as a *conduit*, which has the effect of amplification that influences the volume, speed, reach and level of involvement in a conflict. 2) The *language* used tends to frame and assign performative agency that influences the aspects of representation, performance and dramaturgy of the event in question. 3) Media are a social institution as well as part of the public sphere that makes them part of the *environment* that are involved in co-structuring power relations over the course of a conflict (Eskjaer et al. 2015: 9–10). When communications are well aligned and orchestrated, the chances of effective persuasion and influence of the target audience to think in a particular way increase. Although, mass media may not necessarily determine what an individual thinks at any particular time, it can influence what they think about.

The ability for different actors (including non-state actors) to communicate during armed conflicts is becoming increasingly easier, even if they do not possess the means of production for mass communication (such as printing presses or TV transmission facilities). A result of this is evident in terms of creating a contest for hearts, minds and narratives. "There is a mounting pressure for Western states to engage in information-based strategies such as 'perception management' when conducting military campaigns. In particular, operations must be seen to be conducted efficiently and without incurring casualties if states are to avoid undermining the legitimacy of a war campaign in the public sphere" (Maltby 2007: 3). The public information sphere has become a much more complicated environment with time.

Historically news management used to be more easily enforced, but this has been gradually changing and especially in the 21st century as non-Western media outlets (such as Al Jazeera, CCTV and RT) have become more active, and the World Wide Web (including social media) provides a multitude of alternatives sources of information. It has been noted that this does not radically alter the way that mainstream and traditional media operate, but it does affect the rules of the game for military-media and political-media relations and how they interact (De Franco 2012: 169; Maltby & Thornham 2016; Samei 2016). There are some signs that the West is seeking to regain its lost information dominance, at least to some degree, by attempting to create a spiral of silence through such as what some have labelled as being a return to McCarthyism[4] with the *Washington Post* article[5] accusing various outlets to be useful idiots and sources of Russian propaganda.

In Chapter 6, Chifu tackles the issue of informational warfare that is practised by Russia, where the element of communication is an integral component of the process. The information communicated through these channels is subjective and is intended to fulfil a certain foreign policy agenda. A significant problem is how to differentiate between news and opinion, and subjective informational flows. This requires a certain degree of information and environmental literacy and awareness. One of the communication tactics mentioned is the use of Internet trolls as a virtual means to simultaneously communicate one's own message, while interrupting an adversary's message and communications.

Chifu also raises some points concerning the information and communications conducted by terrorist organisations. They are engaged in a hybrid form of warfare, where information and communication are a critical part of the perception and opinion forming process. The fact that they are able to communicate so widely and instantaneously speaks for the idea of the information dominance of state-based actors being slowly eroded by new non-state actors entering the scene in international relations. They are also able to interrupt the information flows of those state-based actors, thereby fulfilling Arquilla's criteria of being a good information strategist.

Across Chapters 2, 7, 8, 9 and 10, there is a clear element of politics interacting with information and communication. It is clear that positive news on a conflict is less likely to attract resistance and opposition, hence the tendency to try and spin good news and minimise bad news. To paraphrase Winston Churchill, sometimes the truth is so precious that it needs to be wrapped in a lie. Narratives and frames are extremely important for determining the projected reality around an event or a process. This is clear in the subversion that is occurring in Ukraine, where there are two competing sets of narratives and realities surrounding the events of Euromaidan. The 2008 Georgian–Russian War was a battle of competing and clashing sets of messages and narratives too. These are presented in a form that is not dissimilar to a Clash of Civilisations theory, but related to choice between a 'positive' and a 'negative' civilisational choice by the people of the target country.

The elements of propaganda and deception are very evident in the Western-backed regime changes (succeeded and attempted) in Libya and Syria. The manner in which the communication is handled is reasonably consistent in the logic and approach, which tends to narrate these events as a story that has little regard for reality on the ground. There is a *hero* of the story (rebels, 'opposition activists' and other such labels) that holds sets of values and norms just like people in the

West. The logic goes, they want to enjoy the same freedoms and rights as people in the West (in order to build a sense of empathy for them). They are prevented from doing that by the *villain* of the story, a non-caring, repressive and autocratic dictator who holds the opposite values and norms and is often having some Nazi association (with Hitler, the Holocaust … etc.). The hero of the story often requires the help of a *saviour* to live their dream of a free and democratic life, enter leading Western countries and organisations, such as NATO. There is a *victim* in these storylines, which is usually the civilian population of a target country. Their interests and views are often spoken for on their behalf by the *hero* and the *saviour*. Sometimes the *hero* and *saviour* characters are thwarted by a *spoiler*, who prevents the inevitable progress towards Western liberal values at a critical time, enter such countries as China, Iran and Russia and such organisations as Hezbollah. This makes a very complex, often geopolitically tainted conflict seem to be very easily comprehensible to a non-expert audience. The question and goal is to try and 'own' the narrative of the story in order to accumulate the necessary public opinion and perception that is required for the sense of political legitimacy, and to hobble the adversary by depriving them of that sought after legitimacy.

Politics and armed conflict

Politics and war have a very long and interconnected history between them, which has been taken into account and explained by history's great thinkers on the subject. Sun Tzu noted that war was only to be undertaken after all other possibilities were exhausted and that national unity was "an essential requirement of victorious war" (Tzu 1971: 39). Centuries after Sun Tzu, von Clausewitz also made the connection between politics, deception and war. He saw war as being an integral part of the human condition and an act of competition. War "is also a conflict of human interests and activities; and it is still more like State policy, which again, on its part, may be looked upon as a kind of business competition on a great scale. Besides, State policy is the womb in which War is developed, in which its outlines lie hidden in a rudimentary state, like the qualities of living creatures in their germs" (von Clausewitz 182: 202–203). These lead to his famous dictum that "war is a mere continuation of policy by other means" (ibid: 119) and that "they may all be regarded as political acts" (ibid: 120). Over the centuries war has been considered a deeply political act, where war is used as a means to compel an object to comply with a set of certain demands.

More modern thinkers concerning the dilemmas and problems with concepts, such as total defence, are wrestling with questions such as, what is being defended and what are the threats? In light of these questions, one line of thought was that the integrity of a nation needs to be ensured, and maintaining its identity requires more than mere military strength. A common sense of identity and purpose are seen as a means to ensuring national unity, which makes a target country less vulnerable to attack (in the physical and psychological senses) (Bowen 1997). Currently, with the convergence of the disastrous foreign policy of the West in the

Middle East and North Africa, beginning with GWOT and currently with the Arab Spring, has caused significant upheaval in the wider region and is creating numerous security risks and threats to the West. Given the situation described in the chapter on Syria, little seems to have been learned by policy makers. However, rather than relying on the tangible destruction, policy makers seem to rely on the public's intangible faith.

> Despite a lengthy list of military fiascos, the pretension of certain knowledge of what will transpire should we fail to take up arms pervades pro-military rhetoric, leading time and time again to a general acquiescence to the alleged *necessity* of war. (Calhoun 2013: 189)

The above illustrates the importance of reputation management and brand development in being able to increase the power of ethos within the significant influencers from the ranks of politics and the military. If we look at the case of Colin Powell standing before the UN and stating that the US had irrefutable proof of Iraq's possession of Weapons of Mass Destruction and links to terrorism,[6] which has been subsequently found without merit, his credibility (ethos) in this instance was linked to the power of his personality and reputation. Within the field of propaganda studies on observer noted that there are five common themes of conflict propaganda, which are used to support the political legitimacy of armed intervention. These are: 1) the portrayal of the leader figure; 2) the portrayal of the enemy; 3) the military threat; 4) the threat posed to international stability; and 5) the use of technological warfare (Willcox 2005: 91–141). Those aspects all combine and contribute to the façade of political legitimacy of some pending action that may not otherwise be considered as legitimate. It has a tendency of moving politics from a rational to an emotional basis of logic. This means that a target public can be more easily primed and mobilised.

There are also a number of constraints at play on the leeway of the policy of war by interest groups and governments. One of these is the issue and nature of uncertainty, access to alternative sources of information, public perception and opinion. During the time of the Vietnam War, Kissinger noted the strategy disadvantages faced by the militarily superior (stronger in its tangible aspects) United States. There were two 'disabilities' that they suffered, namely the nature of guerrilla warfare and "the asymmetry in the definition of what constituted unacceptable losses" (Kissinger 1969: 212). The West has grown to be very adverse to the notion of taking casualties, which is evidently understood by the messaging done by the political and military establishment in attempting to whitewash the human element from the public representation of war (except in the case where deaths and suffering are caused to build a case for war in order to 'save' them).

The interaction of politics and armed conflict is evident across all of the chapters of this volume. In Chifu's chapters from 3 to 6, there is a clear line of the influence of politics on how the kinds of conflicts, and especially those of a hybrid nature, are imagined and fought. He notes that some of the armed conflicts that Russia has engaged in are specifically calibrated for the current political environment so as not to trigger a larger armed conflict, being just below the threshold of a military response. A political response has occurred in so far as there are a regime of sanctions currently in force against Russia for events in Ukraine and Crimea in particular. This was illustrated with the example of the appearance of the 'Little Green Men.'

In Chapter 5, Chifu engages with the topic of lawfare, which combines the elements of a legal framework within military operations. This is situated within the sphere of hybrid warfare too. The operationalisation of the concept is intended to bestow a certain sense of legitimacy of actions undertaken in the pursuit of attaining military and strategic targets. This concept has been developed and applied by China and Russia, and has caused problems in formulating a united global effort against terror groups, such as ISIS. Lawfare creates certain lethargy in response as it either confounds or bypasses the 'normal' decision-making triggers among the global political and military leadership.

In the chapters by Simons, the armed conflicts within the context of the Arab Spring, such as Libya and Syria are both highly political conflicts. Although, according to Sun Tzu war should be an absolute last resort, the West has resorted very quickly to the use of covert and overt armed conflict in both Libya and Syria. Although, these conflicts have a façade of reluctance about them according to tentative political statements, the West acts as a powerful broker and not an honest one as various small-scale wars have become seemingly commonplace as a means of foreign policy. No matter the lack of success and the list of damning reports on the results of various wars, there is still a call from some quarters to engage in wars of choice elsewhere. These are often caged along the lines envisaged and outlined by Willcox and his five common themes. Chapters 8 and 9, on Libya and Syria, do seem to bear this out.

Simons in Chapters 7 and 10 (Georgian–Russian War and Ukraine) also demonstrates the role played by politics and especially the quest for political legitimacy in these conflicts. Ukraine has turned into a geopolitical stalemate, neither side is prepared to move their position for fear of yielding any ground and giving advantage to their opponent. This conflict has a number of political dimensions from the very beginning of Euromaidan with assumptions of a struggle of civilizational trajectory, along the lines of a choice between Western and Soviet-like or a fascist future or independence – depending on which side of the conflict is consulted. There were similar political choices projected in the 2008 Georgian–Russian War with projections of democracy versus authoritarianism, independence versus Russian occupation. These methods are part of the information strategy that was described by Arquilla earlier in the conclusion.

Armed conflict as a crisis

A crisis is a certain set of simultaneously occurring sets of conditions that affect the risk and threat experienced a particular community at a particular point in time. Stern argues that there needs to be three perceptions that are simultaneously affected – a threat to basic values, a sense of urgency, and an air of uncertainty

(2003: 8). This is the tangible aspect of a crisis; the intangible aspect of a crisis is that it creates an opportunity for a political call for action and mobilisation. War and armed conflict fulfil Stern's entire criterion for being a crisis, and there is certainly a vast level of evidence of political calls for action in order to 'resolve' a crisis.

During an outbreak of what is framed as being a 'crisis' there is an attendant political call for a solution. Among the conceptual frameworks that provide a 'solution' to an armed conflict termed as a crisis are tools that include Just War and Responsibility to Protect (R2P). As seen in the introduction of this volume and in the chapters, these are controversial in nature, especially owing to what has been characterised as being the selective invocation and application of these concepts. For example, China and Russia (among others), have strongly criticised the US-led West as using these concepts as a deceptive means to achieve the other foreign policy goals as regime change. Yet, since 2008 and again in 2014, Russia has seemingly utilised at least in part the notion of R2P in the armed conflicts in Georgia and Ukraine (Baranovsky & Mateiko 2016). The sense of a crisis also becomes evident in a number of the chapters contained in this book.

In Chifu's chapters there is a distinct appearance of the element of crisis. This crisis not only concerns the three elements enumerated by Stern (2003) concerning the resulting military operations, but also the crisis faced by Western political and military decision-makers that struggle to meet the challenges posed by these new or at least unusual, forms of warfare. He calls for revised or new ways to engage in these problematic aspects that are represented by hybrid warfare. In addition, there is a crisis involving the integrity of informational security and flows in the Western segments of the public sphere.

The chapters by Simons also demonstrate the relevance of the crisis lens in understanding the case studies, especially Libya, Syria and Ukraine examples. In the cases of Libya and Syria, the Arab Spring provided Western governments with the three dynamics of mediatised conflicts discussed by Eskjaer et al. (2015), at least initially. These were portrayed selectively and subjectively in the mass media as one-way humanitarian crises, while not being forthright and honest about why people were dying or the depth of involvement by the US-led coalition that was seeking regime change rather than anything more selfless. Ukraine has also been represented subjectively by the different sides of the conflict as a crisis – of democracy, humanitarian, independence, influence of the far-right – each side attempting to enhance their influence and attempt to disadvantage their adversary. The result has given the impression of turning Ukraine into an object, rather than a subject of international relations.

What does the future hold?

In the current times there is a great deal of instability and armed conflict, which is being fanned from numerous directions. There seems to be very little in the way of critical self-reflection by the main actors, rather the expedient use of assigning the blame to other convenient actors in order to skirt acknowledging ownership or responsibility of the problems created. A good example is the hyped rhetoric concerning what the Russians and especially Putin are responsible for, which does not mean that they are completely innocent. But to say that Putin has 'weaponised' refugees not only adversely affects the credibility of the messenger, but fails to solve the problem of a massive refugee crisis. This crisis being fuelled not by Putin but by the continuous sets of regime changes in the MENA region that have directly and indirectly supported by the West, Iraq 2003, Libya 2011 and others that occurred long before direct Russian military involvement in Syria in September 2015. The results have seen millions of people displaced, but little in the way of transparency or accountability of those responsible for it.

An armed conflict is more than often preceded by an intense period of communication via the public information sphere, in an attempt to shape the public's opinion, perception and intangibles. This is a historical continuation of the practice that was established by the formation and the activities of the Committee for Public Information in the United States in 1917. Wars and other forms of military intervention are deliberately projected as being both necessary and defensive in nature as they require a sense of political legitimacy and consensus (or at least to minimise open resistance against) to perform within the liberal democratic framework. However, some of the latest wars of choice, such as Iraq in 2003 and Libya in 2011, have had these façades of communication exposed as false and this has resulted in these events to serve as being potential constraints on future Western-led foreign policy and military interventions.

Currently, according to some observers, the West that rhetorically stands for peace, positive human values and norms is caught in a cycle of "war as the new normal" in a pattern of "forever wars." Publics are becoming increasingly numb to the death and suffering that is being inflicted upon whole countries. And mass media serve as the cheerleaders of the current state of being (Carruthers 2011: 264). This does not necessarily mean that the public are willing to accept more new wars that are being added to the list of ongoing wars. The 2003 Iraq War proved to be a benchmark in terms of the feeling of betrayal by political leaders deceiving the public in to going to war, the Libyan War seems to have reinforced that feeling. The era of the hegemony of the Liberal political order's hegemony over world politics seems to be loosening, the Dutch Referendum on Ukraine, Brexit and the 2016 US elections seem to be indicators of this trend. The question remains exactly what kind of political order shall replace it, if Liberalism does not manage to defend its position.

The results of the political changes with the possible coming of a new political order, which currently manifests itself as a conflict and a divide between political establishment and anti-political establishment, may have an impact upon the nature and pace of armed conflicts to come. Even though in light of history, the 'Liberal' political order has not shied away from engaging in numerous regime changes and subversions of 'non-democratic' states and governments.

In the introduction the following question was posed – does the appearance of different forms of conceiving and waging war constitute a change in the prosecution or warfare or merely signify a greater awareness of those alternative styles?

In answering this question, the chapters have presented a lot of empirical material from numerous conflicts and different actors. The authors tend to agree with Betz's (2015) opinion on the question, insofar as a lot of the different tactics used by Russia and by the West tend not to be anything that is revolutionary and new about how and why wars are fought. The key themes of Clausewitz's Trinity of War – passion, reason and chance – all still exist in the current arena of armed conflict. Information and messaging means are still used by all sides, while they simultaneously defend their own information flows and attack their adversary's. Deception and propaganda are still used by everyone, the actors vying for the edge of political legitimacy that comes with carrying public perception and opinion. What has changed though are the nature and relationships among the actors, and the reach and speed of communications. New ICTs allow non-state actors and alternative actors to become active participants in the new armed conflicts, to communicate and form various politically based relationships. These same means of communication also means that communications are instantaneous and global, having the possibility to reach massive audiences with a clear and consistent message. In practical terms this means non-state actors and those outside of the political mainstream can engage audiences, communicating to them beyond the framework of traditional mainstream media and mobilising and priming those audiences virtually.

Notes

1 https://www.wikileaks.org/podesta-emails/emailid/3774
2 For a related report, please see https://wikileaks.org/clinton-emails/emailid/3122
3 O'Connell, K., *BBC Investigation Exposes Western Aid To Syrian Rebels As 'Wal-Mart' For Extremists,* Mint Press News, http://www.mintpressnews.com/bbc-investigation-exposes-western-aid-to-syrian-rebels-as-wal-mart-for-extremists/213992/, 18 February 2016 (accessed 9 December 2016)
4 Taibbi, M., *The 'Washington Post' 'Blacklist' Story is Shameful and Disgusting*, Rolling Stone, http://www.rollingstone.com/politics/features/washington-post-blacklist-story-is-shameful-disgusting-w452543, 28 November 2016 (accessed 9 December 2016)
5 Timberg, C., *Russian Propaganda Effort Helped Spread 'Fake News' During Election, Experts Say*, The Washington Post, https://www.washingtonpost.com/business/economy/russian-propaganda-effort-helped-spread-fake-news-during-election-experts-say/2016/11/24/793903b6-8a40-4ca9-b712-716af66098fe_story.html?utm_term=.88926e3b8ada, 24 November 2016 (accessed 9 December 2016)
6 *Powell: Iraq Hiding Weapons, Aiding Terrorists*, CNN, http://edition.cnn.com/2003/US/02/05/sprj.irq.powell.un/, 6 February 2003 (accessed 9 December 2016)

Bibliography

Arquilla, J., 'Introduction: Thinking About Information Strategy' in Arquilla, J. & Borer, D. A. (Eds.), *Information Strategy and Warfare: A Guide to Theory and Practice*, New York: Routledge, 2007, pp. 1–15
Baranovsky, V. & Mateiko, A., Responsibility to Protect: Russia's Approaches, *The International Spectator: Italian Journal of International Affairs*, 51(2), 2016, pp. 49–69

Betz, D., *Carnage and Connectivity: Landmarks in the Decline of Conventional Military Power*, New York: Oxford University Press, 2015

Bowen, K., Total Defence – What is Being Defended and What are the Threats?, *OR Insight*, 10(1), January-March 1997, pp. 2–7

Calhoun, L., *War and Delusion: A Critical Examination*, Basingstoke: Palgrave Macmillan, 2013

Carruthers, S. L., *The Media at War*, 2nd Edition, Basingstoke: Palgrave Macmillan, 2011

CIA Red Cell, *Afghanistan: Sustaining West European Support for the NATO-led Mission – Why Counting on Apathy Might Not be Enough*, A Red Cell Special Memorandum, 11 March 2010

De Franco, C., *Media Power and the Transformation of War*, Basingstoke: Palgrave Macmillan, 2012

Eskjaer, M. F., Hjarvard, S. & Mortensen, M. (Eds.), *The Dynamics of Mediatised Conflicts*, New York: Peter Lang, 2015

House of Commons Foreign Affairs Committee, *Libya: Examination of Intervention and Collapse of the UK's Future Policy Options*, Third Report of Session 2016–17, HC 119, 14 September 2016

Kissinger, H., The Viet Nam Negotiations, *Foreign Affairs*, 47(2), January 1969, pp. 211–234

Maltby, S. & Thornham, H., The Digital Mundane: Social Media and the Military, *Media, Culture & Society*, 38(8), 2016, pp. 1153–1168

Maltby, S., 'Introduction – Communicating War Strategies and Implications' in Maltby, S. & Keeble, R., *Communicating War: Memory, Media and Military*, Bury St Edmunds: Arima Publishing, 2007, pp. 1–16

Paul, C., *Information Operations Doctrine and Practice: A Reference Handbook*, Westport (CT): Praeger Security International. 2008

Samei, M. F. A., Public Diplomacy and the Clash of Satellites, *Media and Communication*, 4(2), 2016, pp. 55–68

Simons, G., Selling Conflict in the 21st Century: PR or Advertising the Way to Public Consent?, *Электронное научное издание Альманах Пространство и Время*, 3(2), 2013

Stern, E. K., *Crisis Decision Making: A Cognitive-Institutional Approach*, Volume 6, Stockholm: Swedish National Defence College, 2003

Thussu, D. K. & Freedman, D. (Eds.), *War and the Media*, Thousand Oaks (CA): Sage, 2003

Tzu, S., *The Art of War*, New York: Oxford University Press, 1971

Western, J., *Selling Intervention and War: The Presidency, the Media, and the American Public*, Baltimore: The John Hopkin's University Press, 2005

Von Clausewitz, C., *On War*, London: Penguin Classics, 1982

Willcox, D. R., *Propaganda, the Press and Conflict: The Gulf War and Kosovo*, London: Routledge, 2005

Index